MW01056708

HIKING
THE PACIFIC
CREST TRAIL

OREGON

HIKING THE PACIFIC CREST TRAIL

OREGON

SECTION HIKING FROM DONOMORE PASS TO BRIDGE OF THE GODS

ELI BOSCHETTO

MOUNTAINEERS
BOOKS

IN MEMORY OF MY GRANDMOTHER, RUTH

MOUNTAINEERS BOOKS

Mountaineers Books is the publishing division of The Mountaineers, an organization founded in 1906 and dedicated to the exploration, preservation, and enjoyment of outdoor and wilderness areas.

1001 SW Klickitat Way, Suite 201, Seattle, WA 98134
800.553.4453, www.mountaineersbooks.org

Copyright © 2016 by Eli Boschetto

All rights reserved. No part of this book may be reproduced or utilized in any form, or by any electronic, mechanical, or other means, without the prior written permission of the publisher.

Printed in China

Distributed in the United Kingdom by Cordee, www.cordee.co.uk

First edition: first printing 2016, second printing 2018, third printing 2019

Copyeditor: Jane Crosen
Design and layout: Peggy Egerdahl
Cartographer: Pease Press
Cover photograph: *Sunset alpenglow lights up Mount Jefferson from Scout Lake.*
Frontispiece: *A PCT hiker pauses for a big view of Cowhorn Mountain.*
All photographs by Eli Boschetto and Mitzi Sugar, unless noted otherwise.

The background of the leg maps for this book were produced using the online map viewer CalTopo. For more information, visit caltopo.com.

Library of Congress Cataloging-in-Publication Data is on file for this title.

A NOTE ABOUT SAFETY

Safety is an important concern in all outdoor activites. No guidebook can alert you to every hazard or anticipate the limitations of the reader. Therefore, the descriptions of roads, trails, routes, and natural features in this book are not representations that a particular place or excursion will be safe for your party. When you follow any of the routes described in this book, you assume responsibility for your own safety. Under normal conditions, such excursions require the usual attention to traffic, road and trail conditions, weather, terrain, the capabilities of your party, and other factors. Keeping informed on current conditions and exercising common sense are the keys to a safe, enjoyable outing.

—Mountaineers Books

Mountaineers Books titles may be purchased for corporate, educational, or other promotional sales, and our authors are available for a wide range of events. For information on special discounts or booking an author, contact our customer service at 800-553-4453 or mbooks@mountaineersbooks.org.

ISBN (paperback): 978-1-59485-876-5
ISBN (ebook): 978-1-59485-877-2

CONTENTS

ACKNOWLEDGMENTS

In every walk with Nature one receives far more than he seeks.
—John Muir

NEAR THE END of my third summer on Oregon's Pacific Crest Trail, hiking and researching for this guidebook, I sat perched on Indian Mountain, high above the Columbia River Gorge, admiring a panorama that stretched far and wide. I was just a couple days away from having crossed the entire state of Oregon on foot. And as my journey neared its end, I spent a few moments recalling the experiences that led to this moment—many of which would wind up in this guidebook. Of course, despite having hiked across Oregon largely by myself, I was hardly near the end of a solo adventure. This effort was aided by numerous family members, friends, and colleagues to whom I owe tremendous thanks for their assistance and support.

First and foremost, I could never have done this without the amazing help of my wife, Mitzi. For the hiking portion, she assisted with menu planning, double-checking pack loads, and cross-state trailhead shuttles. During the writing and research phases, she supported me through endless days of copywriting and poring over every PCT map and reference ever created. She celebrated with me through the highs and kept my spirits up through the lows—including helping me coordinate a hasty escape route via satellite phone when I found myself surrounded by wildfires in the Sky Lakes Wilderness in the summer of 2014.

Of course, I need to thank my dear friend and colleague Tami Asars who, in 2012, over margaritas and chimichangas, shared her concept of a new series of PCT guidebooks and invited me to join her on this venture. Additionally, thanks to Kate Rogers at Mountaineers Books for entrusting this fledgling author with the entire state of Oregon, and for all of the direction, patience, and support needed to tackle this immense project.

Special thanks also go out to the following people for their time and patience in answering my endless questions and assisting with copious information requests: Anthony Benedetti, recreation operations for Fremont-Winema National Forest; Jennifer Gifford, trails manager for Crater Lake National Park; Dylan McCoy, lead wilderness ranger for Willamette National Forest; Aaron Pedersen, recreation assistant manager for Mount Hood National Forest; Brad Peterson, wilderness and trails manager for Willamette National Forest; and Ian Nelson and Dana Hendricks with the Pacific Crest Trail Association.

Additional thanks go out to my dad, Allen, his wife, Taffy, and Jim Trindle for assistance with transportation and logistics; Julie Campagnoli (JAM Media Collective), Carl Johnson (Backbone Media), and Angie Houck (Darby Communications) for the Osprey packs, Big Agnes tents, and Vasque boots used on trail; and the gracious baristas at Marino Adriatic Café in Portland for allowing me to camp out in their coffee shop with laptop, books, and maps spread out all over their tables as I worked to bring this guidebook together. And finally I would like to thank these PCT hikers for sharing their tips, stories, campsites, trail camaraderie, spare batteries, and moral support during the course of this adventure: Dirt Wolf, DaVinci, Freedom, Bob, Jan and Chuck, Smitty, Mr. President, Hike On, Foxfire, and Janelle.

And thanks to you, the reader, for considering taking your own journey on Oregon's Pacific Crest Trail. The simple fact that you're holding this book signifies that you have already taken your first step. You only have a few thousand more to go—and what fantastic steps they are. My own experience on the PCT to develop this guidebook was an unforgettable adventure. So, no matter whether you're going for a few miles, or a few hundred miles, your own rewards are sure to be as great. See you on the PCT!

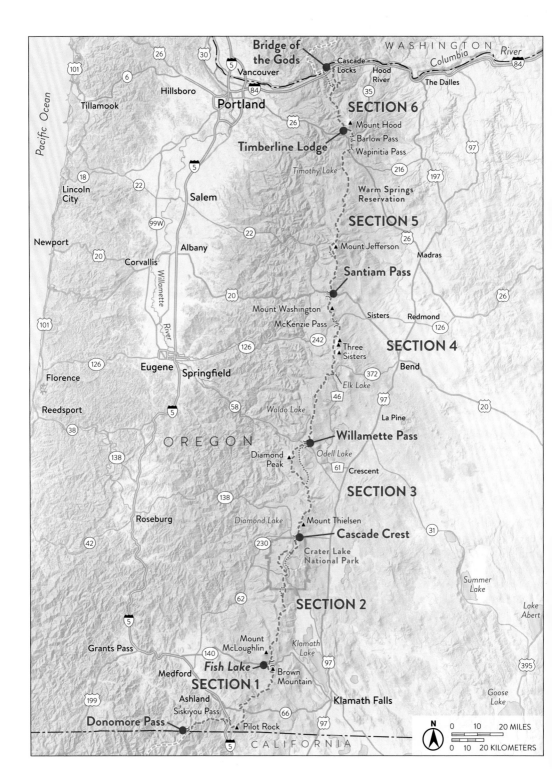

WASHINGTON

Columbia River

Bridge of the Gods

Cascade Locks

Hood River

The Dalles

Vancouver

Portland

Hillsboro

Tillamook

Pacific Ocean

Lincoln City

Newport

Corvallis

Albany

Salem

Willamette River

OREGON

Eugene

Springfield

Florence

Reedsport

Roseburg

SECTION 6

Mount Hood

Timberline Lodge

Barlow Pass

Wapinitia Pass

Timothy Lake

Warm Springs Reservation

SECTION 5

Mount Jefferson

Madras

Santiam Pass

Mount Washington

McKenzie Pass

Sisters

Redmond

Three Sisters

SECTION 4

Bend

Elk Lake

Waldo Lake

Willamette Pass

La Pine

Diamond Peak

Odell Lake

Crescent

SECTION 3

Diamond Lake

Mount Thielsen

Cascade Crest

Crater Lake National Park

SECTION 2

Summer Lake

Lake Abert

Mount McLoughlin

Klamath Lake

Fish Lake

Brown Mountain

SECTION 1

Grants Pass

Medford

Ashland

Siskiyou Pass

Klamath Falls

Goose Lake

Donomore Pass

Pilot Rock

CALIFORNIA

N   0   10   20 MILES
     0   10   20 KILOMETERS

INTRODUCTION

Not all those who wander are lost.
—J. R. R. Tolkien

A PATH OF UNPARALLELED adventure, the Pacific Crest National Scenic Trail is where you make memories, realize your dreams, and find out exactly what you're made of. The 2669-mile trail leads from the scorching deserts of Southern California and over the skyscraping passes of the Sierra Nevada to culminate amid Washington's alpine meadows and ragged, glacier-carved ridges. In between, it traverses the lush forests and rugged volcanic terrain of Oregon.

A journey along the PCT is as much an opportunity for backcountry exploring as it is about discovering yourself. It's an enchanting and challenging experience measured in stark contrasts, where amazing scenery is combined with annoying blisters, unhindered freedom is juxtaposed by lonely isolation, and a stretch of simple existence is punctuated with dirt, sweat, and tears. But in the end, the rewards outweigh the struggles, leaving you with the memories of an incredible experience to last a lifetime.

This guidebook will lead you along Oregon's 455-mile stretch of the PCT, from the California border, near Ashland, to the Washington border at the Bridge of the Gods on the Columbia River. From the rolling grasslands of the Soda Mountain Wilderness to the barren volcanic plains of the Central Cascades to the doorstep of Oregon's tallest peak, Mount Hood, Oregon's stretch of the PCT has something to entice everyone who steps on the trail. Your adventure is calling!

A BRIEF HISTORY OF THE PCT

Among the PCT-traversing states, Oregon was the first to establish a cross-state, long-distance hiking and equestrian trail. Designated in 1920 by Fredrick W. Cleator of the US Forest Service, the 260-mile Oregon Skyline Trail (OST) spanned the Beaver State north-to-south from Mount Hood to Crater Lake. It wasn't completely cross-state, as the areas north of Mount Hood and south of Crater Lake were, at the time, deemed unsuitable for passage or crossed private lands. Unlike the modern-day PCT, the OST did not traverse the spine of Oregon's Cascades but remained lower in elevation, linking numerous lakes and valleys.

The concept of a cross-country route from Mexico to Canada was proposed a few years later, in 1926, when Catherine Montgomery, a schoolteacher from Bellingham, Washington, casually proposed the idea. A few years later, Clinton C. Clarke, chairman of the Mountain League of Los Angeles, organized the Pacific Crest Trail System Conference in 1932 to market the trail idea. This earned him the moniker "Father of the PCT." Unfortunately, Miss Montgomery is only unofficially credited as "Mother of the PCT," and passed away unaware of the impact her suggestion eventually had.

The PCT System Conference was a group of outdoor clubs and nonprofits led by Clarke and dedicated to creating one trail system made up of new and old trails that would extend from Mexico to Canada, cresting the mountainous states. Clarke inspired and planned the YMCA PCT relays—forty teams of young hikers between the ages of fourteen and eighteen who were the first to scout routes for the trail. In 1935, the teams, under the guidance of an outdoorsman named Warren Rogers, left Campo on the Mexican border and meticulously noted their route and adventures. Each subsequent summer, the teams picked up where they had left off, until they reached what is now Monument 78 on the Canadian border on August 5, 1938. Their journey proved that through combining trails, open country, and existing roads a person could get from Mexico to Canada along a scenic alpine route. Much of the original PCT through Oregon utilized stretches of the preexisting Oregon Skyline Trail.

In the 1960s, backpacking and hiking gained popularity, and in early 1965 President Lyndon B. Johnson sent a special message to Congress stressing the importance of environmental conservation and the development and protection of trail systems. Not long after, Secretary of the Interior Stewart L. Udall instructed the Bureau of Outdoor Recreation to head up a nationwide trail study. This study led to the National Trail System Act, enacted by Congress in 1968. The new law facilitated the development and operation of National Scenic Trails and National Historic Trails. As a result, the Appalachian Trail and the Pacific Crest Trail were the nation's first scenic trails.

In 1970, the Pacific Crest National Scenic Trail Advisory Council was appointed, a mix of local recreationists, ranchers, tribal members, timber and mineral representatives, and members of conservation groups. At the council's second meeting, in 1971, it suggested a "Guide for Location, Design and Management," which was approved and published by the US Secretary of Agriculture. This document is still the official management plan used by various agencies. In January 1973, the advisory council, in agreement with the Bureau of Land Management, Forest Service, and other participating agencies, published the official route of the PCT in the *Federal Register*, another big step in creating the trail. In 1988, two monuments were placed at the southern and northern terminuses of the PCT. The trail, however, wasn't officially complete until 1993, with much of the stretch in southern Oregon, south of Crater Lake, among the last (and most expensive) to be constructed. It was also in the 1990s that several sections of the PCT in Oregon were rerouted off the older OST into higher elevations to be more true to maintaining the concept of trekking across the *crest* of the Cascades.

The trail is primarily managed and maintained thanks to the stewardship of volunteers and employees of the Pacific Crest Trail Association (PCTA). Founded in 1977 as the Pacific Crest Trail Conference, the PCTA is a very active nonprofit that coordinates with the Forest Service, private landowners, and other agencies. One of the group's primary goals is to help you, the backpacker, experience the magic of walking this scenic and historic trail.

PCTA: YOU CAN HELP!

The Pacific Crest Trail Association (PCTA) needs you! Volunteers can help with trail repairs, trail widening, drainage improvements and other projects that keep the PCT passable and hikers safe. Become a member and help with all manner of critical trail needs, such as trail maintenance, protection, and promotion, by donating an annual, monthly, or one-time gift. The PCTA website (www.pcta.org) alone is worth a mint in the information it provides.

OREGON'S PCT: AN OVERVIEW

The Green Tunnel—that is usually how thru-hikers sardonically refer to the PCT through Oregon. Yes, there's a lot of forest in Oregon, a product of all that wonderful rain the state receives. But what fascinating forest it is, brimming with all manner of flora and fauna. Far from being homogenous woodland, Oregon's forests display a rich diversity of vegetation through a variety of elevations and ecosystems. And when the trail pops out of the forest into an alpine meadow or onto the flank of a glacier-capped volcano, it's just the cherry on top of an already amazing sundae!

True, Oregon doesn't possess the skyscraping granite spires and sprawling alpine meadows of California's Sierra Nevada—or the rugged and imposing valleys and passes of Washington's North Cascades. What Oregon does feature is a towering chain of striking, glacier-clad volcanoes, interspersed with intimate meadows, charming lake basins, craggy volcanic plains . . . and trees. You can be hiking along Oregon's PCT on a forested ridge when suddenly it opens up to an expansive view of big mountains in the distance, sparkling lakes in wide valleys, and trees as far

The vast and colorful plains below sprawling Diamond Peak beckon PCT hikers deep into Oregon's wilderness areas.

as the eye can see. So many trees it will boggle your mind.

Unlike the wicked ups and downs of the PCT in California and Washington, the trail through Oregon is a pleasant stroll over generally moderate terrain, as it cruises along the Cascade Crest past crumbling mountains cloaked in ancient legends, ambles through idyllic wildflower- and huckleberry-choked parks laced by glacial streams, and winds among ragged lava flows and narrow ridges formed by millennia of volcanic activity and glacial erosion. In Oregon, there are no wind-sucking climbs up 12,000-foot passes, or knee-grinding traverses of 4000-foot-deep canyons. As the PCT casually snakes its way through Oregon, immense swaths of mixed forest separate the major landmarks. But these wooded divides allow you to appreciate every stunning panorama, every amazing scene for its own unique aspects.

On Oregon's PCT you can easily escape to the woods with little effort. While the PCT traverses ten wilderness areas across the length of the Cascades, access to trailheads is often by way of good highways, and less than a couple hours' drive from most major cities. If you're a local, that makes it especially inviting to bug out for a long weekend and take a good long PCT hike without having to travel far. If you're traveling to Oregon to fulfill your PCT dreams, you'll have access to plenty of cities and services nearby, and a number of hiker-friendly resorts and lodges along the route that offer amenities in the form of convenient camping and lodging, resupply services, frosty milkshakes, and more.

STATE MILEAGE AND ELEVATION GAIN AND LOSS

The PCT's total mileage in Oregon is 455.2 miles, with a total elevation gain of 69,340 feet and a loss of 75,930 feet. This makes the PCT passage through Oregon quite the comfort cruise and perfect for breaking in your long-distance hiking legs.

Whether you're a seasoned hiker, or you've just bought your first pair of hiking boots, Oregon's PCT is an all-access adventure where you can get out and enjoy the great Northwest outdoors at your own pace, without being overwhelmed. So get ready to marvel at huge volcanoes and bask on the shores of glittering lakes. Prepare to witness how glaciers sculpted rocky spires and where the earth cracked open to spill forth molten rock. Bring an appetite for juicy mountain berries and an eye for a kaleidoscope of wildflowers. And be ready for lots and lots of trees.

HOW TO USE THIS GUIDE

With hiking boots and a few days off, just about anyone can hike the PCT through Oregon, the "easiest" of the PCT states. This guidebook is designed for those who want to hike bite-sized portions of the PCT, starting and ending at logical points. This book organizes the Oregon PCT into six sections, south to north, that range from about 50 to 95 miles each, so that a section is hikable within about a week's time. The two longer sections (4 and 5) can even be easily split in two, creating even more reasonable trail sections when vacation limitations dictate. Each section consists of several "legs" that proceed from landmark to landmark; typically, these are recommended campsites and water sources. The leg arrangement presents a reasonable itinerary for a moderate hiker, with leg distances averaging between 8 and 14 miles. There are also suggestions for alternate itineraries with longer-mileage days for more advanced hikers or thru-hikers. And of course, you can also customize your own itinerary.

The accompanying **section and leg maps** in this guidebook show the "official" PCT in bright orange dashes; suggested side routes (for water, camping, or resupply) and alternate routes are drawn in orange dots; additional PCT segments (e.g., continuing into the next leg, skipping a portion, etc.) are light orange dashes; and all other connecting trails are shown with black dashes.

Oregon's PCT Sections

Each of the state's six sections begins with an information block. The **distance** is the overall mileage for the section. Each section's mileage begins at 0. Cumulative **state distance** is the running measurement of the entire trail through Oregon, through

PCT SECTION LETTERS AND MILEAGE

The PCTA employs the popular lettering system to identify PCT sections from Mexico to Canada, based on the trail's section divisions in older guidebooks. This guidebook, aimed at section hiking the PCT, divides the trail into manageable portions and therefore doesn't correlate exactly with the lettering system. For your reference, each section does include the corresponding PCT letter(s).

The PCTA also counts overall PCT mileage from mile 0 at the Mexico border to mile 2668.98 at the Canada border. For hikers who are tackling multiple sections at once, this guide gives cumulative *state* mileage for each section, starting from mile 0 at Donomore Pass at the California–Oregon border to mile 455.2 at the Bridge of the Gods. In some cases, section mileage is adjusted to account for alternate route recommendations, but statewide cumulative mileage remains the same.

The distances indicated in this guidebook were measured by GPS receiver and correlated against the 2015 Halfmile PCT map, currently the most accurate measurement of the PCT in *distance*. All waypoints and references in this guidebook are confirmed accurate; however, you may see variances of up to 0.1 mile. Elevation measurements were also collected by GPS receiver and calculated using the CalTopo mapping program, resulting in more accurate topography and elevations than seen in older trail maps and guides.

MAPS AND APPS

These are the most useful maps and apps for hiking the PCT Oregon:

National Geographic Trails Illustrated PCT maps (www.natgeomaps.com) cover the entire PCT through Oregon in two pocket-sized booklets. Released in 2019, these maps were created in cooperation with PCTA and Halfmile maps and were reviewed by this guidebook's author for their information and accuracy. Trails Illustrated maps are updated on a regular basis to keep their information as current as possible.

Halfmile PCT maps (www.pctmap.net) are free to download and easily print at home or at your local copy shop. Maintained by PCT hiker "Halfmile" and his PCT-mapping team, these maps are updated annually. They are very accurate, with recent versions including more helpful waypoint and location information. The popular Halfmile smartphone app was discontinued in 2019.

US Forest Service (USFS) PCT maps (www.fs.usda.gov/main/pct/maps-publications) are large, easy-to-read, full-color, waterproof topo maps that include elevation profiles and historical notes. These maps are pretty out-of-date, and their large size and lack of mileage information limits their usefulness, but they do provide a good trail overview for planning.

Green Trails (www.greentrailsmaps.com) publishes topographical maps for recreational areas in Oregon, Washington, and parts of California. These maps include good road, trail, and access information, and are frequently updated. Unfortunately, Green Trails only covers the PCT through about half of Oregon, from the Three Sisters Wilderness to the Columbia River.

Guthook Guides PCT app (www.atlasguides.com) is a popular PCT hiking smartphone app for iOS and Android devices. It is available in five portions: three for California, one for Oregon, and one for Washington. The app provides plenty of trail beta, photos, and a social platform.

all sections. **Elevation gain/loss** tallies the cumulative ups and downs over the section, and **high point** is just that—the highest point in elevation the trail crosses. **Best time of year** lets you know the optimal hiking season for the PCT section, typically the summer months—although some stretches can be accessed in late spring (weather and snow depending), and some sections are best hiked in autumn.

To help with your trip planning, each section also notes the corresponding **PCTA section letters**, as well as the **land managers** for the areas you'll be passing through and any **passes and permits** required. (The appendixes in the back of this book have more reference and contact information for resupply locations and land management agencies. Before you head out, always

check with the relevant land managers to get the latest on trail and water conditions, forest fires, detours, trailhead safety, and much more.) Then there is a list of the section's trip **legs** between major landmarks.

Following the information block, each section overview briefly highlights what you'll encounter along the way, from dense evergreen forests to colorful alpine meadows to ragged volcanic peaks, detailing the area's terrain, flora and fauna, and geology. Next, you'll find **access** directions to the section's starting and ending trailheads.

Notes give you a heads-up on what's coming. **Services** is a brief summary of near-trail towns or resorts that can help you prepare for your hike or support you along the way with food, lodging, and resupply options. **Camping** explains any limitations or permit requirements. **Water** notes stretches where water is scarce or not available, so you can plan ahead and not run out. Good water sources are called out in trail descriptions with the ⭕ symbol; even if these water sources are seasonal, they're often reliable in all but the driest summers. **Hazards** tells you about a section's challenging river crossings or other potential dangers so you can plan a safe trip within your comfort zone. Finally, each section's opening details end with **suggested itineraries** from camp to camp, including daily mileage.

Section Legs

The leg descriptions start with the landmark-to-landmark **distance** followed by the cumulative **elevation gain/loss** for that leg and its **high point**. The list of **connecting trails and roads** tells you what major trails and roads you'll cross on that leg that could serve as alternate or emergency entry and exit points. This doesn't necessarily mean you'll be near a trailhead when you reach one of these connectors, but the route will eventually lead back toward civilization.

The **on the trail** descriptions, covering every mile of Oregon's PCT, will tell you what's around each bend—from camps to water sources, wildflowers to awesome views—leaving enough for you to imagine and discover firsthand on your trip. **Maps** and **elevation profiles** for each section and each leg link up with the trail descriptions, so you can easily find a place that's mentioned and see how much up and down it'll take to get there. Each leg ends with a list of **camp-to-camp mileages**, so you can plan ahead or change your mind at the last minute, knowing that another snooze spot is just a mile or two ahead.

Camps

Just about any and every flat space along the PCT has likely been used as a camp at one time or another. Some of these spots are suitable as Leave No Trace (LNT) campsites, perhaps even named and signed. Others may not technically follow

---

MAP SYMBOLS

- - - - - - -	Featured PCT leg or segment
··············	Alternate or recommended trail
– – – – –	Adjacent PCT leg or segment
- - - - - - - -	Connecting trails
═══════	Divided highway
───────	Highway
───────	Paved road
▭▭▭▭▭▭	Unpaved road
⑤ ⑨⓪ ②⓪⑤	Interstate highway
② ⑫ ⑩①	US highway
④ ②⓪ ①②③	State route
24 200	Forest road
60	County road

●—	Start/end of leg or segment
🅣	Main trailhead
🆃	Other trailhead
■	Point of interest
▲	Peak
🅐	Frontcountry campground
Camp 2▲	Camp
ford ⌒	Caution
no fires ◣	Restricted area
⋍	Pass or gap
-⋍-	Footbridge
→⌐ ⌐←	Tunnel
────	Ski lift
↦⊣	Gate

▭	Park or forest boundary
▭	Boundary between forests
⌐ ⌐	Wilderness boundary
⌐ ⌐	State or county boundary
▢	Fire area
▬	Lava field
⌒	River or creek
⊣⊦	Fall
⬭	Water
⚲	Spring
⭕	Water source (on profiles)
🅝	True north

When choosing where to bed down, look for existing campsites on durable surfaces that adhere to Leave No Trace practices.

LNT guidelines (100 feet from trail and water) but, as "established" campsites, present the best available options. It's impossible to list every place to camp along the PCT, but this guide includes camps that are close to the PCT and in logical locations. Camps in fragile areas, such as meadows or wetlands, or those discouraged by the land management agency—even though they exist—are not included in this guide. Practice good outdoor ethics and avoid such camps.

Numbered camps are one-offs or trailside pullouts, often useful for solo travelers or small groups. In this guide these camps are numbered sequentially over an entire section and are called out on the section's maps and elevation profiles. **Named camps** are established destination locations, generally with multiple sites (and more visitors). These are recommended for convenience, ideal for larger groups, and may often be located near water. Some of the named camps are actually **car campgrounds**, managed by national forests, national parks, or private entities. Such campgrounds usually show up near trailheads and can be handy for PCT hikers (and any friends you've sweet-talked into meeting you with your favorite treats!). Unlike backcountry camps, most campgrounds offer some conveniences, such as drinking water and trash facilities; they often charge a moderate fee.

PLANNING AND PREPARATION

Taking a hike along the PCT requires proper and thorough preparation, no matter if you're weekending over a few legs or thru-hiking multiple sections—regardless of what some other literature may imply. Before you step foot on the trail, spend some time getting acquainted with trail distances and elevation variances. Plan realistic hiking days based on your own experience and ability. Study the locations of campsites and water sources and the distances between them; this will help you be prepared for challenging sections and potentially long, dry stretches. Become acquainted with your gear: know how each item works, what its limitations are, and practice using it; read gear instructions *before* getting on trail, then leave them home. Finally, read this guide thoroughly. It will provide you with everything you need to fulfill your own personal PCT journey—as well as plenty of inspiring images to get you excited for your own adventure.

When to Hike

In Oregon, **summer is the ideal season** for hiking the PCT, usually beginning in early to mid-July when days are long and the weather is typically sunny. This is also when the trail is (mostly) snow-free, and water sources are usually reliable. Late July through early August is best for vivid wildflower displays, while late August through September is best for huckleberries, and early October gives a peek at rich fall colors. Until the hiking season begins, the PCT is mostly under a blanket of deep snow and largely inaccessible— and unadvisable unless you're an experienced winter hiker—however, in Oregon, you may get lucky and find a few of the low-elevation areas hikable earlier in the year.

There are a few trade-offs to consider when choosing when to hike the PCT. While early summer offers wildflowers and plenty of water, it is also

Your most common company on the PCT will be these cute little critters.

when gazillions of blood sucking mosquitoes can be a tantrum-inducing nuisance. If you're willing to brave the bugs to frolic in the flowers, be prepared with bug-resistant clothing and heavy-duty repellent. In later summer, the bugs are considerably diminished, making for a much more peaceful and pleasant experience—but so are the flowers and reliable water sources. By the end of summer, seasonal springs usually run dry and small lakes and ponds become murky and undesirable, making opportunities for access to good water fewer and farther between, another reason to plan carefully ahead of your hike.

South to North or North to South?

Most PCT section hikers choose to hike the trail south to north, like their thru-hiking cousins. For the thru-hikers, this is to help them get through California's southern deserts before the scorching summer sets in, and end in Washington in late summer or early autumn, in that small window between winter snowpacks. Fortunately for PCT hikers in Oregon, those issues are of little concern. With the majority of the trail being largely accessible through most summer and fall months, it is feasible to hike the trail in either direction, based on personal preference. However, keep in mind that in Oregon there is more elevation gain going south than there is going north, so depending on how good your knees are, you may prefer grinding uphill instead of downhill through some sections. In keeping with the traditional thru-hiking method, **this guide is arranged south to north**, but if you choose the north-to-south option, it's not difficult to reverse the suggested itineraries.

Weather and Water

Oregon summers are usually moderate and comfortable; spring is usually wet, and fall is when the temps start to dive. But because the PCT runs along the spine of Oregon's Cascades, weather can be a mixed bag at any time of year. Even in the heart of summer, fickle mountain weather can throw curveballs at you. Rain, sometimes torrential, can occur at any time during the summer months, especially when higher temperatures result in fast-building thunderstorms over the Cascade Crest, particularly in the southern and central parts of the state. On rare occasions, it has even snowed along the Crest in the middle of summer.

When planning your own PCT hike, short or long, it is best to start watching the weather patterns and temperature forecasts to give you an idea of what to expect during your journey—and to help you get prepared. This makes the case for always packing your raingear—no matter what the forecast says. Oregon can also be susceptible to near-triple-digit temps during summer heat waves, which can be quite grueling when trekking across exposed, miles-long lava beds or burned forests.

Despite the amount of rain Oregon receives, the PCT remains largely waterless through long stretches of trail. This is due to numerous factors, the most obvious being that as the PCT traverses along the *crest* of the Cascades, it is staying high above the valleys and lake basins where the majority of this rain collects. The other significant factor is that much of Oregon's volcanic topography is extremely porous, and the rain seeps directly into the ground rather than running down its surface. This can result in springs that suddenly pop out of hillsides but are dependent on frequent replenishment (i.e., rain) to keep them flowing. After long dry spells, heat waves, and near the end of summer, many springs and creeks run dry.

Before setting out on your adventure, check the PCTA's water report for updates and warnings. Pack along an extra water container to help get you through the long, dry stretches. Collapsible containers and bladders are ideal because they weigh very little and require minimal pack space when not in use. Although this guide's suggested itineraries have been selected to keep you on course (or suggest where you should deviate from your course), be prepared to travel off the PCT to get water at nearby lakes and springs. This will usually entail a little extra mileage on some of your hiking days. Never rely on water caches, as there's no guarantee that they will be where indicated—or that they'll be full.

Passes and Permits

PCT section hikers do not need a PCT-specific permit. Instead, you'll need to follow the rules

PCT PERMIT FOR THRU-HIKERS

If you intend to hike **500 or more miles continuously** along the PCT, you'll need to secure a permit from the PCTA. This free permit comes with permission from federal land management agencies to travel and camp along the PCT corridor. Since the Oregon portion of the PCT is only 455 miles long, a thru-hike across Oregon does not qualify for this pass, unless you are starting and/or finishing in California or Washington, depending on which direction you're hiking. If you do choose to add mileage, and your hike qualifies for the PCT thru-hikers permit, be sure to include your start and ending locations along the PCT proper instead of the nearest city, national park or forest, or wilderness area.

The PCTA begins processing long-distance permit requests in **early February** and will send your permit via US mail. Each hiker must secure his or her own permit. If you're **younger than eighteen**, you'll need a signed letter from your parent or guardian stating the dates and locations of your trip. Keep the letter with you at all times when you're on the PCT.

for permits and passes depending on what agency manages the land you're hiking on. In Oregon, that is largely the US Forest Service, but there are also stretches on National Park Service, Oregon Bureau of Land Management, and Warm Springs Indian Reservation lands.

Wilderness-Use and Camping Permits

Some Oregon wilderness area trailheads have a small kiosk and wooden box containing a bundle of carbon-copy-style wilderness-use permits. These permits are free, and you're required to fill them out when you come to them—*each time* you come to them. Each wilderness area is its own jurisdiction, and the agency in charge relies on you to help keep track of who's using what and when. The information helps agencies apply for trail-funding grants and also tells someone where you are, which is essential to getting you out safely in case of a natural disaster such as a wildfire or landslide.

Fill in the name and address of the party leader, the number of nights you intend to camp, your trip beginning and end dates, points of entry and exit, and the number of people, stock, and dogs in your party. Then sign the form, stating that you agree to the laws, rules, and regulations of the area. (Most permits list the local wilderness regulations and guidelines.) Leave one copy in the box and attach the other copy to your pack.

In addition to general wilderness permits, there are four areas in Oregon that require special permits for camping on or near the PCT. You must obtain and be in possession of the required permit to camp in these areas, or risk a hefty citation. When planning your trip and applying for these permits, you can improve your chances of getting the dates and locations you want by avoiding weekends and holidays. You will find more information on these requirements in each area's respective section description.

Crater Lake National Park (Section 2) requires all PCT and backcountry hikers to obtain a park wilderness permit for camping within the park boundaries. Camping is limited to designated wilderness areas, and recommended in five established backcountry camp locations. Camping is not permitted anywhere between the park road and the rim of the crater. Permits must be obtained in person from the Steel Visitor Center on Munson Valley Road (between Mazama Village and Rim Village) or at the Rim Village visitor center.

Willamette and Deschutes National Forests, beginning in 2020, will require some PCT hikers to obtain limited-entry permits for hiking in the Three Sisters, Mount Washington, and Mount Jefferson wilderness areas. This requirement affects 110 miles of the PCT, including large portions of Sections 4 and 5 in this guide. This action follows a multiyear study of increasing visitor and hiker impacts in these areas. Many feel that this is a deeply flawed decision by the Forest Service that fails to address real wilderness use issues, and does not ensure equitable access among

WILDERNESS AREA REGULATIONS

People venturing into wilderness areas must obey the following rules:

- **Maximum group size is 12 bodies,** which includes any combination of people and stock
- **Motorized and mechanized use** of any kind is prohibited.
- **Camps must be 100 feet** from lakes and the PCT. This rule applies everywhere in wilderness areas, but especially in sensitive environments.
- **Pack-and-saddle stock must be 200 feet** from lakes when grazing, hitched or hobbled.
- **Caching equipment, property, or supplies** for longer than 48 hours is prohibited.

all hikers, PCT and other. This new restriction will require some hikers to plan much more—and perhaps hope for a bit of luck—to access and enjoy a hike on the PCT through these sections.

Here's a quick rundown on how it will work:

- **PCT thru-hikers** holding a 500-mile permit are allowed entry and exit through these wilderness areas at will.
- **PCT section-hikers** are required to obtain an entry permit for the southern or northern wilderness boundaries—limited to just a few per day.
- **PCT backpackers,** and some day hikers, are required to obtain limited wilderness permits for specific trailheads.

All these permits will be available through the www.recreation.gov website. The whole system is very confusing and convoluted. For more information, visit www.pctoregon.com.

Parking Permits

Many of the trailheads located on national forest lands require the vehicle to display a **Northwest Forest Pass.** Daily passes are $5 and annual passes are $30 (there may be additional service fees with some retailers). For multiday—or multiweek—treks along the PCT, the obvious choice is the annual pass.

The alternative to the Northwest Forest Pass is the $80 **Interagency Annual Pass**, which covers trailhead parking on US Forest Service lands as well as BLM, US Army Corp of Engineers, US Bureau of Reclamation, and US Fish and Wildlife Service lands. This pass also covers entrance fees to all US national parks—convenient for starting and/or ending your PCT jaunt in Crater Lake National Park. The **Interagency Senior Pass** is available for people aged 62 and older for the one time, bargain-basement cost of just $10. Additionally, if you have a permanent disability, you may qualify for a free **Interagency Access Pass**. Passes are sold at Forest Service offices and ranger stations, national park visitor centers, and at some retail stores, as well as online (see appendix 1).

Getting to and from Trailheads

Getting to Oregon's PCT trailheads, or getting picked up from one, requires some advance planning. The good thing about the way Oregon's PCT sections have been divided in this guidebook is that they are all (mostly) accessible by main east–west highways, between Interstate 5 on the west side of the Cascades and US Highways 97 and 26 on the east and north sides. The exception to this is accessing the PCT at the actual California–Oregon border crossing, which requires a remote forest road—but it's not too challenging. There are several state highways and Forest Service roads that can access the PCT at midsection crossings and via lateral trails that require varying degrees of effort to access.

If you're hiking in a group, you can always leave a shuttle car at your ending trailhead. This can require several extra hours of driving before you start—in addition to several extra hours at the end of your hike to retrieve the vehicle left at your starting trailhead—but it means a guaranteed ride at the end of a long trip. Don't forget to pack your waiting vehicle's keys!

If you need to solicit a ride to and from trailheads, try researching local online hiking forums

PCT hikers can fill out their own backcountry permits for most of Oregon's wilderness areas.

and Facebook pages related to the PCT. This is a great way to meet new friends who might give you a lift or even join you on your hike. In Oregon, Oregon Hikers (www.oregonhikers.org) is an active forum for hiking in general, and it's a good way to get acquainted with fellow backpackers.

An advantage to hiking the PCT through Oregon in late summer is the bounty of fresh mountain berries to be enjoyed.

As for **buses and trains**, most public transit and private companies go to towns, not trailheads. But you can always take a cab or rent a car for your final hop to the trail. If all else fails, you might just consider good old-fashioned hitchhiking, which is legal in Oregon. If you're going to rely on hitchhiking, your odds of catching a ride are greatly improved by presenting yourself as clean, friendly, and nonthreatening.

Fueling the Beast of the Belly

Food (and water) will account for the majority of the weight in your pack, but getting plenty of calories and replenishing electrolytes are important on the PCT. Dehydrated and freeze-dried foods can help you consume more calories for less weight. But whether you purchase prepackaged food or prepare your own, it should be things that you like to eat—or you could find yourself running out of gas fast. This is often referred to as "bonking." Simple foods high in carbs, proteins, and fats are best. But that doesn't mean it has to be boring—this is your chance to splurge!

Whether you cook your own or buy premade meals, **sample your food selections before getting on the trail**, as there's nothing worse than ending a day on the trail by having to force down a pot of unappetizing gruel. Use the time before your trip to try out different types of foods and meals to see what tastes the best—with no unfavorable reactions. You can also determine serving sizes to ensure that you're getting the proper number of calories to keep you going.

Once you've selected your menu, repackage all of your food in zip-top baggies, and use a permanent marker to write any preparation instructions directly on the bags. This will help reduce the amount of space your food takes up in your pack as well as reduce the amount of waste you'll need to pack out. On the trail, make your trash tiny by stuffing your baggies and food wrappers inside the largest bag you've emptied. Squeeze all the air out and zip it closed. If you do this daily, you'll end up with a small, flat, and manageable trash bag to toss when the chance comes.

Carry your food and trash in a durable bag, and plan to hang that bag in camp every night to keep it away from critters. Drybags and waterproof stuff sacks make good food bags, as they can be left outside and your food will still be protected from rain. The alternative is to carry your food in a bear-proof canister. Canisters are not required anywhere along the PCT in Oregon, and they're heavy and bulky, but they can conveniently double as a camp stool. For the ultimate in lightweight food storage and protection, consider investing in a critter-proof Ursack (www.ursack.com). **Never store your food in your tent!**

When in camp, never cook in your tent. Food aromas attract wildlife, and you risk fire and carbon monoxide poisoning. Cook outside, away from your tent, and enjoy the beauty of nature. It's a good idea to pack along a couple of no-cook meals just in case of rain or swarming bugs so you can still refuel even if you can't fire up the stove.

Resupplying Food and Supplies

Most backpackers need 1 to 2 pounds of food per day, which quickly adds up in pack weight and space, especially if you're out for more than a week. As a section hiker, you can usually carry all you need for a week on the trail—but you don't have to! There are numerous resorts and other facilities on or near the PCT in Oregon that can save you a lot of pack weight.

For a convenient resupply strategy, you can do one of three things: mail a box to a resort or designated resupply retailer or facility near the trail, buy as you hike from stores at or near the trail or trailheads, or talk a friend into meeting you somewhere along the way with a food or supply cache. Each section (as well as appendixes 3 and 4) lists resorts and services near the trail and trailheads, including where you can send packages for pickup.

HOW MUCH FUEL?

This depends entirely on how you like to eat in the backcountry. Many efficiency-minded hikers are fine just boiling water for freeze-dried meal pouches, while camp gourmets may prefer preparing saucy pasta dishes with sautéed fresh veggies. If you're in the camp of the former, you can probably get away with packing along one large fuel can for a weeklong trek; if the latter, you'll probably want to carry an extra can. Also keep in mind that temperature, wind, and elevation can all affect stove performance.

Most places will hold your package for free or a small fee. For longer, multisection trips, or a state-spanning thru-hike, try enlisting a friend to mail your packages on agreed-upon dates. If you go this route, don't seal your packages before you leave—that way, you can ask your supply guru to add things you might be missing, or might need extra of (e.g., Moleskin or GPS unit batteries). Maybe they'll even add in a few extra treats! Some PCT hikers employ a bounce box for resupplying on the trail. This is a box that gets mailed from one resupply facility to the next, and often contains things like phone and camera chargers, batteries, first-aid supplies, extra bug spray and sunscreen, and so on. Some hikers even bounce small laptops or tablet computers to email friends and family, update blogs, and share photos of their trail progress.

If you buy as you hike, you can end up with glorious fresh food, but it can also cost you time off the trail and some head-scratching to figure out your nutritional needs for the stretches of trail still ahead. You also may not find exactly what you're looking for. If you have specific dietary needs or restrictions, you may find the mail-ahead strategy a better (and necessary) option. You'll find more information on the types of food supplies offered at the facilities mentioned in this guide in appendixes 3 and 4.

At some locations, you might find a hiker freebie box for long-distance trail users. Items often found in these boxes include oatmeal, ramen, trail mix, drink powders, sunscreen, and partially used fuel canisters. It is all free for the taking. These boxes are also a good way for you to unload your own extras that you don't need—and perhaps help out a fellow hiker. The contents of hiker freebie boxes vary greatly—some overflowing with discarded extras, some with not so much as a trail bar—so it's best not to depend on these as suitable resupplies, and consider yourself lucky if you score a few suitable extras.

If you need to resupply stove fuel during your hike, follow these guidelines:

- *Never—ever—mail flammable substances!*
- If you have a white gas or alcohol stove, research ahead where you can buy fuel along the way, typically at trailhead towns or resorts.
- If you use a compressed-fuel (isobutane) stove, research ahead where you can buy new full canisters and/or carry extras with you.

THE MOUNTAINEERS' TEN ESSENTIALS

No backpacker should set foot on trail without these essential items, no matter how experienced they are. These items will not only ensure your safety and comfort on the trail, they may also save your bacon should something unforeseen happen.

1. Navigation (map and compass)
2. Illumination (headlamp or flashlight)
3. Sun protection (hat, sunglasses and sunscreen)
4. First-aid supplies (especially for feet)
5. Repair kit including a knife or multi-tool
6. Fire materials (fire starter and matches or lighter)
7. Hydration (extra water and filtering device)
8. Insulation (extra clothing, rain gear)
9. Nutrition (extra food)
10. Emergency shelter (tarp or bivy)

GEAR AND CLOTHING

The best type of clothing you can wear on the trail are lightweight, breathable, moisture-wicking wool or synthetic garments. Many of these materials will also help minimize odors when gone unwashed for several days. Plan your clothing in layers, which will let you make easy adjustments to accommodate for variances in weather and temperature. Even in summer, it can still get cold at night, so pack along a warm jacket, hat, and gloves. It is best to avoid cotton clothing at all costs.

When it comes to gear and clothing for the PCT, **weight matters**. You've probably heard stories of thru-hikers who cut off their toothbrush handles and measure each bag of granola to the exact ounce needed. (Ironically, these are often the same folks toting ukuleles and iPads down the trail, too!) That's a great way to trim pack weight if you're planning on being on the trail for several weeks, or months, and want to knock out 25–30-mile days. For section hiking the PCT, in spurts of a week or two, you still want to watch your load weight, but you can indulge in a few creature comforts as well—and you don't have to drop a ton of cash on a hyperlight pack system.

As a general rule of thumb, your **pack weight should not exceed 25–30 percent of your body weight**. When choosing the gear and clothing that's going with you, divide it into two piles: "must-haves" and "wanna-haves." Things that belong in your must-have pile are your tent or shelter, sleeping and cooking gear, extra clothing, raingear (no matter what the forecast says!), and your Ten Essentials. Things that belong in your wanna-have pile are your camp chair, unabridged copy of *The Lord of the Rings*, full-frame DSLR with a 300-millimeter lens, and 2-pound bag of peanut M&Ms.

Start by filling your pack with your must-haves. Don't forget to include your food and a full load of water. Then put your pack on and test its weight. If you need help getting up, chances are there are a few things that should've gone in your wanna-have pile and you need to do some reevaluation. If the load is moderately comfortable, then consider how much room you still have available and start selecting from your wanna-have pile for those extra items that will add a little more comfort to your endeavor. Remember, you're hiking the PCT for fun and recreation, not for punishment. You don't need to deprive yourself of a few extras—especially essentials—just to save a few ounces. If your pack is properly balanced and adjusted, once you hit your stride on the trail, you're likely to forget it's even on your back. So go ahead and pack along that inflatable pillow and ultralight camp chair—you'll be glad you did.

Boots and Socks

Keeping your feet happy on the trail is paramount, and your footwear can make or break your PCT hiking experience. These days, many experienced long-distance backpackers use trail-running shoes. These shoes are lightweight, extremely breathable, and can handle a variety of trail conditions. But they're not for everyone, and it takes a lot of training to tackle a trail like the PCT in runners. Conversely, a good pair of sturdy hiking boots offers more foot protection and ankle support, which can improve the management of your pack load. Many styles of boot also incorporate a GoreTex liner that enables breathability while also keeping your feet dry when the elements decide to show themselves—a common occurrence in the Northwest. Regardless of what type of footwear you choose, remember your feet will swell as you hike, so size up at least a half size so your feet don't become smashed and painful in your shoes.

Choose the right socks. As with clothing, wool and synthetic fibers are breathable, moisture-wicking, and minimize odors. Do not wear cotton. Choose a mid- to heavyweight hiking sock with good cushioning that's not too snug in your boots. Consider adding a micro sock liner to protect your feet from friction and rubbing.

Trekking Poles: Your Metal Arm Extensions

Trekking poles can give you more support and help you manage the load on your back. They'll help you ascend the long, uphill slogs, and save your knees on the steep downhill pitches, not to mention give you extra stability when fording streams and rivers. They make great splints or tarp supports too.

TIPS FOR LIGHTENING YOUR LOAD

If you're determined to go as minimalist as possible, consider these options to help shave extra ounces from your load:

- **Use tiny travel containers.** Never carry a full tube or can of anything, and purchase travel-sized toiletries.
- **Discard all pouches.** Ditch your pack's raincover case, mattress stuff sack, and so on.
- **Pare down your first-aid kit.** Carry only the realistic "what-ifs" and those items you use most frequently.
- **Lighten up your potty paper.** Remove the cardboard core from your TP, or buy rolls at your outdoor retailer that come without.
- **Get creative with multipurposing.** You can use a piece of cord as a clothesline, backup shoelace, or guyline for your tent or to secure a splint. Your puffy jacket or a stuff sack filled with clothes can be your pillow, and so on.
- **Wash your clothes.** Instead of overloading on fresh undergarments and socks, use a large zip-top bag (or Scrubba bag) as your on-trail washing machine, and refresh your essentials every few days.

High-Tech Gadgets

Like it or not, tech gadgets have invaded the backcountry. But they're not all bad. GPS units can help you track your mileage and elevation, and smartphones can carry apps that can help you pinpoint your location, identify wildflowers, and take photos. Oregon has such prolific cellular coverage that you can even make phone calls and post to your Facebook profile from many places on the trail.

If you do choose to bring the toys, remember that they're only as good as long as their batteries last. Carry extra batteries for your essential electronics, or mail extras ahead in your resupply caches. You can also recharge at many of the resorts on or near the trail. Putting your smartphone in airplane mode when you're not using it can often buy you an extra few days of battery power. Portable chargers are convenient but add weight to your pack, and solar chargers don't work so well when you're forest-bound, so consider your options carefully.

ON THE TRAIL

You're almost there! You've done all your packing, you know where you're going, and you're headed for the great outdoors. Even so, you still have some things to think about.

Wilderness Ethics and Multiuse Trails

In Oregon, the PCT passes through different federal, private, and reservation lands used by many people. Being aware of a few simple principles can ensure a rewarding and memorable experience.

PCT TRAIL NAMES

Odd trail nicknames are part of the PCT's unique subculture, even for section hikers. Your trail name becomes part of your persona.

Traditionally, you don't choose your own trail name. Other hikers, based on a story you tell or trait you exhibit, crown you with a nickname. You can choose whether or not to accept it, and those who bestow it should make an effort to avoid outright offense. Once you accept it, that name becomes who you are on the trail. Sometimes, you'll bond with other PCTers and never learn their real names, livelihoods, or histories, but none of that matters. Learning about a person through a trail name is like getting to know someone on fast-forward.

Plan ahead and be prepared. Bring what you need and double-check your lists. Mountain weather can change quickly and dramatically, despite what the forecast says, so don't skimp on extra clothing and raingear just because there's blue sky outside.

Travel and camp on durable surfaces. Avoid camping on vegetation or in meadows and fragile alpine areas, and look for existing campsites before making a new one. When you stop for a break, step off the trail and set yourself and your pack on logs, rocks, or other durable surfaces.

Dispose of waste properly. Dig cat holes 6 to 8 inches deep—at least 100 feet from the trail and campsites and 200 feet from water sources—to bury human waste. Pack out all toilet paper. Do not use rocks or downed wood to hide waste piles. Pack out everything you bring along, including uneaten food, wrappers, and trash.

Leave what you find. Your pack will be heavy enough, and you'll quickly start cursing that pretty piece of obsidian you picked up. Additionally, it is illegal to remove rocks, plants, and Native American artifacts from protected areas and national parks.

Minimize fire hazards. Only use fire pits in areas where fires are permitted, and in campsites where a fire pit already exists. Keep fires small and use only downed, dead sticks and wood. Don't burn any trash in fire pits, and make sure your fire is completely extinguished before you go to bed or leave camp.

Respect wildlife. Keep your food to yourself, and store your food properly by hanging it from a tree or using an animal-proof food container. When photographing animals, keep a respectable distance away and never approach animals with young.

Be considerate of others. Keep your voice low so others can enjoy the quiet. If you're hiking in a group, go single file when passing others, and grant uphill hikers the right-of-way. If you enjoy listening to your tunes on trail, keep them to yourself by using headphones. In camp, respect "quiet time," typically 10 p.m. to 8 a.m.

Horses are permitted on the entire length of the PCT. While horse droppings can be irritating, volunteer equestrian groups are often the ones supporting trail maintenance by packing in

The origins of some features' names become obvious when you get to know them, as is the case with Shale Butte whose open slopes offer excellent views.

tools, food, and gear for backcountry trail crews. When approaching horse riders or a pack string, announce your presence by calling ahead with a friendly "hello!" This will keep the horse from becoming spooked by your sudden appearance. Then step to the downhill side of the trail and allow the equestrians to pass.

Mountain bikes and motorized vehicles are prohibited on the PCT. Ongoing pressure from the mountain-biking community in recent years has sparked debate about allowing bikes on the trail. The Forest Service, however, continues to uphold its 1988 order keeping the PCT closed to mountain bikes.

Fishing can be a fun diversion when camping along the PCT, and may score you a tasty meal. If you're interested in casting a line in one of the many backcountry lakes, follow the Oregon Department of Fish and Wildlife regulations (see appendix 1). If you do get lucky and catch dinner, avoid attracting furry, four-legged critters by cleaning and cooking your fish away from where people camp.

Staying Found

In places, the PCT can be challenging to follow, despite the familiar PCT blazes that often mark the route. Some signs are missing or misleading, some trail turns are not second nature, and some stretches follow reroutes or rock cairns. Fog and inclement weather can also throw you off. If it feels wrong, it most likely is! Stop and reassess your surroundings and direction, using landmarks, map, and compass. If for some reason you get lost or find yourself in an uncomfortable situation, here are a few tips that may help.

Always let someone know where you're going and when you plan to return home. Leave your itinerary with a friend or family member. Give them a map with your route marked, and leave a list of the land management agencies and contact numbers for the areas you'll be passing through. Specify a date and time that you will check in at the completion of your journey, and when to contact rangers should you not check in on time. Be sure to

BLAZES OF GLORY

Navigating along the PCT is fairly straightforward thanks to trail blazes and signs on trees and signposts, all the way from Mexico to Canada. Blazes come in a variety of shapes, depending on their age. Some very old ones are white and diamond-shaped, with green lettering that says "Pacific Crest Trail System" and an image of a tree. Newer blazes feature the PCT emblem with black, white, and teal coloring, with the wording "Pacific Crest Trail, National Scenic Trail" and an image of a mountain and a tree. In other places, wooden signs say "Pacific Crest Trail" with an arrow. Other markers include plain silver diamonds and tree notches in the shape of an "i." Despite this variety of navigational aids, not every section is clearly marked, and long stretches will offer few or no markings, thus making it imperative that you still travel with a map and compass.

give yourself a buffer for weather or unforeseen circumstances.

Stay put and don't panic if you're lost or injured! It's easier to locate a fixed target than a moving one. Use your waiting time to gather firewood, filter water, and examine your food situation. Try to relax your mind with positive, constructive thoughts, and settle into a daily routine that will help ease the situation.

Use your cell phone, satellite phone, or personal locator beacon for help. Almost everyone takes a cell phone into the backcountry these days, and reception has become surprisingly reliable, even in remote areas. Satellite phones have become cheaper and smaller, making them a better option if you travel frequently in the backcountry. Additionally, personal locator devices (e.g., SPOT Satellite Messenger) connect to private satellite networks and can alert friends, family, and emergency personnel if you trigger an SOS. However, keep in mind that the reliable service provided by electronic communication devices is not a replacement for common sense.

Treating Water

To filter or not to filter should not even be a question worth asking. It only takes one bad swig to ruin your entire trip. Even if water looks clear and clean, it may contain tasteless protozoa such as *Cryptosporidium* and *Giardia*. These waterborne pathogens cause flulike symptoms, including vomiting and diarrhea, lasting one to six weeks or in some cases, up to a year.

With all the current options for treating and/or filtering water, it's not worth risking. **Water-treatment devices** range from UV-light pens that kill bacteria and viruses, to carbon or ceramic filters that eliminate bacteria and unpleasant tastes. Almost all are lightweight, portable, and extremely effective. Or, use **water-treatment tablets**, usually made with iodine or chlorine dioxide (the latter is better for not having a nasty taste). And you can always **boil water**—that's the only 100 percent effective way to kill waterborne pathogens, but it consumes fuel and eats up trail time if you're not in camp.

If you do use a filter, avoid silted and murky water if possible. Oregon's glacier-fed rivers of milky-colored water contain silt and silica (glass!) that can clog a filter and cause digestive problems.

Taking Care of #2
There are few backcountry privies along the PCT, meaning that you must typically engage in the backcountry squat.

- Find a spot that's at least **100 feet from camps and the trail** and at least **200 feet from water**.
- **Dig a hole** 6 to 8 inches deep. If you dig too deep, the bacteria won't be able to properly break down the waste.
- **Dispose of toilet paper** in a small baggie and take it with you.
- **Cover up the waste** completely after stirring in some dirt to ensure that it will decompose efficiently.
- **Apply a squirt of hand sanitizer** and you're good to go.

Hazards
For as well-traveled as the PCT is, there are still challenges to be faced along the way, largely due to weather and the forces of nature.

No Bridge over Troubled Water
Arriving at a sturdy bridge over running water is always a comfort and relief. Unfortunately, not all rivers and streams along the PCT offer this luxury. When the need arises to cross a bridgeless waterway, a little know-how goes a long way.

Cross early in the morning, when water levels are at their lowest. If you're hiking solo and the conditions look questionable, consider waiting for other hikers to come along and cross together.

Look for straight, shallow, wide, and gentle water. You don't need to cross directly at the trail if the conditions look threatening. Scout up- and downstream for a safe crossing with calmer water.

Don't cross if it's above your knees. Any higher than your knees, and the current can suck you downstream. If the water is flat, however, you could probably bend this rule of thumb.

Watch for hidden debris. Keep a close eye out for small logs or downed trees that might be hidden underwater.

Unbuckle your pack's waist belt. Your pack might shift slightly as you walk, but having an easy exit strategy could save your life if you go for an unexpected plunge.

HAVE AN ESCAPE PLAN

You're likely going to spend weeks, if not months, planning your perfect PCT hike. During that planning phase, spend a little time plotting for "what if" moments, when you might need to make a quick exit. While having to bail from the trail is not an appealing prospect, unforeseen incidents do occur—critters raiding your food supply, water filter breaks, minor injury or illness, inclement weather, trail hazards, wildfires. As such, familiarizing yourself with the area you'll be hiking through, and other trails on and near the PCT, is beneficial.

Under ideal conditions, the easiest way to exit is either continuing forward or backtracking to the PCT trailheads for the section you are hiking, as these are located at easily accessible main highways. If you're in the middle of a section and need a quicker exit, or the direction you're heading is suddenly blocked or hazardous, there are often numerous lateral trails that connect to the PCT that exit to other nearby trailheads; you'll find these listed for each leg under "Connecting Trails and Roads." Identify the trails that will best help you exit to where you are most likely to get assistance, typically major trailheads on good roads or near maintained camp areas. Conversely, know which trails end at remote trailheads on poor roads where you are less likely to receive assistance. During your planning, mark these preferred exit routes on your map. They'll be good to know, just in case.

Maintain at least two points of contact. Use trekking poles or find a big stick to help you balance.

Log crossings can be hazardous. Crossing on a downed log might seem like the best bet for keeping your shoes dry, but could also be hazardous. Is the bark completely intact? If not, it could peel off and send you tumbling into the water. Likewise, wet logs without bark can be slipperier than ice and also send you reeling. Before proceeding, check for good traction and keep your gaze focused on the log or opposite riverbank. Don't look at the rushing water beneath you, as it can cause dizziness.

Never cross in bare feet. When there are no logs to cross or rocks to hop over, you may just have to bear down and get your feet wet—but keep your shoes on! Bare feet can easily slip on mossy rocks and wet logs, plus you run the risk of jamming or breaking toes or puncturing your feet on sharp rocks or sticks—all of which can bring a swift ending to your journey and a sudden need of assistance. If you don't carry an extra pair of water-crossing shoes, just tighten up your boots and plunge through.

Landslides Might Bring It Down

Should you encounter a landslide, only attempt to cross if you think the ground is stable enough. Slides can be a result of years of soil erosion, water runoff, or volcanic activity, and the soil and debris often shifts when you step on it. Probe the debris with your trekking poles or a long stick to ensure that it's stable. Carefully kick in steps and keep your weight centered above your feet as you move. Move as quickly as you can to clear the area.

Where There's Smoke, There's Fire

With warm, dry weather comes the threat of wildfires, often sparked by lightning from summer thunderstorms. At least once a season, it seems, fires close parts of the PCT. In recent years, as summer temperatures have been climbing, and drought conditions have been worsening, wildfires are becoming more common and more destructive.

While California is generally the hardest hit, fires can pop up just about anywhere, including in the usually damp Pacific Northwest. In the early 2000s, several massive wildfires blackened Oregon's Mount Washington and Mount Jefferson wilderness areas and burned across more than 40 miles of the PCT. In 2014, wildfires closed the entire stretch of the PCT in the Sky Lakes Wilderness, and in 2015, half of the stretch through Crater Lake National Park.

If you encounter thunderstorm activity while hiking, be extra-vigilant of your surroundings. Descend from high ridges and retreat from any sharp, exposed peaks. If you observe smoke or an active wildfire anywhere in your vicinity, head out to a road via the nearest safe route. Wildfires can spread incredibly fast, so don't assume that because a fire is in the distance, you're safe. Wildfire updates are often posted on the land management agency and PCTA websites to help you stay on top of new developments and trail closures.

Dangers can also remain in past burn areas. Use extra caution when hiking in areas with blackened, dead-standing trees and loamy, loose soil, as trees may become unstable, especially in high winds. Don't camp in areas with charred trees, even if they look sturdy.

Hunting Season

Oregon's hunting seasons vary from year to year depending on the health of the game population being hunted and other factors. For complete hunting regulations and seasonal openings, visit the Oregon Department of Fish and Wildlife website (see appendix 1). Here are some general guidelines if hiking during hunting season:

Wear bright-colored clothing. Pick a hat, shirt, jacket, or pack that will be clearly seen and identify you as a hiker. Orange and red are recommended; avoid white, khaki, and brown.

Make noise as you hike. Hunters typically avoid high-traffic areas that frighten away game. Talk, sing, or whistle to let hunters know that there are hikers in the area.

Avoid peak times of day. Hunters favor dawn and dusk when animals are most active. If hiking in low light, wear a headlamp.

Avoid off trail travel. Hunters are scoping for game away from populous trails, so avoid tromping through brush where a hunter might be awaiting his next target.

Black bears roam the length of Oregon's Cascades. Count yourself lucky if you spy one of these shy creatures.

Leave Fido at home. If you hike with a dog, hunting season is a good time to leave him at home. If you have to have your pup on the trail with you, put him in his own brightly colored vest and keep him leashed and at your side.

Animal Encounters

On your PCT journey, you're likely to see more wild animals than other humans. Most pose little threat, but always exercise common sense and follow accepted safe behaviors when you encounter larger beasts.

Bear Know-How

The only type of bear found in Oregon is the black bear, and seeing one on the PCT is largely a matter of chance. And luck. From late spring through midsummer, bears are most active in the morning and early evening hours. In fall, as they're gorging on berries and grubs to fatten up for their long winter naps, they are more active throughout the day.

Black bears are extremely wary of people, and prefer to be left alone to forage, feed, and raise their young. When on the trail, **watch for bear signs** such as footprints, scat piles, and scratched-up trees. Make noise by talking loudly, singing, or clapping when hiking through overgrown brush or when approaching blind curves.

Black bears are rarely aggressive and typically run away when people come near. **If you do encounter an aggressive bear**, it's likely feeling threatened and defending its cubs or food source. Startled bears will pop their jaws, huff, and slam their paws to the ground to tell you that you've crossed the line. **Avoid eye contact** (which bears perceive as a challenge) while talking calmly and backing away slowly. **Never turn your back on a bear and never, EVER run**. Occasionally, a bear

Crater Lake is one of Oregon's natural scenic wonders, and is worth a detour off the PCT to take it in.

will bluff-charge (charge, stop short, and run away) to try to scare the wibbles out of you. Stand your ground and avoid eye contact. Don't take even a half step backward. If a black bear does attack, fight back with all you've got.

Cougar Country

The odds of seeing a cougar (a.k.a. mountain lion) on the PCT in Oregon are quite slim. You're likely to not even see a footprint from these shy, solitary animals. Similar to bears, cougars are often in the wind long before you're aware they were even nearby.

In the ridiculously rare instance where you do cross paths with a cougar and it gets curious about you, there are a few things you can do. **Maintain eye contact**. Cougars rely on being stealthy and hidden. Staring a cat down tells it you're aware of its presence. **Make noise and get crazy**. Wave your trekking poles or pull your jacket up over your head to make yourself look like a formidable enemy. If you have children or a dog with you, pick them up and keep them high, as cougars usually target the easiest prey.

Never run from a cougar. This may trigger the cat's instinctive urge to chase. Back away slowly and never turn your back on the animal. If a cougar does attack, fight back and fight dirty. Throw rocks, punch it, and poke it in the eyes.

Snakes

The PCT runs through landscapes that are home to several varieties of snakes, most of which are nonthreatening. **Oregon is home to two varieties of rattlesnake**: the western rattlesnake and the Northern Pacific rattlesnake. They have a hard time eking out a living in the mild, damp Northwest, but are sometimes seen sunning themselves on or near the trail (mostly in the southern and eastern parts of the state) in the warm summer months. Like most creatures, they're rarely aggressive unless they feel threatened, and are courteous enough to give you a warning tail shake to let you know they're nearby.

You can minimize your chances of encountering a rattlesnake by **watching your footing** in dry areas with low brush and tall grass, in scree fields, and on rocky outcroppings. **Use trekking poles.** Snakes are sensitive to vibration and might feel you before they hear you. If you're hiking with your pup through rattlesnake country, keep him on a short leash. If you encounter a snake on the trail, back away slowly, and don't make any sudden movements. Keep your distance and allow the snake to vacate the area first.

Insects

Mosquitoes, gnats, blackflies, ticks, and horseflies are some of the annoying biting, burrowing, buzzing bugs you may have to battle on the PCT. Thankfully, walking at a good clip tends to discourage most of them from landing or attaching.

The best way to keep the buggers at bay is to **wear a loose-fitting long-sleeve shirt and pants** and employ a **good insect repellent.**

The most common and effective repellents contain **DEET.** This pesticide makes some folks nervous, but the US Environmental Protection Agency has given it a thumbs-up and human-health complications are rare. Gentler (but somewhat less effective) mosquito repellents include a wide variety of herbal products, often with ingredients such as citronella and essential oils. You might also consider treating your clothing and gear with a chemical called **permethrin.** One application is usually effective for up to six weeks and through six washings.

Bee stings and horsefly bites can cause severe allergic reactions. If you get stung or bitten and develop hives, wheezing, or swelling of the lips, throat, or tongue, seek help immediately. If you know you are allergic to insect bites, it's a good idea to carry precautionary medications and/or an EpiPen.

Staying Safe and Crime-Free

Thankfully, most criminals are lazy and committing crimes on trails is usually too much effort. That said, staying vigilant and keeping a healthy level of awareness is always a good idea.

Never leave valuables in your vehicle. Take (or hide) anything and everything that might look interesting. Even if it's empty, a closed sunglasses case might look like it contains an expensive pair of Oakleys; a smartphone charger might make a prowler think the phone is still in the car.

Case the place. When you arrive at a trailhead, look for anything or anyone that seems out of place—for example, people sitting in cars as if they're waiting. Criminals rely on stealth, and may spook and leave if they see you watching them. If you smell a rat, write down the license plate number, vehicle make and model, and a description of the person in question. A moment of diligence may make the world of difference should something happen later on.

Trust your instincts. If you sense that someone you meet has bad intentions, allow yourself to be guarded and rude if necessary.

Never tell anyone you meet where you're planning to spend the night, especially if you're alone. Be vague—"I'm just hiking until I get tired."

Never mention your party size. If you're hiking alone, using "we" statements might confuse a criminal. Shouting "Hurry up, Tony" or "Let's get

BE A CONSIDERATE HIKER

As you're hiking the PCT, you are bound to meet all manner of hikers, people from far and wide who all share a common interest in getting out and experiencing wilderness in a big way. For the most part, PCT hikers are a friendly, helpful bunch who only want to see everyone succeed at their own PCT dreams. You are bound to meet people along the way whom you will share rest breaks and campsites with, swap stories with, and perhaps provide assistance to (or receive assistance from) when in need. Being a considerate hiker can go a long way with fellow hikers while on trail, and with other campers and recreationists when off trail—perhaps even so far as to score you an extra treat.

Be ready for lots and lots of trees.

going, Natasha" into the bushes may deter someone who thinks you're an easy solo target.

Avoid hiking with headphones. When in the backcountry, try listening to birdsong, squeaking pikas, and whistling marmots instead of blasting your favorite U2 album. Paying attention to your surroundings will help you hear someone or something coming. If you need the extra energy boost of some high-tempo tunes to get you up a big climb, or down a long, monotonous stretch, keep the volume low so you can still detect surrounding noises.

TRAIL WISDOM

> *Do, or do not. There is no try.*
> —Yoda

I am not a thru-hiker by nature. My idea of a great hike is one to two weeks on trail, covering 70 to 80 miles in an amazing place, and calling it a trip well-spent. This is largely because my hiking to-do list is too long to spend too much time in one place. Additionally, I'm a slow hiker. I like moderate trail days, where I can amble along, enjoy the sights, photograph flowers, admire rocks, take naps near lakes, and quit early enough in the day to enjoy lounging in camps and watching sunsets. That's what drew me to participate in this new series of PCT guidebooks—the everyperson's approach to taking on a big trail and enjoying it in easy-to-manage pieces.

I spent three summers researching this book, hiking the PCT through Oregon in a variety of pieces and lengths to experience the entire trail through the state. Some portions I hiked more than once so I could experience the trail at different times of year, or so I could capture different moods in photos. Even as a "professional" hiker, with thousands of trail miles under my boots, I still learned many lessons along the way while undertaking this effort and immersing myself in the PCT for those three summers. As you start preparing for your own PCT experience, I'd like to share a few additional, helpful thoughts to help ensure that you have an amazing journey of your own.

Hike your own hike. This is perhaps the most important thing I would like to impart to all potential PCT hikers. Hiking the PCT is not just for uber-athletes and hardcore thru-hikers. For the most part, the PCT is an all-access trail that can be hiked by just about anyone in reasonably good health, and who is willing to live in the dirt for an extended period of time. This guidebook is designed to help anyone who is interested in hiking the PCT in a manner that suits individual interests, while giving potential hikers a realistic template for taking on a big trail in a way that fits in with "real life."

Know your limits. When planning your hike, be realistic with your expectations. Hiking the PCT is not a contest, and it's not a proving ground to show off how tough you are. Plan your hiking journey based on your current ability, not your ideal ability. Pushing yourself quickly beyond your known limits only compromises your chances of success, and often results in bonking and burning out. As you're planning, familiarize yourself with distances and elevation variances, and where the good water and campsites are. As you're hiking, you can modify your itinerary up or down to go farther if you're feeling good, or slow down if you find yourself struggling.

Don't be "that guy." Every now and then, you're bound to meet a real tool on trail—the hiker who scoffs at anyone he considers less hardcore, less experienced, or not toting the latest in hyperlight backpacking gear. These are the folks who are usually not fun to be around, and who will only diminish your own experience. These are also the people who, in recent years as the PCT has become more and more popular, have been the reason that many Trail Angels have stopped serving hikers and that some resort and establishment owners no longer welcome PCTers. Remember, "manners maketh man"—and woman. In the end, you want to have a memorable experience for the right reasons, not the wrong ones.

Enjoy the whole experience. Many PCT hikers disparage Oregon as being the boring "Green Tunnel." And there are many long, viewless stretches through Oregon that can—and likely will—get monotonous over the miles. This is where you need to discover more about what's beneath you than what's on the horizon. Oregon has a fascinating geologic story, much of it found in the colorful

DON'T THROW YOUR BOOTS OVER A CLIFF

While it was a humorous moment from a recent popular story, throwing your boots over a cliff—or anything, for that matter—is still littering, and violates Leave No Trace practices. Many sensitive areas in Oregon's wilderness areas and along the PCT are getting trashed by overuse and by careless hikers and campers, which results in more restrictions and more permit requirements by land managers. Practice the mottoes of "Pack it in, pack it out" and "Take only photographs, leave only footprints." This will ensure that our wild places stay wild, and we can continue to enjoy and appreciate them as they're meant to be seen.

lavas, basalts, and pumices on and near the trail. The other story comes in the form of the plants, mosses, lichens, flowers, berries, and fungi seen throughout the state. Pack along small field guides, or download a smartphone app (Oregon Wildflowers is a great one to have handy). Keep a log of your finds along the way and see how many you can identify. Give yourself bonus points if you find the elusive calypso orchid or a morel mushroom.

With a little planning, a little know-how, and a little get-up-and-go, you'll soon be on your way to enjoying the spectacular Pacific Crest Trail and its grand landscapes. As you wander amid fragrant meadows and take in misty-eyed views of wide mountain panoramas, you'll be making memories for years to come. Your journey awaits!

For more information, trail news, resources, and updates, visit www.pctoregon.com.

DONOMORE PASS TO FISH LAKE

WHEN YOU ARE READY to hike the Pacific Crest Trail through Oregon, there's no better place to start than where the trail enters the Beaver State at Donomore Pass. This remote starting point—often overlooked or skipped by many a PCT hiker—offers more quiet and solitude than many of the northern sections, and navigates terrain that is generally mild. As a convergence zone of three distinct mountain ranges, it also exhibits some unique geology and a variety of flora unseen on any other section of Oregon's PCT, including rolling grasslands, oak woodlands, granite outcrops, and passage under a prominent natural landmark. Along the way are wildflower meadows, glaciated valleys, and panoramic views over the Siskiyou Mountains, all leading to the foot of Oregon's volcanic Cascade Range. The first two legs of this section are some of the most view-packed, making it worth the extra effort to include them and not skip ahead to the easier starting point at Siskiyou Pass.

The PCT enters Oregon in the western **Siskiyou Mountains**, the oldest mountain range in the state and just southwest of the city of Ashland. From the border the trail bears east, traversing the ridgeline that separates the **Rogue River–Siskiyou National Forest** and **Klamath National Forest**. This is because in California the PCT has taken a wide westward turn to navigate around Mount Shasta, proceed up through the Trinity Alps and Marble Mountain wilderness areas, then cross the Seiad Valley before climbing into Oregon. This is referred to as the PCT's "Big Bend," where it takes nearly 300 trail miles to cover a direct distance of only 50 miles. Here at the start of Leg 1, just beyond the apex of this westward circuit, the PCT bows back east to continue its northward trajectory along the crest of the Cascades.

DISTANCE 82.1 miles

STATE DISTANCE 0–82.1 miles

ELEVATION GAIN/LOSS
+13,480 feet/–14,660 feet

HIGH POINT 7110 feet

BEST TIME OF YEAR July–Aug

PCTA SECTION LETTERS A, B

LAND MANAGERS Rogue River–Siskiyou National Forest, Klamath National Forest, Oregon Bureau of Land Management (Cascade-Siskiyou National Monument, Soda Mountain Wilderness), Fremont-Winema National Forest

PASSES AND PERMITS NW Forest Pass required for parking at Summit Sno-Park trailhead.

MAPS AND APPS
- National Geographic PCT: Oregon South 1005, maps 10–15
- Halfmile PCT: California R6–Oregon B8
- Guthook PCT: Oregon

LEGS
1. Donomore Pass to Long John Saddle
2. Long John Saddle to Siskiyou Pass (I-5)
3. Siskiyou Pass (I-5) to Hobart Bluff TH
4. Hobart Bluff TH to Hyatt Lake
5. Hyatt Lake to Burton Flat Road
6. Burton Flat Road to Fish Lake (Summit TH)

Opposite: *The brilliant contrast of blue sky, green trees, black lava, and red cindery trail near Brown Mountain is just one of many unforgettable stretches of the PCT through Oregon.*

The PCT enters Oregon at the remote Donomore Pass. This weathered sign marks your starting line.

The PCT then crosses Interstate 5 at **Siskiyou Pass**. Here the trail takes a southward bend—which will surely throw your internal compass out of whack—and enters the **Cascade-Siskiyou National Monument** and the **Soda Mountain Wilderness**, where it makes a wide circuit to regain high ground on a trajectory to intersect with the crest of Oregon's Cascade Range. The trek through the monument—largely on Bureau of Land Management (BLM) land and easements crossing private lands—is mostly pleasant, effortless, and enhanced by the significant biological diversity and impressive views. The monument is known as a birder's nirvana, where more than 200 species of birds are known to make their home or a migratory pass-through. More than 100 species of butterflies are known to reside in the area, giving further proof of the region's natural diversity.

The final portion of Section 1 leaves the BLM and private lands behind and reenters the **Rogue River–Siskiyou National Forest**. This mid-elevation region has been heavily logged over the years, but the PCT (thanks to easements) remains largely in a corridor of second- and old-growth forest, spared from most of the unsightly clear-cuts. Where the trail finally reaches the Cascade Crest just south of **Brown Mountain**, the terrain and scenery change suddenly and dramatically, showcasing Oregon's volcanic nature—and whetting your appetite for more and bigger scenery ahead. The section ends at the Lake of the Woods Highway (OR 140), just east of **Fish Lake**, which is easily accessible from points both west and east.

While the terrain through this section remains generally mild, the challenge comes in

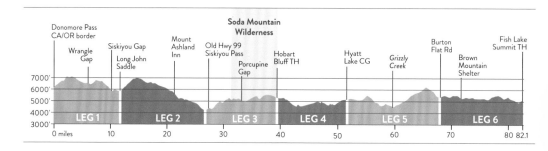

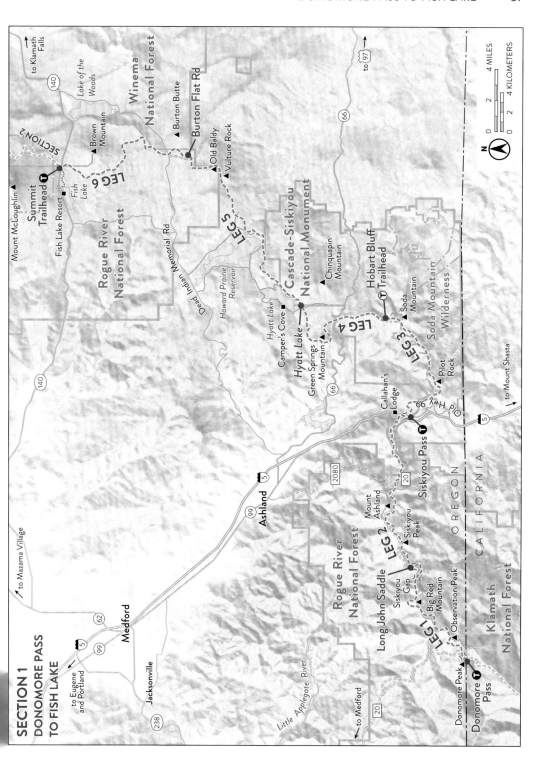

SECTION 1
DONOMORE PASS
TO FISH LAKE

to Eugene
and Portland

to Mazama Village

Jacksonville

Medford

Ashland

to Medford

Little Applegate River

Rogue River
National Forest

Long John Saddle

Siskiyou
Gap

Mount
Ashland

Siskiyou
Peak

Big Red
Mountain

Observation Peak

Donomore Peak

Donomore
Pass

LEG 1

LEG 2

Klamath
National Forest

OREGON
CALIFORNIA

Callahan's
Lodge

Siskiyou Pass

Pilot Rock Hwy

Pilot
Rock

LEG 3

LEG 4

Soda
Mountain

Soda Mountain
Wilderness

Hobart Bluff
Trailhead

Chinquapin
Mountain

Cascade-Siskiyou
National Monument

Green Springs
Mountain

Hyatt Lake
Camper's Cove

Hyatt Lake

LEG 5

Howard Prairie
Reservoir

Dead Indian Memorial Rd

Rogue River
National Forest

to Mount Shasta

to Klamath
Falls

Lake of the
Woods

Winema
National Forest

Brown
Mountain

Burton Butte

Burton Flat Rd

Old Baldy

Vulture Rock

LEG 6

SECTION 2

Mount McLoughlin

Summit
Trailhead

Fish Lake Resort

Fish
Lake

to Klamath
Falls

N

0　2　4 MILES

0　2　4 KILOMETERS

Wide views and sprawling wildflower meadows await in the Siskiyou Mountains.

less-than-ideal camping locations. Aside from a couple of recreational reservoirs with established campgrounds, this section offers few ideal trailside campsites. There is also little access to fresh or running water, sometimes only one source through each leg, resulting in potentially long stretches of dry trail. This makes it necessary to top off your hydration containers at every opportunity and be prepared for dry camping in some areas.

All this may not sound like the typical wilderness hiking experience you would expect from the Pacific Crest Trail, but it presents an opportunity to explore a portion of trail that is unlike any other. You'll receive a pleasant starter to Oregon's mixed forests (the product of all that rain the state receives every year), a bevy of wildflowers, abundant birds and wildlife, plus an introduction to the geology of a dynamic landscape. Welcome to Oregon's Pacific Crest Trail.

ACCESS
Donomore Pass

From Medford, take exit 30 for the Crater Lake Highway (OR 62). Turn west on Rossanley Drive (OR 238) and head through town for 5.8 miles, turning left (south) on Hanley Road to stay on OR 238. At an intersection, turn right on East California Street, continuing on OR 238 for another 7.8 miles. When the road forks, veer left (south) onto Upper Applegate Road and proceed 9.2 miles.

Just past the Applegate River bridge, turn left (east) onto Beaver Creek Road (FR 20). This road is paved for the first few miles, then turns to good gravel. Despite the confusing spiderweb of intersecting forest roads on most maps, FR 20 remains the main road and easy to navigate. At 14 miles, the road comes to a wide four-way junction at Silver Fork Gap; proceed straight through the junction onto FR 2025 for 4.1 winding miles to Donomore Pass and a small trailhead parking area.

Siskiyou Pass

If you want to avoid the lengthy backroad trip to the Donomore Pass border trailhead, you can opt for the easy access point on Old Highway 99 (OR 99), just off I-5. Take exit 6, 25 miles south of Medford, and merge onto OR 99 south. Proceed approximately 0.9 mile to a large pullout on the east side of the road where a large PCT trail marker indicates the continuation of the trail north.

Fish Lake (Summit Trailhead)

From Medford, take exit 30 for the Crater Lake Highway (OR 62). Turn east and proceed 5.6 miles through town. Turn right (east) on Lake of the Woods Highway (OR 140) and drive 32 miles. The PCT crosses the highway approximately 2 miles east of the entrance to Fish Lake Resort. The Summit Sno-Park trailhead is on the north side of the highway just beyond the crossing. From the Klamath

TRYING THE TRAIL

If you are new to long-distance hiking, Section 1 of Oregon's Pacific Crest Trail is the perfect stretch to give it a try. The section is divided up fairly evenly, and every second day ends at a lodge or resort, each with its own restaurant and other amenities. By carrying a minimal food load and just hiking from resort to resort, you can build up your thru-hiking legs and enjoy your hike, not overly weighed down by carrying a week's worth of food from the outset. Some refer to this as "slackpacking," a derogatory hiker term for taking advantage of creature comforts versus "roughing it." But if you're not accustomed to long trail miles day after day under the weight of an oversized pack, it can quickly become exhausting and discouraging. Give it a shot and reward yourself. Then you'll be primed to go farther on your own into the next section, and beyond.

Small springs offer cool refreshment in early summer months.

Falls area, drive 36.2 miles north, then west on Falls Highway (OR 140) to the trailhead parking area. You can access the PCT from the parking area via the 0.25-mile Summit Spur Trail (#3732).

NOTES
Services
This section of Oregon's PCT presents the unique opportunity to visit up to four mountain resorts where you can enjoy tasty meals, get lodging, and purchase limited supplies, each within just a couple days' hiking of each other: Callahan's Lodge at the I-5 crossing (end of Leg 2), Green Springs Inn on OR 66 (middle of Leg 4), Camper's Cove at Hyatt Lake (end of Leg 4), and Fish Lake Resort (end of Leg 6) on OR 140. Cities near the southern trailhead are Medford and Ashland, where you can find gas, groceries, lodging, restaurants, and gear supplies. Fish Lake Resort, at the northern trailhead, has camping, lodging, dining, and limited grocery supplies. (See appendixes 3 and 4 for more info.)

Camping
Finding campsites along the trail in southern Oregon can be challenging, with obvious and convenient sites being few and far between. While you can camp anywhere in wilderness and national forest, this section crosses a wide swath of BLM and private lands where camping is limited or restricted. As such, a few less-than-ideal camping locations are suggested, including trailheads and roadsides.

Water
The southern portion of Oregon can experience hot, dry temperatures through the summer months, with seasonal springs and creeks often drying up by midsummer. This can make for long stretches of waterless trail, so plan to top off your containers at every opportunity.

SUGGESTED ITINERARIES

The following distances do not include off-PCT miles (up to 2 miles) to water sources, campsites, alternate routes, or resupply locations. For more information about trail distances, see How to Use This Guide in the introduction.

6 DAYS

		Miles
Day 1	Donomore Pass to Long John Saddle	11.9
Day 2	Long John Saddle to Siskiyou Pass (I-5)	15.3
Day 3	Siskiyou Pass (I-5) to Hobart Bluff TH	12.1
Day 4	Hobart Bluff TH to Hyatt Lake	11.3
Day 5	Hyatt Lake to Burton Flat Road	16.9
Day 6	Burton Flat Road to Fish Lake (Summit TH)	14.2

5 DAYS

Day 1	Donomore Pass to Grouse Gap Shelter	16.5
Day 2	Grouse Gap Shelter to Porcupine Gap	16.9
Day 3	Porcupine Gap to Hyatt Lake	17.6
Day 4	Hyatt Lake to Burton Flat Road	16.9
Day 5	Burton Flat Road to Fish Lake (Summit TH)	14.2

4 DAYS

Day 1	Donomore Pass to Mount Ashland Campground	18.2
Day 2	Mount Ashland Campground to Hobart Bluff TH	21.5
Day 3	Hobart Bluff TH to Big Springs	23.9
Day 4	Big Springs to Fish Lake (Summit TH)	18.5

1 DONOMORE PASS TO LONG JOHN SADDLE

DISTANCE 11.9 miles

ELEVATION GAIN/LOSS
+2100 feet/−2300 feet

HIGH POINT 7110 feet

CONNECTING TRAILS AND ROADS
FR 2025 (unpaved), FR 20 (Siskiyou
Summit Road, unpaved), FR 2030
(Little Applegate Road, unpaved),
FR 41S12 (unpaved)

ON THE TRAIL

Looking at the driving distance and maze of old forest and logging roads to access the remote trailhead closest to the PCT's California–Oregon crossing (especially when there's a much easier access right off Interstate 5), you may ask yourself, "Is it really worth the effort just to start at the 'official' border?" The short answer is "Yes!" While it requires additional time and logistics, the PCT's 27 trail miles between the state border crossing and I-5 offer some of the best scenery in Section 1: wide-open slopes above meadowy basins, big panoramas of the Siskiyous and Mount Shasta, and gads of summer wildflowers. The recommended campsite at the end of the leg is no award-winner, but it sets you up for a fairly reasonable next day's hike. The ideal way to start here is to ask, beg, or bribe a friend or family member to shuttle you to the trailhead. Don't count on hitchhiking, as there's not a lot of traffic on these outlying, unpaved roads.

Once you've arrived at the secluded Donomore Pass trailhead on FR 2025 in the **Rogue River–Siskiyou National Forest**, on a saddle just east of **Donomore Peak**, you're a mere 0.3 mile north of the official border crossing. For now, leave your gear in the car (except your camera and GPS receiver) and take a short walk south on the PCT, under tall, shady conifers. The trail bends east, descending along the contour of a high slope above Donomore Meadows (in California). A few openings in the trees present wide vistas to the south of the **Siskiyou Mountains**. On the north side of the trail, you'll find your official starting line in the form of a weathered wooden sign: "Welcome to Oregon / Interstate 5: 28 / Hyatt Lake: 51 / Washington: 498 / Canada: 962."

Mounted to the side of the sign is a rusty metal box containing the trail register, usually a spiral-bound notebook. Here, you can enter your name and date of entry as an official PCT hiker. Once you've signed the register, taken the obligatory photo, set your GPS unit's odometer to 0—and the gravity of your imminent endeavor

Oregon sunshine blossoms brighten up the trail.

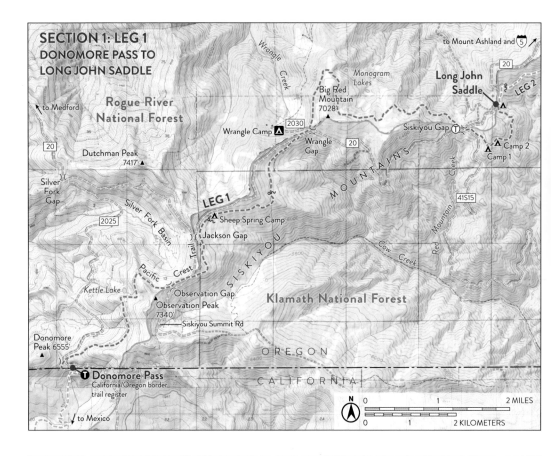

SECTION 1: LEG 1
DONOMORE PASS TO
LONG JOHN SADDLE

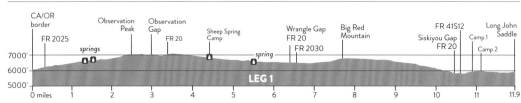

sinks in, whether you're undertaking a section or two, the whole 455.2 miles to the opposite Oregon border, or beyond—retrace your steps north back to the trailhead and your patiently waiting loaded backpack. If you're starting midday, midsummer, your route ahead will offer lots of exposure and little water, so be sure your bottles are topped off, put on sunscreen, and wear a hat. All that's left is to thank your shuttle driver, shoulder your pack, and start walking.

The trail gently contours up around 7340-foot **Observation Peak**, alternating between sun-dappled hemlock and fir forest and exposed, recovering clear-cut slopes dotted with manzanita, weathered stumps, and rocky outcrops. Wildflowers splash the trailsides with color—purple lupine and penstemon, yellow aster and buckwheat, red paintbrush, pink fireweed, and more. Watch out for hummingbirds darting between flowers. It's not long before the trail crosses a couple small,

OBSERVATION PEAK

The first of many, many high points to come along the Pacific Crest Trail's journey through Oregon, Observation Peak can be reached by a short cross-country ascent. On the peak's northern ridge, around 2.5 miles, where the PCT turns southeast, strike out straight up the ridgeline, past a false summit to where a large cairn and post mark the true summit amid a grassy plateau. There may or may not be a peak register for you to leave your mark. The view from the top takes in Mount Shasta and the Marble Mountains to the south, and stretches all the way to Mount McLoughlin—your destination—to the northeast.

seasonal springs ◐ at 1.3 and 1.5 miles—good for a refreshing splash on your face, or wetting a bandanna to keep you cool. The trail contours around a wide drainage high above Kettle Lake, then reaches the leg's high point on Observation Peak's northern ridge. Here, the path levels to make a high circuit above the grassy, green meadows of **Silver Fork Basin** to **Observation Gap**, at 3 miles, where a rocky saddle showcases panoramic views south to 14,179-foot **Mount Shasta**. This landmark will be a welcome sight in the days and miles to come.

Moving away from the gap, the PCT makes the first of many crossings of the **Siskiyou Summit Road** (FR 20), at 3.4 miles, before turning north briefly on a shallow, contouring descent, paralleling the road, to just below **Jackson Gap,** where it turns east again. At 4.4 miles, the sound of trickling **Sheep Spring** ◐ will perk your ears, and just below the trail to the right (east) you'll spot a modest clearing at the end of an old jeep road: **Sheep Spring Camp**. Just ahead, the PCT crosses the jeep road, so turn right (south) and follow the road to the piped spring which streams out of the hillside. Just beyond, the open clearing at the end of the road can accommodate a couple tents, and the view here is expansive. If you get a late start,

this is an ideal location to bed down for the night; if you're continuing on, be sure to take advantage of the spring and top off your water bottles. You may find a trickling spring another mile ahead, but the next semi-reliable water source isn't for another 8 miles.

Leaving the spring behind, the PCT continues its parallel path below FR 20, gently descending along the east side of the crest across a sprawling, grassy slope. The bright yellow, daisy-like flowers decorating the hillsides are Oregon sunshine. To the east, a noticeable pointed peak—**Pilot Rock**—can be seen in the distance. Just as the pioneers of days past used Pilot Rock as a navigation point, PCT hikers, too, can refer to this rocky prominence as a bearing. At 6.4 miles, the PCT crosses FR 20 again, then just beyond crosses **Little Applegate Road** (FR 2030) at the ridgetop saddle of **Wrangle Gap**. At this junction, FR 2030 descends 0.5 mile west to **Wrangle Camp**. This campground has five tent sites with fire rings and picnic tables, a shelter with a woodstove, and a vault toilet; there is no water available here.

SUMMIT ROAD

For much of the first two legs of Oregon's PCT from the border to Siskiyou Pass, the trail parallels the Siskiyou Summit Road (FR 20). The continuation of the road used to access the trailhead nearest the border, the summit road proceeds all the way down to the Mount Ashland Ski Resort where it turns into the paved Mount Ashland Ski Road and connects with OR 99 and I-5. Some sections of this road are rough and often in disrepair, making the trailhead approach from the west easier, albeit longer. In early season and heavy snow years, many PCT hikers choose to hike the easy-to-follow road instead of route-finding on the trail. The road intersects, or is reasonably near to, the same water sources and campsites indicated in the trail description.

Ridgetop views abound as the PCT circuits Silver Basin near Observation Peak.

With convenient campsites limited through long stretches, this makes another fine option for calling it a day, especially for late starters. Beyond the gap, the PCT continues north on a mild ascent around 7028-foot **Big Red Mountain**, now on the west side of the crest.

After circling Big Red's dry, rocky slopes, the trail gains a few hundred feet to the leg's second high point, where it then levels out and begins undulating east across several meadowy slopes sprinkled with paintbrush and columbine, with wide views to the north. Unseen in the valley below are the small Monogram Lakes and Little Applegate River. The PCT then begins descending again, crossing more open slopes dotted with sparse trees and rocky outcroppings, and traverses the head of another wide basin on a high and narrow stretch of trail. The downgrade increases, allowing

WATER ALERT!

If you arrive at Long John Saddle and your water situation is dire, you can drop your pack and proceed 0.3 mile farther up the PCT to a small, seasonal spring that runs across the trail.

you to pick up some speed and arrive at **Siskiyou Gap** at 10.4 miles. (Some maps show two springs crossing the trail in the mile before Siskiyou Gap; don't count on finding them running.) Unfortunately, there's no decent camping to be found at the gap; just a small trailhead parking area next to a field of tall grass.

Crossing FR 20, the PCT proceeds along a south-facing slope to circuit a 6223-foot knob. The high slopes are covered with grasses and shrubbery and speckled with bright red skyrocket; tree cover increases as the trail continues descending. At 10.6 miles, the path crosses unpaved FR 41S12, branching off FR 20 just to the north. A short 0.3 mile past the road crossing is a large campsite tucked back in the trees, right (south) of the trail (**Camp 1**). This large site has enough room to accommodate a few tents. Unfortunately, there is no nearby water. Just beyond, at 11.1 miles, another campsite can be found just right (south) of the trail (**Camp 2**). This tiny campsite has a flat spot for one tent, and a pretty decent southeast view.

The trail then plunges back into forest as it continues its mostly downward circuit of the knob. In the denser forest, lady fern lines some portions of the trail and adorns the slopes. Where the trail reaches the north side of the knob at 11.9 miles, it pops out of the forest to the ridgetop, five-way road junction at **Long John Saddle**. The PCT continues straight through the junction, but ahead to the left (west), along the east side of FR 20, is **Long John Saddle Camp** in the trees, with a fire ring, a couple downed logs for sitting, and room for a few tents. This roadside campsite is by no means choice, but it serves its purpose after hiking a full day. If you proceed just a little ways up the road to a gap in the forested ridge, you may enjoy a colorful sunset panorama over Sevenmile Ridge and the wider Rogue River–Siskiyou National Forest.

CAMP-TO-CAMP MILEAGE

Donomore Pass to Sheep Spring Camp 4.4
Sheep Spring Camp to Wrangle Camp
      junction 2.2
Wrangle Camp junction to Camp 1. . . . . 4.3
Camp 1 to Camp 2 . . . . 0.2
Camp 2 to Long John Saddle Camp 0.8

Stalks of purple larkspur add splashes of color on open slopes.

2 LONG JOHN SADDLE TO SISKIYOU PASS

DISTANCE 15.3 miles

ELEVATION GAIN/LOSS
+2240 feet/–3930 feet

HIGH POINT 7030 feet

CONNECTING TRAILS AND ROADS
Grouse Gap Road (unpaved), FR 40S15
(unpaved), FR 20 (Mount Ashland Ski
Road), FR 2080 (Tolman Creek Road),
Callahan's Cutoff Trail, OR 99

ON THE TRAIL

The next leg is a pleasant stroll toward, and then below, the green slopes of Mount Ashland. The PCT makes an ascending traverse of the north ridge of Siskiyou Peak before beginning the long descent to the I-5 crossing at **Siskiyou Pass**. Along the way there are plenty of wide views to be enjoyed amid more slopeside meadows brimming with wildflowers, as well as a peek at this region's plutonic origins. There are also several opportunities to refill your water along the way—a refreshing improvement over the previous leg. The first half is considerably exposed, so keep applying your sunscreen. Another thing to take note of through this leg is that you will be losing nearly 4000 feet of elevation, descending from high, breezy slopes into a (potentially) very warm, dry valley by midday. Take advantage of shade breaks, and keep yourself hydrated.

From **Long John Saddle**, the PCT continues northeast on level terrain under shaded forest. At 12.2 miles, the trail makes a right turn where a dribbling spring **○** crosses the trail in a lush green draw. Striking orange-and-black Columbia lilies are profuse through here in midsummer. This tiny spring is a fairly reliable water source, even late into the hiking season, and a good place to top off your supply. (Many of the mapped springs and creeks in the miles to come are often dry.) Moving forward, the

trail begins a moderate, forested ascent toward 7149-foot **Siskiyou Peak** on trail adorned with lupine, aster, and bunches of white cow parsnip. This is followed by an open, rocky plain, dotted with pink mountain heather.

The trail then bends southeast for the final short ascent to the rocky northern ridge of Siskiyou Peak at the edge of a broad, open slope painted yellow with buckwheat in summer; below is an expanse of barren gullies where springs and winter runoff once flowed down the hillside. The PCT contours across this wide clearing, once again coming parallel with FR 20, and presents more wide views to the east toward Pilot Rock (getting closer). Near the end of the traverse, around mile 14.6, a small campsite can be found near a lone tree in the gravelly clearing between the trail and the road (**Camp 3**). Here, big views to the southeast of Mount Shasta's familiar profile will likely prompt you to pause, while Mount Ashland to the northeast beckons you forward.

After a short, moderate descent, the trail makes a shallow, contouring ascent across another open slope. Here the exposed rocks and gravelly surface take on a noticeably different characteristic: granite. This small exposure of the **Wooley Creek Suite**—a biotite granite formation estimated to be around 160 million years old, and a part of the Siskiyou

TRAIL TRIVIA

The name *Siskiyou*, a Chinook word for "bobtailed horse," has been given to many features in the area, including a peak, a mountain range, and a county. The original designation occurred in 1828 when an official with the Hudson's Bay Company lost a prized horse in a snowstorm while crossing the area. His party, in honor of their chief, named the place the "Pass of the Siskiyou."

The PCT passes through grassy meadows and groves of aspen at Grouse Gap.

Mountain Range—is pressed up against the younger rocks of the volcanic Cascade Range and the Klamath Mountains. The traverse across this parklike slope is extremely pleasant, with more wide views south over the Siskiyous and Mount Shasta. At 15.6 miles, the trail crests the divide in a low saddle. From this point, it's all (mostly) downhill.

The PCT drops over the crest on a short series of moderate switchbacks through alternating shady forest and sunny pocket meadows; summer wildflowers beautify the open areas. At 16.5 miles, the trail exits the forest and levels out amid a sprawling, grassy clearing and once again meets FR 20 at **Grouse Gap**; 0.3 mile south on a gravel spur road is **Grouse Gap Shelter**. More often used as a winter warming hut for snowshoers and cross-country skiers, the shelter has a picnic table and a fire pit, with a vault toilet nearby. The sloping and uneven terrain around the shelter doesn't invite ideal camping

SISKIYOU PEAK

This summit can be claimed via a fairly steep, 0.3-mile ascent on a well-trodden path. Look for it around 14.2 miles—where the PCT turns north, the summit trail veers off south. The open, meadowy summit offers a wide panorama over the entire area.

but will suffice in a pinch; if the spring and summer runoff is particularly high, there may be water running in a creeklet nearby, but don't count on it.

Proceeding onward, the PCT takes a level path through a grove of pretty aspen, beginning a contouring traverse of a wide, shallow basin on the flank of 7532-foot **Mount Ashland**. The trailside shrubbery becomes dense and tall, creating a green

47

corridor where lupine, cow parsnip, Columbia lily, red columbine, and purple delphinium are profuse at the peak of summer; watch for buzzing bees and darting hummingbirds. At 17 miles, hop over the first (small and dribbling) of several springs ⬤ that cross the trail. The sound of running water will be music to your ears. After the last (largest) spring crossing at 17.4 miles, the next reliable water source will be more than 4 miles ahead, so this makes a good spot to top off and refresh yourself. The trail passes through another grove of aspen, then ducks back under the cover of older coniferous forest, with bright green Methuselah's beard draped from trunks and boughs.

The trail undulates through the forest on a pleasant, shallow descent, working its way around the southern flank of Mount Ashland; FR 20 is just upslope, once again paralleling the trail. At 18.2 miles, the trail crosses FR 40S15, which branches off FR 20, 0.5 mile northeast. Near this road junction is the **Mount Ashland Campground**. With the limited camping options available along this leg, the Mount Ashland Campground makes the most convenient place to call it a day if you're not going all the way to Siskiyou Pass. The campground has nine free, first-come, first-served walk-in sites with picnic tables and fire pits. There is a vault toilet, but no water or trash service.

The PCT then winds down across several wide, waterless draws. At this point, the wide views diminish to brief peeks beyond the increasingly forested surroundings. At 19.9 miles, the PCT pops out of the trees to arrive at a trailhead on paved **Mount Ashland Ski Road** (FR 20).

Crossing the road and continuing to descend, the forest opens a bit, with more sky overhead. High on the trees above the snow line, blue trail

ASHLAND

At the FR 2080 crossing, many PCT thru-hikers in need of a resupply will exit the trail here and proceed to the town of Ashland, 12.2 miles to the north. In Ashland you'll find a post office, grocery store, lodging options, restaurants, drugstore, and an outdoor gear shop. To get there, hike north on Tolman Creek Road (FR 2080) to Bull Gap. At the junction, continue north on FR 200, to the next junction with the Ashland Loop Road. Keep going north and descend all the way into Ashland. To get back on the PCT, you can retrace your route, or proceed through Ashland to I-5 and hitchhike (legal in Oregon) to the PCT crossing at Siskiyou Pass.

markers indicate the route for winter travelers. The trail then crosses **Tolman Creek Road** (FR 2080, see sidebar about town of Ashland), beyond which is a small campsite in the trees, right (south) of the trail at 20.8 miles (**Camp 4**); there is room for a couple small tents, but no views and no water. Shortly past this campsite, at 21.1 miles, is the boundary of the Rogue River–Siskiyou National Forest, with a large sign beside the trail. For the next 40-plus miles, the PCT traverses Oregon Bureau of Land Management (BLM) land. Crossing the threshold onto BLM land and now on a south-facing slope, you'll likely notice a distinct change in the landscape: as the greener forest gives way to dry scrubby woods, the trail surface transitions from softer duff to gravel and dirt. As your elevation decreases in this drier

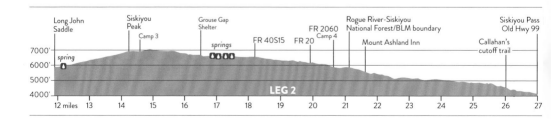

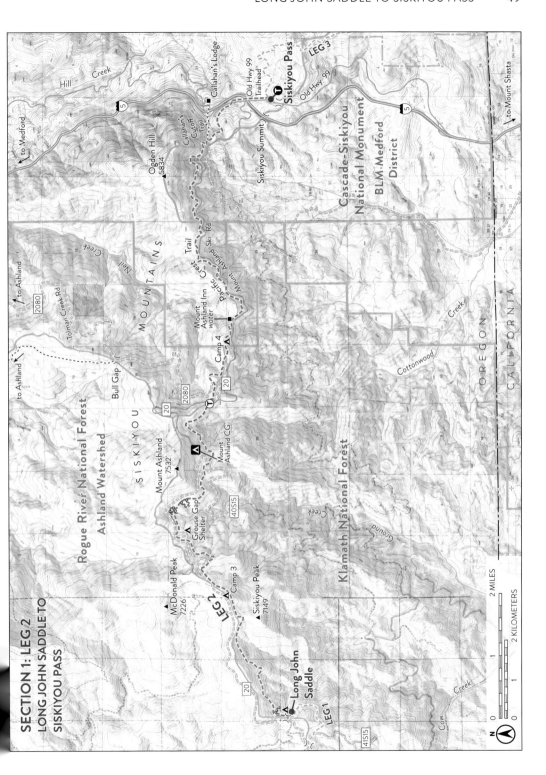

SECTION 1: LEG 2
LONG JOHN SADDLE TO
SISKIYOU PASS

Willowherb colors open, rocky ground.

Tiger lilies often adorn moist spring channels.

Skyrocket paints brushy trailsides.

CALLAHAN'S MOUNTAIN LODGE

At Siskiyou Pass on I-5, Callahan's Mountain Lodge offers a variety of hiker-friendly services, including an area for camping, laundry service, showers, resupply package hold, a restaurant, and luxury lodging accommodations (see appendices 3 and 4). A tiny souvenir store stocks a selection of candy bars and sodas. Most attractive for thru-hikers is the lodge's restaurant and bar with nightly live music. For dinner at the end of a long day, the restaurant offers a hiker special: bottomless spaghetti with meat sauce—a real treat! The well-stocked bar can mix a variety of concoctions, as well as serve up a selection of local and domestic beers. Before departing in the morning for the next leg, fuel up with a hearty breakfast and hot coffee on the open-air deck as hummingbirds flit here and there.

To get there, turn off the PCT at the signed cutoff junction (mile 26) and proceed 0.7 mile down a steep, narrow trail to a railroad track; cross the tracks, veering left, and continue down a brushy service road in a narrow gully to exit the trail beside I-5. Walk the road under the freeway to get to the lodge, just on the other side.

environment, it may also become perceptibly warmer.

The grade of descent increases considerably, with a few expansive views to the south to keep things interesting; Mount Ashland Ski Road parallels the trail below. At 21.5 miles, a small sign on a trailside tree indicates that you are entering private land. For the next several miles, hikers are required to stay on the PCT and camping is not permitted—though there aren't really any suitable camping options along these steep, brushy slopes anyway. Just 0.1 mile farther the trail exits the tree cover beside what used to be the **Mount Ashland Inn** 0. Now a private residence, the inn no longer serves hikers, though they have maintained a picnic table and water faucet near the old parking area as a courtesy. Though camping is not permitted here, it makes a fine place to drop your pack for a break and refill your water bottles. Moving away from the inn, the trail makes a short, moderate ascent to regain the hillside, then continues meandering alongside the road, bearing northeast.

Over the next few miles the trail becomes brushy and sometimes overgrown. Through these lower, drier environs, mountain rhododendron and tall Oregon grape line the trailsides. Some maps will show a couple of springs crossing the

trail through this area, but don't count on finding them running later in the season or in drier years. The trail makes a short ascent as it circuits the base of 5837-foot **Ogden Hill**, then enters a pretty section of Douglas-fir forest, followed by another short ascent. Turning south for its final descent, the PCT crosses a couple old jeep roads, and comes to the junction with the **Callahan's Cutoff Trail** at 26 miles. If you're planning to take advantage of the services at **Callahan's Lodge (Camp)** 0, turn off here (see sidebar); if skipping Callahan's, proceed past the cutoff junction and descend a final steep mile to **Old Highway 99**. The PCT continues its northward journey on the opposite side of the highway 0.6 mile south. Since there aren't any good camping or water sources for quite a few miles to come, Callahan's is the ideal location to end the day.

CAMP-TO-CAMP MILEAGE

Long John Saddle to Camp 3 . . . . 2.7
Camp 3 to Grouse Gap Shelter junction 1.9
Grouse Gap Shelter junction to Mount
    Ashland Campground junction 1.7
Mount Ashland Campground junction
    to Camp 4 . . . . 2.6
Camp 4 to Callahan's Cutoff Trail 5.2

3 SISKIYOU PASS TO HOBART BLUFF TRAILHEAD

DISTANCE 12.1 miles

ELEVATION GAIN/LOSS
+3010 feet/−2080 feet

HIGH POINT 5570 feet

CONNECTING TRAILS AND ROADS
Road 40-2E-33 (unpaved), Road 41-2E-3
(unpaved), Pilot Rock Trail, Baldy
Creek Road (unpaved), Soda Mountain
Trail (unsigned), Soda Mountain Road
(unpaved)

ON THE TRAIL

As the Pacific Crest Trail continues across BLM and private lands, some may view the next few legs as being somewhat undesirable. Accessible water and good campsites continue to be spare, and the proximity to civilization makes it feel more like hiking in Portland's Forest Park (not that that's a bad thing) than on one of the world's longest and most renowned wilderness trails. The silver lining is this section's ecological and geographic diversity. Through the next many miles, you're not chasing big views and alpine environs, but rather

A landmark for early pioneers, Pilot Rock does the same for PCT hikers in the Soda Mountain Wilderness.

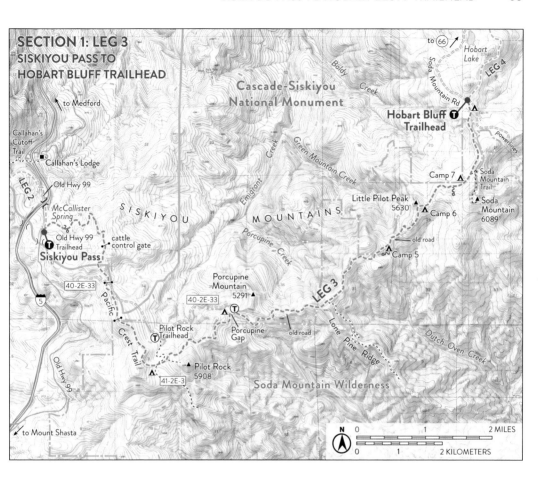

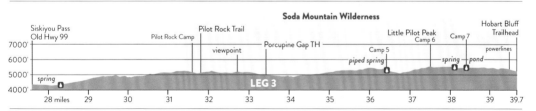

an abundance of wildflowers, wildlife, birds, and interesting geology. Plus, the mild terrain continues to help break in your trail legs for the more challenging miles ahead.

Continuing north from Old Highway 99, the PCT dives east into a grassy woodland where Oregon grape lines the trailside. A little less than a mile from the highway, at 28.3 miles, the trail crosses a gully on a small wooden bridge; just beyond the bridge, a short bootpath leads left (north) to marshy McCallister Spring. If you didn't tank up your water supply at Callahan's, this is the only water for another 8 to 10 miles—and you have a moderate amount of dry, exposed climbing ahead. Beyond the spring, the trail begins ascending grassy slopes, turning south

into the **Cascade-Siskiyou National Monument**, and alternating between open, airy stretches with partial views and closed-in groves of oak, aspen, and Douglas-fir sprinkled with thimbleberry and chicory. Unlike the previous days on soft, duffy trail, the tread through here is mostly hard-packed and rocky. At 30 miles, crest a shallow ridge and pass through a cattle control gate, followed by a gravel jeep road; 5908-foot Pilot Rock begins looming in the nearer distance as the PCT enters the **Soda Mountain Wilderness**.

Shortly beyond, the PCT crosses gravel Road 40-2E-33, then begins contouring a low hill, offering a few views into California, with I-5 now far below. Continuing the mostly exposed ascent southeast, a new variety of tree begins occupying

One of many varieties of brightly colored buckwheat that adorn rocky, sandy trailsides

CASCADE-SISKIYOU NATIONAL MONUMENT AND PILOT ROCK

Established in 2000 and expanded in 2017, the Cascade-Siskiyou National Monument protects more than 85,000 acres of mountains, forests, and grasslands in southern Oregon where three distinct mountain ranges converge: the Klamath Range to the south, the Siskiyou Mountains to the west, and the Cascade Range to the north. Within the monument, the **Soda Mountain Wilderness**, established in 2009, adds further protection to 24,700 acres of this unique landscape, characterized by its tremendous biodiversity. More than twenty species of trees thrive among the monument's hills and valleys, including several species of fir, pine, maple, and oak, as well as juniper, madrone, dogwood, aspen, ash, alder, and incense cedar. In addition to Roosevelt elk, black bears, and cougars, a remarkable number of birds (approximately 200 species!) make their homes in the wilderness area, including hawks, grouse, woodpeckers, owls, terns, swallows, wrens, and hummingbirds. Some reside there year-round, while others stop in the wilderness as part of their migration. The monument and wilderness are managed by the Oregon Bureau of Land Management. Approximately 8 miles of the PCT winds within the northwest boundary of the wilderness area.

The most notable geologic formation within the monument is **Pilot Rock**. Dated at more than 25.6 million years old, the andesite and basalt monolith is all that remains of an even older volcano, long since eroded away. The rock's 570-foot prominence can be distinguished from both the Shasta and Rogue valleys up to 40 miles away. It was commonly used as a navigation aid, and received several name changes over the years. The original Native American designation was *Tan-ts'at-seniphtha*, meaning "stone standing up." It was changed to Boundary Mountain by early area settlers, then again to Emmons Peak following an expedition by the US military. In the mid-1800s it was changed to its present name of Pilot Rock as a reference point for pioneers migrating from California.

Take in wide panoramas of Mount Shasta from the shoulder of Pilot Rock.

the slope: juniper, notable for its twisted trunks, tiny, scalelike leaves, and small blue berries. Here, the trail levels in an open, gravelly saddle between two low hills; clumps of buckwheat create a patchwork mosaic on the ground in yellow, orange, and red, depending on the season, while the sparse juniper trees offer a few patches of shade. The trail reenters tree cover at the south end of the saddle and contours around the next hill, followed by a short descent east into a forested valley. At 31.6 miles the PCT passes the **Pilot Rock Trailhead (Camp)** on dirt Road 41-2E-3; the large camp area has room for three to four tents. The **Pilot Rock**

PILOT ROCK

A 1.2-mile trail branches off the PCT (mile 31.6) to the base of Pilot Rock, a prominent landmark and popular destination for rock climbers. From here, a harrowing Class 3 scramble ascends a narrow chute to the summit. (This is the only non-technical option.) The view from the top takes in Black Mountain, Mount Ashland, Mount Shasta, and peaks in the Siskiyous and Marble Mountains.

Trail breaks off the PCT just 0.2 mile farther. The PCT turns northeast, undulating below the north slope of Pilot Rock, then makes a short eastward ascent to a rocky saddle with an impressive view of Pilot Rock and Mount Shasta far to the south. Right of the trail, a bare patch of dirt offers a primitive, exposed tent site.

From the saddle, the trail makes a meandering descent northeast and crosses 40-2E-33 again to the **Porcupine Gap Trailhead (Camp)** at 33.4 miles. A modest campsite left of the trail has room for up to three tents and logs for benches. Continuing east, the PCT makes a curving ascent around 5291-foot **Porcupine Mountain** to a high ridgetop lined with snowberry and scrub oak. The trail now intersects and parallels an old logging road along the ridgetop and proceeds through a series of unsigned forks and crossings over the next couple miles as it undulates eastward. After traversing a wide, grassy slope, offering another pleasing view of Mount Shasta, the trail descends into another forested valley, crosses an open meadow, then arrives at a piped spring ⬤ at 36.4 miles. The spring, marked by a post in a grassy clearing right (east) of the trail, is little more than a rocky puddle where a pipe trickles cold, clear water. By this point, you'll have gotten used to

taking full advantage of every water source—do the same at this one. Just 0.1 mile beyond the spring, in the trees left (north) of the trail, is a nice secluded campsite with room for one tent (**Camp 5**).

The PCT descends into a grassy swale alongside a dry creekbed, then intersects the old Baldy Creek Road, which goes along Lone Pine Ridge, at 36.8 miles; at this unsigned fork, the PCT bears right and begins another moderate ascent. After a series of switchbacks, the trail eases and then ascends the southeast slope of 5630-foot **Little Pilot Peak**.

WATER ALERT!

The small pond near the campsite at 38.4 miles is the last reliable water source until reaching the Little Hyatt Reservoir outlet 11.1 miles north, just shy of the end of Leg 4. About halfway through the next leg, there *may* be a pond at 45.4 miles, but this can be murky later in the season. Take advantage of this location to top off all your bottles for a dry camp at the end of the day, and to get you through the majority of the next day.

Look for pretty chickory in the oak groves of the Cascade–Siskiyou National Monument.

Camping on the edge of this open meadow at the Hobart Bluff trailhead offers brilliant sunrises and sunsets.

Crossing over to the west side of the ridge, you'll find the peak's rocky top left of the trail at 37.5 miles. A level, bare patch at the base of the peak has a decent campsite for one tent (**Camp 6**), and offers a wide view west toward Mount Ashland. Continuing northwest, the trail passes through alternating grand fir forest and open, grassy slopes, contouring across the northwest flank of **Soda Mountain**; you may find a (seasonal) trickling spring ○ crossing the trail around 38.1 miles. For a better chance at water, look for a bootpath left (west) that leads to a moderate campsite tucked next to a grove of trees at 38.4 miles (**Camp 7**); this space can accommodate two small tents. Just beyond the campsite is a fenced-in pond ○. If this site is available, it's worth grabbing.

The trail intersects another old road, this time forking to the left, then crosses an open, rocky slope that offers a view of **Little Pilot Rock** (not

SODA MOUNTAIN

Near the northern boundary of the Soda Mountain Wilderness, 6089-foot Soda Mountain is one of the few remaining wilderness fire lookout sites in active service. A 1-mile path branches off the PCT and climbs to its summit. Look for a side trail cutting off to right (east) shortly past the campsite and pond at 38.4 miles; the path is often marked with a small rock cairn. Climb 0.2 mile to the lookout access road, then turn right (south) and walk the dirt road 0.8 mile to the lookout at the top. The original lookout was established in 1933, and replaced with the current one in 1962. The view south looks over the Iron Gate Reservoir to Mount Shasta and the Marble Mountains.

the same as Little Pilot Peak); it then makes a shallow ascent to an exposed crest. Views from this rocky prominence are expansive to the west, but the scrubby, rocky, uneven terrain doesn't offer any convenient camping options. Rounding the east side of the hill, and exiting the Soda Mountain Wilderness, the PCT gradually descends a grassy slope where you'll spy a series of powerline towers cutting through the valley ahead and, soon enough, hear the buzzing of the powerlines overhead. At 39.7 miles the trail bottoms out in a shallow valley at gravel **Soda Mountain Road**; across the road is the **Hobart Bluff Trailhead (Camp)**. There is really nothing appealing about camping at this roadside trailhead other than it being a flat

space, but this is the last reasonable option for many miles to come. If you can manage to ignore the sound of the nearby buzzing powerlines and the lack of wilderness surroundings, the wide-open area presents an opportunity for nice sunsets and decent stargazing. Remember, sometimes it's all about silver linings.

CAMP-TO-CAMP MILEAGE

Callahan's Lodge to Pilot Rock Camp 4.7
Pilot Rock Camp to Porcupine Gap Camp . . . 1.8
Porcupine Gap Camp to Camp 5 . . . . 3.0
Camp 5 to Camp 6 . . . . 1.1
Camp 6 to Camp 7 . . . . 0.9
Camp 7 to Hobart Bluff TH Camp 1.3

4 HOBART BLUFF TRAILHEAD TO HYATT LAKE

DISTANCE 11.3 miles

ELEVATION GAIN/LOSS
+1980 feet/–2180 feet

HIGH POINT 5340 feet

CONNECTING TRAILS AND ROADS
Hobart Bluff Trail, Green Springs Highway (OR 66), Green Springs Loop Trail, Old Hyatt Prairie Road (unpaved), Road 39-3E-32 (unpaved), East Hyatt Lake Road

ON THE TRAIL

The next leg of the Pacific Crest Trail is largely a means to an end: to get to a nice campsite near a forested lake—and if you plan accordingly, pick up a resupply box. The trail forward is a bit of a roller-coaster, over terrain similar to that of the previous leg, with moderate grassy slopes, forested stretches, and an absence of running water—so be sure to top off your supply at the previous leg's last source. Another thing

to note (if you've been paying attention to your map and compass) is that you are now heading northeast. You still have a good number of miles to go before reaching the crest of the Cascades, but at least you're starting to move more forward and less sideways.

Leaving the trailhead, the PCT makes a short ascent into Douglas-fir forest to contour around the unremarkable 5542-foot **Hobart Peak**. Bunches of low grass and mixed shrubbery splash swaths of green across the otherwise drab, debris-littered forest floor. In early summer, white trilliums and pink fawn lilies make the path a little more cheerful. The trail dips to a saddle, then makes another short ascent to the leg's high point at 40.6 miles. Here, the spur trail to **Hobart Bluff** cuts off to the left (west). The PCT then begins making a steady descent north. On a shallow grade, the trail contours around another low hill, crosses an open, grassy slope, then proceeds along a narrow ridgetop. From here, the descent increases through a short series of forested switchbacks, levels a bit, then crosses another wide, grassy slope.

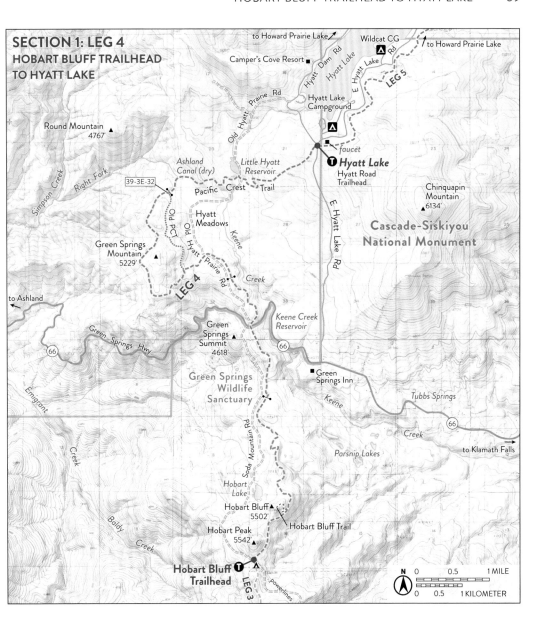

SECTION 1: LEG 4
HOBART BLUFF TRAILHEAD TO HYATT LAKE

to Howard Prairie Lake

Wildcat CG

to Howard Prairie Lake

Camper's Cove Resort

Hyatt Dam Rd

Hyatt Lake Rd

E Hyatt Lake Rd

LEG 5

Hyatt Lake Campground

Round Mountain 4767'

faucet

Hyatt Lake

Hyatt Road Trailhead

Ashland Canal (dry)

Little Hyatt Reservoir

Simpson Creek

Right Fork

39-3E-32

Pacific Crest Trail

Chinquapin Mountain 6134'

Old PCT

Hyatt Meadows

Cascade-Siskiyou National Monument

Green Springs Mountain 5229'

Old Hyatt Prairie Rd

Keene

LEG 4

Creek

to Ashland

Green Springs Hwy

Green Springs Summit 4618'

Keene Creek Reservoir

66

Green Springs Inn

Tubbs Springs

66

Emigrant

Creek

Green Springs Wildlife Sanctuary

Keene

Creek

66

to Klamath Falls

Soda Mountain Rd

Parsnip Lakes

Hobart Lake

Hobart Bluff 5502'

Hobart Peak 5542'

Hobart Bluff Trail

Baldy Creek

Hobart Bluff Trailhead

LEG 3

powerlines

N   0   0.5   1 MILE

0   0.5   1 KILOMETER

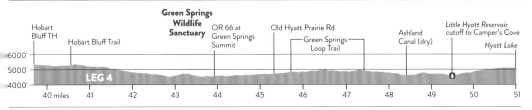

Hobart Bluff TH

Hobart Bluff Trail

Green Springs Wildlife Sanctuary

OR 66 at Green Springs Summit

Old Hyatt Prairie Rd

Green Springs Loop Trail

Ashland Canal (dry)

Little Hyatt Reservoir cutoff to Camper's Cove

Hyatt Lake

6000'
5000'
4000'

LEG 4

40 miles   41   42   43   44   45   46   47   48   49   50   51

Open, grassy plains in the Green Springs Wildlife Sanctuary and near the Ashland Canal offer plenty of sunshine and wildflowers.

HOBART BLUFF

This short side trail off the PCT winds 0.4 mile west to summit Hobart Bluff. From the top of this 5502-foot rocky prominence, you can take in a 360-degree view of southern Oregon's Siskiyous and beyond: Soda Mountain, Pilot Rock, Mount Ashland, Mount Shasta, and, to the northwest, snowy Mount McLoughlin beckons you forward.

The trail temporarily exits BLM land at 42.7 miles, passing through a gate and entering private land belonging to the **Green Springs Wildlife Sanctuary**. Established in 2010, the sanctuary is a 154-acre conservation easement in a recovering logging area noted for its grassy plains and groves of oak trees. As you pass through it for the next mile, starting with a traverse across a low saddle, then a short ascent to gain an unnamed bluff, keep your eyes peeled for some of the area's roaming residents: deer, elk, black bears, coyotes, bobcats, and smaller scurrying critters, as well as a host of owls, hawks, woodpeckers, and songbirds.

From the top of the bluff, you may be able to spy a highway and reservoir in the valley below. The trail now turns northwest and begins a steady descent through a viewless corridor. As you near the bottom, the trail passes the sanctuary's residence and outbuildings, ducks through one more short stretch of trees, then comes to the shoulder of the **Green Springs Highway** (OR 66) at 43.9 miles. There aren't any services here, but a large kiosk offers information about the sanctuary's flora and fauna. If you're in need of water, you can proceed east along the highway for 0.25 mile to the **Keene Creek Reservoir ❶** for a refill, where a few flat spots near the shore can accommodate camping, or walk the highway for 2 miles east to **Green Springs Inn**.

GREEN SPRINGS INN

Located on OR 66, just east of where the PCT crosses, Green Springs Inn is an easy 2-mile road walk (or hitchhike). This cozy resort offers comfortable lodge rooms (some with hot tubs), private cabins (with cozy decks), and a pleasant dining room that features big breakfasts, tasty burgers, and upscale dinners. Very hiker-friendly, they will hold mailed resupply packages for PCT hikers free of charge. The 4-mile roundtrip to this location is a bit more of a detour off the trail, but if you're modifying your itinerary to skip Camper's Cove on Hyatt Lake, Green Springs makes an attractive alternative with better hours (see appendix 4).

Leaving the Cascade-Siskiyou National Monument behind (and back on BLM land), the PCT continues north directly across the highway. It then bends northeast across a dirt road, proceeds through the trees, then crosses the road again before turning northwest and entering a surprisingly pretty (considering the proximity to a highway and vestiges of civilization) stretch of green forest. Just beyond 44 miles the trail passes through another gate, this one indicating the Mt. Fir Lumber Company, a now-defunct logging operation. Beyond the gate, the trail continues gently up through the forest, crossing Old Hyatt Prairie Road at 45.3 miles; then, back in the forest, it passes a small murky pond that fills a shallow, grassy basin right of the trail.

Following a crossing of Road 39-3E-32, a narrow dirt service road, the trail comes to a fork at 45.7 miles. Here, at the southern junction of the **Green Springs Loop Trail**, the PCT forks left to circuit 5229-foot **Green Springs Mountain**'s south and west flanks. This newer section of trail was opened in 2011 to offer hikers a more pleasant viewing experience than the original route, along a stretch of old logging road. The trail begins a gentle ascent through more forest—note the mountain

The cold, clear water spilling out of Little Hyatt Reservoir is a refreshing delight for hot and thirsty PCT hikers.

HYATT LAKE CAMPGROUNDS

Hyatt Lake offers several conveniences for PCT hikers, including a selection of campgrounds and a small resort. **Hyatt Lake Campground**, with 54 sites, caters mostly to the car-camping and small RV crowds—an ideal place to pitch your tent if you like being lulled to sleep by the thrumming of generators. Near the center of the camp are seven walk-in sites with picnic tables, fire pits, and a restroom. There is also a walk-in PCT Camp on the west side of the campground, accessible by a short side trail.

Just 1.5 miles west on Hyatt Dam Road (or 0.5 mile if you hike up Old Hyatt Prairie Road) is **Camper's Cove Resort**. This near-lakeside resort offers 25 rustic cabins, a restaurant that serves up pizzas, burgers, and hearty breakfasts, and a tiny store with a selection of basic foods, snacks, cold drinks, and a few first-aid supplies. They also accommodate resupply packages for hikers. Whether you're staying at the resort or the campground nearer the trail, it's worth sending yourself a package here to help minimize your load for your first few days—especially since you'll probably be carrying the additional weight of extra water. (See appendix 4 for more info.)

If you want to avoid a potentially crowded, noisy campground—especially on summer weekends—and don't need to resupply at the resort, the alternative is to camp at the **Wildcat Campground**. This small campground has 12 sites on a small peninsula, about 2 miles north of the main campground. Amenities include a water pump, vault toilet, and trash service. (See Leg 5 for directions.)

strawberry beginning to adorn the trailsides—then pops out to traverse a grassy savanna with views into the valley to the southwest. On this open hillside yellow star thistle, moth mullein, and purple camas add splashes of summer color. The PCT continues up around the mountain, back under tree cover for a short stretch—you may notice the bright red bark of ponderosa pines and pink flashes of common thistle and checker mallow—then traverses another grassy swath above Soda Creek's wide valley. The trail eventually descends to the northern junction of the Green Springs Loop at around 47.4 miles.

At 48.1 miles, the PCT crosses Road 39-3E-32 for the last time, passes through another gate, and makes a shallow descent into a wide, grassy swale—the northwestern extent of **Hyatt Meadows**. The trail proceeds across the open space, dipping to cross the dry Ashland Canal running through the middle. On the opposite side, it's back into the trees for a moderate ascent over a low ridge, then a quick descent to the outlet of the **Little Hyatt Reservoir 🅾** and Old Hyatt

Prairie Road at 49.5 miles. A sturdy bridge crosses the outlet just below the check dam to meet the road. If your itinerary includes a stay or resupply at **Camper's Cove Resort**, you want to hop off of the PCT here and proceed up gravel Old Hyatt Prairie Road for 2 miles to paved Hyatt Dam Road; Camper's Cove is 0.5 mile north. To continue on the PCT to the **Hyatt Lake PCT Camp**, proceed across the road and through recovering logging land to the junction of Hyatt Dam and East Hyatt Lake Roads at 51 miles. For the campground, proceed 0.1 mile down the access road to the entrance booth; for the PCT Camp, take the short side trail west, just past the road fork and before the entrance booth.

CAMP-TO-CAMP MILEAGE

Hobart Bluff TH Camp to Camper's Cove
    junction 9.8
Camper's Cove junction to Hyatt Lake CG
    junction 1.5
Hyatt Lake CG junction to Hyatt Lake CG
    (off PCT) 0.1

ALTERNATE ROUTES: OLD HYATT PRAIRIE ROAD OR "OLD" PCT

From the shoulder of Green Springs Highway (OR 66), you will notice **Old Hyatt Prairie Road** just left of the trail ascending north. This dirt-and-gravel road proceeds 4.5 miles to Hyatt Lake and parallels the PCT much of the way—a convenient alternate if the PCT is snowbound, or you want to shave off a few miles to get to the lake and call it quits earlier in the day.

For a shorter, albeit viewless, route on the "old" PCT, take the 0.75-mile right fork of the **Green Springs Loop Trail**. This option cuts 1.5 miles off the trail with a circuit around Green Spring Mountain's forested east and north flanks; elevation gain is minimal. The trail parallels **Road 39-3E-32**, crossing it several times, to meet the northern loop junction.

5 HYATT LAKE TO BURTON FLAT ROAD

DISTANCE 16.9 miles

ELEVATION GAIN/LOSS
+2740 feet/–2440 feet

HIGH POINT 6230 feet

CONNECTING TRAILS AND ROADS
Wildcat Glades Road (unpaved), Eve Springs Road (unpaved), Klum Landing Campground spur trail, Moon Prairie Road (unpaved), Keno Access Road, Big Springs spur trail, Big Draw Road (unpaved), Burton Flat Road (unpaved)

ON THE TRAIL

Refreshed after your stay at Hyatt Lake, it's time to get back on the trail. The day's travel will bear generally northeast to get you closer to the Cascade Range, skirting the Cascade-Siskiyou National Monument for a few more miles, before finishing in greener pastures back in the Rogue River–Siskiyou National Forest. The leg ahead is a bit longer than previous ones, due to the lack of good water (with one reliable source two-thirds of

the way through the leg) and camping locations—something you're likely accustomed to by now. The scenery through this stretch won't be much to write home about. But at the end of the leg, after a sizeable ascent and a moderate descent, you'll be primed to meet the volcanic Cascades on the final leg of this section.

Starting from the trailhead/junction at **East Hyatt Lake Road**, the PCT dives under tree cover on relatively flat terrain, heading northeast. At 51.1 miles, just 0.1 mile from the road, is a short spur left (north) that leads to a horse-watering faucet and trough **O**; take advantage of this easy water opportunity if you haven't already filled up. Paralleling the East Hyatt Lake Road, the PCT meanders north, leaves tree cover to mount a small, grassy hill, then drops back into forest. Around 53 miles, the PCT crosses an old jeep road that leads 0.5 mile west to the paved road and **Wildcat Campground**. The trail then crosses another jeep road and exits national monument land.

To get to the Wildcat Campground, look for a trailside kiosk near an overgrown logging road. Veer left (northwest) to paved East Hyatt Lake/ Hyatt Dam Road; go left (west) just around a bend to the campground access road. Turn right (north)

The PCT crosses a number of open, brushy and rocky slopes as it exits the Cascade-Siskiyou National Monument—a good reason to apply your sunscreen!

onto the access road, veer right (northeast) at the fork, and proceed into the campground.

The PCT then crosses a wide, shallow, grassy basin littered with stumps and debris piles, remnants of an old logging operation. This is another parcel of private land that the PCT passes through on its easement. On the north side of the basin, the trail starts climbing gradually northeast, crosses a couple bone-dry creek beds, dips through a shallow draw, crosses the dirt **Wildcat Glades Road**, and resumes climbing. The trail comes to a crest at

55.1 miles with a view south to Mount Shasta—always a welcome sight. Descending east from the crest, you're back on private land, indicated with a trailside sign, in mixed forest; near 56.7 miles is one of your only peeks at **Howard Prairie Lake**. The trail levels near the bottom of the descent, where it crosses gravel **Eve Springs Road** near 57.5 miles, and comes alongside the paved **Howard Prairie Road**.

The PCT then crosses several dirt and gravel spur roads—including one particularly confusing

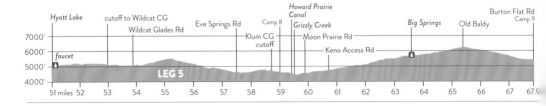

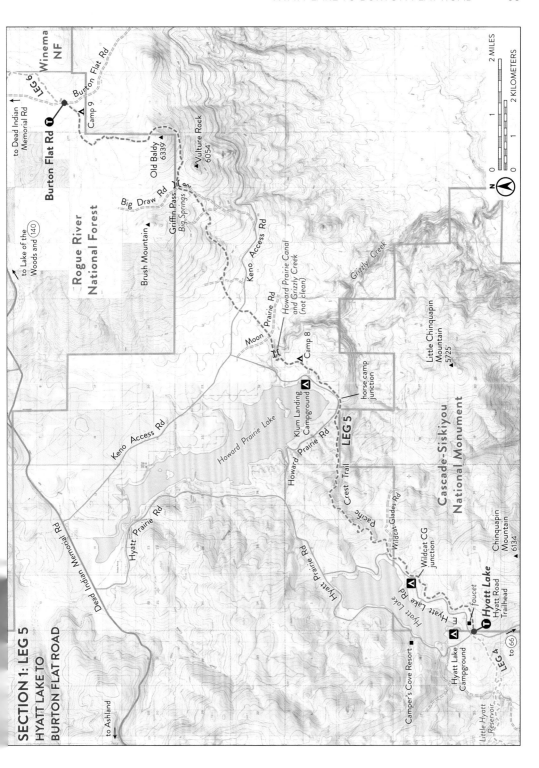

SECTION 1: LEG 5
HYATT LAKE TO
BURTON FLAT ROAD

Winema NF

LEG 9

Burton Flat Rd

to Dead Indian Memorial Rd

Burton Flat Rd

Camp 9

Old Baldy 6339'

Vulture Rock 6054'

Rogue River National Forest

Big Draw Rd

Griffin Pass

Big Springs

Brush Mountain

Keno Access Rd

to Lake of the Woods and 140

Moon Prairie Rd

Howard Prairie Canal and Grizzly Creek (not clean)

Grizzly Creek

Camp 8

Little Chinquapin Mountain 5725'

Keno Access Rd

Klum Landing Campground

Howard Prairie Lake

horse camp junction

LEG 5

Cascade-Siskiyou National Monument

Howard Prairie Rd

Pacific Crest Trail

Wildcat Glades Rd

Dead Indian Memorial Rd

Hyatt Prairie Rd

Hyatt Prairie Rd

Wildcat CG junction

Chinquapin Mountain 6134'

Hyatt Lake Rd

faucet

Hyatt Lake

Hyatt Road Trailhead

LEG 4

to 66

Hyatt Lake Campground

Camper's Cove Resort

Little Hyatt Reservoir

to Ashland

N

2 MILES

2 KILOMETERS

Enjoy your last big look at Mount Shasta from high on the slopes of Old Baldy.

KLUM LANDING CAMPGROUND

The Klum Landing Campground on the shore of Howard Prairie Lake offers 30 sites with picnic tables and fire rings; it also has water, restrooms, and a shower building. Get there by turning left (west) off the PCT onto the old jeep road at 58.7 miles. Follow the jeep road to paved Howard Prairie Road and turn left (southwest). Proceed across the road into the camp area.

Klum Landing Campground 0.3 mile west. After the jeep road, pass a trailside campsite (**Camp 8**) at 59 miles, just before another spur road crossing. Tucked back in a grove of trees, this large site can accommodate up to four tents.

Crossing another dirt road, the trail bends northwest, then northeast, and descends a couple forested switchbacks to cross the concrete canal coming out of Howard Prairie Lake at 59.4 miles. You'll quickly notice that the water is dirty and oily, not recommended for drinking. However, the shaded, grassy bank makes a fine spot to take a break and eat lunch next to actual running water (even if you can't drink it). Across the canal, and the gravel service road alongside it, the PCT dips into the wide, lush floodplain below the dam. High shrubbery lines the trail through here to a bridge over **Grizzly Creek**, in a marshy channel below. Same as the canal water, you don't want to drink this.

The trail continues northeast to cross numerous old logging roads and comes to the **Keno Access Road** at 60.7 miles. Directly across the road, the PCT continues under shady forest, now beginning a gentle ascent toward **Griffin Pass**. Just past another road crossing, the trail turns east and climbs, circuiting the lower flanks of **Brush Mountain**. After about 0.5 mile, the trail turns northeast again and begins climbing a fairly steep (dry) drainage in one of the most unsightly sections of forest in all of Oregon: dry and closed-in, grand and Douglas-firs barely let any sunlight penetrate

crossing over a wide, gravelly plain. Look for trail cairns marking the way forward and proceed up an overgrown jeep road, then break off left (north), back on the trail. A large PCT marker on a tall ponderosa pine will confirm you're on the right path, which goes on to traverse a dry, forested hillside. Shortly beyond, a signed spur trail indicates a horse camp 0.7 km (0.4 mile) west. As the trail turns northeast away from the lake, it reenters greener forest of fir, pine, and cedar. Near 58.7 miles, the trail crosses another jeep road, leading to to the blowdown- and deadfall-littered floor. Thankfully, this unpleasant stretch only lasts for about a mile before cresting the slope and dipping into a saddle and returning to greener woodland.

At 63.6 miles you arrive at the junction to this leg's only reliable water source, **Big Springs ❶**. (The next water source is some 8 miles north at Brown Mountain Shelter.) If your supply is low, you don't have to worry about missing Big Springs, as the junction is clearly signed amid a wide opening in the forest cover. Descending 100 yards right (east) of the trail on an overgrown bootpath, the spur crosses gravel **Big Draw Road**—yes, you're still crossing roads—then a boggy meadow on wooden puncheon (boardwalk) to a gated fence. Opposite the gate in the trees is a tiny flat spot that could accommodate a tent. Through the gate, at the end of the puncheon, "Big" Springs is a rubber pipe dribbling cold, clear water into a rocky puddle; Vulture Rock rises directly eastw.

Once you've topped off at Big Springs and are back on the PCT, 5740-foot Griffin Pass is just ahead, at the border of the Rogue River–Siskiyou National Forest. Here, the PCT turns east, staying on BLM land, and begins a gentle, counterclockwise ascent of 6339-foot **Old Baldy**, once the site of an old fire lookout. Unlike many other "bald" mountains named for rocky or barren summits, southern Oregon's Old Baldy derived its name from the meadowy slopes adorning its southern and western flanks. The massive clear-cut on its southeastern flank only adds to its namesake character. The trail, however, remains pleasantly wooded, with patches of greenery lining the trailside. As it circuits around the eastern side, the forest cover gives way to high shrubbery which opens up a splendid panorama (thanks to the aforementioned clear-cut) to the south over the Fremont-Winema National Forest's Kent Peak and Buck Mountain, and all the way to that big familiar mountain to the south.

The PCT reaches its crest for this leg on the northeast slope of Old Baldy, just below the summit. Here, you're offered one more sweeping view of Mount Shasta before the trail dips back under the cover of trees and reenters the Rogue River–Siskiyou National Forest at 65.4 miles.

TRAIL TRIVIA

Grizzly Creek and **Grizzly Prairie** (now Howard Prairie) were named for the grizzly bears that once populated the area and preyed on settlers' cattle in the latter half of the 1800s. **Grizzly Peak**, northeast of Ashland, was similarly named following a near-fatal encounter between a local settler and one of the brutish bruins.

Now the PCT begins its steady descent along the west-facing slope of Old Baldy's northern ridgeline, beginning with a gentle northwest descent, then bending due north on a more moderate grade. As if passing through some kind of invisible barrier, the scenery—though still in dense forest—improves markedly. The trees, older, taller, greener, and draped with moss and lichen, rise above the slope over a carpet of fern and other shrubbery; a variety of forest wildflowers, such as cute, pink pipsissewa, splash color amid the greenery.

The PCT continues down the ridge, winding through tight bends on a modest grade—enough to make you glad the ascent wasn't similarly steep. As it nears the bottom to enter a wide saddle, the trail bends northeast again, descends a little more, then levels out in thinner forest. At 67.9 miles it meets **Burton Flat Road (Camp 9)**. Approximately 25 yards before the road, a couple of small campsites can be found just right (east) of the trail. These are fairly primitive, each with enough flat space for one tent. The location is not optimal, but having hiked a 16.9-mile day it's serviceable. The alternative is to continue another 3.7 miles to Brown Mountain Shelter.

CAMP-TO-CAMP MILEAGE

Hyatt Lake Campground to Wildcat
    Campground junction. 2.0
Wildcat Campground junction to Klum
    Landing Campground junction 5.7
Klum Landing Campground junction
    to Camp 8. . . . . 0.3
Camp 8 to Camp 9 . . . . 8.9

6 BURTON FLAT ROAD TO FISH LAKE

DISTANCE 14.2 miles

ELEVATION GAIN/LOSS
+1410 feet/−1730 feet

HIGH POINT 5520 feet

CONNECTING TRAILS AND ROADS
Dead Indian Memorial Road, Brown
Mountain Shelter spur trail, FR 3720,
Brown Mountain Trail (#1005), High Lakes
Trail (#6200), Fish Lake Trail (#1013),
Summit Trail (#3732)

ON THE TRAIL

By day six, you're probably ready for a change
of scenery—and here it comes! Back in national
forest, you'll start to feel like you're once again
in a wilderness setting. Through the next leg the
PCT takes a pleasant rolling route north to **Brown
Mountain**—where the change of scenery becomes
sudden, obvious, and striking—then contours west
around its base to the Fish Lake junction. There's
only one reliable water source through this leg, so
you'll want to be sure to top off your containers—
especially since the latter half of the leg can get
quite hot at the peak of summer. If you're ending
the section at Fish Lake, you'll have an opportunity to take a dip in the lake (or take a shower) and
get a tasty meal. This also makes a good staging
point for continuing your trek into Section 2, as
you can pick up or purchase a resupply.

From **Camp 9** near **Burton Flat Road**, the PCT
continues north under pleasant, mossy woodland

where the ground cover becomes noticeably more
prolific with the introduction of trailside shrubbery. Bearing northeast, the trail makes a gentle,
viewless ascent over the lower western flank of
6090-foot **Burton Butte**, then bends north and
drops down to a large trailhead parking area beside
Dead Indian Memorial Road at 69.9 miles. The
only suitable option for camping here is to pitch
your tent in the trees at the edge of the parking
area. After crossing the road, the trail continues
north to climb another low hill and reaches the
first high point of the leg in a shallow saddle. Here,
the trail bends northeast and begins a short, steady
descent before leveling out.

At 71.6 miles the PCT reaches a junction
with an old roadbed. Here, a tall sign indicates
Canada 889 miles to the north and Mexico 1779
miles to the south. More immediately appealing,
it also indicates the **Brown Mountain Shelter**—
water!—100 yards to the left (west). The small log
building has a woodstove inside but is usually dirty
and cluttered with trash left by less-considerate
visitors; a picnic table outside makes a fine place
to take off your pack for a snack break. Near the
shelter is a large hand-pump well **◑**. It takes several vigorous pumps to start drawing water, then
only a few more to fill a 1-liter bottle. There are no
obvious campsites near the shelter, but a few bare
spots could suffice if you don't mind a few lumps
underneath.

Topped off and back on the trail, you'll head
north, crossing gravel logging road FR 3720, then
northeast again on easy, undulating tread. While
this section of the Rogue River–Siskiyou has been

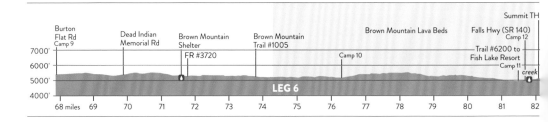

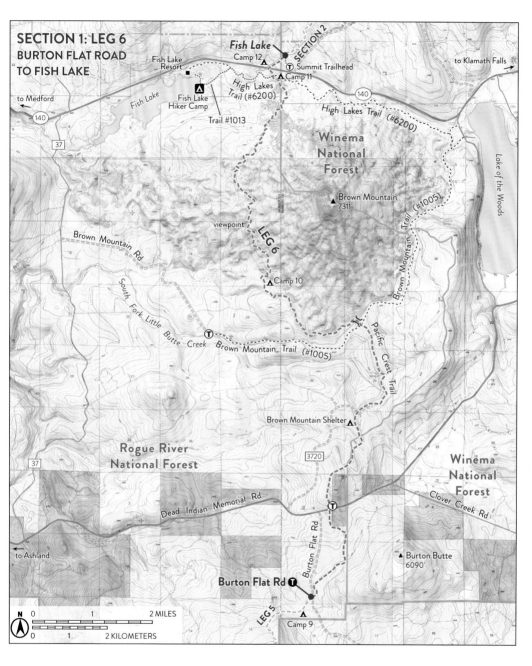

SECTION 1: LEG 6
BURTON FLAT ROAD
TO FISH LAKE

heavily logged, you're pleasantly unaware as the trail remains in a corridor of dense forest which impedes most views of the nearby clear-cut and recovering areas, even as you transition from older forest to younger. At 73.8 miles the PCT comes to a junction with the **Brown Mountain Trail** (#1005), which proceeds 2.9 miles west to a trailhead on FR 3705 and 5.1 miles east to **Lake of the Woods**; 0.2 mile past the junction, the trail crosses a dry creek gully on a small single-rail bridge as it

Early morning sunlight illuminates mossy forest near Brown Mountain.

turns west to begin its circuit around the wide base of Brown Mountain.

Around 74.3 miles you'll start to notice a gradual change of scenery, beginning with the crossing of a flow of basaltic lava rock. The trail plunges back into the forest, then pops out again to cross a wider lava flow, transitioning from forest duff to a carpet of red volcanic cinders—a marked color contrast with the dense black lava rock, rich green forest, and, quite possibly, vivid blue sky overhead. The next couple miles continue to wind and undulate northwest through alternating stretches of shady old growth and exposed lava flows. Looking up, you may catch a few glimpses of Brown Mountain's 7311-foot summit; looking down, you may spot Douglas squirrels and pikas darting between the rocks. If the day is a hot one, you may find yourself speeding across the hot black lava flows to get back under the cooler cover of the trees.

Under the cover of shady forest, the PCT skirts an older, moss-covered lava flow, and at 76.3 miles reaches a decent campsite right (east) of the trail in a small clearing (**Camp 10**). The partially exposed space has room for a couple small tents; unfortunately, there is no water. This makes a fine place for a snack or lunch break before the day's only significant climb of just a few hundred feet. The trail then jogs west before turning east and then north for a higher traverse around the mountain's west flank, continuing to meander through trees and over lava as it navigates around larger flows and jumbly basins. You may find these adorned here and there with tall hedges of chinkapin—just look for the spiky "porcupine egg" seedpods.

The payoff comes around 78.1 miles, near the crest of the traverse, with an expansive view north to **Mount McLoughlin**. Oh, yeah, *that's* why you're hiking this. The view is quite grand, so be sure to enjoy it for the next 0.5 mile or so—once you dip back into the trees, you won't see this 9495-foot peak again until you're far north of it (in section 2). From the crest, the trail begins a moderate descent under more shady Douglas-firs, bends northeast, then continues winding steadily down. As the trail begins to level and veer back to the northwest, it comes to a wide junction with the **High Lakes Trail** (#6200) at 81.5 miles. To the left (west) is **Fish Lake Resort**; to the right (east) is **Lake of the Woods**. Just right of the wide junction is a small campsite with enough room for a couple small tents (**Camp 11**).

At this point, you determine whether your trek ends, pauses, or continues on. Either way, it's

BROWN MOUNTAIN

Brown Mountain is the first of Oregon's cascade volcanoes you will encounter on the Pacific Crest Trail, some 75 miles north of the California–Oregon border. The mountain is one of Oregon's smaller volcanic peaks, estimated to be between 12,000 and 60,000 years old. The wider base of Brown Mountain consists of an andesitic shield volcano while the steeper upper reaches and summit are composed of a large cinder cone. As recently as 2000 years ago, a flood of basaltic aa lava poured down its north and west flanks. Despite being surrounded by old-growth forest, the lava flows have seen minimal erosion (basalt is an extremely dense, hard rock and resistant to rapid weathering), and vegetation—other than some multicolored lichen—has been slow to take root on the jumbly slopes. Where the PCT crosses over these lava flows, much of the trail has been built of small red cinders. Meticulously constructed across numerous lava branches, small and large, these short few miles proved to be one of the last and most costly portions of the 2650-mile PCT to build.

worth building a visit to Fish Lake Resort into your itinerary. There, you can camp, rent a rustic cabin, clean up, resupply, and get a refreshing drink and hearty meal. There is also a small PCT hiker camp area near the resort and lakeshore. Get there by hanging a left (west) on the High Lakes Trail. The wide, graded trail (marked and used as a winter recreation route) starts with a short incline, then proceeds mostly on a shallow downslope, winding through blocky basalt lava flows. Where the trail forks, veer left onto the **Fish Lake Trail** (#1013), a narrow dirt bootpath (slightly shorter than continuing on the High Lakes Trail). As you near the lake, the trail crosses a dirt service road, then gets brushy and rugged as it winds the final length over a jumbly lava bed and comes to the hiker

campsites. For the resort and restaurant, take a user trail right (north) into the RV campground and follow the gravel road around to the resort entrance.

To bypass Fish Lake and finish the section, or continue on into Section 2, proceed another 0.2 mile north through the trees to where the trail spills out onto the shoulder of the **Falls Highway** (OR 140). Carefully cross the highway and plunge back under the cover of forest. Just left of the trail is a large campsite with room for a few tents (**Camp 12**). For water, proceed 0.1 mile farther up the trail to a small creek ⚫ crossing; this may be low or even dry by late summer. To get to the **Summit Trailhead** and the end of Section 1, continue northeast to the trailhead junction at 82.1 miles, hang a right (south)

The junction for the Brown Mountain shelter will be a welcome sight—there's water close by!

FISH LAKE RESORT

Fish Lake paints a refreshingly pretty picture at the end of Section 1.

Tucked among the forest on the northern banks of Fish Lake, **Fish Lake Resort** offers a full range of services for campers, hikers, and vacationers. The lake itself is not what you would call "picture-perfect," resting in a forested saddle between Brown Mountain and Mount McLoughlin (you can't see either), but it is refreshingly pleasant if you've just come off several days of hot, near-water-less trail. In addition to the popular RV camping area on the east side of the lake, the resort also offers eleven cabins at reasonable prices and six tent sites. If you'd rather avoid the crowds—and it does get crowded through the summer months—there are a couple small hiker campsites on the east side of the lake.

At the resort, the **Tadpole Cafe** offers both indoor and outdoor seating—the shaded deck is especially nice—and serves up a good selection of hearty breakfasts (the loaded breakfast skillet is a real winner!), sandwiches, burgers, milkshakes, and nightly dinner specials. A modest store caters mostly to the camping/fishing crowds with food staples, snacks, candy, and plenty of cold drinks. They also stock a small selection of freeze-dried backpacker meals and energy bars, and there's usually a hiker box where you might find—or donate—a food item or two. In addition to the food and camping conveniences, the resort also offers showers and a laundry room, and handles resupply packages for hikers. (See appendix 4 for more info.)

The southernmost of Oregon's big volcanoes, 9495-foot Mount McLoughlin dominates the scene from the lava beds around Brown Mountain.

off the PCT on Trail #3732, and find the large trailhead parking area just 0.3 mile farther at the Summit Sno-Park.

Now that you've completed the first section of Oregon's PCT, you've only just scratched the surface. There are still several hundred more miles of lush old-growth forest, pristine lakes, wildflower-choked meadows, and rugged volcanic peaks yet to come—including some spectacular wilderness areas and a visit to Oregon's gem of a national park, Crater Lake. When you're ready for more, move on into Section 2.

CAMP-TO-CAMP MILEAGE

Camp 9 to Brown Mountain Shelter 3.7
Brown Mountain Shelter to Camp 10 . . . . 4.7
Camp 10 to Camp 11 (Fish Lake Junction). . . . 5.2
Camp 11 (Fish Lake Junction to Camp 12). . . . 0.2

FISH LAKE TO CASCADE CREST

AT THE FOOT OF OREGON'S Cascade Range, the Pacific Crest Trail forges north into a vast wilderness built by millennia of volcanic activity, then worn away by the grinding weight of ice and the steady march of time and gravity. This becomes the central setting for the PCT through much of the rest of the state: a landscape dominated by crumbling volcanoes and high ridges separating wide glacial basins pocked with lakes and blanketed with rich, dense forest. From here on, the PCT takes a comfortable, moderate, mid-elevation course, traversing mountains and crossing valleys. Section 2 begins at the base of southern Oregon's tallest volcano, **Mount McLoughlin,** and concludes with an unforgettable passage through **Crater Lake National Park**, one of the state's most iconic natural features.

The trail continues just north of **Fish Lake** on the **Falls Highway** (OR 140), in the **Fremont-Winema National Forest**. In contrast to the remote trailhead of Section 1, access to Section 2 is a breeze—just an easy hour's drive east from Medford, or west from Klamath Falls, on good, paved highway. Almost from the get-go, the PCT enters the **Sky Lakes Wilderness**. The name invokes images of countless pools of cerulean mountain water (yes, there are) amid high peaks and ridges (plenty of those, too), all under expansive, dreamy skies (often present in summer). Ironically, however, the PCT bypasses all of the lakes in the area, which must all be accessed by a variety of lateral trails winding through the wilderness. A cruel trick by trail designers? Not so much. It was simply their efforts at keeping the Pacific Crest Trail as near to the actual crest of the mountains as possible—otherwise it might need to be renamed the "Pacific Lakes and Valleys Trail." Thankfully for

DISTANCE 68.8 miles (recommended); 73.4 miles (official)

STATE DISTANCE 82.1–156.3 miles

ELEVATION GAIN/LOSS +9680 feet/–9060 feet

HIGH POINT 7740 feet

BEST TIME OF YEAR Aug–Sept

PCTA SECTION LETTER C

LAND MANAGERS Fremont-Winema National Forest (Sky Lakes Wilderness), Rogue River–Siskiyou National Forest (Sky Lakes Wilderness), Crater Lake National Park, Umpqua National Forest

PASSES AND PERMITS NW Forest Pass required at Summit Sno-Park and North Crater trailheads; Crater Lake National Park wilderness permit required for camping within park boundary.

MAPS AND APPS
- National Geographic PCT: Oregon South 1005, maps 5–10
- Halfmile PCT: Oregon C1–C12
- Guthook PCT: Oregon

LEGS
1. Fish Lake to Island Lake
2. Island Lake to Seven Lakes Basin
3. Seven Lakes Basin to Stuart Falls Junction
4. Stuart Falls Junction to Mazama Village
5. Mazama Village to Grouse Hill (via Rim Trail)
5A. Alternate: Mazama Village to Grouse Hill (via PCT)
6. Grouse Hill to Cascade Crest

Opposite: The sight of Wizard Island rising from the azure depths of Crater Lake is a worthy reason for detouring off the PCT for a few miles.

section and thru-hikers, it's less than a mile to many of these placid pools, making them suitable options for refilling, refreshing, camping, and additional exploration.

The highlight of the section—and certainly a highlight in all of Oregon—is **Crater Lake**. This 6-mile-wide (east–west) lake filling a nearly mile-deep volcanic caldera is a sight to behold. The color of the water is unlike any other lake you've likely ever seen. It's so . . . *BLUE!* It can only be likened to similar other surreal landscapes, like standing at the edge of the Grand Canyon in Arizona, or gazing across the vast Haleakala Crater on the island of Maui. You may want to consider building in a "zero day" (thru-hiker-speak for a day off) to catch the Crater Lake Trolley for a tour around the rim, or spend a day on the lake with a boat tour and visit to Wizard Island. Of course, like any national park, it will be crowded, especially at the peak of summer. It may be a bit of a culture shock after being on a quiet trail for several days before arriving, so try to plan your visit to the park for midweek.

The challenge of this section comes between the lake-filled basins of the Sky Lakes Wilderness and the southern boundary of the national park. Here, the PCT passes through the hot, dry burned area of the **790 Fire**, followed by the hot, dry **Oregon Desert**—all smack in the middle of a 21-mile stretch of waterless trail. Mercifully, there is an alternate route (used by many thru-hikers) that detours off the PCT to a happy little camp area near a refreshingly pleasing waterfall. But if you want to stay true to the PCT and power through this stretch, start early and carry extra water. That makes the reward—the soda fountain at Mazama Village—that much sweeter.

One thing to be aware of—very aware of—is that all the water in this forested lake country makes it homey for hordes of ravenous mosquitoes. The peak of this murderous, blood sucking misery usually comes in early summer and lasts through late July. By August, the little buggers are usually gone—or at least significantly diminished. Even then, it's advisable to armor-up by wearing long pants and sleeves, a hat, bug repellent—and a head net might help you keep your sanity.

So whether you're continuing your journey from Section 1, or just starting with Section 2, the trail ahead has everything you're coming to hike the PCT for: remote wilderness, expansive views, oodles of high-country flora and fauna, and a national park to boot. This is the Pacific Crest Trail, Oregon-style.

ACCESS
Fish Lake (Summit Trailhead)
From Medford, take I-5 exit 30 for the Crater Lake Highway (OR 62). Turn east on OR 62 and proceed 5.6 miles through town. Turn right (east) on Lake of the Woods Highway (OR 140) and drive 32 miles. The PCT crosses the highway approximately 2 miles east of the entrance to Fish Lake Resort; look for the trailhead at the Summit Sno-Park area on the north side of the highway just beyond.

From Klamath Falls, drive 36.2 miles north then west on Falls Highway (OR 140) to the trailhead parking area. You can access the PCT from the parking area via the 0.25-mile Summit Trail (#3732). If you're starting from Fish Lake Resort, it's just a 2-mile jaunt down the High Lakes Trail (#6200) to the PCT junction.

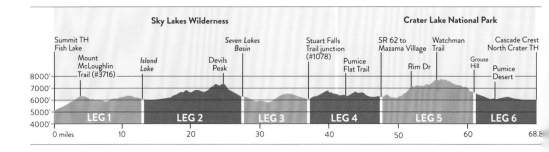

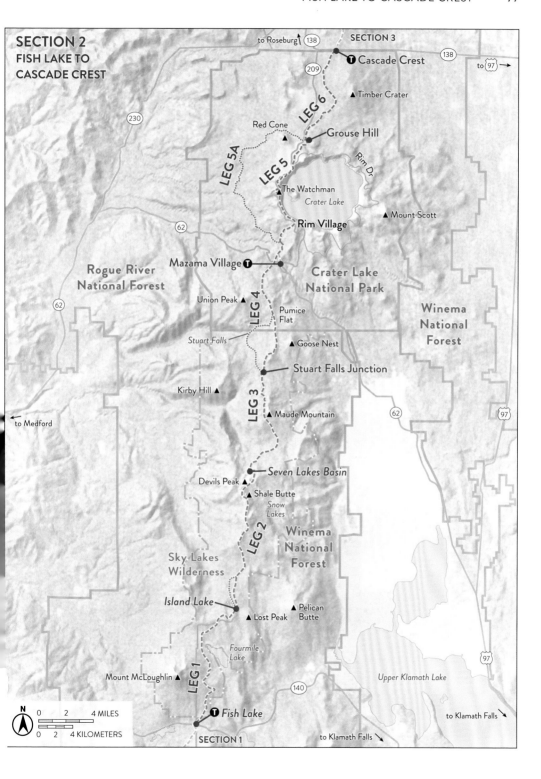

SECTION 2
FISH LAKE TO
CASCADE CREST

to Roseburg (138)   SECTION 3

(209)   Cascade Crest   (138)

to (97)

▲ Timber Crater

(230)

LEG 6

Red Cone   Grouse Hill
▲

LEG 5A   LEG 5

Rim Dr.

The Watchman
▲   Crater Lake   ▲ Mount Scott

(62)   Rim Village

Mazama Village   Crater Lake
National Park

Rogue River
National Forest

Union Peak ▲   LEG 4   Pumice
Flat   Winema
National
Forest

(62)   Stuart Falls   ▲ Goose Nest

Stuart Falls Junction

Kirby Hill ▲   LEG 3

to Medford   ▲ Maude Mountain   (62)   (97)

Seven Lakes Basin

Devils Peak ▲
▲ Shale Butte
Snow
Lakes   Winema
National
Forest

LEG 2

Sky Lakes
Wilderness

Island Lake   ▲ Pelican
▲ Lost Peak   Butte

Fourmile
Lake   (97)

LEG 1

Mount McLoughlin ▲   Upper Klamath Lake

(140)

to Klamath Falls

N
0   2   4 MILES   Fish Lake
0   2   4 KILOMETERS   to Klamath Falls
SECTION 1

Luther Mountain serves as a notable landmark as the PCT winds through the Sky Lakes Wilderness.

Cascade Crest

From Roseburg, take I-5 exit 124 for the North Umpqua Highway (OR 138). Proceed through town, following signs for OR 138 and Crater Lake National Park. Continue east for 87 miles, passing the turnoff for Diamond Lake Resort. Continue 0.9 mile past the Crater Lake north entrance road (OR 209) and turn left (north) onto a side road signed for the North Crater trailhead. Proceed 0.3 mile to parking and trail access at the end of the turnaround.

From Bend, drive south on US 97 for 75 miles. Turn right (west) on OR 138 and continue 14 miles to the turnoff for the North Crater trailhead.

NOTES

Services

The nearest services to the southern trailhead can be found at Fish Lake Resort, 2 miles west of the PCT (see Section 1). The cities of Medford and Klamath Falls are approximately 1 hour west and east, respectively, with all the usual services and accommodations of larger towns. Mazama Village in Crater Lake National Park has good services for hikers, including camping, dining, and opportunities to resupply; there are additional, albeit limited and more costly, services in the Crater Lake Rim Village. Services nearest the northern trailhead at Cascade Crest are very limited, the closest being 14 miles east at the junction of OR 138 and US 97; there are additional, albeit still limited, services in the small town of Chemult, 10 miles north of this junction on US 97. (See appendixes 3 and 4 for more info.)

Camping

There are plenty of good near-trail campsites through the Sky Lakes Wilderness, as well as an abundance of side trails that lead to pleasant lake basins and a bevy of camping options. Camping within Crater Lake National Park is limited to five designated camp areas and specific wilderness zones. All require a park wilderness permit, which must be obtained in person at the Steel Visitor Center or in the Rim Village (See Passes and Permits in the introduction for more info.)

Water

Access to near-trail water is a challenge through this section. Camp locations, both near- and off-trail, have been selected for their access to water, but the PCT between locations remains largely dry, requiring some short detours, and a recommended alternate route, to resupply. The longest waterless sections are 15 and 21 miles, so carrying extra containers to get through these areas is a good idea.

Wildfire Damage

In the summer of 2017, the Blanket Creek and Spruce Lake fires burned across several miles of the PCT in the Sky Lakes Wilderness and Crater Lake National Park, causing extensive damage. Portions of trail in these areas may experience extended closures or detours as the Forest Service and National Park Service assess damage and undertake repairs. Contact the forest or park for the latest information on trail accessibility.

SUGGESTED ITINERARIES

The following distances do not include off-PCT miles (up to 3.7 miles) to water sources, campsites, alternate routes, or resupply locations. For more information about trail distances, see How to Use This Guide. Listed in the first two itineraries, Stuart Falls Junction is not an ideal place to spend the night; either proceed on the PCT or take the recommended alternate route. The last two itineraries use the alternate recommended route around Crater Lake.

6 DAYS: RECOMMENDED ROUTE

		MILES
Day 1	Fish Lake (Summit TH) to Island Lake	13
Day 2	Island Lake to Seven Lakes Basin	14
Day 3	Seven Lakes Basin to Stuart Falls junction	9.7
Day 4	Stuart Falls junction to Mazama Village	10.4
Day 5	Mazama Village to Grouse Hill (via Rim Trail)	12.6
Day 6	Grouse Hill to Cascade Crest	9.1

6 DAYS: OFFICIAL ROUTE

Day 1	Fish Lake (Summit TH) to Island Lake	13
Day 2	Island Lake to Seven Lakes Basin	14
Day 3	Seven Lakes Basin to Stuart Falls junction	9.7
Day 4	Stuart Falls junction to Mazama Village	10.4
Day 5	Mazama Village to Red Cone Spring Camp (via PCT)	13.6
Day 6	Red Cone Spring Camp to Cascade Crest	12.7

5 DAYS

Day 1	Fish Lake (Summit TH) to Island Lake	13
Day 2	Island Lake to Seven Lakes Basin	14.2
Day 3	Seven Lakes Basin to Mazama Village	19.9
Day 4	Mazama Village to Grouse Hill	12.6
Day 5	Grouse Hill to Cascade Crest	9.1

4 DAYS

Day 1	Fish Lake (Summit TH) to Sky Lakes Area	18.2
Day 2	Sky Lakes Area to Ranger Spring	12.3
Day 3	Ranger Spring to Mazama Village	16.6
Day 4	Mazama Village to Cascade Crest	21.7

1 FISH LAKE TO ISLAND LAKE

DISTANCE 13 miles

ELEVATION GAIN/LOSS
+1990 feet/–1050 feet

HIGH POINT 6320 feet

CONNECTING TRAILS AND ROADS
Summit Trail (#3732), South Rye Trail,
Mount McLoughlin Trail (#3716), Twin
Ponds Trail (#993), Cathill Way Trail
(#992), Red Lake Trail (#987), Long Lake
Trail (#3758), Blue Canyon Trail (#982)

ON THE TRAIL

The first leg of Section 2 begins your journey north into the **Sky Lakes Wilderness** with a moderate climb over Mount McLoughlin's eastern flank to reach the crest of the Cascades. Views are spare, with much of the stretch remaining under cover of varied forest; however, you may notice the ground cover becoming greener and fuller than seen in sections south, with new varieties of flowers and berries appearing trailside. The initial climb is moderate, and the following walk pleasant. You can even work in a side adventure to the summit of southern Oregon's highest peak. At the end of the leg, there are a couple serviceable campsites near the PCT, or you can take a side trail to a large camp area near the shore of a lovely forested lake.

From the Summit Sno-Park trailhead, just north of Falls Highway (OR 140), hike 0.3 mile northwest to connect with the Pacific Crest Trail. At the junction, set your GPS unit odometer to 0,

turn right, and let your journey begin. Here, the mixed forest of fir and hemlock is thick with vegetation: huckleberry, snowberry, red elderberry, and prickly currant. Moving forward, the PCT begins a moderate ascent northeast on comfortable tread to circuit the wide base of **Mount McLoughlin,** entering the Sky Lakes Wilderness just 0.4 mile up the trail; 0.1 mile over the boundary is a decent campsite right (east) of the trail with room for a couple small tents (**Camp 1**). Shortly beyond, the carpet of forest greenery is briefly replaced with dry, tangled debris and deadfall, soon returning to livelier green underbrush.

At 0.8 mile, the PCT comes to the junction with the old **South Rye Trail**. The PCT meanders forward through the forest, comfortably gaining elevation and crossing a dry drainage and a few ancient lava flows. At 2.5 miles is another campsite right (east) of the trail with room for two tents (**Camp 2**). Over the next mile, the PCT passes through forest alternating between lush and green and dry and brown, traverses another

TRAIL TRIVIA

As with many mountains, **Mount McLoughlin** went through many name changes over the years: *M'laiksini Yaina*, Malsi, Mount Pitt, Big Butte, and Mount Shasty. It finally became Mount McLoughlin in 1838, named for Dr. John McLoughlin of the Hudson's Bay Company, who was known to aid weary settlers making their way along the Oregon Trail.

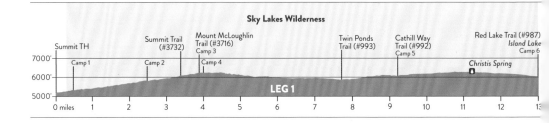

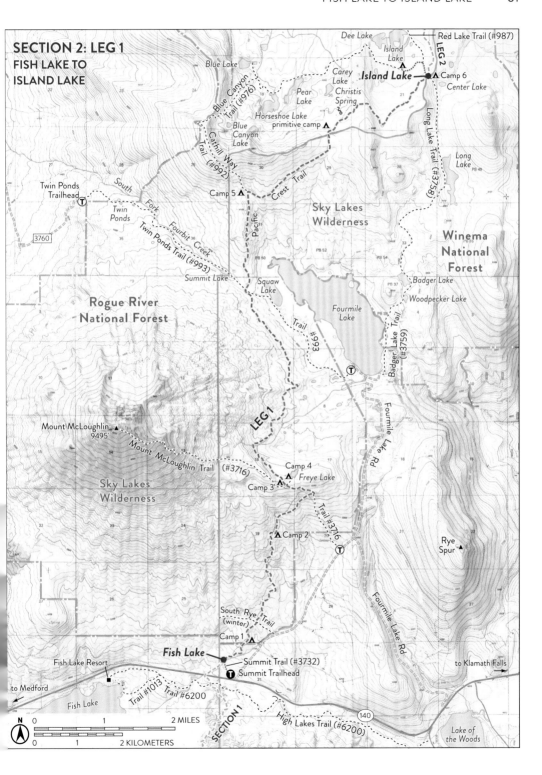

SECTION 2: LEG 1
FISH LAKE TO ISLAND LAKE

Red Lake Trail (#987)

Dee Lake

Island Lake

Blue Lake

Island Lake   Camp 6

Carey Lake   Center Lake

Blue Canyon Trail (#976)

Pear Lake

Christis Spring

Horseshoe Lake
primitive camp

Blue Canyon Lake

Cathill Way Trail (#992)

Crest Trail

Camp 5

Long Lake Trail (#3758)   Long Lake

Twin Ponds Trailhead

South Fork

Twin Ponds

Pacific

Sky Lakes Wilderness

Winema National Forest

3760

Fourbit Creek

Twin Ponds Trail (#993)

Summit Lake

Squaw Lake

Badger Lake

Woodpecker Lake

Trail #993

Fourmile Lake

Badger Lake Trail (#3759)

Rogue River National Forest

LEG 1

Mount McLoughlin
9495'

Mount McLoughlin Trail (#3716)

Fourmile Lake Rd

Camp 4
Freye Lake

Camp 3

Sky Lakes Wilderness

Camp 2

Trail #3716

Rye Spur

South Rye Trail (winter)

Fourmile Lake Rd

Camp 1

Fish Lake   Summit Trail (#3732)

Summit Trailhead

to Klamath Falls

Fish Lake Resort

to Medford

Fish Lake

Trail #1013   Trail #6200

SECTION 1

High Lakes Trail (#6200)

140

Lake of the Woods

N

0   1   2 MILES

0   1   2 KILOMETERS

MOUNT MCLOUGHLIN

Dominating the southern portion of the Sky Lakes Wilderness is Mount McLoughlin, Oregon's sixth-highest peak. With its snow-capped 9495-foot summit, it is visible for miles from almost any direction—except if you're on the PCT nearby where it remains largely hidden by dense forest. This volcanic peak underwent several stages of mountain-building, with the formation of an unusually tall cinder cone atop an older shield volcano. That was followed by several periods of andesitic lava flows emanating from both the summit crater and lower vents. During the last ice age, a large glacier gouged out the northeast flank. A small glacier continued to occupy the eroded cirque until the early twentieth century.

A rough, fairly strenuous 3.9-mile trail climbs 3300 feet from the PCT to its summit, ascending through rocky forest before rising above the treeline. The trail from there on is marked by stone cairns and posts. Views from the summit take in Mount Shasta and Mount Lassen (in California) to the south and the peaks around Crater Lake and Mount Thielsen to the north. This side trip would likely require adding an extra day to your itinerary. If you choose to climb this summit, be sure to pay close attention to your route on your map or GPS receiver and descend by the same path you ascend. Many hikers make the mistake of descending the southern ridge instead and wind up lost and needing to be rescued.

drainage, then intersects the **Mount McLoughlin Trail** (#3716) at 3.4 miles. The east branch of this trail descends 0.9 mile to a trailhead on Fourmile Lake Road.

From this junction, the PCT and Mount McLoughlin Trail continue forward as one, turning sharply northwest and gaining elevation to another junction at 3.9 miles. On this small plateau, the Mount McLoughlin Trail breaks off to continue its westward climb toward its namesake peak; unfortunately, the trail junction remains closed-in by trees with no views of the summit. A small campsite can be found just right of this junction with room for one tent (**Camp 3**); nearby is the 0.2-mile spur trail that leads northeast to small **Freye Lake**, with a partial view of the mountain and a couple more campsites.

Moving away from the junction, the PCT comes to a low crest (the high point of the leg—now it's easy cruising from here) and a trailside campsite with room for two tents and a nice view of the sky (**Camp 4**). The trail then begins a shallow descent, still bearing northwest, through forest increasingly green and pleasant. After crossing another drainage (likely dry), the trail turns northwest and levels out, still contouring around Mount McLoughlin's lower eastern slope. Along the way a window in the trees offers a peek at the forested hills ahead, but little is to be seen of the hulking volcano you're standing on.

Turning northwest again, the trail proceeds to a junction with the **Twin Ponds Trail** (#993) at 7.7 miles in a shallow saddle. Just before the junction you may notice a grassy meadow through the trees to the right (northeast) of the trail—the remnant of a long-gone pond. This lateral trail heads 0.5 mile east to **Squaw Lake ⬤** and northwest 3.3 miles to the Twin Ponds and a trailhead at the end of FR 3760. (The Twin Ponds Trail uses a portion of the Rancheria Trail, an old wagon road that dates back to the 1860s and was used to supply Fort Klamath.) There aren't any suitable campsites at this junction, but a couple of trailside logs make decent benches for taking a break. From this low point, the trail begins its next ascent north to crest a minor ridge with a brief view of **Fourmile Lake** to the east and a forested peak directly ahead. Just below this peak, at 9.2 miles, the forest opens up and the trail takes a sharp turn to the east. At this turn is the junction with the little-used **Cathill Way Trail** (#992); a small campsite can be found left (west) of the trail with room for one tent (**Camp 5**).

The PCT now bears northeast through an area of young noble firs—somewhat resembling a Christmas tree farm—to traverse a forested ridge

Much of the PCT through the Sky Lakes Wilderness remains forest-bound, with big views being few and far between.

on the back side of a glaciated basin, where it offers a partial view south at Mount McLoughlin—*there it is!* Where the trail passes through a forested saddle, around 11 miles, it crosses the crest into the Rogue River–Siskiyou National Forest, where a primitive campsite with room for two tents can be found in a clearing left of the trail. A short distance farther, at 11.2 miles, is the signed spur trail to **Christis Spring** . To top off your containers with cold, clear water, take this brushy bootpath

Island Lake, a short detour off the PCT, makes a fine place to camp in the Sky Lakes Wilderness.

100 yards west to the seeping spring. This is usually a reliable water source even late into the season. From the spring the trail meanders northeast around another low hill, then drops to the

TRAIL TRIVIA

If staying at the camping area on the south side of Island Lake, you may notice a tree with a wooden railing around it. This large Shasta red fir is the **Judge Waldo Tree**, and marks the spot where Judge John B. Waldo and his party camped in 1888 on their expedition from Willamette Pass to Mount Shasta. Take note of this name, as you will see it pop up again later.

southeast before returning to its previous bearing. Because the trail remains forested through much of this area, there are no notable landmarks to help you determine your exact location or surroundings—you just have to trust your map, compass, and occasional tree blazes.

At 13 miles, the PCT meets the four-way junction of **Red Lake Trail** (#987) and **Long Lake Trail** (#3758). The latter passes through a saddle, then drops into a shallow basin with (usually dry) Center Lake, then proceeds south to Long Lake and beyond to the eastern shores of Fourmile Lake. Here, at the end of the leg, the options are to camp at the junction—a small camp can be found right (east) of the trail with room for one tent (**Camp 6**)—or proceed 0.6 mile off the PCT to **Island Lake Camp**, via the Red Lake Trail. It's definitely worth the easy side trip to Island Lake. Get there by turning off the PCT on a gentle descent northward to a fork with the **Blue Canyon Trail** (#982). Veer left (west) on the Blue Canyon Trail to circuit around the south side of the lake. You won't see much of the lake through the dense forest, but watch for an unsigned (usually flagged, though) bootpath right (north) that proceeds to a large camping area near the lakeshore. The open area has room for several tents, with a large fire ring in the center. A footpath from the camping area leads through the trees to a section of grassy lakeshore for water access and a nice view.

CAMP-TO-CAMP MILEAGE

Summit Trailhead to Camp 1 . . . . 0.5
Camp 1 to Camp 2. . . . . 2.0
Camp 2 to Camp 3 . . . . 1.4
Camp 3 to Camp 4 . . . . 0.1
Camp 4 to Camp 5 . . . . 5.2
Camp 5 to Camp 6 . . . . 3.8
Camp 6 to Island Lake Camp (off PCT) 0.6

2 ISLAND LAKE TO SEVEN LAKES BASIN

DISTANCE 14 miles

ELEVATION GAIN/LOSS
+2290 feet/–2100 feet

HIGH POINT 7380

CONNECTING TRAILS
Red Lake Trail (#987), Sky Lakes Trail (#3762), Divide Trail (#3717), Snow Lakes Trail (#3739), Devils Peak Trail (#984), Seven Lakes Trail (#981)

ALTERNATE TRAILS
Red Lake Trail (#987), Sky Lakes Trail (#3762), Isherwood Trail (#3729), Cherry Creek Trail (#3708), Donna Lake Trail (#3734), Divide Trail (#3717), Snow Lakes Trail (#3739), Nannie Creek Trail (#3707), Devils Peak Trail (#984), Seven Lakes Trail (#981), Sevenmile Trail (#3703)

ON THE TRAIL

The next leg of the Pacific Crest Trail continues its journey through the **Sky Lakes Wilderness**, yet again does not come into direct contact with any of its namesake lakes. You will see a few from ridgetop traverses, but exploration of the lake basins (and access to clean water) requires side trips of varying mileages. The high point of this leg, literally and figuratively, is the traverse around **Lucifer and Devils Peak**, which affords some of the grandest views yet to be seen in southern Oregon. The route takes a generally northward bearing, walking the crest that divides the Rogue River–Siskiyou (west) and Fremont-Winema (east) national forests, all the while gaining elevation at mostly gentle and moderate grades. From the leg's high point down to several camping options—and water!—you will lose almost all of the day's elevation gain in a big drop, in just a quarter of the day's mileage.

Fully tanked up and ready to push on, leave the Red Lake Trail junction in your dust. (If you're interested in more lakes, you can take the alternate **Red Lake Trail** (#987) north from the junction prior to the PCT. This trail reconnects to the PCT 2.8 miles north.) The trail proceeds north in pleasant, sun-dappled forest, beginning with a fairly level first mile. This is followed by a shallow ascent as the trail jogs slightly west to contour along the base of a forested ridge. You won't be greeted with any big views yet, but the morning sunlight streaming into the forest paints an enchanting picture and warms the soul.

At 15.7 miles, you'll pass the easy-to-miss upper junction with the Red Lake Trail. Shortly

WATER ALERT!

North of the Sky Lakes Trail junction, most maps show the PCT taking a northward course to **Fly Lake**—a potential water source—then turning south to climb steeply up the ridge west of the Dwarf Lakes Area. This is inaccurate. The trail actually veers northwest for a more gradual ascent of the ridge and doesn't go near Fly Lake. Plan your water accordingly.

beyond, the trail veers northeast, still on its gentle, forested ascent; at 16.2 miles is a small primitive campsite. The next junction comes as a fork at 16.6 miles with the **Sky Lakes Trail** (#3762), branching right (northeast) into the Sky Lakes area to weave around numerous small and large forested lakes (see alternate routes sidebar). The PCT (left fork) begins a more moderate ascent of the ridge west of the **Dwarf Lakes Area**. As you gain elevation, ground cover alongside the trail begins to increase with a smattering of grasses, low shrubs, and lupine; you may spot a grassy meadow (what used to be a small pond) right of the trail. At approximately 17 miles you'll hit an invisible milepost: the 100-mile mark of the PCT in its journey through Oregon. You may find a little trail graffiti in the form of small rocks or sticks spelling out "100." If you started at the border with Section 1 and have gotten here, give your partner, or yourself, a high five.

Continuing the ascent, the forest begins to fall behind as the trail enters more open slopes with lots of sky overhead. The views begin to open

as well, giving you a semblance of your location within the surrounding wilderness. To the east, a forested ridge rises above the tree-choked lakes basin; just visible behind the ridge is the pointed apex of 6623-foot **Cherry Peak**; in the farther distance is the Upper Klamath Lake basin. The trail then turns west, passing a decent campsite left (south) of the trail at 18.2 miles (**Camp 7**). This nice, open space has room for two tents and logs for sitting. Past the camp the trail switchbacks up a rocky slope dotted with pink fireweed, then heads north to, and through, a saddle between two prominences.

From this high point, the trail descends the west side of the northern prominence, and opens up limited views to the west. When the trail levels out, look for a bootpath around 18.8 miles that branches off to the left (west) of the trail, leading to an open viewpoint above a rocky outcropping. Here you can count the ridges of mountains fading into the western distance. Just beyond this viewpoint, at 18.9 miles, is a large trailside campsite with room for up to four tents, a fire ring, and conveniently situated logs (**Camp 8**). The PCT then quickly ascends the next ridgeline prominence on a short series of switchbacks to circuit around its eastern side and comes to its exposed crest. Here, the ground is covered with red volcanic cinders; from this high point you're presented with another view into the lake basin to the east. You may not guess it, but the shape and contour of the landscape gives indication of the area's glaciated history.

Then it's down again, as the trail proceeds north into the trees, through a few switchbacks, then veers northeast. At 19.9 miles, a small camp can be found west of the trail with room for a couple tents (**Camp 9**). As the trail continues

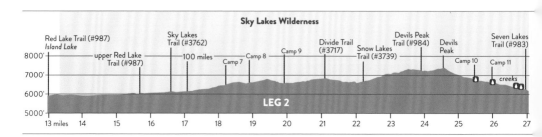

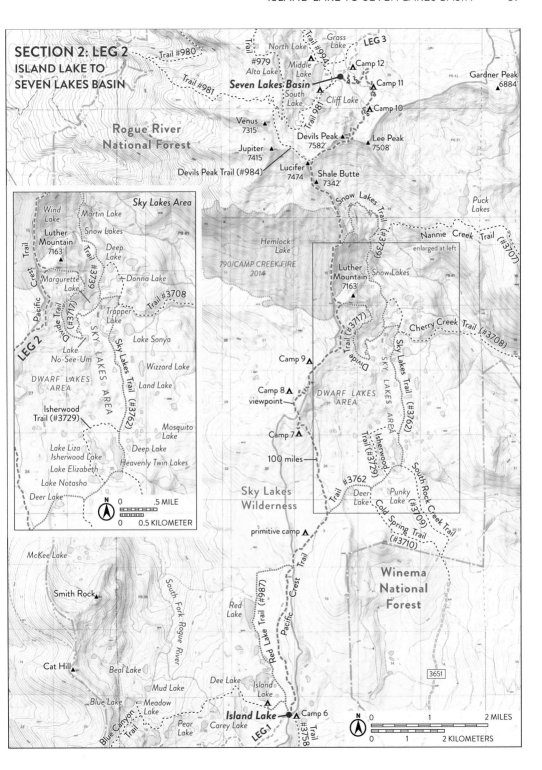

SECTION 2: LEG 2
ISLAND LAKE TO
SEVEN LAKES BASIN

Trail #980

Trail #981

Trail #994

LEG 3

North Lake

Grass Lake

Camp 12

#979 Alta Lake

Middle Lake

Seven Lakes Basin

South Lake

Cliff Lake

Camp 11

Camp 10

Gardner Peak
6884'

PB 43

PB 37

Venus 7315'

Devils Peak 7582'

Lee Peak 7508'

Jupiter 7415'

Lucifer 7474'

Devils Peak Trail (#984)

Shale Butte 7342'

Snow Lakes Trail (#3739)

Puck Lakes

Nannie Creek Trail (#3707)

Rogue River National Forest

Sky Lakes Area

Wind Lake

Martin Lake

Luther Mountain 7163'

Snow Lakes

Deep Lake

Trail #3739

Margurette Lake

Donna Lake

Trail #3708

Divide Trail (#3717)

Trapper Lake

Hemlock Lake

PB 41

790/CAMP CREEK FIRE 2014

enlarged at left

Luther Mountain 7163'

Snow Lakes

PB 41

Divide Trail (#3717)

Cherry Creek Trail (#3708)

Pacific Crest Trail

LEG 2

Lake Sonya

Wizzard Lake

SKY LAKES AREA

Sky Lakes Trail (#3762)

Land Lake

DWARF LAKES AREA

Lake No-See-Um

SKY LAKES AREA

Sky Lakes Trail (#3762)

Camp 9

Camp 8
viewpoint

DWARF LAKES AREA

Isherwood Trail (#3729)

Mosquito Lake

Lake Liza

Isherwood Lake

Lake Elizabeth

Lake Notasha

Deep Lake

Heavenly Twin Lakes

Camp 7

100 miles

Trail #3762

Deer Lake

Punky Lake

South Rock Creek Trail (#3709)

Deer Lake

N

0   .5 MILE

0   0.5 KILOMETER

Sky Lakes Wilderness

Cold Spring Trail (#3710)

Winema National Forest

McKee Lake

primitive camp

Smith Rock

South Fork Rogue River

Pacific Crest Trail

PB 39

Red Lake Trail (#987)

Red Lake

3651

Cat Hill

Beal Lake

Mud Lake

Dee Lake

Blue Lake

Meadow Lake

Blue Canyon Trail

Pear Lake

Island Lake

Carey Lake

LEG 1

Island Lake

Camp 6

Trail #3758

N

0   1   2 MILES

0   1   2 KILOMETERS

Storm clouds build above the Sky Lakes Wilderness, a common occurrence in warm summer months.

Mountain traverse near the end of Section 1). Moving northward from the point, the trail contours the steep eastern slope of the next ridgeline, the grade increasing to a moderate degree. As it wraps around the ridge, alternating through groves of trees and across exposed talus slopes, you're presented with a view of 7163-foot **Luther Mountain** directly ahead.

At 21.1 miles, the PCT comes to the saddle between Luther Mountain to the northeast and an unnamed 7042-foot prominence to the southwest. This is also where the PCT meets the **Divide Trail** (#3717). From the saddle, the PCT veers northwest while the Divide Trail breaks off eastward to traverse the lower slope of Luther Mountain before making an 800-foot circuiting descent to **Margurette Lake** in the Sky Lakes Area. Just beyond the junction, a wide panorama to the north opens up—a safer option for those who aren't interested in a summit scramble. The view here showcases the rocky escarpment that rises above the Snow Lakes in the wide valley below, with the bare slopes of **Lucifer** and **Devils Peak** creating the horizon in the farther distance. That's where you're headed—but don't let the forbidding names intimidate you.

Progressing forward, the trail begins a shallow descent along the spine of a narrow ridge that burned in the very hot, dry summer of 2014. This ridge divides the Snow Lakes basin to the east and the upper Big Ben Creek valley to the west. The ridge reaches a low point affording a few views before the trail begins climbing again, veering northeast. At 22.2 miles, the **Snow Lakes Trail** (#3739) breaks off to the right (east). If you're focusing more on your climb than your

working its way up along the ridge, it comes to a point with a fantastic southward view. Here, you finally get a big look at Mount McLoughlin, now a considerable distance behind. Note the deep, glaciated cirque and sharp ridges above the treeline on the north and eastern flanks—quite a different appearance than the gradual, even slopes of the south and western sides (seen from the Brown

LUTHER MOUNTAIN

There is no trail to the summit of Luther Mountain, but it can be reached via a short, steep scramble from the saddle junction with the Divide Trail near mile 21.1. On the summit, you'll be treated to a 360-degree view over the entire Sky Lakes Wilderness.

FIRE NOTE: 790 FIRE

In 2014 the 790 Fire burned more than 3000 acres in the Sky Lakes Wilderness, including 2 miles of the PCT, between Luther Mountain and Shale Butte. The entire section of trail through the wilderness area was closed to hikers for nearly one-and-a-half months as fire crews fought to suppress the blaze. During the closure, thru-hikers were required to make a lengthy detour around the closure and pick up the trail again in Crater Lake National Park.

surroundings, it's easy to miss this junction. Just beyond, the PCT winds north steadily up across an open, rocky plateau offering a wide panorama to the south, including a far-off glimpse of Mount Shasta. Here, the trail bends northwest, now on rocky, shale-like tread, to proceed along the top of another narrow ridge to circuit around the west slope, and just below the peak, of 7342-foot **Shale Butte**; high points to the northwest are 7415-foot **Jupiter** and 7315-foot **Venus**. The PCT then hops through a narrow gap to the east side of the ridge, where a whole new panorama opens up to the east, and begins a curving northeastward traverse under the layered and twisted basaltic summit of 7474-foot Lucifer.

At 23.9 miles, the **Devils Peak Trail** (#984) breaks off to the west and descends into the **Seven Lakes Basin**, another alternate route for exploring the area's lakes. Beyond this junction, the PCT continues through a corridor of trees, still making its bending traverse high on the steep-sided ridge. It then crosses another exposed slope of rocky talus, to reach the 7370-foot crest of the trail just below the jagged, crumbly dome of 7582-foot **Devils Peak**. If you're watching your GPS unit's odometer, you should be at approximately 24.6 miles. Take a moment here to enjoy the view. The surrounding trees consist of, among others, whitebark pine, found only in the highest reaches of the area and often notable for their mangled and skeletal appearance, due largely to their exposure

to the elements. Mount McLoughlin rises prominently to the south, now seemingly very far off; to the east, the wide Klamath basin can be seen beyond the forested ridges and valleys below; and to the north, a whole new panorama opens up before you, including—what you may not realize at first—the wide base of ancient Mount Mazama: the rim of Crater Lake.

After nearly 12 miles of sustained climbing through this leg, you're probably ready for some downhill action to pick up speed and make up time. The PCT drops over the eastern ridge of Devils Peak on a series of steep-enough switchbacks to make you glad you're going down and not up, reenters open, green forest, and brings you to a delightful sight at 25.5 miles: running water ◐. Just beyond the creek crossing is a nice campsite with room for a couple tents and an admirable view of Devils Peak and a panorama to the west (**Camp 10**). There are several more creek crossings and camping options in the next couple miles, but this one offers the nicest view.

From this point, the trail eases to a gentler grade, still descending, and begins meandering northeast through open, sunny forest. A wide, grassy meadow right (east) of the trail signals that you're near the next water source, a chilly spring that crosses the trail at the north end of the meadow, at 26 miles ◐. Try to contain your glee. Here, too, is a good campsite just off the trail, large enough to accommodate up to three tents, with

TRAIL TRIVIA

The steep, narrow ridges that the PCT traverses through this section of the Sky Lakes Wilderness are actually glacial formations called **arêtes**. These ridges are a result of parallel valley glaciers or opposing mountain glaciers grinding away at the rocky basins that contain them. If an arête is particularly narrow and steep-sided, often in alpine terrain, it may also be called a knife-edge ridge.

ALTERNATE ROUTES AND SIDE TRIPS: SKY LAKES

RED LAKE TRAIL

This trail is used to access the campsites at **Island Lake**, beyond which it parallels the PCT for a few miles, passing **Dee** and **Red lakes**, each with secluded campsites. Whereas the PCT ascends gradually north from this junction, the Red Lake Trail proceeds over fairly level terrain and remains near water for much of its 3.1-mile length. The final 0.5 mile climbs steeply to reconnect with the PCT at mile 15.7. Use of this alternate route adds only 0.4 mile to the leg, but the nice stroll beside forested lakes and running water makes it a fair trade-off.

SKY LAKES TRAIL (SHORT)

If the opportunity to explore a few of the Sky Lakes Wilderness's forested pools is too good to pass up, there are numerous options for adding short or long side trips. The shortest makes a loop around **Isherwood** and the **Heavenly Twin lakes**. This 3.4-mile lollipop also nets smaller Notasha, Elizabeth, Liza, and Florence lakes. For this option, veer northeast off the PCT at 16.6 miles onto the **Sky Lakes Trail** (#3762). This route drops into the adjacent wooded basin, passing **Deer Lake**.

At the junction with the **Cold Spring Trail** (#3710), turn left (northeast) for a short stretch, then left again onto the **Isherwood Trail** (#3729) and begin traipsing clockwise around the loop, weaving between lakes and smaller ponds. When the path meets the Sky Lakes Trail again, turn right (south) to complete the loop, passing the **South Rock Creek Trail** (#3709); at the junction with the Isherwood Trail again, retrace your steps back to the PCT. You may want to consider adding an extra day to your itinerary for this side loop, what with all the extra camping options—plus the fishing at Isherwood Lake is said to be especially good.

SKY LAKES TRAIL (LONG)

This alternate route through the Sky Lakes Wilderness parallels the Pacific Crest Trail through a sizeable portion of the leg, cutting out up to 4.5 miles of PCT, and adding up to 6.6 miles of weaving trail among countless lakes and ponds. The first half of the route remains generally mild, passing one lake cluster after another—a welcome reprieve from several miles of viewless ridge-walking. The second half, for reconnecting to the PCT, is fairly steep and strenuous. But, for lake lovers, this one's a no-brainer. Turn off the PCT onto the **Sky Lakes Trail** (#3762) at 16.6 miles, and proceed along the same route of the short option to where the **Isherwood Trail** (#3729) then rejoins the Sky Lakes Trail. Turn left (north) and proceed past **Land Lake** and numerous small ponds to large **Trapper Lake**. Continue through two junctions, first the **Cherry Creek Trail** (#3708), then the **Donna Lake Trail** (#3734), and loop around the north shore of Trapper Lake. At the next junction, on the east side of **Margurette Lake** (camping not permitted), veer left (south) onto the **Divide Trail** (#3717) and climb 2.9 miles to the saddle on the PCT below **Luther Mountain** (mile 21.1). An even longer alternate route through the **Snow Lakes Basin**, featuring Tsuga, Snow, Wind, and Martin lakes, adds a couple more miles and reconnects to the PCT even farther north, but this area was heavily burned in 2014 so is not recommended.

Look for pink monkeyflower beside streams along the trail.

SEVEN LAKES BASIN

This 3-mile alternate route into the Seven Lakes Basin, west of the PCT, traverses the ridgeline below **Lucifer**, **Jupiter**, and **Venus** before dropping into the forested lake basin. From the partially exposed ridge are good views northward over tree-ringed lakes and crumbly ridges to where the forest floor drops into the head of the **Middle Fork Canyon**. This route also offers a milder descent than the PCT's, potentially saving you from a fairly knee-crunching decline. The price for this alternate is missing out on the leg's high point on the flank of **Devils Peak** and its own stellar views. Look for the junction with the **Devils Peak Trail** (#984) at 23.9 miles, just northeast of Lucifer, and turn left (west). The trail descends gradually for 1.1 miles, contouring below Jupiter and Venus to a junction with the **Seven Lakes Trail** (#981). Turn right (south) continue descending, passing the **Alta Lake Trail** (#979), into the head of the basin between **South** and **Cliff lakes**, below an exposed escarpment. Here is where you can start looking for dispersed camping around the lakes. Note, however, that because this area is heavily used, the Forest Service is attempting to restore some locations and has marked them as closed. The trail forks on the north side of Cliff Lake, where the right (east) branch reconnects with the PCT at mile 27; the left (north) branch continues as the **Sevenmile Trail** (#3703) to **Middle, North,** and **Grass lakes**. If camping at any of these upper lakes, you can also reconnect to the PCT, via the Sevenmile Trail at mile 27.8, northeast of Grass Lake.

logs for sitting (**Camp 11**). Continuing down, the trail makes a small switchback west, followed by a larger sweeping switchback to circuit a shallow basin, and crosses two more running creeks **O**, at 26.7 and 26.8 miles, one of which cascades down a small, rocky outcropping in a lush gully bursting with yellow monkeyflower and purple larkspur. This is quickly followed by the junction with the **Seven Lakes Trail** (#983) at 27 miles.

If you haven't stopped at one of the previous campsites, here you need to decide on where to end your day. The **Seven Lakes Basin (Camp) O** trail breaks off to the left (southwest), leading to Cliff Lake and another junction to South, Middle, North, and Grass lakes. Many of these lakes have established backcountry camps for hikers and equestrians, as well as dispersed camping. Some of the lakeshores have sensitive areas that have been closed for rehabilitation, so be aware of any posted area closures. If you would rather stick to the PCT for convenience, there is one more option for water and camping just ahead, where the trail bends back northeast and crosses the area's last stream **O** at 27.2 miles (**Camp 12**). Here, two of the creeks that you crossed previously converge and cross the PCT one more time. Nearby are a few small campsites in the trees near and above the creek, and one more about 50 yards farther down the trail. This creek is considered the last reliable water source for the next 21 miles. You will want to end your day at any of the creeks or lakes in this area so that you can replenish your water the next morning before continuing on—it's a long way to the next drink.

CAMP-TO-CAMP MILEAGE
Camp 6 to Camp 7 . . . . 5.2
Camp 7 to Camp 8 . . . . 0.7
Camp 8 to Camp 9 . . . . 1.0
Camp 9 to Camp 10 . . . . 5.6
Camp 10 to Camp 11 . . . . 0.5
Camp 11 to Seven Lakes Trail junction 1.0
Seven Lakes Trail junction to
    Camp 12 (Leg 3) 0.2

3 SEVEN LAKES BASIN TO STUART FALLS JUNCTION

DISTANCE 9.7 miles

ELEVATION GAIN/LOSS
+990 feet/–1180 feet

HIGH POINT 6480 feet

CONNECTING TRAILS
Sevenmile Trail (#3703), Ranger Spring Trail (#1077), Big Bunchgrass Trail (#1089A), McKie Camp Trail (#1089), Stuart Falls Trail (#1078)

ON THE TRAIL
There is no easy way to tackle the next two legs of the PCT continuing north—nearly 21 miles of waterless trail through dry forest, a wide, exposed burn area and across the Oregon Desert. You just have to suck it up and power through it—and pray that the time you're hiking is not during a summer heat wave. The end of this leg is not an ideal stopping point, which splits the stretch in half and presents a couple options for how to wrap up the day. If you have the strength and endurance, it is best to continue straight through the next leg (Leg 4) and end your day at Mazama Village in Crater Lake National Park—a rewarding finish with cold drinks, tasty food, and a backpacker's camp. Or you can take the Stuart Falls alternate route for a decent camp area and water source, then meet up with the PCT again farther north inside the park boundary. Whatever you decide, keep your sunscreen accessible and carry as much extra water as you can manage. Just

The small creeks near the Seven Lakes Basin are the last reliable water source before the long, hot, waterless stretch to Mazama Village.

consider these next two legs the Brussels sprouts before your dessert.

Beginning at the Seven Lakes Trail junction, the way forward continues its forested descent. Shortly after getting underway, at 27.8 miles, the **Sevenmile Trail** (#3703) cuts off to the left (west) to descend to Grass and Middle lakes. From here, the PCT and Sevenmile Trail continue as one for the next 2.7 miles, meandering north and northeast though airy, viewless forest. At 28.3 miles, the trail crosses **Honeymoon Creek**. Don't count on finding drinkable water here; except in the heaviest of runoff years, it's only a mucky puddle, if anything. Shortly thereafter, the PCT crosses another dry creek and bends east again, crossing the crest into the Fremont-Winema National Forest for a short stretch. At 30.4 miles, the PCT and Sevenmile Trail part ways, the former forking left (north), while the latter breaks off right (northeast) to a remote trailhead at the end of FR 3334.

The nearest reliable water source on this leg of the PCT is **Ranger Spring 0**. The junction to the spring comes at 30.5 miles, where a spur trail (#1077) cuts off to the left (west) and descends to the small spring, which eventually grows into the

Middle Fork Rogue River. A trip to the spring will add 1.6 miles to your day's total, so you'll have to consider the lesser of two evils: carrying a little extra water from the start of the day, or taking a lengthy side trip to top off your supply just shortly after getting under way. Near the junction are a couple of small camping areas right (east) of the trail with enough space to accommodate up to three tents (**Camp 13**). Just beyond the spring

WATER ALERT!

The small creeks 0.2 mile north of the Seven Lakes Trail junction are the last reliable near-trail water source through Legs 3 and 4 until reaching **Mazama Village** inside of Crater Lake National Park, 20.9 miles farther. There are two off-PCT options for accessing water, Ranger Spring near the start of the leg, the other utilizing an alternate side route. The following leg descriptions offer information for both, but you will definitely want to top off your containers going forward and be prepared for some hot, dry trail ahead.

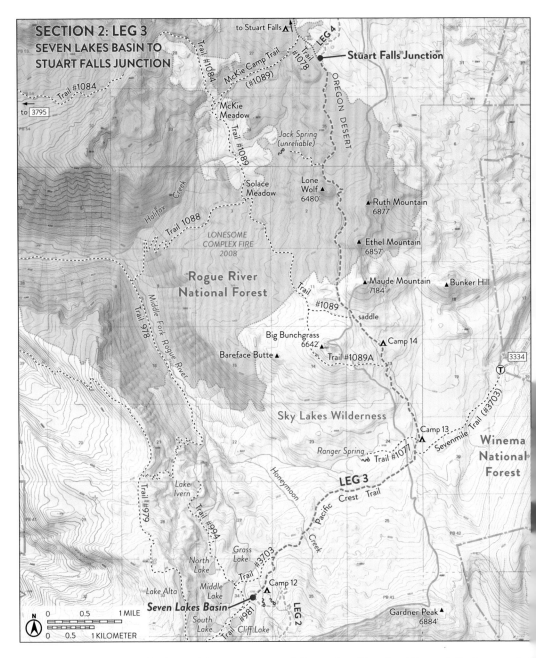

SECTION 2: LEG 3
SEVEN LAKES BASIN TO
STUART FALLS JUNCTION

to Stuart Falls

LEG 4

Stuart Falls Junction

Trail #1084

Trail #078

McKie Camp Trail
(#1089)

OREGON DESERT

Trail #1084

to 3795

McKie
Meadow

Trail #1089

Jack Spring
(unreliable)

Solace
Meadow

Lone
Wolf ▲
6480'

Ruth Mountain ▲
6877'

Halifax Creek

Trail 1088

LONESOME
COMPLEX FIRE
2008

Ethel Mountain ▲
6857'

Rogue River
National Forest

Trail
#1089

Maude Mountain ▲
7184'

Bunker Hill ▲

Middle Fork Rogue River

Trail 978

saddle

Big Bunchgrass
6642' ▲

Camp 14 ▲

3334

Bareface Butte ▲

Trail #1089A

T

Sky Lakes Wilderness

Sevenmile Trail (#3703)

Camp 13 ▲

Winema
National
Forest

Ranger Spring

Trail #1077

LEG 3

Lake
Ivern

Trail #979

Pacific   Crest   Trail

Honeymoon   Creek

Trail #994

Lake
Alta

North
Lake

Grass
Lake

Trail #3703

Middle
Lake

Camp 12 ▲

Seven Lakes Basin

LEG 2

Gardner Peak ▲
6884'

South
Lake

Trail #981

Cliff Lake

N   0   0.5   1 MILE
     0   0.5   1 KILOMETER

junction, continuing north, the trail bottoms out at the leg's low point before beginning a steady northwest ascent to pass between 6642-foot **Big Bunchgrass** and 7184-foot **Maude Mountain**. Another decent camp can be found right (east)

of the trail at 32 miles (**Camp 14**); this wooded site has room for a couple tents. Where the trail crests, directly between the two low peaks, the forest peels back to reveal a wide, grassy meadow and lots of lupine; just beyond, at 32.6 miles the **McKie Camp Trail** (#1089) branches off westward.

The PCT now crosses back into the Rogue River–Siskiyou National Forest and begins a gentle descent north along the western flank of Maude Mountain. Here, the scene dramatically changes into one of complete devastation, as the PCT enters the sprawling burn area of the 2017 **Blanket Creek Fire**. To the right (east) of the trail, are the charred humps of 6857-foot **Ethel Mountain** and 6877-foot **Ruth Mountain**; directly north is the burned hulk of 6480-foot **Lone Wolf**. Before 2017, this area had been

recovering from 2008's **Lonesome Complex Fire**. This wildfire burned more than 20,000 acres of the Sky Lakes Wilderness and Rogue River–Siskiyou National Forest, but the area had become green and lively again with young lodgepole pines intermingling with a carpet of beargrass, while vibrant pearly everlasting, fireweed, and lupine adorned the slopes. Then lightning ignited the Blanket Creek Fire, which wiped out all of that young forest. The flames of that blaze laid waste to more than 33,000 acres of the northern Sky Lakes Wilderness and southern Crater Lake National Park—including nearly 10 miles of

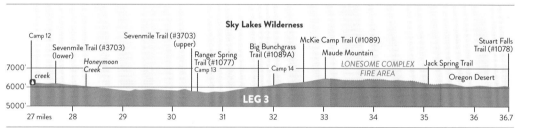

ALTERNATE ROUTE: STUART FALLS

Due to the long waterless stretch of trail between the Seven Lakes Basin and Mazama Village inside Crater Lake National Park, this side loop to a good-flowing creek and camp area makes an attractive option for splitting the 21 dry, lackluster miles of Legs 3 and 4 in half. The trip to **Stuart Falls** adds 3.7 undemanding downhill miles for a moderate total of 13.4 miles for the day. Reconnecting with the PCT the next day requires a moderate 2.8-mile ascent, which deposits you well inside the park boundary at PCT mile 42.2, and within striking distance of **Mazama Village**, just 5.9 miles farther. This under-10-mile day can have you dropping your pack in camp by midday with time to spare for taking advantage of some of the village's amenities.

To take the alternate route, veer left (northwest) off the PCT and onto the **Stuart Falls Trail** (#1078) at 36.7 miles, shortly after reentering the forest on the north side of the Oregon Desert. The trail gradually descends through mostly shady old-growth forest, where it meets the northern junction with the **McKie Camp Trail** (#1089) after only 0.4 mile. The trail steepens as it bends northwest and begins navigating across a network of stream and spring gullies, passing a junction with the **Lucky Camp Loop Trail** (#1083) after another 2 miles. Turning northward again, the trail crosses a few more drainages, passes the **Red Blanket Trail** (#1090), crosses **Stuart Creek**, and arrives at the 40-foot falls, which cascade down an escarpment of columnar basalt. Several small campsites can be found in the area around the base of the falls. (See route map in Leg 4.)

The 2017 Blanket Creek Fire laid waste to a large swath of the Sky Lakes Wilderness, including nearly 10 miles of the PCT.

the PCT. When the smoke finally cleared, there wasn't much trail left through the area.

But that didn't stop PCT trail crews from getting right back in there the following summer to clear the debris and reestablish the trail—a Hulk-sized task considering the area's remote, wilderness location. Despite their efforts, the way forward leaves much to be desired. You can still expect to encounter frequent blowdowns and burned snags blocking the trail, a common problem in burned forests. Some of these obstacles may require you to detour around them. Trail markers are few and far between, so look for flagging, cairns, and other signs to help lead the way forward—and consult your map regularly!

When the trail reaches the base of Lone Wolf, around 34.5 miles, it turns west to circuit the

burned mound, descending as it turns back to the northwest. Along the way you're afforded a view north to the peaks on the rim of Crater Lake, now getting closer and higher. At 35.1 miles,

TRAIL TRIVIA

The three ladies along the Pacific Crest Trail—**Maude, Ethel,** and **Ruth mountains**— were named by Lee C. Port, a Forest Service worker in the early 1900s. Ethel, his wife, also worked for the Forest Service as a telephone operator and fire dispatcher; the other two were names of fellow Forest Service workers' spouses.

the PCT levels and enters a small grove of shady, unburned, trees. Nearby, the 0.7-mile side trail to **Jack Spring** heads west. Before the fire, this spring was unreliable at best. Now it's not worth the effort—if you can even find the old trail. There aren't any established camps here, but the ground is flat enough for a primitive setup, and the tall trees offer some respite from the sun and heat. If nothing else, at least take a break here—the next 1.4 miles will be a rough slog in the heat of the day.

The way forward is not difficult, just hot. Continue the gentle descent through mostly burned forest until you come to the dry expanse of the **Oregon Desert**, a flat, dry basin that retains little water due to its porous pumice surface. Slather on your sunscreen, put on your floppy hat, and go. There is sparse trailside vegetation, and the sad, crispy lodgepole pines offer little shade. The trail is mostly ash and sand, so despite being generally flat, you won't go as fast as you might like. At 36.7 miles you'll reach the junction with the **Stuart Falls Trail** (#1078). There is no good camping nor water at this junction, and the forest is heavily burned. Here you have to decide your way forward, and how many more miles you're going to put in before calling it a day: 2.2 miles to a trailside camp; 3.7 miles to Stuart Falls; or 11.4 miles for a marathon trek to Mazama Village.

CAMP-TO-CAMP MILEAGE

Seven Lakes junction to Camp 12 . . . . 0.2
Camp 12 to Camp 13 . . . . 3.3
Camp 13 to Camp 14 . . . . 1.5
Camp 14 to Stuart Falls junction 4.7
Stuart Falls junction to Camp 15 (Leg 4) 2.2
Stuart Falls junction to Stuart Falls
    Camp (alternate, off PCT) 3.7

4 STUART FALLS JUNCTION TO MAZAMA VILLAGE

DISTANCE 10.4 miles

ELEVATION GAIN/LOSS
+1510 feet/–1390 feet

HIGH POINT 6770 feet

CONNECTING TRAILS AND ROADS
Pumice Flat Trail, Stuart Falls
Trail #1078 (south), Union Peak Trail,
Crater Lake Highway (OR 62)

ON THE TRAIL

If you choose to forgo the Stuart Falls alternate route (see Leg 3), then the way forward is a rolling course into the forested southern section of Crater Lake National Park. The grades are mostly gentle to moderate, both up and down, making the hiking fairly effortless; however, there is still no water until you reach Mazama Village for another 12 miles—be sure to conserve some of your supply to make it last that far. You also have several more miles of dismal, burned forest to contend with. Take advantage of shade where you can find it, and keep an eye on your map or GPS to ensure you're staying on track. If there's a silver lining,

SHORTCUT: PUMICE FLAT TRAIL

The **Pumice Flat Trail** is sometimes used by PCT thru-hikers as an alternate route to Mazama Village. Once the trail ends at the highway, it requires an additional 3 miles of walking road (or hitchhiking) to get to the village. The tradeoff is sparing yourself several hundred feet of elevation gain on a roundabout route through mostly viewless forest.

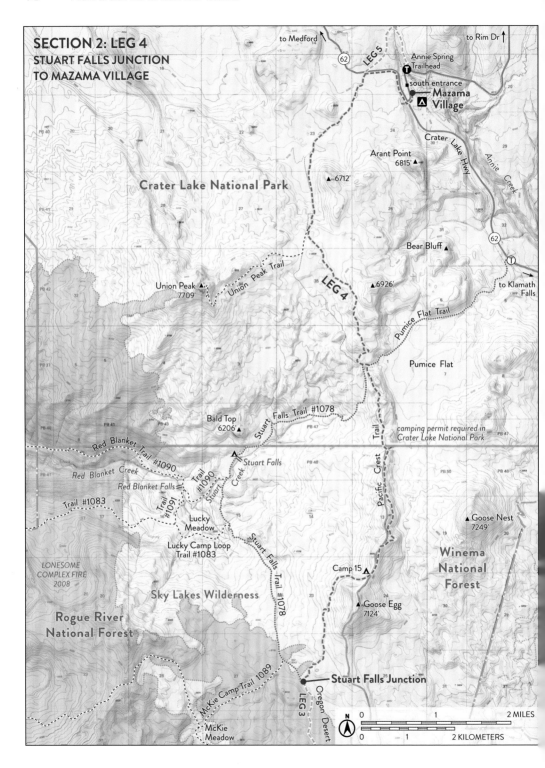

SECTION 2: LEG 4
STUART FALLS JUNCTION
TO MAZAMA VILLAGE

it's that you get a few more views over the wide valleys surrounding the area. The payoff is the soda fountain at the Mazama Village store and the restaurant that serves up a pretty decent (and reasonably priced) burger.

Under the partial shade of charred conifers, the PCT climbs away from the Stuart Falls Trail junction, winding northeast. After about 0.5 mile, at the edge of an open clearing, it heads north, contouring around the base of a 7124-foot volcanic butte called the **Goose Egg**, then east. Just right (south) of the trail at 38.9 miles is a small campsite (**Camp 15**) that can accommodate one tent, the only noticeable camp between the start of the leg

and the national park boundary. Moving along, the trail ascends north along the eastern slope of a narrow volcanic ridge; here the trail surface begins turning to mixed dirt and cinders, belying the volcanic landscape you're crossing. At 39.3 miles, the PCT reaches its high point on the leg in a shallow saddle and presents a wide panorama to the west. Over a rolling sea of trees you can make out the deep valley containing Red Blanket Creek and the rocky pyramid of 7709-foot **Union Peak**.

The trail then makes a gentle, contouring descent along the divide, undulating northward to parallel the **Pumice Flat** (sorry, no views) until it enters **Crater Lake National Park** at 40.9 miles.

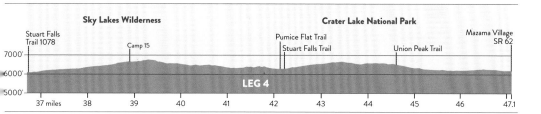

CAMPING IN CRATER LAKE NATIONAL PARK

Crater Lake National Park has very specific regulations about camping on the rim—despite what you may see in the movies. There is absolutely no camping permitted between Rim Drive and the edge of the caldera. Wilderness camps, while permitted, must be at least 1 mile off trail and/or away from the road. There are five established wilderness camps available to PCT hikers. The first available camp for PCT hikers is **Dutton Creek Camp**, just south of the trail, at 49.2 miles; there is good water at this camp. This is followed by **Bybee Creek Camp** at 54.8 miles and 0.3 mile west of the PCT, and **Red Cone Spring Camp** at 61.5 miles and just a short distance off the trail; of these two, the former has a good perennial creek nearby, while the latter has a small, seasonal-at-best water source.

For Rim Trail hikers (the recommended route in this guide), **Lightning Spring Camp** is a moderate 0.8-mile descent west of the PCT near 53.9 miles, and **Grouse Camp**, just off the Rim Trail at 60.5 miles; the former of these two does have the advantage of being near a mostly reliable water source. There is no water at Grouse Camp, but if you plan ahead you can cache water in the bear box at the Red Cone Spring trailhead, 0.5 mile north. The trail descriptions of each offer more info on these camps.

All backcountry camping in Crater Lake National Park requires a park wilderness permit. These can be obtained at the Steel Visitor Center on Munson Valley Road and at the park visitor center in Rim Village. See "Passes and Permits" for more information.

A short, moderately strenuous trail climbs to the top of Union Peak for grand views of Oregon's southern Cascades.

The very unceremonious entry is a trailside sign that indicates you're entering the park, and permits are required for camping. Once on the west side of the ridge, the trail begins ascending again, veering slightly northwest, and arrives at a T-junction at 42.1 miles. To the right (east) the **Pumice Flat Trail** crosses a lodgepole pine basin for 2.7 miles to connect with the **Crater Lake Highway** (OR 62). The PCT continues left (west), making a gentle, contouring ascent along a grassy slope where it meets the northern junction of the Stuart Falls Trail (#1078) at 42.2 miles, coming in from the south. Here the PCT continues right (northwest).

From the junction the trail arcs east before resuming a northwest bearing. Unless you have an extremely good internal compass, you may begin to wonder if you're going the right way—don't worry, there are plenty of highly visible PCT trail markers guiding you. The trail finally reenters green, lively forest adorned with grassy slopes

UNION PEAK

Rising more than 800 feet above the surrounding forest, Union Peak is the remnant core of an ancient volcano, and the oldest mountain within the park area. If you have an interest in claiming this rocky spire, the PCT meets the peak trail at 44.6 miles. The spur branches 1.7 miles southwest to the base of the peak where it then climbs 0.8 mile over a series of steep, rocky switchbacks to the tiny summit area. Views from the top stretch south over the entire Sky Lakes Wilderness and north to Mount Thielsen and beyond, but Crater Lake is not visible. For its exposure, the peak is frequently struck by lightning during thunderstorms, so this is not the place to be if you see a storm brewing.

MAZAMA VILLAGE

Located at the southern entrance to Crater Lake National Park, 1 mile east of the PCT, Mazama Village offers a large campground, as well as a number of rentable cabins; there is also a small backpacker's camp. The **Annie Creek Restaurant** serves a variety of hearty meals, including decent pizzas and satisfying breakfasts, all very reasonably priced (and much better than what you'll find at the rim snack bar). Additionally, a modest grocery store stocks plenty of camping and hiking foods, cold drinks and ice cream, and handles resupply packages. Attached to the store are shower and laundry facilities. Summer weekends are typically, expectedly, crowded for this being Oregon's only national park. If you can manage it, try to visit Mazama Village and resupply midweek to avoid the masses of bus-riding tourists. (See appendix 3 for more info.)

dotted with lupine and other low shrubs. As you continue to climb, wider panoramas are fairly limited, but a small window through the trees presents one more view of Union Peak, now almost directly west. Where the trail crests again at 44.6 miles, it meets the junction with the **Union Peak Trail**.

Next, the trail dives back under tree cover to round an unnamed, 6712-foot butte. The forest, a mixture of hemlock, fir, and ponderosa pine, takes on an idyllic quality, making the gentle descent pleasant, the wide, smooth trail joyfully effortless. You may spy a couple of tempting, primitive campsites as you progress, but if you do not have a national park wilderness permit, you risk getting a citation—besides, your payoff is just a few miles away. The trail makes one final, insignificant rise and fall over the low flank of a small knob, then arrives at the trailhead parking area at **Crater Lake Highway** (OR 62) at 47.1 miles.

Directly across the highway, the PCT continues north. But here is where you want to jump off the trail and hang a right onto the road and stroll a last mile east, then south, along the highway to **Mazama Village (Camp) ◑**. (It is recommended that you walk along the shoulder *against* traffic.) This detour cuts out approximately 1 mile of viewless PCT, between the highway and the junction with the **Annie Spring Trail** (which you'll use to reconnect with the PCT for the next leg, so if you're tracking your mileage with a GPS receiver, plan to adjust it accordingly). At Mazama Village, you'll have just about every amenity a hot, thirsty, hungry, sweaty, tired hiker could want: cold drinks, hot food, showers and laundry service, and an established campsite. Treat yourself to an icy beverage and a bag of salty snacks for a well-done trek across 21 miles of parched trail, then prepare yourself for the next day's leg around the sapphire jewel of Oregon: Crater Lake.

CAMP-TO-CAMP MILEAGE

Stuart Falls Junction to Camp 15 . . . . 2.2
Camp 15 to Crater Lake Highway 8.2
Crater Lake Highway to Mazama Village
 (via road) 1.0
Crater Lake Highway to Dutton Creek Camp
 (via PCT) 2.2

ALTERNATE ROUTE: DUTTON CREEK CAMP

If you choose to bypass the crowds and conveniences at Mazama Village, you can continue on to the Dutton Creek Camp, but this will add another 2.2 miles to your (potentially) already long day. Get there by crossing the highway and proceeding on the PCT with a gradual climb for another 0.8 mile to meet the Annie Spring Trail junction. From here, the trail levels to an easy grade before descending 1.4 miles to a couple creek crossings, followed by a large trail junction and the short spur left (south) to the camp area. This small, hiker-only camp has two large, designated tent spaces. (See Leg 5 for more info.)

5 MAZAMA VILLAGE TO GROUSE HILL (VIA RIM TRAIL)

DISTANCE 12.6 miles

ELEVATION GAIN/LOSS
+2610 feet/–2330 feet

HIGH POINT 7740 feet

CONNECTING TRAILS AND ROADS
Annie Spring Trail, Dutton Creek Trail,
Rim Trail, Rim Drive, Lightning Spring Trail,
The Watchman Trail

ON THE TRAIL

No matter whether you started your trek with Section 1 from the Oregon border, or Section 2 from Fish Lake—or even just beginning your trek from Mazama Village—you are now staged to hike one of the most gobsmacking sections of Oregon's PCT: the circuit around the vivid cerulean expanse of Crater Lake. Technically, the Rim Trail around Crater Lake is not the PCT's official route, which stays low in the trees around the base of the big caldera. But most hikers choose to deviate from the official path and use the Rim Trail, one of the scenic highlights in the state, as the preferred alternate—and since you're probably ready for some scenic "wow" at this point, the following description covers the highly recommended alternate route. (The official PCT route can be found on page 110, along with suggested itinerary modifications.)

The leg begins with a steady climb up Crater Lake's forested, southwestern rim. From the point you reach the rim, your course circuits and roller-coasters around the high points of the western side of the drowned, 6-mile-wide caldera. You will have a few opportunities to refill your water supply at creek crossings on your way up the rim, then again at **Rim Village**. Beyond the upper village, the trail is dry again for the next 27-plus miles, so you'll want to top off your bottles and prepare yourself for a dry camp on the north side of the park.

Once you're packed up in Mazama Village and are prepared for the visual feast in store for you, head north through the village, past the A Loop of the campground, to the **Annie Spring Trail**. Take this trail north to cross **Munson Valley Road** (which becomes Rim Drive) to a small trailhead where, nearby, Annie Spring gushes out of the hillside. Continue north on the Annie Spring Trail, climbing steadily up a series of forested switchbacks that will get your heart pumping. The trail eases after about 0.5 mile to a more moderate grade, then reaches a slight crest amid pleasant pine and hemlock forest.

Just about 1 mile up you'll arrive at the junction where the Annie Spring Trail ends at the PCT. (If you're tracking your mileage via a GPS receiver, you want to be at 47.9 miles; see trail note.) To continue north to the rim, turn right (east) and proceed along the pleasingly level trail. The

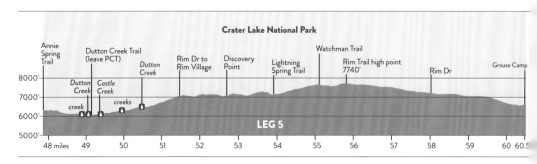

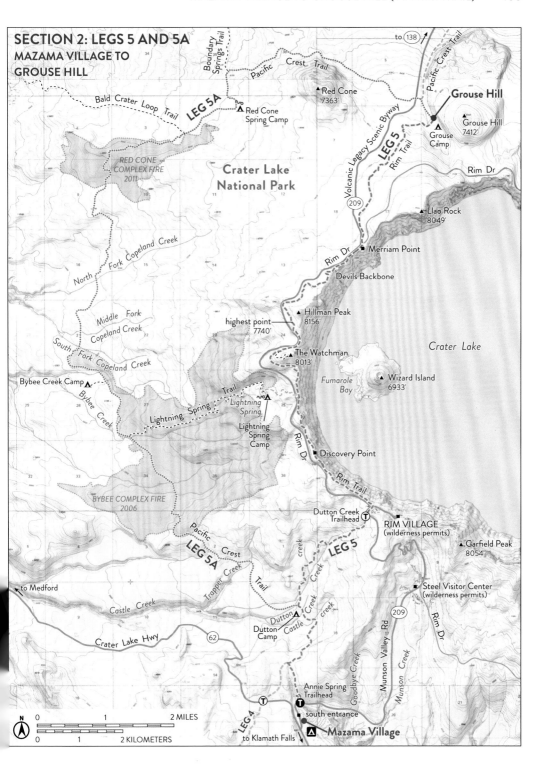

SECTION 2: LEGS 5 AND 5A
MAZAMA VILLAGE TO GROUSE HILL

Boundary Springs Trail

Pacific Crest Trail

to (138)

Pacific Crest Trail

Bald Crater Loop Trail

LEG 5A

Red Cone Spring Camp

Red Cone 7363'

Grouse Hill

Grouse Hill 7412'

Grouse Camp

RED CONE COMPLEX FIRE 2011

Crater Lake National Park

Volcanic Legacy Scenic Byway

LEG 5

Rim Trail

Rim Dr

(209)

Llao Rock 8049'

North Fork Copeland Creek

Rim Dr

Merriam Point

Devils Backbone

Middle Fork Copeland Creek

highest point 7740'

Hillman Peak 8156'

Crater Lake

South Fork Copeland Creek

The Watchman 8013'

Bybee Creek Camp

Lightning Spring Trail

Lightning Spring

Fumarole Bay

Wizard Island 6933'

Bybee Creek

Lightning Spring Camp

Discovery Point

Rim Dr

Rim Trail

BYBEE COMPLEX FIRE 2006

Pacific Crest Trail

LEG 5A

Dutton Creek Trailhead

RIM VILLAGE (wilderness permits)

Garfield Peak 8054'

LEG 5

to Medford

Trapper Creek

Dutton Creek

creek

Steel Visitor Center (wilderness permits)

(209)

Rim Dr

Castle Creek

Dutton Castle creek

Crater Lake Hwy

(62)

Dutton Camp

Munson Valley Rd

Munson Creek

Goodbye Creek

Annie Spring Trailhead

south entrance

Munson Creek

to Klamath Falls

LEG 4

Mazama Village

N

0   1   2 MILES

0   1   2 KILOMETERS

TRAIL NOTE: ANNIE SPRING VIA PCT

If you don't want to miss a single mile of the PCT, the alternative to using the Annie Spring Trail spur to reconnect to the PCT from Mazama Village is to walk the **Crater Lake Highway** (OR 62) 1 mile west to the PCT crossing and climb 0.8 mile north to the upper **Annie Spring Trail** junction. This will add another mile to the leg's distance, but doesn't afford any additional views or access to water.

trailside vegetation begins to become noticeably interesting again (following the previous long miles of mostly deadfall and debris) with spots of red skyrocket and yellow ragworts.

The PCT then makes a gentle descent on a few sweeping switchbacks into a verdant basin. Unlike the dry forest of earlier miles, this forest looks and feels lush and lively, with plenty of green carpeting the forest floor. Look for stalks of purple penstemon and monkshood, and little pink bleeding hearts; nearer water you'll find pink monkeyflowers and small white violets. Speaking of water, at 48.9 miles, the trail crosses a wonderful little wooded creek ⬤. After another 0.2 mile of nearly flat trail, cross the wider, more melodic **Dutton Creek** ⬤, then come to a large junction at 49.2 miles. To the left (south), a side trail descends 0.1 mile to **Dutton Camp**, a hiker-only backcountry site; to the right (north) the **Dutton Creek Trail** begins climbing toward Crater Lake's rim; and straight ahead (west), the PCT continues its undulating, forested (longer and viewless) circuit around the lower base of the ancient mountain. The two routes meet

Choose from the scenic Rim Trail or the official PCT route at the trail junction near delightful Dutton Creek.

TRAIL TRIVIA

Annie Spring was named in 1865 for Annie Gaines, one of the first white women known to climb to the rim of Crater Lake and descend to the water below. She later married and became the sister-in-law to Frederick Schwatka, a famous arctic explorer.

again 11.7 miles and 16.3 miles, respectively, north of the crater rim.

Turning right onto the Dutton Creek Trail, the path immediately begins ascending the forested slope on a moderate grade, then soon crosses the happily musical **Castle Creek ⬤**. The trail then begins a more strenuous ascent climbing directly up the contours of the drainage. There are a couple more creek crossings at 50 miles and 50.5 miles, giving the opportunity to splash icy water on your likely sweaty brow. The trail continues its steady climb for another 0.5 mile, then begins to ease as it nears the top, where you might begin to detect the sound of automobiles nearby. At 51.5 miles, the trail abruptly ends at the Dutton Creek trailhead on **Rim Drive**, depositing you just steps away from the rim of **Crater Lake**. Cross the road and take in your first view of the deepest, clearest lake in the United States. Directly below, conical **Wizard Island** rises from the azure water. After the work it has taken you to get here, it's worth dropping your pack and snapping a victorious selfie with the spectacular panorama behind you.

The route continues left (northwest) on the **Rim Trail**. Before proceeding, however, you'll want to turn right and visit the **Rim Village**. Here, you can top off your water at the fountain, utilize a real restroom if needed, and purchase a sandwich, snack, or souvenir. You'll also want to **visit the Rim Visitor Center to pick up a wilderness camping permit** (see the note about camping in the park). There are also a few viewpoints with interpretive displays that describe the lake and caldera's history, features, and geology. Once you've taken care of business at the rim, hop on the paved (only for a short distance) Rim Trail and begin your clockwise

circuit around the edge of the caldera, paralleling Rim Drive.

Once the Rim Trail reverts back to a dirt surface, it immediately begins a series of steep, roller-coaster ups and downs—contrary to the deceptively smooth-looking circuit on most topo maps. You won't be thinking much about the exertion through these rises and falls because you'll be too distracted with every next view of the deep blue lake directly below you—sometimes *very* directly below, as the trail hugs the caldera rim, sometimes precariously above very steep and sheer drops; watch your footing through some of these areas. At 52.7 miles, the trail reaches **Discovery Point**, a popular viewpoint just off the road for a picture-perfect view of Wizard Island and brilliant blue-green **Fumarole Bay**. The trail then pulls away from the road to continue along the rim, more up, more down, then connects with the road again at 53.9 miles. Here, depending on the time of day, and your own itinerary, is where you'll find the spur trail to **Lightning Spring Camp ⬤**, just 0.1 mile farther up the road, on the opposite (west) side. The trail to the camp descends 0.8 mile and 300 feet through pumice meadows dotted with penstemon, phlox, buckwheat, and lupine to the small, hiker-only camp, with two large, designated campsites. These sites can each accommodate at least two tents and have fire rings. **Lightning Spring**, right at the trail fork, runs fairly reliably year-round; however

WATER ALERT!

With the exception of **Lightning Spring** (0.8 mile west of the Rim Trail, at mile 53.9), the water fountains at **Rim Village** are the last near-trail water supply through the end of the section, and more than 8 miles into the next—that's a total of 26.3 waterless miles. With significant exposure, the rim route can get very warm at the peak of summer, despite its elevation. This is followed by a dry camp at Grouse Hill, then several miles of very dry lodgepole forest to the park's northern boundary. Tank up as needed.

One of Oregon's not-to-be-missed scenic highlights, Crater Lake can be enjoyed from the Rim Trail alternate route.

Despite possessing a wealth of natural and scenic wonders—Mount Hood, the Columbia River Gorge, the Painted Hills, and its spectacular Pacific coastline, to name but a few—Crater Lake is Oregon's only national park. The lake was "discovered" by three gold prospectors in 1852 and was originally named "Deep Blue Lake." (No prize for originality there.) But at the time, pretty lakes weren't a priority for the hardscrabble settlers trying to eke out their livelihoods in the untamed Northwest. It wasn't until 1870 that William Gladstone Steel was captivated by the lake and spent the rest of his life and fortune working for its preservation. In 1902, Crater Lake was designated America's fifth national park. To promote tourism, and backed by Steel, the historic Crater Lake Lodge was opened in 1915, and Rim Drive was completed in 1918.

Of course, Crater Lake's history dates back more than just a century, and is steeped in rich Native American legend. According to the ancient Klamath peoples who witnessed the explosive event approximately 7700 years ago, Chief Llao, who resided within Mount Mazama, did battle with Chief Skell. The climax of the confrontation was the complete destruction of the mountain.

Geologically speaking, the tale dates back even farther, with Mount Mazama beginning its formation more than 420,000 years ago in a series of overlapping lava and pyroclastic flows. It is estimated that the summit of Mount Mazama once reached more than 12,000 feet. After a long period of dormancy, the mountain came back to life around 30,000 years ago in a new series of eruptions that created many of the area's features seen today. Then, around 5700 BC, a cataclysmic eruption decapitated the mountain by more than 3500 feet, sending a column of ash more

than 6 miles into the sky and distributing more than 12 cubic miles of magma, pumice, and ash across the greater Northwest and southern British Columbia areas. Some pyroclastic deposits near the mountain-filled valleys to a depth of 300 feet.

When the dust settled, all that remained was a nearly mile-deep hole where a mountain once stood. Eventually, rainwater and snowmelt started filling the caldera, taking approximately 250 years to reach the current level. Without any natural inlets or outlets, the water level rises and falls annually by only a few feet, maintaining a balance between precipitation, evaporation, and seepage. Because of the lack of organic material within the caldera, the water in the lake is exceptionally pure, with clarity being measured at up to 134 feet. There is still hydrothermal activity that occurs in the deepest parts of the lake, where the fractured floor allows water to be heated by hot, subterranean rock.

Only two features breach the lake's surface, the most prominent being Wizard Island, on the west side of the lake. This large cinder cone began erupting following Mount Mazama's major blowout, and grew over the following centuries as the caldera began filling with water. At the current (average) lake level, Wizard Island rises about 760 feet above the water, and more than 2300 feet above the caldera's floor; the 500-foot-wide crater at the summit of Wizard Island is ominously named the "Witch's Cauldron." The smaller prominence, poking above the surface near the southern rim, is the Phantom Ship, named for its sometimes ghostly appearance. This remnant of a lava fissure rises 170 feet above the water. Crater Lake is still considered an active volcano.

Mount Thielsen looms in the distance over Crater Lake's Pumice Desert.

it may diminish to a light dribble by the end of summer.

Pulling away from the road again, the Rim Trail begins a steady, contouring ascent, westward, around the middle flank of **The Watchman**. This 8013-foot high point on the western rim is capped with an historic fire lookout that was manned until 1974. Along the way, from open meadows and exposed slopes, you are presented with sprawling views to the south and west. Pick out Union Peak's barren slopes in the nearer distance, and the silhouette of Mount McLoughlin—where you started several days ago—far back on the southern horizon. The trail then bends east around the north side of The Watchman to a wide gravel side trail (road) at 55.1 miles; this makes a switchbacking, 0.8-mile, 400-foot ascent to the lookout on top,

worth making the trip. From this high perch, you'll have an unparalleled, bird's-eye view over the entire lake and parklands. Try to find the jagged formation of **Phantom Ship** rising out of the lake near the southeastern rim.

Now on old road (the same one that continues up The Watchman), the trail makes a shallow

RIM HIGH POINT

The 7745-foot high point on the Rim Trail alternate route is not considered the "official" high point on Oregon's PCT. The official high point is 7560-foot Tipsoo Pass, some 30 miles farther north. Just consider this point a bonus achievement.

descent to Rim Drive and another busy, roadside viewpoint at 55.5 miles. Here, there are picnic tables and an outhouse offering a few creature comforts if you're ready for a break. If you put your pack down, watch for scurrying chipmunks (obviously tourist-fed) looking to share your snack with you. The trail continues on the north end of the parking area, making a shallow, northwestward ascent to circuit around 8156-foot **Hillman Peak**. The long views continue to impress, now adding vistas to the north as you pass through a high point at 7745 feet. Along the trail, splotches of color take the form of spiky, orange paintbrush, puff-like yellow buckwheat, and little purple phlox. Then, slightly above the road, the trail bends northeast and makes a shallow descent across more rolling, wide-open slopes of the back side of the **Devils Backbone**, meeting Rim Drive again at 57.4 miles.

Turn right on the road and walk the shoulder for 0.5 mile to a wide roadside viewpoint. Once you're around the imposing slope of the Devils Backbone, there are numerous braided paths along the rise between the road and the rim, but it's just as convenient to walk through the viewpoint parking areas. Here, at **Merriam Point**, take in a final view of Crater Lake, now from the north side, looking back at The Watchman, Castle Crest, and 8054-foot **Garfield Peak**; to the southeast, 8929-foot **Mount Scott** is the highest point on the caldera.

Now the Rim Trail crosses Rim Drive at 58.5 miles, just east of the junction with the **Volcanic**

WATER CACHE

In 2016, the national park installed a bear box at the **Lightning Spring trailhead**, on the park's north entrance road (OR 209), specifically for water caches to help PCT hikers get through the park's long, dry miles. The park does not service this cache. You need to plan ahead and leave your own water container ahead of your hike. Be sure to put your name and expected pickup date on your container, and plan to pack it out with you. Via the recommended Rim Trail route, the cache is approximately 0.1 mile west of the junction of the Rim Trail and PCT at 60.9 miles (0.5 mile from Grouse Camp); via the PCT, the cache is located right where the trail crosses the park road at 65.4 miles (mileages adjusted for respective routes).

Legacy Scenic Byway (OR 209), and gradually descends north across an open cindery plain dotted with grasses, wildflowers, and an abundance of knotweed, which turns bright red in the fall and carpets the entire slope in crimson. The trail then bears northeast, winding among groves of trees and more open plains. Upslope, the view is mostly the forested backside of **Llao Rock**; downslope, you're

Patches of phlox splash cheerful color along the rocky trailside.

able to pick out the highway through the trees. As the surrounding forest begins closing in, the grade of descent increases moderately; you may be able to spot 7412-foot **Grouse Hill** to the northeast.

Following a short eastward jog, the trail eases to a shallow pitch once again, traverses through a dry drainage, then bends northwest. At 60.5 miles, the junction to **Grouse Camp** appears to the right (east). A short side trail leads to the forested, hiker-only camp at the base of a steep talus slope. The camp area is fairly large, with two designated sites, each able to accommodate a few tents while still affording a little bit of privacy. The open center of the camp contains a large fire ring and several log benches. There is no nearby water,

so remember to conserve some of your supply to get you through the night and the next day. As far as camps go, it's a decent, albeit, sadly, viewless, place to end the day—and because it's one of the only convenient camps for a long stretch of miles, you're likely to have company to share a campfire and watch the stars.

CAMP-TO-CAMP MILEAGE

Annie Spring Trail junction to
　　Dutton Camp 1.3
Dutton Camp to Lightning Spring
　　Trail junction 4.7
Lightning Spring Trail junction
　　to Grouse Camp. 6.6

5A ALTERNATE
MAZAMA VILLAGE TO GROUSE HILL (VIA PCT)

DISTANCE 17.6 miles

ELEVATION GAIN/LOSS
+1230 feet/–820 feet

HIGH POINT 6500 feet

CONNECTING TRAILS
Lightning Spring Trail, Bald Crater Loop Trail, Boundary Springs Trail, Volcanic Legacy Scenic Byway (OR 209)

ON THE TRAIL
The PCT's official route circuits the base of Crater Lake's rim in mostly viewless forest, and holds to the PCT designers' intent to keep the trail stock-friendly and steer clear of busy and popular locations. This route is somewhat milder than the upper Rim Trail which climbs steeply to the rim, then circuits the edge of the crater on several narrow, twisting paths that parallel the rim road—definitely not suitable for horses. The upside for taking the official route is that there is

much more access to running water, as opposed to the long, waterless miles along the rim, and there are several more camping options. As the mileage for this leg runs higher than others, the ideal way to tackle this section is to hike to the camp area at **Red Cone Spring** (see Trail Note), to Grouse Hill and the final leg (6) the next day.

TRAIL NOTE: FIRE DAMAGE
Several miles of the PCT's official route around the base of Crater Lake were badly burned in the 2017 Spruce Lake Fire. This fire resulted in significant trail damage, and the destruction of the camp area at Red Cone Spring. Hikers should exercise caution, and expect to encounter downed trees and debris on the trail. In lieu of camping at Red Cone Spring, the park is permitting dispersed camping through this area. Hikers should adhere to standard LNT guidelines; water at the spring is no longer reliable.

For the purpose of this guidebook—and for obvious scenic reasons—the Rim Trail route is the default main route, with mileage reflected accordingly. The official PCT route will continue the established section mileage from 47.9 miles (at the Annie Spring junction) and will end at the junction with the Rim Trail near Grouse Hill, at 65.5 miles. However, at this point, mileage forward will revert back to the default main route, requiring a subtraction of 4.5 miles to the section's remaining mileage.

To remain on the official route of the PCT, follow the same directions at the beginning of Leg 5, from Mazama Village to the Dutton Creek Trail junction. Instead of turning, continue straight through the junction, where the the trail immediately crosses **Castle Creek** 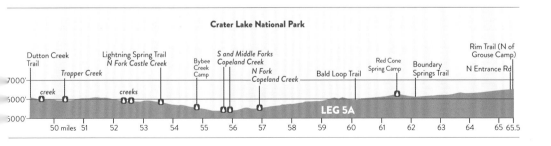, then winds northwest through mixed conifer forest on a shallow descent. It crosses another seasonal creek at 49.6 miles, and **Trapper Creek** at 50.4 miles, which often diminishes later in the season. Continuing on, the trail gently climbs a low ridge, then descends north into an area recovering from a years-ago wildfire, reaching a couple more seasonal streams at 52.4 and 52.6 miles. Continuing northwest, the trail reenters forest and descends to cross **North Fork Castle Creek** at 53.6 miles, meeting the **Lightning Spring Trail**. Here, the Lightning Spring Trail climbs 4 steep miles to meet the Rim Drive (and the Rim Trail). About 3.2 miles up, **Lightning Spring Camp** offers a couple campsites (see Leg 5). Stock is not permitted within 0.25 mile of the rim road; a hitching post can be found near the trail.

The descent continues, turning onto a winding northward track. To the east, patches of the

WATER ALERT!

Red Cone Spring is the last near-trail water supply through the end of Section 2, and into Section 3 at Thielsen Creek--that's 20.9 miles ahead. The first half of this stretch is 12.7 miles of very dry, and potentially very warm, lodgepole forest to the park's northern boundary. Continuing into Section 3, you'll have an additional 8.2 miles of waterless, albeit shadier, trail. Fill up as needed.

recovering 2006 **Bybee Complex Fire** area are still visible through the trees; to the west, dense green forest persists. Around 54.8 miles, a side trail descends left (west) 0.3 mile to **Bybee Creek Camp**, where happy little **Bybee Creek** flows reliably down the hillside beside the camp area. Just 0.1 mile beyond the camp spur, the PCT crosses Bybee Creek, then turns sharply west. The descent runs out at 55.4 miles, at the westward extent of the PCT's circuit around the base of the rim. The trail then makes an abrupt turn north, and from here to the Grouse Hill junction the way is mostly a gentle ascent, relieved by a few small descents.

Just as the trail begins its ascent, around 55.7 miles, it crosses **South Fork Copeland Creek** and enters the Spruce Lake Fire burn area. You can probably expect to encounter plenty of downed trees and snags for the next few miles, so exercise caution. The Middle Fork channel follows at 55.9 miles, and the North Fork at 56.9 miles. The trail then turns north, back under the cover of

Crater Lake National Park

One day, this trail blaze will disappear.

blackened forest, and begins climbing more moderately for the next few miles. Just prior to cresting a low ridge at 59.4 miles, the trail passes through the small area burned by the 2011 **Red Cone Complex Fire**. It then bears east and mostly downhill until reaching the **Bald Crater Loop Trail** at 60.1 miles. This 13.9-mile loop trail (connected with the Boundary Springs Trail) circuits 6478-foot Bald Crater in the northwest corner of the national park. On the southwest corner of the loop, the trail skirts the Sphagnum Bog and Crater Springs, a wide wetlands area where elk often roam.

The PCT then reaches the crest of the next moderate rise at 61.5 miles, after which, a side trail branches off east to **Red Cone Spring Camp** (See Trail Note on page 110. Inquire with park about current status of camp area.) On this route, this is the last camp area available within the park

boundary—unless you want to proceed to the Grouse Hill junction and backtrack 0.4 mile on the Rim Trail to Grouse Camp—but that makes for a pretty long day. As previously noted, the small spring here is exceptionally fickle, so plan accordingly. Still largely forest-bound, there aren't any prize-winning views to be had here, but the open meadow gives the opportunity for some good stargazing before turning in.

From Red Cone Spring, there's 4.1 more miles to the Rim Trail junction. Start by descending north to the junction with the **Boundary Springs Trail** at 62.1 miles. From here, the trail turns east and exits the burn area to traverse the northern flanks of 7363-foot **Red Cone**, the largest and youngest of the three cinder cones in the northern park area, named for the red-colored cinders exposed near its summit. The cone's lightly glaciated north flank is mostly forested, so you won't get a good look at its notable lava features. Once over the cone's north slope, the trail descends into dry lodgepole forest before gradually climbing to reach the **Volcanic Legacy Scenic Byway** (OR 209) at 65.4 miles. On the west side of the road is a large trailhead parking area, with a bear box for water caches. Cross the road and proceed 0.1 mile to the junction with the Rim Trail. At this point, turn left (north) to begin the final leg of your Section 2 journey.

CAMP-TO-CAMP MILEAGE

Annie Spring Trail junction to Lightning
    Spring Camp junction. 5.7
Lightning Spring Camp junction
    to Bybee Creek Camp. 1.2
Bybee Creek Camp to Red Cone
    Spring Camp. 6.7
Red Cone Spring Camp to Grouse Camp 4.4

NATIONAL CREEK COMPLEX FIRE

In the summer of 2015, the National Creek Complex Fire burned more than 15,000 acres in the northwest corner of Crater Lake National Park. This was the largest wildfire in the history of the park. The Bald Crater Loop, Boundary Springs, and Bert Creek trails were closed to hikers, as well as the PCT between Lightning Springs and OR 138. While the PCT remained unscathed, the northern portions of the Bald Crater Loop, north of Sphagnum Bog, and Boundary Springs trails burned heavily.

6 GROUSE HILL TO CASCADE CREST

DISTANCE 9.1 miles

ELEVATION GAIN/LOSS
+290 feet/–1010 feet

HIGH POINT 6620 feet

CONNECTING TRAILS AND ROADS
Pacific Crest Trail, Volcanic Legacy Scenic
Byway (OR 209), North Crater Trail

ON THE TRAIL

After spending an amazing, view-packed day
circuiting the sapphire wonder of Oregon's only
national park, it would be ideal to complete the
last leg and finish the section on a high note—no
such luck. The section's final 9 miles are hot, dry,
and utterly viewless. The consolation is that nearly
the entire stretch is a moderately shady, shallow

descent, so if you break camp early you can make
quick time getting to the trailhead and your waiting vehicle, ride, resupply, or water cache.

From **Grouse Camp**, the **Rim Trail** continues
its gently descending circuit around the base of
Grouse Hill, remaining largely closed-in by scrag-
gly lodgepole pine forest. At 60.9 miles, the Rim
Trail meets the **Pacific Crest Trail**, which comes in
from the west. Continuing once again on the PCT,
the trail advances north for another mile between
the base of Grouse Hill and the Volcanic Legacy
Scenic Byway (OR 209), the park's north entrance
road, then begins veering northeast, peeling away
from both. The grade eases to an almost level
walk for the next couple miles amid airy, viewless
forest, the trail tread turning soft and sandy, to an
unsigned T-junction at 63.6 miles at the edge of
the **Pumice Desert**. Only marginally visible from
the trail, this vast, barren expanse of cinders was

The camp area at Grouse Hill makes a nice, albeit viewless, place to end a long day of hiking.

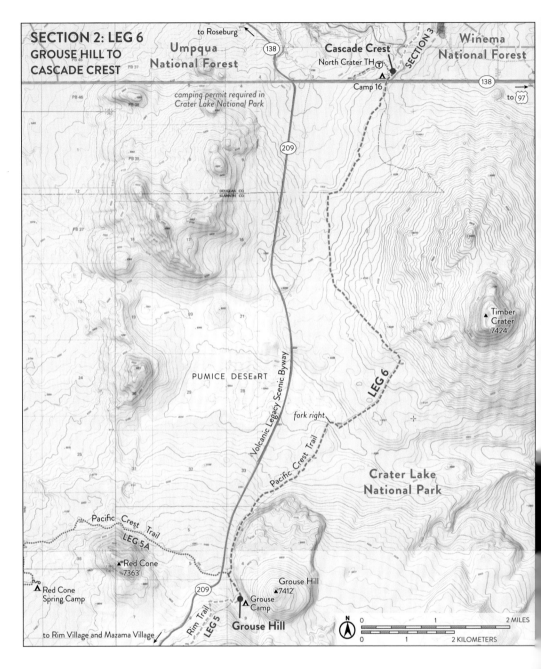

deposited (up to 200 feet deep) by the eruption of Mount Mazama. The porous nature of the area inhibits growth, so only a handful of hardy lodgepole pines adorn the inhospitable plain. If you're hiking through here during the heat of summer, you can thank the trail designers that the way forward circuits the plain amid shady trees instead of crossing straight through.

The PCT now continues right (east) jogging forward on the defunct Timber Crater Trail for 0.2

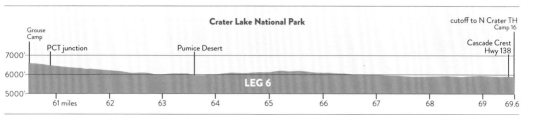

mile, then turns sharply northeast, toward 7424-foot **Timber Crater**. You might catch a glimpse of the forested peak through the trees. Near 65 miles, the trail suddenly veers northwest, making a short, gentle ascent over the crater's lower slope in greener, shadier forest before descending north into sunnier woodland. Over the last 3 undulating miles to the highway, you may notice a profusion of diamond-shaped trail blazes in the trees, marked by the trail names of past PCT hikers—cute, creative, and funny—a welcome break from the viewless monotony, but still vandalism, and it is not recommended that you follow suit. Then, without warning, the trail pops out of the tree cover onto the red cindery shoulder of **OR 138** at 69.5 miles.

With no parking or noticeable signage at this highway crossing, the end of the section is just a little bit farther. Carefully cross the highway, exiting Crater Lake National Park and entering the **Umpqua National Forest**; just east of the crossing a large roadside sign marks the nearby boundary

of the **Fremont-Winema National Forest** at the **Cascade Crest.** Proceed another 0.1 mile to a more obvious junction marked with an assortment of trail signs; a small camp can be found just left (west) of the trail with space for one tent (**Camp 16**). This junction marks the end of the section. If you're finishing here, turn left (west) on the **North Crater Trail**, leaving the PCT at 69.6 miles (remember, mileage adjusted for the recommended route, not the official route). Follow this flat, forested path the last 0.2 mile to the **North Crater Trailhead** and your waiting vehicle. Plan ahead and make sure you have a refreshing drink stashed under a seat waiting for you. If this is the end of your trek, post an awesome photo of your trip and brag about your achievement. If your journey continues, you're about to plunge into the **Mount Thielsen Wilderness**, where an icy stream and a good campsite await just a few miles ahead.

CAMP-TO-CAMP MILEAGE
Grouse Camp to Camp 16 . . . . 9.1

CASCADE CREST TO WILLAMETTE PASS

NORTH OF CRATER LAKE National Park, the Pacific Crest Trail wends its way into Oregon's Central Cascades region. Along the way, the route crosses two wilderness areas, a national recreation area, and touches four national forests as it works its way north, taking a wide, lazy, S-shaped track. The landscape becomes more pronounced and rugged as the PCT begins skirting volcanic peaks, ridges, and spires notably sculpted by ice age glaciers, affording some impressive scenery. In addition to the dramatic new landscape, a profusion of new flora and fauna enters the mix, keeping things interesting along the way when the forest closes in. All the while, the trail maintains its relatively moderate path, with undemanding ascents and descents through increasingly pleasant forest and subalpine settings.

The section gets underway just north of Crater Lake National Park, near the **Cascade Crest** in the **Fremont-Winema National Forest**. Access to the trailhead is easy from west or east; there's a good parking area with a few campsites and a vault toilet for last-minute pit stops. The PCT soon enters the **Mount Thielsen Wilderness**, with the prominent peak of Mount Thielsen guiding the way forward. In the days and miles ahead, this pointed peak on the southern horizon will mark the distance you've covered. After crossing the length of the wilderness area, the PCT enters the **Oregon Cascades Recreation Area**, where the route traverses high ridges between wide, glaciated valleys and skirts two more volcanic peaks before presenting a glorious sight for every thirsty hiker: water—and lots of it.

The climax of the section comes in the final stretch, where the PCT comes to the shore of gorgeous **Summit Lake** at the foot of the **Diamond Peak Wilderness**, after which it traverses a

DISTANCE 60 miles

STATE DISTANCE 156.3–216.3 miles

ELEVATION GAIN/LOSS
+8280 feet/–9110 feet

HIGH POINT 7560 feet

BEST TIME OF YEAR Aug–Oct

PCTA SECTION LETTER D

LAND MANAGERS Umpqua National Forest (Mount Thielsen Wilderness), Fremont-Winema National Forest (Mount Thielsen Wilderness), Deschutes National Forest (Mount Thielsen Wilderness, Diamond Peak Wilderness), Willamette National Forest (Diamond Peak Wilderness)

PASSES AND PERMITS NW Forest Pass required for parking at North Crater and Willamette Pass trailheads; self-register wilderness permits available at some trailhead kiosks.

MAPS AND APPS
- National Geographic PCT: Oregon South 1005, maps 1–5
- Halfmile PCT: Oregon D1–D10
- Guthook PCT: Oregon

LEGS
1. Cascade Crest to Thielsen Creek
2. Thielsen Creek to Maidu Lake
3. Maidu Lake to Windigo Pass
4. Windigo Pass to Summit Lake
5. Summit Lake to Willamette Pass
4/5A. Windigo Pass to Willamette Pass (via OST)

Opposite: Somewhat resembling Tolkien's Mount Doom, Mount Thielsen is often referred to as the "lightning rod of the Cascades."

skyscraping, glacier-carved mountain before meandering through lush, forested lake country. But the joy doesn't just come in the big panoramas and alpine high country. Pretty little wildflowers adorn the forest floors and rocky ridges. Berries—*so many berries!*—make for delightful snacks as you're strolling along at the right time of summer. And then you may see mushrooms and lichens and little critters that dart across the trail in front of you, and pesky gray jays that lurk over your shoulder waiting for you to drop a cracker or turn your head so they can get into your trail mix. Big critters roam the area as well, but are seen less frequently. You are more likely to see the evidence of their presence in the form of footprints or a pile of scat in the middle of the trail.

The challenges in this section are the continued lack of frequent and easy access to water—due in large part to the porous nature of the volcanic soils that make up much of Oregon's mountainous crest, and (if following the recommended five-day itinerary) the increasingly longer mileage days from one camp location to the next. At a little more than 17 miles, the last leg can be especially challenging if you're not used to trail days that long. Not to worry, however; that leg can easily be split in two for a six-day itinerary. Just be sure to monitor your water situation and carry extra to accommodate dry camps. Depending on the season, there are a few stretches where you might still find snow-covered trail, even into the summer months, specifically on the north side of Mount Thielsen and around Cowhorn Mountain. If you run into snow-covered trail where the route is not obvious and well-trod by previous hikers, you should only proceed with map and compass (or GPS receiver) and have good routefinding skills.

This route also presents an opportunity to deviate from the PCT and onto an older stretch of the Oregon Skyline Trail (OST), predecessor of the PCT. This alternate route breaks off from Windigo Pass, near the midpoint of the section, and parallels the PCT to the east where it skirts several idyllic lakes over easier terrain. It offers some nice views, more water access, and a shorter journey by about 10 miles, but you sacrifice one of the section's highlights: the traverse under Diamond Peak. If hiking this section in especially hot, dry years, this alternate is a no-brainer for its water access alone. During normal seasons, though, the official route is recommended.

Now, as the PCT begins taking on a Middle Earth–like quality—and you're less likely to begrudge "green tunnel" syndrome—you'll find joy in pleasant, mossy forests interrupted by high-point panoramas, and delight in one of the prettiest trailside lakes in the entire state. And as you're watching the moon rise from your backcountry or lakeside campsites, you can take comfort in knowing that the PCT has plenty to offer—you just have to find it.

ACCESS
Cascade Crest
From Roseburg, take I-5 exit 124 for the North Umpqua Highway (OR 138). Proceed through town, following signs for OR 138 and Crater Lake National Park. Continue east for 87 miles, passing the turnoff for Diamond Lake Resort. Continue 0.9 mile past the Crater Lake north entrance road

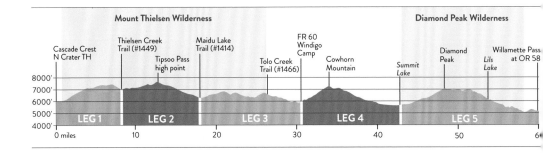

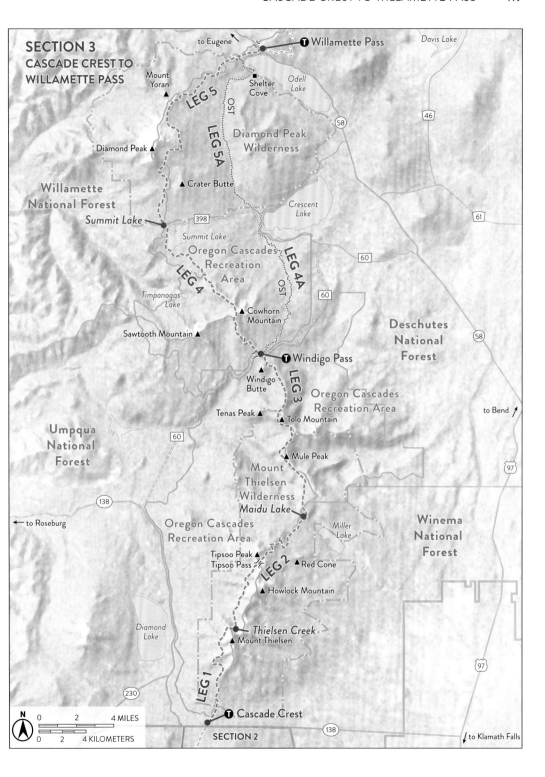

SECTION 3
CASCADE CREST TO
WILLAMETTE PASS

to Eugene
Willamette Pass
Davis Lake

Mount
Yoran
Shelter
Cove
Odell
Lake

LEG 5
OST
LEG 5A
Diamond Peak
Wilderness
58
46

Diamond Peak

Crater Butte

Crescent
Lake

Willamette
National Forest
Summit Lake
398
61

Summit Lake
Oregon Cascades
Recreation
Area
LEG 4A
60

LEG 4
OST

Timpanogas
Lake
60

Cowhorn
Mountain

Deschutes
National
Forest
58

Sawtooth Mountain

Windigo Pass
LEG 3

Windigo
Butte
Oregon Cascades
Recreation Area
to Bend

Tenas Peak
Tolo Mountain

Umpqua
National
Forest
60
97

Mule Peak

Mount
Thielsen
Wilderness
Maidu Lake
Miller
Lake

138
to Roseburg

Oregon Cascades
Recreation Area

Winema
National
Forest

Tipsoo Peak
Tipsoo Pass
LEG 2
Red Cone

Diamond
Lake
Howlock Mountain

Thielsen Creek
Mount Thielsen

97

LEG 1
230

Cascade Crest
138
SECTION 2
to Klamath Falls

N
0   2   4 MILES
0   2   4 KILOMETERS

Take in this scene of Diamond Peak over Summit Lake from a hidden campsite on the lake's south shore.

(OR 209) and turn left (north) onto a side road signed for the North Crater trailhead. Proceed 0.3 mile to parking and trail access at the end of the turnaround.

From Bend, drive south on US 97 for 75 miles. Turn right (west) on OR 138 and continue 14 miles to the turnoff for the North Crater trailhead.

Willamette Pass

From Eugene, take I-5 exit 188 for the Willamette Highway (OR 58) east. Drive 62 miles to the Pacific Crest Trailhead on the north side of the highway, just past the Willamette Pass ski area.

From Bend, drive south on US 97 for 46 miles. Turn right (west) on Crescent Road for 12 miles to the junction with OR 58. Turn right (west) and continue 10.5 miles to the trailhead, shortly past Odell Lake.

NOTES
Services

The nearest limited services to the southern Cascade Crest trailhead are 14 miles east at the junction of OR 138 and US 97; there are additional services 10 miles north of this junction in the small town of Chemult. Shelter Cove Resort, approximately 2 miles south and east of the PCT and the northern

Willamette Pass trailhead, has a small store, cabin rentals, and will accept and hold resupply packages; camping can be found adjacent to the resort at the Trapper Creek Campground. There are no resupply opportunities through this section.

Camping
Obvious and convenient campsites are plentiful throughout this section, both along the PCT and at several nearby lakes.

Water
Water through the first half of this section can be challenging to come by. Most legs begin and/or end at a water supply, but there is little to be found along the way. Midsection, there is a 17-mile waterless stretch, that may be serviced by a cache at Windigo Pass. Be sure to top off all your containers with enough to get you through each whole day, and plan for one dry camp mid-section.

SUGGESTED ITINERARIES

The following distances do not include off-PCT miles (up to 0.9 mile) to water sources, campsites, alternate routes, or resupply locations. For more information about trail distances, see How to Use This Guide. For the five-day itinerary via the PCT, you can break the last day up even further by hiking from Summit Lake to Camp 19 or 20 (7.1 and 8.7 miles, respectively), then finishing to Willamette Pass the following day.

5 DAYS
		Miles
Day 1	Cascade Crest to Thielsen Creek	8.2
Day 2	Thielsen Creek to Maidu Lake	9.7
Day 3	Maidu Lake to Windigo Pass	12.4
Day 4	Windigo Pass to Summit Lake	12.4
Day 5	Summit Lake to Willamette Pass	17.3

5 DAYS (VIA OST)
Day 1	Cascade Crest to Thielsen Creek	8.2
Day 2	Thielsen Creek to Maidu Lake	9.7
Day 3	Maidu Lake to Windigo Pass	12.4
Day 4	Windigo Pass to Crescent Lake	9.0
Day 5	Crescent Lake to Willamette Pass	11.1

4 DAYS
Day 1	Cascade Crest to Tipsoo Pass	12.8
Day 2	Tipsoo Pass to Windigo Pass	17.5
Day 3	Windigo Pass to Summit Lake	12.4
Day 4	Summit Lake to Willamette Pass	17.3

3 DAYS
Day 1	Cascade Crest to Maidu Lake	17.9
Day 2	Maidu Lake to Summit Lake	24.8
Day 3	Summit Lake to Willamette Pass	17.3

1 CASCADE CREST TO THIELSEN CREEK

DISTANCE 8.2 miles

ELEVATION GAIN/LOSS
+1690 feet/−640 feet

HIGH POINT 7370 feet

CONNECTING TRAILS AND ROADS
North Crater Trail, FR 961, Mount Thielsen
Trail (#1456), Thielsen Creek Trail (#1449)

ON THE TRAIL

Beginning just north of Crater Lake National Park, in the **Umpqua National Forest**, the PCT quickly enters the Mount Thielsen Wilderness. This leg's way northward is largely forested, offering few views until reaching the lower flanks of Mount Thielsen—and then the views become dramatic. The trail is also dry, devoid of any running water or nearby lakes until the end of the leg at Thielsen Creek, nearly 8 miles ahead. This area of southern Oregon, despite its moderate elevation, can get exceptionally warm in midsummer, so set out with plenty of water, hat, and sunscreen. The leg's ascent is a moderate one, with a nice finishing descent to a well-established camp area near an icy, cascading creek.

Setting out from the **North Crater Trailhead**, take the flat, winding spur trail east 0.2 mile to its junction with the PCT. (If you're coming from Section 2 of the PCT, from Crater Lake National Park, this junction is 0.1 mile north of OR 138.) Here, reset your GPS unit odometer to 0, point yourself north, and move out. The trail heads slightly northeast on good tread, through lodgepole pine and mountain hemlock forest that is open and airy, offering little bits of shade; ground cover is sparse, with just a few grasses and low shrubs here and there. After 0.4 mile, the trail crosses a dirt road (FR 961), where a trailhead sign indicates distances ahead for Mount Thielsen and Maidu Lake. At this point, the trail has sidled slightly eastward into the **Fremont-Winema National Forest**.

At approximately 1 mile, a sign on a tree indicates the boundary of the **Mount Thielsen Wilderness**. As the trail rises, the surrounding forest becomes denser, and trailside greenery begins to appear, including Oregon grape and huckleberry. If you're hiking through during berry

MOUNT THIELSEN WILDERNESS

Designated in 1984, the Mount Thielsen Wilderness encompasses more than 55,000 acres in southern Oregon, just north of Crater Lake National Park. The centerpiece in this region of volcanic peaks and ridges scoured away by ice age glaciers is 9182-foot **Mount Thielsen**, an extinct shield volcano and Oregon's 22nd-highest peak. Along with alpine forests and meadows, where mountain hemlock and various fir species cling to slopes and high ridges, the wilderness is also home to the headwaters of the Wild and Scenic North Umpqua River. The rolling lower elevations, east and west of the Pacific Crest, are blanketed with dense lodgepole pine and Douglas-fir forest. The local residents include black bears, bobcats, mule deer, Rocky Mountain elk, and a variety of smaller scurrying critters, in addition to more than 200 varieties of birds, either permanent or migratory. Fewer than 80 miles of trails cross the area, 25 of which are on the PCT as it crosses the entire length of the wilderness. The remaining trails, mostly on the west side of the crest, climb to the high peaks or visit the small lake basins; the 79-mile **North Umpqua Trail** originates at Maidu Lake.

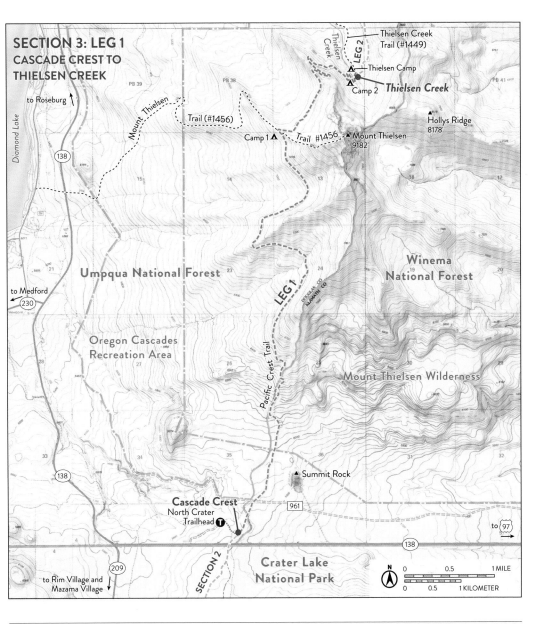

SECTION 3: LEG 1
CASCADE CREST TO
THIELSEN CREEK

Thielsen Creek
Trail (#1449)

LEG 2

Thielsen Camp

Camp 2   *Thielsen Creek*

Hollys Ridge
8178'

to Roseburg

Mount Thielsen

Trail (#1456)

Camp 1   Trail #1456   Mount Thielsen
9182'

Diamond Lake

138

Umpqua National Forest

Winema
National Forest

to Medford
230

LEG 1

Oregon Cascades
Recreation Area

Pacific Crest Trail

Mount Thielsen Wilderness

138

Summit Rock

Cascade Crest
North Crater
Trailhead

961

to 97

138

SECTION 2

Crater Lake
National Park

to Rim Village and
Mazama Village

209

N   0   0.5   1 MILE

0   0.5   1 KILOMETER

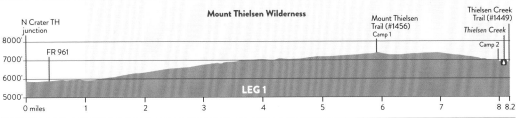

Mount Thielsen Wilderness

N Crater TH
junction

Mount Thielsen
Trail (#1456)

Camp 1

Thielsen Creek
Trail (#1449)

Thielsen Creek

Camp 2

8000'

FR 961

7000'

6000'

LEG 1

5000'

0 miles   1   2   3   4   5   6   7   8 8.2

Spy Diamond Lake from the PCT as you ascend the flanks of Mount Thielsen.

season, consider yourself lucky, as the sweet, juicy huckleberries are a tasty and refreshing substitute for the lack of water. About 2 miles in, the grade increases, gaining the divide that straddles the Fremont-Winema and Umpqua national forests. As the trail gains elevation, more ground cover appears, displaying tall flower stalks in season: lupine with delicate purplish-blue flowers, and beargrass with large white blooms.

The trail makes a short bend to the west, once again in the Umpqua National Forest, then continues its northward ascent along the lower flanks of Mount Thielsen. You may notice a shift in the ground cover and trail surface as you continue forward: the addition of light-colored volcanic cinders—pumice debris from the eruption of Mount Mazama. As the trail gains in elevation, curving west to traverse a wide, glacier-carved basin, the forest parts to reveal views south to the peaks atop Crater Lake's rim, including Llao Rock, The Watchman, and Mount Scott. Just before the trail dips back under dense tree cover, you're offered a view of sparkling **Diamond Lake**, resting quietly

beneath the slopes of 6309-foot **Hemlock Butte** and 8368-foot **Mount Bailey**.

The trail skirts the northwest extension of a glaciated ridge, contours north along the ridge, then bends east to traverse the next glaciated basin. A few breaks in the forest cover present a few more views west over Diamond Lake; to the east, a sheer, rocky ridge rises skyward. Finally, the trees part and offer the first grand view of spire-like **Mount Thielsen**. You'll get to enjoy this view for a short stretch before the trail ducks back under cover of old-growth forest. The trail then passes below a wide, open slope covered with more pumice before reaching a junction at the crest of a westward-extending ridge at 5.9 miles. Here, the **Mount Thielsen Trail** (#1456) climbs from the Diamond Lake area to the west, and continues upward to the pointed peak of Mount Thielsen. Just left (west) of the PCT is a nice campsite with room for a couple tents, and a prize view of the mountain (**Camp 1**). From the junction, the Mount Thielsen Trail continues steeply east and up toward the summit.

MOUNT THIELSEN

Look and listen for cute little pikas in the sprawling talus slopes beneath Mount Thielsen.

First, it was referred to as *Hischokwolas* by the native Chinook people. Early settlers then named it Big Cowhorn for its pointed summit spire. Finally, in 1872, it was designated Mount Thielsen in honor of Hans Thielsen, a leading railroad builder of the time. One of Oregon's older volcanic peaks, it is estimated to be around 290,000 years old, composed mostly of basaltic andesite, breccia, and tuff. Eruptive activity halted more than 100,000 years ago, leaving the mountain susceptible to heavy erosion through the following ice ages. Glaciers carved away at the peak from all sides, wearing down its flanks and exposing its core interior. The numerous arêtes (ridges) radiating from the central peak are what separated one glacier from the next.

When the glaciers receded and disappeared, all that remained of the mountain was the uppermost summit and its hornlike spire. The shape of this spire makes it prone to lightning strikes, hence its nickname, "the lightning rod of the Cascades." The abundant lightning strikes on the pinnacle have resulted in the formation of a rare mineral called fulgurite, which appears as dark, glassy splotches. A steep trail (#1456) ascends the mountain from the west, crosses the PCT (mile 5.9), and continues to the summit. The route is nontechnical, but the upper reaches are a steep scramble on loose rock. Views from the top take in the entire central and southern Cascade Range.

With your climbing done for this leg, take in the expansive view north over the terrain that lies ahead, including far-off **Diamond Peak**. The trail then drops over the north side of the ridge and proceeds steadily down, directly toward the immense talus and debris slope that makes up the northwestern flank of Mount Thielsen. From this vantage, you can see the mountain's needlelike summit, which inspires its moniker, "the lightning rod of the Cascades." If you are passing through this section of trail during a thunderstorm, you don't want to be anywhere on or near the exposed slopes of Mount Thielsen. This peak is struck by lightning regularly, hence the snappy nickname. The grade eases where the trail meets the talus slope, then turns north to contour across the jumbled mass. Listen for the "eeeeep!" of cute, furry pikas, then try to spot them scurrying amid the rocks.

The PCT reenters forest on the opposite side of the talus slope, offering one more peek back at the pointed prominence. Here you can make out more of the layered and twisted volcanic strata that make up the mountain, all largely exposed by the massive amount of glaciation that took place. The trail then bends northwest to begin a series of sweeping switchbacks into the next glacial basin, this one on the north side of the peak—and the only one that still has consistent running water.

The forested and viewless descent drops quickly, and nearing the bottom, the sound of running water will perk your ears—especially if you've hiked here from Crater Lake in Section 2, where your last access to water was nearly 30 miles past. Just before the final switchback, with the creek now in sight, a small camp can be found just right (east) of the trail at 8 miles (**Camp 2**).

After the last switchback, the trail proceeds across a small, forested clearing with another peek at Mount Thielsen, to where **Thielsen Creek ⓞ** crosses the trail at 8.1 miles. Thielsen Creek flows reliably well, even late into the hiking season; the crossing is an easy rock-hop. Now that you've reached your water source, it's time to make camp. Continue another 0.1 mile to **Thielsen Creek Camp**, at the junction with the **Thielsen Creek Trail** (#1449), at 8.2 miles. In the trees around this busy trail junction are several dispersed campsites, some with fire rings, some without; some secluded, some not. None offer any views, but the convenient access to fresh water is a suitable substitute, and makes a fine place to end the day before the next long, waterless stretch.

CAMP-TO-CAMP MILEAGE

North Crater junction to Camp 1 . . . . 5.9
Camp 1 to Camp 2 . . . . 2.1
Camp 2 to Thielsen Creek Camp 0.2

2 THIELSEN CREEK TO MAIDU LAKE

DISTANCE 9.7 miles

ELEVATION GAIN/LOSS
+960 feet/–1710 feet

HIGH POINT 7560 feet

CONNECTING TRAILS
Thielsen Creek Trail (#1449), Howlock Mountain Trail (#1448), Maidu Lake Trail (#1414), Miller Lake Trail (#1446)

ON THE TRAIL

The next leg remains largely under the hemlock, fir, and cedar slopes of the Umpqua National Forest, with the notable exception of reaching the official high point of the Pacific Crest Trail in Oregon and Washington: Tipsoo Pass. Near the pass, on either side, subalpine meadows and cindery plains offer panoramic views in alternating directions. The forest also takes on some new characteristics in draping lichens and new shrubs and ground cover unseen over previous miles.

SECTION 3: LEG 2
THIELSEN CREEK TO
MAIDU LAKE

Maidu Lake

Maidu Lake Camp

LEG 3

Maidu Lake Trail (#1414)

Camp 6

Maidu Lake

Miller Lake Trail (#1446)

Miller Lake

Umpqua National Forest

Oregon Cascades
Recreation Area

Tipsoo Peak Trail (#1472)

100

Tipsoo Peak
8034'

Camp 5

Red Cone
7271'

Tipsoo Pass 7560'
(Oregon/Washington
PCT high point)

Pacific Crest Trail

LEG 2

7410'

8122'

8096'

Mount Thielsen Wilderness

Howlock Meadows

Camp 4

Camp 3

Howlock Mountain Trail
(#1448)

Howlock Mountain
8324'

8207'

Winema
National Forest

Thielsen Creek Trail (#1449)

Thielsen Creek

Sawtooth Ridge

7652'

7843'

Thielsen
Camp

Camp 2

Thielsen Creek

LEG 1

Mount Thielsen
9182'

N

0   1   2 MILES

0   1   2 KILOMETERS

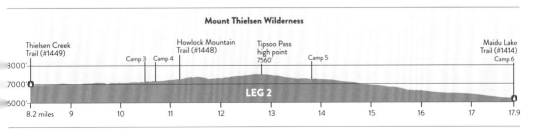

Mount Thielsen Wilderness

Thielsen Creek
Trail (#1449)

Howlock Mountain
Trail (#1448)

Tipsoo Pass
high point
7560'

Maidu Lake
Trail (#1414)

Camp 3   Camp 4

Camp 5

Camp 6

9000'

7000'

5000'

LEG 2

8.2 miles   9   10   11   12   13   14   15   16   17   17.9

The PCT circuits wide, grassy meadows under Howlock Mountain, south of Tipsoo Pass.

As before, however, this leg also has no running water for its entire length, and access to water at the end requires a side trip to nearby Maidu Lake, a pretty pool with good water and lots of campsites. Before setting off, be sure to top off at the creek for whatever water you'll need for the day. Then take one more look at Mount Thielsen's imposing northern face, now presenting an entirely different aspect as jumbles and pinnacles of volcanic rock rise out of the lower talus slope.

From **Thielsen Creek**, the trail makes a shallow ascent through somewhat open, airy forest. About a mile along, the forest closes in and becomes noticeably older, with wispy Methuselah's beard draping from trunks and boughs, and big mushrooms bursting out of the ground along the trailsides. Here the PCT bends east to begin the long northeast traverse of **Sawtooth Ridge**. As the trail contours the ridge on its generally mild ascent, the slope steepens across the trail, climbing high to the east and falling away sharply to the west.

Occasional windows through the forest give peeks of the rocky ridgetop above and the wide valley below. Cast a look behind and see Mount Thielsen rising ominously above the forested ridgeline looking not unlike Tolkien's Mount Doom.

Now with elves, orcs, and hobbits on the brain, continue forward as the trail bends northwest to contour a lateral extension of the ridge, then back

TRAIL TRIVIA

Howlock Mountain was originally named Walker Mountain, after W. T. Walker, who explored the Middle Fork Willamette River in 1852. When it was realized there was another Walker Mountain relatively close by, the name was changed to its current designation in honor of a central Oregon Piute Indian chief.

TIPSOO PEAK

From the high point on the PCT at **Tipsoo Pass**, a faint bootpath breaks off to ascend the moderate southern slope of **Tipsoo Peak** to the summit. Head straight up the ridge-line, bearing slightly northwest to connect with the Tipsoo Peak Trail (#1472) just below and west of the summit. The final stretch is a scramble up a rocky ridge for 100-mile panoramic vistas as far north as Mount Jefferson and south to Mount Shasta.

Give yourself a "high" five at Tipsoo Pass, the PCT's highest point in Oregon and Washington.

o its previous heading. At 10.5 miles, a very nice campsite can be found in the trees, left (west) of the trail, with room for two or three tents, and some convenient log stumps for seating (**Camp** 3). Another 0.2 mile ahead the trail comes to a light crest to cross an open plain of light-colored cinders; about halfway across, a small cairn of red and black volcanic rocks sits beside the trail. Left (west) of the trail, a lone tree rises amid the rocky ground; a small campsite rests behind with space for one tent (**Camp 4**). On the opposite side of the plain the trail dives back under shady tree cover—but not for long.

Following a rounding traverse below 8324-foot **Howlock Mountain** (a view comes shortly ahead), the PCT meets the **Howlock Mountain Trail** #1448) at 11.2 miles, climbing from the Diamond Lake area. Interestingly, the latter ends here at the PCT and offers only the sparest of looks at its namesake peak. As the PCT continues onward, still gaining elevation on a very easy grade, open spaces in the forest begin to reveal grassy meadows and wider views of the rocky peaks and pinnacles of Sawtooth Ridge, including—finally—a look at Howlock Mountain. (You wouldn't know it to look at it, but Howlock Mountain was once a large shield volcano; heavy glacial erosion reduced the mountain to a spiny ridge characterized by small horns and sharp arêtes.) The PCT then makes a

short ascent on a couple switchbacks to cross the next lateral extension in a shallow saddle. From this vantage, you're offered a view of your destination: the forested saddle to the right of red-hued **Tipsoo Peak**.

The trail drops over the ridge on a gentle descent—yes, you start down, knowing you should be going up—to traverse the final northward extension of Sawtooth Ridge. The trail is fairly open, offering a few views over the western valleys. The descent doesn't last long, and the trail once again resumes its gradual ascent; at 12.1 miles, it passes a wide grassy basin divided by the shallow gully of a long-gone creek. The trail then bends east to reach the plateau of **Tipsoo Pass**. (*Tipsoo* is Chinook jargon for grass.) Here, the open cindery plains and grassy meadows present a big view back over Sawtooth Ridge before arriving at the anticlimactic 7560-foot **OR/WA PCT High Point** just past 12.8 miles. There is no big view to be had here as the crest area is surrounded by trees; a post with a small sign signifies the location. Opposite the crest marker, a small, primitive campsite can be found under tree cover. Just a few yards farther grants a view of the brilliant red cindery mound of 8034-foot Tipsoo Peak.

Proceeding onward, the PCT begins its long, meandering descent northeast to the lakes junction, crossing into the Fremont-Winema National

Enjoying the sunset from Maidu Lake, just a short side trip off the PCT, makes a nice way to end a day of hiking.

Forest and circuiting the southeastern flank of Tipsoo Peak. Through the initial descent, the trail crosses open slopes, pocket meadows, and—unfortunately—dry creekbeds. Near 13.8 miles, an exposed campsite with space for a couple tents can be found right (east) of the trail on a rocky ledge (**Camp 5**); there is a nice panorama eastward overlooking 7271-foot **Red Cone** rising above the trees. The trail then dives back under tree cover and continues its winding descent to the extension of the ridge. Here, just below an unnamed 6975-foot outcrop, the trail passes through a rocky notch and makes a sharp turn south down into viewless forest. The grade eases as the trail bends back to the northeast and continues to a four-way junction with the **Maidu Lake Trail** (#1414) and **Miller Lake Trail** (#1446) at 17.9 miles.

With Maidu Lake (the headwaters of the North Umpqua River) being the only water source until Six Horse Spring, another 6.5 miles ahead, it makes a worthwhile—and scenic—destination to end the leg. The trail to the lake breaks off the PCT and proceeds north for 0.9 mile to the lake loop trail just before the lakeshore and **Maidu Lake Camp**. Look for several dispersed campsite in the trees near and left (west) of the fork, al with good water access. At the north end of th 0.8-mile lake loop is another large camp area nea the bridged outlet; a couple secluded primitiv sites can also be found in the trees on the wes and east sides. If you're only interested in wate and less interested in a pretty view, there are

MILLER LAKE CAMPGROUND

Another, longer option for camping and potential resupply is to visit Miller Lake, east of the PCT. This trail breaks off eastward to descend 2 miles and more than 600 steep feet to the Miller Lake Basin. A 0.8-mile side trail then winds around the south shore of the lake to the campground at Digit Point. There are no services available here other than the campground, so any resupply would have to be in the form of well-bribed friends waiting to meet you.

couple small campsites in the trees near the PCT's junction with the Maidu Lake Trail (**Camp 6**), each large enough to accommodate a single tent. It's not too bad to dump your gear, set up camp, then just jog down to the lake and back to refill your containers and set yourself up for the next morning's departure.

CAMP-TO-CAMP MILEAGE

Thielsen Creek Camp to Camp 3 . . . . 2.3
Camp 3 to Camp 4 . . . . 0.2
Camp 4 to Camp 5 . . . . 3.1
Camp 5 to Camp 6 (Maidu Lake junction) . . . 4.1
Camp 69 (Maidu Lake junction)
    to Maidu Lake Camp (off PCT) 0.9

3 MAIDU LAKE TO WINDIGO PASS

DISTANCE 12.4 miles

ELEVATION GAIN/LOSS
+1650 feet/−2040 feet

HIGH POINT 6780 feet

CONNECTING TRAILS AND ROADS
Maidu Lake Trail (#1414), Miller Lake Trail
(#1446) Six Horse Spring Trail (#39), Tolo
Creek Trail (#1466), Windigo Pass Trail
(#1412), Windigo Pass Road (FR 60)

ON THE TRAIL

The next leg of the Pacific Crest Trail continues to traverse the divide between the Umpqua and Fremont-Winema national forests, with the Fremont-Winema (east of the crest) eventually giving way to the **Deschutes National Forest**. The trail also departs the Mount Thielsen Wilderness to enter the **Oregon Cascades Recreation Area**. Instead of remaining below the crest, much of this leg stays high on the ridgetops, on a rolling track skirting Miller Mountain, Mule Peak, Tolo Mountain, Tenas Peak, and Windigo Butte. Despite this, much of the leg remains in the trees, with only a few views to break up the forested uniformity—more time to practice your flower and shrub identification. Once again, water is scarce, with the only reliable source at Six Horse Spring, about halfway through the leg and 0.5 mile off trail.

From the Maidu Lake junction, the PCT continues in sun-dappled hemlock and fir forest on a gentle northeast ascent. The grade quickly increases to switchback to the top of the bluff above the **Miller Lake Basin**. A nice view overlooking the lake and distant Deer Butte can be had where the trail turns north at the edge of the steep precipice. The trail continues to climb, bending west, then north to make a contouring ascent of 7513-foot **Miller Mountain**'s western slopes. At this point, you may start to notice a rather prolific shrub with tiny berries adorning the slopes and trailsides. This is grouse whortleberry, a miniature form of huckleberry. The small, tart berries are a popular food source of large and small animals, though difficult to harvest by hand for their exceptionally diminutive size. This shrub becomes the dominant ground cover for many miles ahead, and if you enter an area at the peak of the blooming season, it will smell like you've walked into a pastry shop with

WATER ALERT!

Though there is occasionally a hiker's water cache at Windigo Pass, **Six Horse Spring** is the last reliable water source near the PCT until you reach Summit Lake at the end of Leg 4, 17.2 miles farther north. It's best to top off everything you're carrying, and be prepared for a potentially dry camp at Windigo Pass.

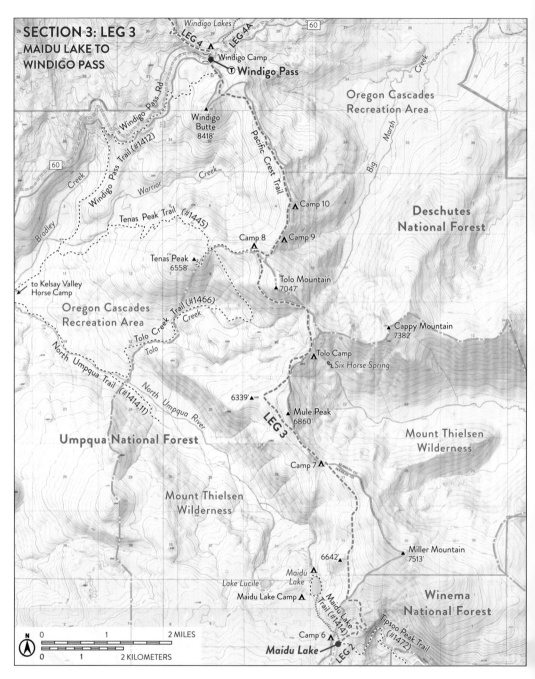

SECTION 3: LEG 3
MAIDU LAKE TO
WINDIGO PASS

the sweet fragrance of fresh-baked blueberry muffins.

Bearing north, the PCT passes through a shallow saddle between Miller Mountain to the east and an unnamed 6642-foot butte to the west—you wouldn't know it however, as the surrounding forest prohibits any views of either. Just a short distance farther, the trail reaches its first, and highest,

The blueberry muffin–like smell of in-season grouse whortleberries will make your mouth water.

crest of the leg, around 20.9 miles, on the steep slope of Miller Mountain's northwestern ridge; a few pockets through the trees afford only partial views to the west over the glacial basin that is the **North Umpqua River Valley** and beyond to 6546-foot **Red Cinder Butte**. From this crest, the trail begins a moderate descent northwest to another shallow saddle, this time atop the ridgeline in very pretty, lush green forest. Here, at 21.6 miles, you'll find a nice campsite left (west) of the trail with room for one tent (**Camp 7**).

The trail continues, hopping over to the east side of the crest on a short, steep ascent to stay high on the ridgeline. Just below a ridgetop prominence, the trail traverses a small slope of rockfall. The northeastward view takes in the forested upper basin of the **Little Deschutes River**; the partially rocky peak across the basin displaying colorful layers of volcanic strata is 7382-foot **Cappy Mountain**. The trail then dives back under tree cover, and proceeds to rise and dip along the ridgetop. Note the proliferation of more greenery

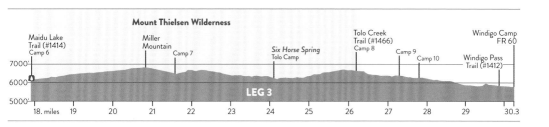

Sunlight illuminates the forest along the PCT near Tolo Mountain.

along the trailsides, including pipsissewa, with its cute, little pink flowers.. The trail and ridge then reach the southern flank of 6860-foot **Mule Peak** where the PCT hops over to the west side of the crest and begins the next steady descent to circuit

TRAIL TRIVIA

It is uncertain when and how **Windigo Pass**, as well as Windigo Butte and Windigo Lake, received their designations, but according to *Oregon Geographic Names*, which cites legends of the Ojibwa Indians, the **Windigo**, or **Weendego**, were "a legendary tribe of giant and ferocious cannibals." Could it be Sasquatch? Let that one sink in while you're sitting around the campfire.

the peak's western slope. The traverse through here alternates between older, shady forest and younger, airy forest adorned with an abundance of red-limbed manzanita on the open, sunny slopes.

Bending back to the northeast, the PCT continues descending, reentering denser forest garnished with ferns, bleeding heart, and mountain strawberry, to the saddle on the ridgeline north of Mule Peak. This is followed by another, shorter traverse along the steep western slope of a smaller prominence to the next saddle, where the trail levels to a pleasant walk and arrives at **Tolo Camp** and the junction to **Six Horse Spring** at 24.1 miles. Here, a large open area can accommodate up to four tents, with a fire ring and a few large logs for sitting; there are also a couple of secluded single-tent sites just outside of the large main area. Despite the lack of views, this location is a good midway lunch spot, and an opportunity to refill your water containers. To reach the spring—via a steep 0.5-mile switchbacking descent on the east side of the ridge—you're best off leaving your heavy pack up top and just carrying down your bottles and filter. Near the bottom are a couple of mucky ponds; for cleaner water, proceed just a little farther down an overgrown bootpath to where the water is flowing down a small cascade.

From Tolo Camp, the trail proceeds on a gently undulating track along the west side of the ridge to a saddle on the southeast side of 7047-foot **Tolo Mountain**. Here, the PCT turns west to circuit the mountain clockwise on a gentle ascent under shady, mossy forest. Along the way, a small opening in the trees presents a quick view to the south, including the tip of Mount Thielsen poking above the forested ridgeline. Where the trail reaches the western slope of Tolo Mountain, it turns north, climbing to reach the crest at the junction with the **Tolo Creek Trail** (#1466, signed Bradley Creek) at 26.2 miles. Near the junction, a nice campsite can be found left (west) of the trail in a glen of low trees (**Camp 8**); there's a log to sit on and enough space for a couple small tents.

From Camp 8 the PCT now heads east, on the north side of the ridge, departing the Mount Thielsen Wilderness and entering the Oregon Cascades Recreation Area. It then turns northeast to traverse along the ridgetop separating the Warrior Creek basin to the west and the Big Marsh Creek basin to the east, while walking the divide between the Umpqua (west) and Deschutes (east) national

TENAS PEAK

If you're feeling claustrophobic and need a respite from the tree cover, take the Tolo Creek Trail (#1466) 1.25 miles west to tag 6558-foot Tenas Peak. From the PCT, the trail descends 300 feet to a saddle and junction with the Tenas Peak Trail (#1445). Proceed southwest on the peak trail to make the steep, circuiting, switchbacking ascent to the summit. Once the site of a Forest Service fire lookout, the peak offers wide views over much of the Mount Thielsen Wilderness.

forests. A couple of small camps can be found along the ridgetop at 27.3 and 27.8 miles, each with space for one tent (**Camps 9 and 10**); the first camp has a partial view over the eastern basin. The trail follows this narrow ridgetop for the next couple miles, gradually descending, with a few views to the east. It then bends west to pass through a saddle between 8418-foot **Windigo Butte** to the west and a lower, unnamed butte to the east, then drops again to the trail junction at **Windigo Pass** at 29.9 miles. Here, the **Windigo Pass Trail** (#1412) breaks off westward for 6 miles into the Bradley Creek valley, where it intersects the Tenas Peak Trail (#1445) then ends at Kelsay Valley Horse Camp on FR 60. The PCT proceeds on a winding,

OREGON CASCADES RECREATION AREA

Sandwiched between the Mount Thielsen Wilderness to the south (and east) and the Diamond Peak Wilderness to the north is the Oregon Cascades Recreation Area. At 157,000 acres, it is the largest unprotected roadless area remaining in Oregon, and is shared among three national forests: Umpqua, Willamette, and Deschutes. The area is largely forested, and is home to two ancient stratovolcanoes: Sawtooth Mountain and Cowhorn Mountain, the latter of which is the highest point in the recreation area. The area was proposed for wilderness designation in Oregon's 1984 wilderness bill, but failed due in large part to the anti–wilderness crusade by Mark O. Hatfield (more on Hatfield's wilderness notoriety in Section 6). The PCT crosses the recreation area for 33 miles, from just north of Tolo Mountain to the north end of Summit Lake. The area is bisected by just one road—Windigo Pass Road (FR 60)—which cuts through at Windigo Pass.

WATER ALERT!

Windigo Camp sometimes has a large water cache for PCT hikers, graciously maintained by local Trail Angels. It is a real treat to find water here, and you are welcome to help yourself to what you need, but please be considerate of other hikers in need as well. You can find the current status of this cache on the PCT Water Report via www.pctoregon.com/pct-info/trail-conditions. The next water source is 11 miles north at Summit Lake.

gently ascending track for another 0.4 mile to cross **Windigo Pass Road** (FR 60) at 30.3 miles. On the north side of the road, near a trailhead parking area and information sign, **Windigo Camp** can accommodate several hiking parties, with spaces for up to six tents; in the central area is a large fire ring with several log benches for seating and cooking.

CAMP-TO-CAMP MILEAGE

Camp 6 (Maidu Lake junction) to Camp 7 ... 3.7
Camp 7 to Tolo Camp..................... 2.5
Tolo Camp to Camp 8..................... 2.1
Camp 8 to Camp 9 .... 1.1
Camp 9 to Camp 10 .... 0.5
Camp 10 to Windigo Camp 2.5

4 WINDIGO PASS TO SUMMIT LAKE

DISTANCE 12.4 miles

ELEVATION GAIN/LOSS
+1660 feet/–1920 feet

HIGH POINT 7210 feet

CONNECTING TRAILS AND ROADS
Windigo Pass Road (FR 60), Cowhorn Traverse Trail (#3641), FR 398

ON THE TRAIL

The next leg of the Pacific Crest Trail climbs to a high ridgeline before dropping into the wide glacial basin holding Summit and Crescent lakes. There are lots more views to be enjoyed along the way—especially some sweeping panoramas from the high point on the shoulder of Cowhorn Mountain—interspersed with some of the most lush and appealing old-growth forest seen so far. Once again, there is no reliable near-trail water to be obtained through this stretch until you reach the south end of Summit Lake. With more elevation and exposure, you definitely want to keep yourself

hydrated, but (depending on water supply from Six Horse Spring or Windigo Camp) be cautious of your consumption, ensuring that you have enough to last to the end of the leg. You'll want to waste no time getting to Summit Lake, where the views and camp options are stellar, to enjoy it before the sun sets—it may even be worth building in a layover day.

From **Windigo Camp**, the PCT climbs gradually northwest on good tread and begins ascending a moderate ridge, right along the crest of the Cascades. This ridge divides two wide glacial basins to the east and west and serves as the boundary between the Umpqua (west) and Deschutes (east) national forests. Shortly after leaving camp, at 30.6 miles, a small campsite can be found just off trail with room for a couple tents (**Camp 11**). Just a few steps beyond, the trail leaves the dense forest cover for the partially exposed west side of the ridge, offering wider views to the west and south. The trail then reaches a minor crest and makes a wide switchback through a gap, then follows the ridgetop northwest. This becomes the norm over the next several miles as the trail works its way to the shoulder of Cowhorn Mountain: meandering

Big views await as the PCT climbs toward Cowhorn Mountain.

and switchbacking upward, west, and east. On the sunny, exposed west sides of the ridge, manzanita lines the trail and covers the slopes; on the shadier, forested east sides, grouse whortleberry becomes the dominant ground cover.

As you work your way up, more views show you where you came from and where you're headed. At one point on the eastern side, you're offered a look over the somewhat swampy **Windigo Lakes**, seemingly so close, yet with no convenient access. After another twisting roundabout to gain the next section of ridgecrest, the trail comes to the edge of a precipitous drop at the top of a steep, rocky slope just past 32.2 miles. This opening in the forest grants a sweeping view eastward over the

sea of trees filling the basin below and across the Deschutes National Forest. It also presents your first clear view of the exposed volcanic slopes of Cowhorn Mountain. From the viewpoint, the trail makes a winding circuit around a low prominence, then turns northwest, ascending again, now back on the west side of the crest. At 32.6 miles, a bootpath breaks off the PCT to the left to descend into a shallow, wooded basin. In the early season, or during wetter summers, there may be a small lakelet in this basin with an opportunity to obtain water. Typically, by midsummer, it's just a muddy bowl. This location should not be counted on for good water, but if you happen to find some, consider yourself lucky.

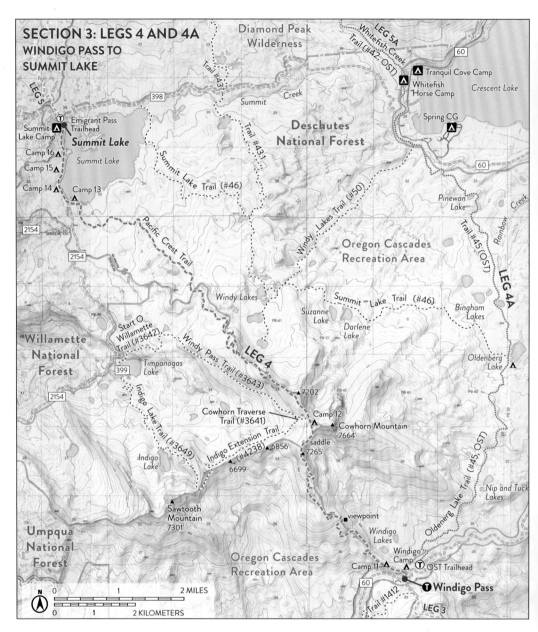

SECTION 3: LEGS 4 AND 4A
WINDIGO PASS TO SUMMIT LAKE

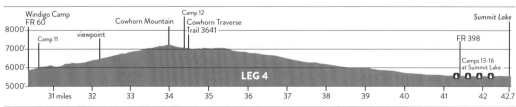

Note: There is no profile for Hike 4A.

The trail continues upward, traversing between the west and east sides of the ridgeline, each offering different views over the surrounding forests, lakes, and basins, including long views back at distant Mount Doom (i.e., Mount Thielsen). At one point, you may find yourself commenting, "*Wow—that's a lot of trees!*" Indeed it is. Nearing the crest, the trail makes one more westward circuit around a 7265-foot prominence and reaches the leg's high point from which a big view of Diamond Peak to the north lures you forward. It then curves northeastward to an open saddle at 34.1 miles on the shoulder of 7664-foot **Cowhorn Mountain**. This point makes a good place to enjoy a snack break and take in the expansive scene before you, with good seating on the porous volcanic rocks beside the trail. Try not to tread on the delicate penstemon or pasqueflower—these alpine plants only have a couple months during the summer to bloom and proliferate before spending the remainder of the year under snow.

The trail continues northeast across the saddle, where it crosses into the Willamette National Forest, now to the west. It then skirts the peak's western slope to another gap on its northwestern ridge, high above a deep glacial basin—and the next "wow" view. Here, you get your first big look (if you don't take the summit trail to bag Cowhorn) at the sprawling forested basin containing **Crescent Lake**. In the middle distance you can identify Redtop, Lakeview, and Maklaks mountains; farther away, you may be able to pick out Mount Bachelor and the Three Sisters. Just beyond this viewpoint, at 34.4 miles, a small camp with room for one tent can be found left of the trail (**Camp 12**). Then, just 0.1 mile farther, at 34.5 miles, is the junction with the **Cowhorn Traverse Trail** (#3641), which descends west to intersect the Windy Pass Trail (#3643), which in turn descends southwest toward Indigo Lake and northwest to Timpanogas Lake and FR 2154.

Descending from Cowhorn Mountain, the PCT takes an even more winding path down the northwestern ridge, remaining on or near the crest, but reentering pleasant forest with pocket meadows and a bevy of summer wildflowers. After traversing the southwest slope of a 7202-foot butte, a new view opens up, taking in **Summit Lake** backed by

ALTERNATE ROUTE: OREGON SKYLINE TRAIL

Here is where you have the option of hopping off the PCT and taking a stroll on the Oregon Skyline Trail (OST), predecessor of the PCT. There are a couple advantages to considering this alternate route, namely, fewer and easier miles and more water. This stretch of trail, which parallels the PCT to the east, possesses generally milder terrain and cuts the total distance (from Windigo Pass to Willamette Pass) by nearly 11 miles. More attractively, the OST comes into contact with more water. The first stretch hops past several small lakes to large **Crescent Lake**, with numerous camping options; the second stretch follows the drainages of Whitefish and Trapper creeks—passing lovely **Diamond View Lake**—all the way to **Odell Lake**, and Willamette Pass shortly beyond. The trade-off is missing some great PCT views at Summit Lake and below Diamond Peak. But if you're hiking through during peak summer and the temps are sweltering, it may be worth it. (See Leg 4/5A for more info.)

a likely still-snowy Diamond Peak; pocked among the forested carpet below, several of the **Windy Lakes** glitter in the midday sun. *This is why you're hiking the PCT.* Try to contain the giddy grin likely to spread across your face. The trail then crosses a jumbly stretch of exposed volcanic rock before hopping to the opposite side of the ridge to circuit the next prominence, followed by a winding, switchbacking descent into verdant forest at the northwestern extent of the ridge. At 37.3 miles, a small primitive camp can be found left of the trail.

The PCT eventually levels out in mixed forest and, now east of the crest proper, meanders northwest, reaching the southern extent of **Summit Lake** at 41.2 miles, where it begins its clockwise track around the lake. At 41.3 miles, look for a bootpath that cuts off right (east) of the trail

From the shoulder of Cowhorn Mountain, you get an idea of just how vast Oregon's forests truly are—that's a lot of trees!

through the huckleberry onto a narrow peninsula. Near the end of the peninsula is one of the choicest campsites on all of Oregon's PCT (**Camp 13**). Sheltered by a glen of trees, this site has a fire ring with a couple of log benches and flat space to accommodate a couple small tents. There is easy access and entry to the lake all around—and the view across the lake to Diamond Peak is

COWHORN MOUNTAIN

Currently ranked as Oregon's 108th-highest peak, Cowhorn Mountain used to be higher on the scale before a storm in 1911 blew off its upper spire. This ragged, 7664-foot volcanic spire along the Cascade Crest is similar to its taller cousin to the south, Mount Thielsen, in that it has suffered from significant glacial erosion. Through the ice ages, glaciers wore away at every side of the mountain, leaving behind a horn-shaped crown and radiating steep-sided ridges. Also similar to Thielsen, that erosion laid bare much of the ancient volcano's interior. Take note of the resistant basaltic vents—the pinnacles rising out of the southern flank's talus slope. Multicolored layers of tilted strata also tell the tale of the mountain's uplift and eruptive history.

To claim the summit, and take in the panoramic view that stretches from Crater Lake to the Three Sisters, follow a moderate bootpath that breaks east off the PCT to ascend the western ridgeline; a steep, nontechnical scramble gains the small summit platform. Look for the faint path around 34.3 miles.

magnificent. This site is still 1.3 miles from the end of the leg, but if you can score it, it's worth making up the distance the next day.

Just beyond, the PCT meets FR 398 at 41.4 miles. This rough jeep road traverses the west side of Summit Lake, north to Emigrant Pass, and south to the Timpanogas Lake area. The PCT crosses the road and dives back into the trees to parallel the road, then crosses two more times farther ahead. Here, you might just prefer to walk the nearly level road for its refreshing views across the lake—oh, so much water!—and access to several nice lakeside campsites. Each of the following campsites indicated along the road has room for one or two tents, fire rings, logs and stumps for sitting, and good lake access.

Continuing along the road, slightly above the wooded lakeshore, the next campsites can be found at 41.6 and 41.9 miles (**Camps 14 and 15**). The PCT then comes in from the left (west) side of the road to cross again into the trees on the right (east). It's worth veering back onto the

trail for the next jaunt, sticking closer to the lakeshore, and gaining access to another nice campsite at 42.2 miles (**Camp 16**). The trail then pulls away from the lake, comes parallel to the road again, and crosses back to the forested side of the road. Here again, you're better off proceeding on the road to access the last, and largest, camp area on the lake at **Summit Lake Camp** at 42.7 miles. This is less of a campground and more of a short spur road and turnaround with a few pullouts for making camp. There's not much in the way of privacy here, but there is a vault toilet, picnic table, and easy access to the lake for swimming and refilling water. A few secluded flat spots can be found in the trees on the small bluff above the road. This is a popular destination for canoe campers who put in the lake with their boats and gear and paddle out to and around the small islands and large, Swiss cheese–like peninsula to find private little lakeside campsites. You may just be able to strike up a conversation with fellow campers, regaling them with tales of your journey

Kick back lakeside at the Summit Lake Campground, with distant views of Cowhorn Mountain and the Calapooya Mountains.

on the PCT—and perhaps score a supportive soda or burger—while enjoying a colorful sunset across the lake with views of Cowhorn Mountain and the Calapooya Mountains.

If the thought of camping at a frontcountry location doesn't float your boat, and you have a little gas left in the tank, you can continue on to one of a couple small, secluded campsites 0.7 and 1.8 miles beyond—each located pond-side for convenient water access—and knock off a little mileage in the next day's travel, the last and longest leg of

the section. Proceed into Leg 5 for more info on these two camps (**Camps 17 and 18**).

CAMP-TO-CAMP MILEAGE

Windigo Camp to Camp 11	0.3
Camp 11 to Camp 12	3.8
Camp 12 to Camp 13	6.9
Camp 13 to Camp 14	0.3
Camp 14 to Camp 15	0.3
Camp 15 to Camp 16	0.3
Camp 16 to Summit Lake Camp	0.5

5 SUMMIT LAKE TO WILLAMETTE PASS

DISTANCE 17.3 miles

ELEVATION GAIN/LOSS
+2320 feet/–2800 feet

HIGH POINT 7040 feet

CONNECTING TRAILS AND ROADS
FR 380, Rockpile Trail (#3632),
Crater Butte Trail (#3844),
Mount Yoran Trail (#3683), Deer Creek
Trail (#3672), Bechtel Trail (#4366),
Willamette Highway (OR 58), FR 5810 (to
Shelter Cove)

ON THE TRAIL

The final leg of Section 3 is a long one, with a choice of ending destinations: the resort at Shelter Cove on Odell Lake, or the trailhead at Willamette Pass on the Willamette Highway (OR 58). This leg can also be easily split in two, trimming the daily mileage and allowing you to take more time to traverse the wide open basin below Diamond Peak and explore the many lakes on the latter half of the stretch. If this option sounds more appealing, consider Camps 19 or 20; the former, while waterless, is a nice space with a great view, and the latter is a charming site beside a small lakelet. Either in whole or in parts, this next stretch is the scenic climax you've been waiting for—huge views of glaciated volcanic peaks, icy streams (perhaps), sprawling meadows bursting with wildflowers and berries, and more easily accessible lakes than you can shake a trekking pole at.

From **Summit Lake Camp**, proceed north up FR 398 to the T-junction, just beyond the upper camp access road. Turn left (west) and walk FR 380 just 40 yards to the PCT crossing and kiosk at the **Emigrant Pass Trailhead**. Fill out your self-registration permit and enter the **Diamond Peak Wilderness**. The PCT continues its northward journey by making a gentle, meandering ascent into the woods, passing several small, boggy ponds

and lakelets. At 43.4 miles, the trail circuits one of the larger, cleaner lakelets where, on the west side, a bootpath cuts off to the right (east) to a nice, secluded campsite just above the lakeshore (**Camp 17**); there you'll find a couple logs for sitting and space for one tent. The trail maintains its easy, winding ascent, now heading north, and passes through the PCT's 200-mile mark (in Oregon) around 43.9 miles. If you started at the California–Oregon border, give yourself a pat on the back—nice work. It then crosses a dry creek gully and rises to a pretty pond that brilliantly reflects the surrounding forest and wide-open sky overhead. Left of the trail here, at 44.5 miles, is a decent campsite with room for two tents (**Camp 18**).

The trail, pleasantly adorned with an abundance of greenery, now begins meandering northeast, still gradually gaining elevation, to intersect the faint and overgrown **Rockpile Trail** (#3632) and **Crater Butte Trail** (#3844) at 45.7 miles. The former cuts off to the left (west) to **Rockpile Lake** and **Marie Lake** (0.7 and 0.9 mile, respectively), then farther west to a trailhead on FR 2160; the latter breaks off right (east) to circuit wide around Crater Butte before splitting off to **Diamond View, Sow Bug, and Effie lakes**. Near the junction is a small, primitive campsite. The trail then eases to a level walk—with huckleberries galore. If you're fortunate enough to be passing through during berry season, you're in for a real treat for the rest of the day. The berry-laden shrubbery eventually dwindles to deadfall and cinders (only for a short spell—the berries come back soon), the duffy tread turning to hardpack, the grade once again increasing to a moderate slope in dry, airy forest. Following another dry creek crossing, the trail turns northwest, traverses a shallow basin, then ascends a slight, rocky ridge southward to an exposed viewpoint at 47.1 miles. Here, as you look over Summit Lake, now many miles to the south, the horizon showcases Cowhorn Mountain, Sawtooth Mountain, Mount Thielsen, and even far-off Mount McLoughlin.

The long passage below Diamond Peak, chock-full of summer wildflowers, icy streams, and panoramic views, may make you feel like you have left Oregon for California's High Sierra.

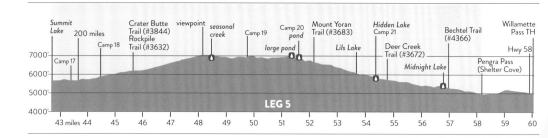

From the viewpoint, the PCT makes a quick hairpin turn north, continuing up the rocky ridge. Patches of bright yellow rabbitbrush and pink bleeding heart and fireweed adorn the exposed slope, and grouse whortleberry becomes prolific (can you smell it?); look for cute little western chipmunks scurrying among the rocks. At this point, you also get your first up-close views of **Diamond Peak**, with bigger and better to come. Just beyond the turn, a large cairn marks a climber's path that breaks off westward to scale the 8421-foot southern summit. The trail then curves northeast and dives back under tree cover through an ugly stretch of dry forest and deadfall. Thankfully it's short, and the greenery and ground cover returns quickly, alternating between lush patches of healthier forest and sunny open spaces. The trail makes another short, moderate ascent, then comes out into the open again (here's where you want to make sure you have sunscreen on) to cross a jumbly flow of multicolored lava rock, winds through a tangled avalanche path, then—*whoa!*

If you've ever hiked among the high passes of the Sierra Nevada, the next view may seem somewhat familiar. If not, welcome to the Oregon Cascades alpine high country. The entire sweeping

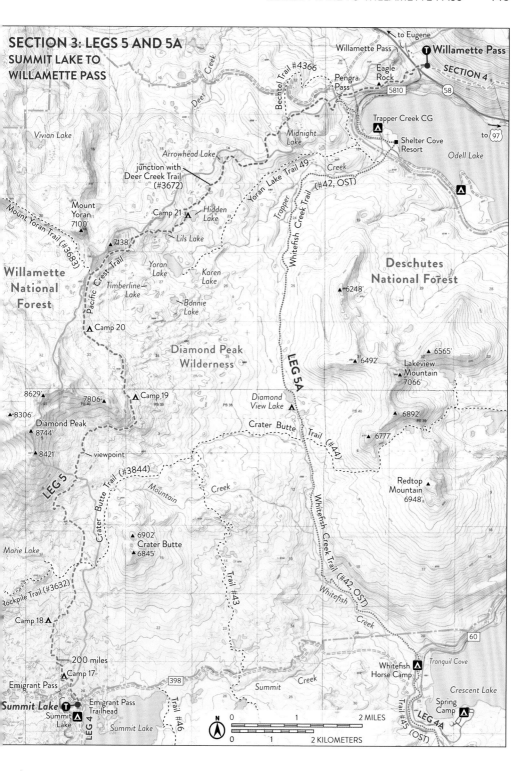

SECTION 3: LEGS 5 AND 5A
SUMMIT LAKE TO
WILLAMETTE PASS

DIAMOND PEAK WILDERNESS

Established in 1964 and encompassing more than 52,000 acres of central Oregon's volcanic high country, the Diamond Peak Wilderness protects one of the state's westernmost volcanic mountains—Diamond Peak. The peak was named for John Diamond, a member of the Road Viewers survey party who was first to reach the summit in 1852. Straddling the Cascade Crest, the wilderness area is surrounded to the north, east, and south by wide glacial basins filled with large lakes: Summit, Crescent, and Odell. The countless small kettle lakes and ponds in the northern section of the wilderness are the result of retreating glaciers, now long gone.

Surrounding all these pools, the wilderness is heavily blanketed with hemlock, pine, and fir forests, where a variety of woodland and alpine creatures, large and small, make their home. Be on the lookout for black-tailed deer, mule deer, elk, black bears, marmots, martens, foxes, and conies. The area is also home to a variety of birds, including Clark's nutcrackers, Oregon jays, and bufflehead and goldeneye ducks. Of the not-so-welcome residents, the area is also usually populated with hordes of bloodthirsty mosquitoes in early summer.

At the center of all this, Diamond Peak is a geologically young shield volcano, composed mostly of basaltic andesite, and is estimated to be less than 100,000 years old. Heavily glaciated on all sides—though not so much as Mount Thielsen to the south, where the mountain's interior was laid bare—Diamond Peak showcases a hornlike main summit (sculpted by up to four different glaciers converging on the mountain) from which narrow arêtes (ridges) radiate to three lower subordinate summits. At one point, the northernmost summit was the primary peak, but the last eruptive episode opened a vent to the south and allowed the mountain to grow the current high point. High on the mountain's flanks, above the sweeping talus slopes, several cirques once held glaciers as recently (geologically speaking) as 100 years ago. Now only the barest traces of the glaciers remain under heavy winter snowpacks.

Despite its moderate size, only 52 miles of trails delve into the wilderness area's old-growth forests and high country, 14 of which are the Pacific Crest Trail, and approximately 10 belonging to the older Oregon Skyline Trail. Several mountaineering trails, of varying difficulty and from all sides of the mountain, lead to Diamond Peak's high points. For its wide-open upper slopes, it is also a popular winter ski mountaineering destination.

extent of 8744-foot Diamond Peak now comes into view, curving from west to north. Lofty ridges and pinnacles vault skyward above expansive talus slopes and glacial moraines; high cirques may still be holding winter snows. Below the steep upper slopes, glades of mixed conifers offer little breaks of shade between wide exposures of rocky, gravelly plains embellished with small saplings, bunchgrass, manzanita, saxifrage, and pink mountain heather. At 48.2 miles, the trail comes to a crest at a rocky plateau, the high point of the leg. The 360-degree view here is all-encompassing—one of those views that makes you consider your own smallness in a very big place. Take a few moments to soak in the enormity of your surroundings.

Just beyond this viewpoint, the PCT continues across the plain on a gently undulating track, patches of stonecrop and heather here and there. You'll cross several bone-dry drainage gullies before coming to one that may actually have running water ⭘ at 48.5

Water—hiker's gold—can be found in numerous ponds, kettles, and lakes as the PCT crosses the Diamond Peak Wilderness.

DIAMOND PEAK

Claiming the 8744-foot summit of Diamond Peak is a nontechnical endeavor; however, the additional mileage (up to 3 miles roundtrip) and elevation gain (more than 2100 feet) may require adding a day to your trip's itinerary. Look for the faint climber's trail, marked by a large cairn, that breaks off the PCT around mile 47.1, just north of the hairpin turn and good viewpoint. The summit route climbs a steep mile up a main ridge on the southern flank to an 8421-foot false summit. From this skyscraping vantage point, the view takes in the wide basins of Odell, Crescent, and Summit lakes, Lakeview and Redtop mountains to the east, and Cowhorn and Sawtooth mountains to the south—not to mention a dizzying view across the knife-edge ridge leading to Diamond Peak's main summit and into the massive glacial cirques on both sides.

If you'll settle for nothing less than the actual summit, you can gingerly work your way another 0.4 mile along the summit ridge, around several pinnacle outcrops, to the true summit and some really overwhelming views. This final stretch is not for the acrophobic! The route is rocky and sporadically marked by cairns and flagging, so be sure to use map and compass or GPS receiver, and pay very close attention to your route and where you came from for the return trip.

SHELTER COVE RESORT

The General Store at Shelter Cove offers cold drinks and plenty of treats.

Approximately 2 miles southeast of the PCT and equally south of the Willamette Highway (OR 58), Shelter Cove Resort on Odell Lake—one of Oregon's larger Cascades lakes, filling a wide, glacial valley—is an extremely hiker-friendly and delightful place to take a layover ("zero day") from the trail and resupply or finish your trek. The resort, spread out on a small abutment along the western lakeshore, is open year-round and caters largely to RV travelers, fishers, skiers, and weekenders. There is a 72-site RV campground with hookups, in addition to eight cabins and a lodge for groups. The resort accepts and holds resupply packages, and usually has a hiker donation box for taking or leaving spare items. There is also a small laundry room available for cleaning your trail-weary clothing. The store carries a variety of cold drinks, popular camp foods, snacks, candy, and ice cream. They also have a counter-service café that serves hearty breakfasts and burgers, pizza, and salads for lunch and dinner. Near the resort the Forest Service operates the **Trapper Creek Campground** (May–October), with 26 single sites and three group sites; all are RV-compatible, but none have hookups.

To get there from the PCT, exit the trail at Pengra Pass and descend the curving dirt road 0.5 mile southeast. Continue past a couple side trails that branch off the road to a railroad track. Cross the tracks, veering right (south), to continue down the dirt road to meet paved FR 5810. Turn right (south) and walk the road 1 mile to the campground and 1.3 miles to the resort. (See appendixes 3 and 4 for more info.)

miles—a glorious sight amid this exposed, often sweltering traverse. The icy-cold creek flows from a high cirque that typically holds snow late into the summer and is perfectly refreshing. If you're planning on splitting this leg in half, you may want to consider topping off all your water containers here in case a dry camp is coming. The trail then bends east, alternating through pockets of shady forest and open slopes, then eventually dips below the treeline. Here you find yourself back under the cool shade of old growth, the wide views now behind you—but more huckleberries in front of you. Again the trail bends, now north, wrapping around the eastern extension of Diamond Peak, descending gradually across the contour of a steep slope. Just shy of 49.8 miles, a bootpath cuts off to the right (east) 30 yards to an exquisite sheltered campsite at the edge of a bluff with a wide view of nearer **Maiden Peak** and farther **Three Sisters** (**Camp 19**); this site has a fire ring, logs for sitting, and room for a few tents. If you're going to split the leg in half—if you have enough water—this would be a great place to do it.

The trail undulates northeast, continuing its course around Diamond Peak, now on its northeastern flank. Occasional breaks in the trees permit views back up at the northern summit point; otherwise the trail crosses one pleasant pocket meadow after another, one of them especially delightful and parklike, brimming with heather and huckleberry, with a peek at 7100-foot **Mount Yoran** ahead. The trail then crosses a rocky drainage (no longer flowing) followed by another short ascent up a rocky ridge, then levels and circuits a clear, pretty pond in a shallow basin at 51.4 miles ⭘. A small campsite with room for one tent can be found in the trees on the east side (**Camp 20**)—another fine selection for splitting the leg in half. Here, the trail turns north again, still descending, passes another small pond (which, by the end of summer is likely a mud puddle), then contours down a steep ridge, just below the crest. At 52.2 miles, the PCT comes to the junction with the **Mount Yoran Trail** (#3683), which cuts off to the left (west) to cross the crest through a low saddle and proceed on to Divide and Notch lakes.

At this point, you've left behind the expansive views of the high country and have entered the forested lakes region of the Diamond Peak Wilderness, an area containing more than a hundred lakes, tarns, and ponds. You won't see them all, but—unlike the earlier portion of this section, or any sections prior—the PCT passes or grants nearby access to many of the pleasant and picturesque pools, with no shortage of clean, clear water. Sticking below the crest, and following the descending, contouring traverse of two unnamed buttes, the trail winds northeast and skirts **Lils Lake**; at 53.8 miles, a steep path descends right (south) to the lakeshore below. Shortly thereafter you'll glimpse **Hidden Lake** ⭘ through the trees; the trail continues around to the north side where, near 54.4 miles, a bootpath breaks off for 50 yards to the lakeshore and a small campsite surrounded by huckleberries with room for two tents (**Camp 21**).

The trail continues its pleasant meandering, passing a few kettles and small ponds, then meets **Deer Creek Trail** (#3672) at 54.8 miles, near a large lily pond. Shortly beyond, the PCT comes to the south end of **Arrowhead Lake**. The lake has no easy, obvious access, and requires a short bushwhack over jumbled and rocky terrain. After passing a large, murky lily pond, the trail then bends east, making another short, moderate descent,

Floral fireworks come in many varieties on the sunny, rocky plains below Diamond Peak, including pink mountain heather.

Shelter Cove at Odell Lake makes a fine place to kick up your weary trail feet and relax.

then north. The surrounding forest transitions from older to younger, verdant to parched; ground cover shifts from lupine and whortleberry to dry, woody debris. At 56.8 miles, a side trail branches off right (south) to unseen **Midnight Lake** in a deep bowl below the crest—a popular destination for summer day hikers and winter snowshoers. Just 0.2 mile farther, the PCT reaches another trail junction, this one for the **Bechtel Trail** (#4366), which breaks off left (north) for 0.5 mile to the Bechtel trailhead and shelter. (This is part of the Gold Lake Sno-Park trail system.)

Now on the leg's homestretch, the PCT makes a steady contouring descent through a closed-in forest corridor along the steep north slope of an unnamed (and unseen) butte; lining the trail is an abundance of lupine, rhododendron, and mountain strawberry. The descent eases to a shallower grade and winds down to exit the wilderness at a trailhead and road crossing at **Pengra Pass** at 58.2 miles. If you're ending or resupplying at **Shelter Cove** on Odell Lake, here is where you get off the PCT and descend southeastward on dirt forest road to FR 5810 for 1.8 miles to the resort. If you're ending the section at the **Willamette Pass Trailhead** on the Willamette Highway (OR 58)—or continuing on to Section 4—cross the forest road and continue northeast on the PCT for another 1.8 miles, skirting the south slope of Eagle Rock. Carefully cross the highway and proceed to the short spur trail at 60 miles that leads to the large parking area behind an ODOT service building. Now that you've experienced a taste of what the PCT offers through Oregon's Central Cascades area, you're likely to want more. When you're ready, move on to Section 4.

CAMP-TO-CAMP MILEAGE

Summit Lake Camp to Camp 17 . . . . 0.7
Camp 17 to Camp 18 . . . . 1.1
Camp 18 to Camp 19 . . . . 5.3
Camp 19 to Camp 20 . . . . 1.6
Camp 20 to Camp 21 . . . . 3.0
Camp 21 to Pengra Pass junction 3.8
Pengra Pass junction to Trapper Creek
    Campground (off PCT) 1.7
Pengra Pass junction to Shelter Cove
    Resort (off PCT) 2.0
Pengra Pass junction to Willamette Pass
    Trailhead 1.8

4/5A ALTERNATE
WINDIGO PASS TO WILLAMETTE PASS
(VIA OREGON SKYLINE TRAIL)

DISTANCE 20.1 miles

ELEVATION GAIN/LOSS
+1490 feet/–2430 feet

HIGH POINT 5930 feet

CONNECTING TRAILS AND ROADS
Windigo Pass Road (FR 60),
Oldenberg Lake Trail (#45), Summit Lake
Trail (#46), Windy Lakes Trail (#50),
Whitefish Creek Trail (#42),
Metolius–Windigo Trail (#99), Crater Butte
Trail (#44), FR 5810 (to Shelter Cove)

ON THE TRAIL

A popular alternate route to Legs 4 and 5 on the
PCT is to take the old **Oregon Skyline Trail**.
This route parallels the PCT to the east, from
Windigo Pass to Odell Lake. This alternate route
trims almost 10 miles off the section's total distance, and reduces the cumulative elevation gain
by nearly 2000 feet. In addition, it offers much
more near-trail access to water, including Nip
and Tuck lakes, Oldenberg Lake, Bingham Lakes,
and Diamond View Lake. The cherry on top of
this alternate route is that halfway through the
stretch the trail skirts Crescent Lake, with access
to several lakeside campgrounds. The downside

If it's a hot, dry summer, consider a detour on the Oregon Skyline Trail to Crescent Lake.

A PCT hiker taking a detour on the Oregon Skyline Trail

to taking this route—besides not hiking the PCT—is missing out on the traverse of Cowhorn Mountain, Summit Lake, and the passage below the spectacularly scenic Diamond Peak. If the summer you're hiking is especially brutal heatwise, you may want to consider this option for its access to water alone.

From Windigo Pass, access the Oregon Skyline Trail by walking Windigo Pass Road (FR 60) east for 0.6 mile to the **Oldenberg Lake Trail** (#45). The gently undulating trail takes off northeast through mixed forest. A little over 2 miles along, it drops into a shallow basin containing **Nip and Tuck lakes ⬤**, ascends to the trail's high point, then descends to a junction on the southwest shore of **Oldenberg Lake (Camp) ⬤** at 4.3 miles. Here, the **Summit Lake Trail** (#46) branches west for 10.9 miles, past the **Windy Lakes**, to the east side of Summit Lake on FR 6010. Access to large Oldenberg Lake is easy, and dispersed campsites can be found around the lakeshore. The trail then

descends north, passing **Bingham Meadow** and winding between a few of the **Bingham Lakes ⬤**, where side trails grant water access.

The OST continues its gentle downgrade, meandering easily northwest past small **Pinewan Lake,** then loops through dry forest to come parallel to **Crescent Lake Road**, just downslope to the right (east). Shortly past the 9-mile mark, about halfway between Windigo Pass and Odell Lake, a short spur trail branches off right (east) to the road and connects to the large **Spring Campground ⬤**, a short distance southeast. If you're ready to call it a day and enjoy the afternoon on the lake, walk the road 0.5 mile south to the campground access road, then another 0.5 mile to the campground. This 77-site area has vault toilets, potable water, and access to a large, sandy beach for kicking back lakeside.

The trail continues north along the west side of Crescent Lake, paralleling the lake road, and comes to the **Whitefish Horse Camp** at 10.2 miles.

At the north end of the camp, the OST forks left (northwest) as the **Whitefish Creek Trail** (#42); to the right (east), the **Metolius–Windigo Trail** (#99) leads to the **Tranquil Cove Picnic Area**, an ideal place to have lunch on the lake. From this point, the OST proceeds northwest up the **Whitefish Creek** drainage, where it enters the **Diamond Peak Wilderness** and begins traversing the lower flanks of 6948-foot **Redtop Mountain**. The route remains mostly under the cover of dry lodgepole pine forest, eventually bending north. Near 14.7 miles the route crosses the **Crater Butte Trail** (#44), which branches off right (east) to **Fawn Lake** and left (west) to 6902-foot **Crater Butte** and connects with the **Pacific Crest Trail**. The grade then eases and the trail comes alongside a small lake at 15 miles; just shortly past, at 15.3 miles, the OST/Whitefish Creek Trail arrives at pretty **Diamond View Lake**. From this vantage point, you're treated to a picture-perfect view of ragged Diamond Peak to the west (hence the catchy lake name). A few small, dispersed campsites can be found around the lake.

Now the alternate route begins descending again, north, and enters an area forested with spruce and fir trees. Around 18 miles, the trail drops down to follow **Trapper Creek 🚰**, a delightful little creek that sings and splashes as you hike along, and where you'll have several access points to the water. The trail then turns east and eases to a gentler grade for the final 1.5 miles until it crosses a railroad track and meets FR 5810, directly across from the **Shelter Cove Resort** on Odell Lake. It's worth popping into the resort for a quick trip to their store, plentifully stocked with cold drinks, ice cream, and snacks. At this point, 2 miles south of the section's end at **Willamette Pass**, you can conclude your journey at the resort, or reconnect to the PCT by walking the road a short distance northward to a jeep road that climbs off to the left (west). Follow this

See shooting stars during the day! Look for these pretty pink and yellow wildflowers near water and in wet meadows.

road to **Pengra Pass** where the PCT crosses, then continue 1.8 miles northward, traversing below **Eagle Rock** before crossing the Willamette Highway (OR 58). The spur to the Willamette Pass trailhead is just beyond.

CAMP-TO-CAMP MILEAGE

Windigo Pass Road to Oldenberg
    Lake Camp 4.3
Oldenberg Lake Camp to Spring
    Campground junction 4.7
Spring Campground junction to Whitefish
    Horse Camp 1.2
Whitefish Horse Camp to Diamond View
    Lake Camp 5.1
Diamond View Lake Camp to Shelter
    Cove Resort 4.8

WILLAMETTE PASS TO SANTIAM PASS

IF YOU HAD TO CONSOLIDATE all of the best wilderness scenery in Oregon into one stretch of the Pacific Crest Trail, the 93 miles between Willamette Pass and Santiam Pass would be it. This section has it all: old-growth forest, pristine lakes, alpine meadows, glacier-capped peaks, and stark volcanic plains. It ups the ante with plenty of panoramic views, good campsites, and mostly reliable and frequent access to water. Throw in a picturesque mountain resort halfway through the leg where you can send yourself a resupply and chow down on a tasty burger, and things are just golden. And if the full section is too much to tackle in one outing, it can easily be split in two by taking advantage of that aforementioned resort (less than an hour's drive from Bend), and knocking out the first half over one long weekend and the second half over another.

The section divides its time between the **Deschutes National Forest** on the east side of the crest, and the **Willamette National Forest** on the west side. Along the way, it crosses two wilderness areas, all the while remaining on mostly moderate, rolling terrain with few big climbs. The general bearing is just slightly northeastward, mostly tracking along the spine, or very near the Crest, with few significant lateral deviations. Of course, true to Oregon's moniker of "the green tunnel," much of that time is still spent in the trees. But unlike many PCT sections to the south, this one adds in countless lakes and tarns in glacial basins, gads of wildflowers throughout the summer, and berries. If you time your passage just right in later summer, you can practically gorge on juicy huckleberries from start to finish. Who needs views, right?

DISTANCE 93 miles

STATE DISTANCE 216.3–309.3 miles

ELEVATION GAIN/LOSS
+12,260 feet/–12,610 feet

HIGH POINT 6900 feet

BEST TIME OF YEAR Aug–Sept

PCTA SECTION LETTERS E, F

LAND MANAGERS Willamette National Forest (Waldo Lake Wilderness, Three Sisters Wilderness, west), Deschutes National Forest (Three Sisters Wilderness, east)

PASSES AND PERMITS NW Forest Pass required for parking at Willamette Pass, Elk Lake, and Santiam Pass trailheads; limited-entry permit required to hike in Three Sisters and Mount Washington wilderness areas; for more information about PCT permit requirements, visit www.pctoregon.com/pct-info/permits.

MAPS AND APPS
▪ National Geographic Oregon North 1004, maps 11–17
▪ Halfmile PCT: Oregon E1–F3
▪ Guthook PCT: Oregon

Opposite: *The Three Sisters Wilderness packs more stunning scenery than any other stretch on the PCT in Oregon. Take your time, and soak it all in.*

LEGS

1. Willamette Pass to Bobby Lake
2. Bobby Lake to Irish Lake
3. Irish Lake to Cliff Lake
4. Cliff Lake to Elk Lake
5. Elk Lake to Mesa Meadow
6. Mesa Meadow to Sunshine Meadow
7. Sunshine Meadow to McKenzie Pass
8. McKenzie Pass to Santiam Pass

The first half of Section 4, from Odell Lake to Elk Lake, begins just east of the Waldo Lake Wilderness in mostly mid-elevation forest. The first few legs are the slow and steady buildup for what's to come. It starts with the longest sustained climb of the whole section—a very moderate 1200 feet over 5 miles. How's that for a cakewalk? The route then traces the Crest through pleasant forest on easy terrain. A few big views are offered up, with a few more available from short side trips. As soon as the trail crosses into the **Three Sisters Wilderness** and enters the **Cascade Lakes Area**, you'll effortlessly traipse from one pleasant forested pool to the next—many with very nice campsites. There are also numerous opportunities for exploring some of the adjacent lake basins—**Winopee Lake** and **Mink Lake**—if you want to extend your trip by a day or two. Then finish the first half at **Elk Lake Resort**, where you can camp, eat, drink, resupply, clean up, and even take some time to paddle around the lake, all while enjoying epic mountain views—a preview of what comes next.

The second half of the section is the icing on Oregon's cake. This is where you spend the next few legs traversing the west side of the **Three Sisters**, three 10,000-plus-foot volcanic peaks all frosted with icy glaciers and lined up in a row—a very unusual and unique formation in the state. The trail changes dramatically with its passage by each, where you'll experience pumice flats, alpine meadows, glacial streams, volcanic plateaus, forested ridges, and jagged lava flows. You may just go into scenery overload—better bring extra memory cards for your camera. All the while, the trail maintains its very moderate passage, with undemanding ascents and leisurely descents between enjoyable strolls where your only concerns are trying to remember the name of the purple wildflowers (likely lupine—it's everywhere!) carpeting one idyllic meadow after the next.

The section wraps up by leaving the mountains and forests behind and crossing a moonscape of volcanic lava rock that showcases the building blocks of the Cascades. Here, the trail weaves through lava flows and around tall cinder cones where little water can be found among the porous surface, and only the heartiest trees, shrubs, and wildflowers eke out their existence fully exposed to the elements. Tolkien buffs will conjure countless landscape likenesses to well-known settings within Middle Earth. This last stretch of the section is the most challenging, not so much for the terrain, which remains moderate to easy, but more for the exposure and lack of accessible water. In the end, however, it is the perfect way to wrap up such a splendid section of trail, by witnessing how fire is both the origin and climax of this dynamic environment.

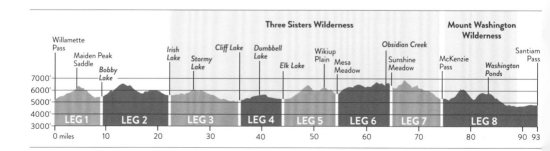

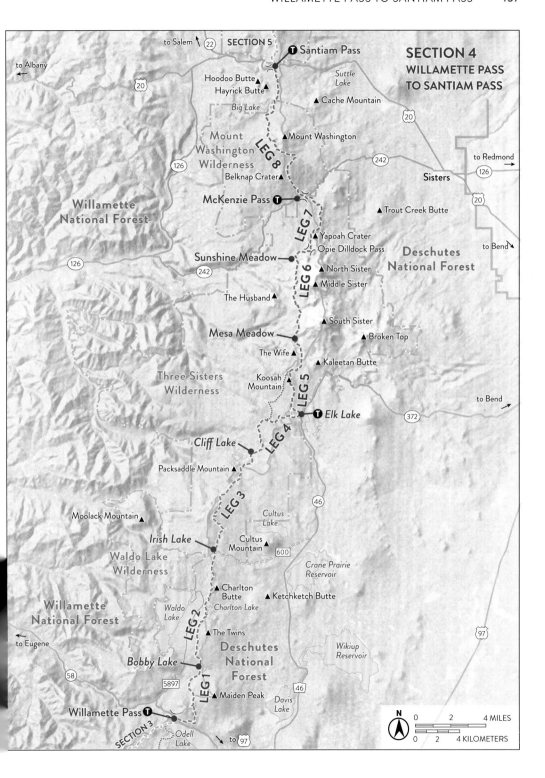

to Salem ↑ (22)   SECTION 5   🛑 Santiam Pass

SECTION 4
**WILLAMETTE PASS
TO SANTIAM PASS**

to Albany ←

(20)

Hoodoo Butte ▲
Hayrick Butte ▲

Big Lake

*Suttle
Lake*

▲ Cache Mountain

(20)

**Mount
Washington
Wilderness**

LEG 8

▲ Mount Washington

(126)

(242)

Sisters

to Redmond →
(126)

Belknap Crater ▲

McKenzie Pass 🛑

LEG 7

▲ Trout Creek Butte

**Willamette
National Forest**

(20)

to Bend ↘

▲ Yapoah Crater
Opie Dilldock Pass

Sunshine Meadow •

(126)

(242)

LEG 6

▲ North Sister
▲ Middle Sister

**Deschutes
National Forest**

The Husband ▲

▲ South Sister

Mesa Meadow •

The Wife ▲

▲ Broken Top

▲ Kaleetan Butte

**Three Sisters
Wilderness**

Koosah
Mountain

LEG 5

to Bend →

🛑 *Elk Lake*

(372)

Cliff Lake •

LEG 4

Packsaddle Mountain ▲

LEG 3

(46)

Moolack Mountain ▲

*Cultus
Lake*

Irish Lake •

Cultus
Mountain ▲

(600)

**Waldo Lake
Wilderness**

*Crane Prairie
Reservoir*

▲ Charlton
Butte
Charlton Lake

▲ Ketchketch Butte

**Willamette
National Forest**

*Waldo
Lake*

LEG 2

▲ The Twins

to Eugene ←

**Deschutes
National
Forest**

*Wikiup
Reservoir*

(97)

Bobby Lake •

(58)

[5897]

LEG 1

▲ Maiden Peak

*Davis
Lake*

(46)

Willamette Pass 🛑

SECTION 3

*Odell
Lake*

to → (97)

N
0   2   4 MILES
0   2   4 KILOMETERS

Reese Lake, high on the volcanic plateau between South and Middle Sister, offers good camping, cool swimming, and picture-perfect views.

All this natural splendor comes with a price: trail companions, of the two-legged and six-legged variety. Because of its proximity to large urban areas east and west of the Cascades (Bend, Eugene, Salem) and its relatively easy access—not to mention the draw of outstanding scenery from nearly 4000 miles of trails—Oregon's central Cascade mountain and lake regions draw a large number of hikers, backpackers, and campers. The other form of company you should be prepared for are the tiny buzzing kind, especially in early summer. With all the water in the lake basins, and all the snowmelt running out of the mountains, mosquitoes are plentiful—and ravenous.

With such outstanding and popular scenery through this section, it's important to follow Leave No Trace practices and leave as minimal an impact as possible in this very heavily used region. In order to preserve these wild and scenic lands for the next generation of PCT hikers to enjoy—and the generations after them—it's up to all of us to be good stewards of Oregon's wilderness and the trails that explore them.

ACCESS
Willamette Pass
From Eugene, take I-5 exit 188 for the Willamette Highway (OR 58) east. Drive 62 miles to the

Pacific Crest Trailhead on the north side of the highway, just past the Willamette Pass ski area.

From Bend, drive south on US 97 for 46 miles. Turn right (west) on Crescent Road for 12 miles to the junction with OR 58. Turn right (west) and continue 10.5 miles to the trailhead, shortly past Odell Lake.

Elk Lake Resort

From Bend, take US 97 exit 139 and travel 1.5 miles west on SW Reed Market Road. At the roundabout with the Cascade Lakes National Scenic Byway, (OR 46) take the third exit, following signs for Mount Bachelor. Proceed 30 miles west, passing the ski resort and eventually curving south around Devils Lake. Shortly beyond, the resort is on the east side of the highway, with a large trailhead parking area directly across on the west side of the highway.

Santiam Pass

From Salem, take I-5 exit 253 for OR 22; turn and drive east for 80 miles. Continue east on US 20/OR 126 for another 5.4 miles to the signed PCT

Trailhead; turn left onto the short spur to the parking roundabout.

From Bend, drive 19 miles north on US 20 to the town of Sisters; continue west on US 20/OR 126 for 20 miles to the trailhead.

NOTES
Services

Near the Willamette Pass trailhead, **Shelter Cove Resort** on Odell Lake has plenty of hiker-friendly services, including a well-stocked store and a laundry room, and they will hold resupply packages. Adjacent to the resort is the **Trapper Creek Campground**. The cities nearest this trailhead are Eugene, 62 miles west, and Bend, 68 miles northeast. Midway through the section, **Elk Lake Resort** is a popular PCT hiker respite with a campground, cabins, restaurant, and showers, and they will hold resupply packages. Near the end of the section, Big Lake Youth Camp offers limited services and will hold resupply packages. If continuing your hike into Section 5, this is the last resupply location for nearly 50 miles. At the northern trailhead at

There are wildflowers aplenty across the Three Sisters Wilderness, including big white Washington lilies.

SUGGESTED ITINERARIES

The following distances do not include off-PCT miles (up to 1.3 miles) to water sources, campsites, alternate routes, or resupply locations. For more information about trail distances, see How to Use This Guide. For the eight-day itinerary, you can break the last day down even further by hiking from McKenzie Pass to Camp 25 at Washington Ponds (8.8 miles), then finishing to Santiam Pass the following day—be prepared for a dry camp.

8 DAYS

		Miles
Day 1	Willamette Pass to Bobby Lake	9.5
Day 2	Bobby Lake to Irish Lake	13.0
Day 3	Irish Lake to Cliff Lake	13.6
Day 4	Cliff Lake to Elk Lake	8.4
Day 5	Elk Lake to Mesa Meadow	10.2
Day 6	Mesa Meadow to Sunshine Meadow	10.3
Day 7	Sunshine Meadow to McKenzie Pass	9.5
Day 8	McKenzie Pass to Santiam Pass	18.5

7 DAYS

Day 1	Willamette Pass to The Twins	13.4
Day 2	The Twins to Stormy Lake	13.8
Day 3	Stormy Lake to Dumbbell Lake	11.9
Day 4	Dumbbell Lake to Mesa Meadow	15.6
Day 5	Mesa Meadow to Minnie Scott Spring	13.4
Day 6	Minnie Scott Spring to Washington Ponds	15.2
Day 7	Washington Ponds to Santiam Pass	9.7

6 DAYS

Day 1	Willamette Pass to Charlton Lake	17.1
Day 2	Charlton Lake to Stormy Lake	10.1
Day 3	Stormy Lake to Elk Lake	17.3
Day 4	Elk Lake to Reese Lake	14.0
Day 5	Reese Lake to McKenzie Pass	16.0
Day 6	McKenzie Pass to Santiam Pass	18.5

Santiam Pass, the nearest services are in the town of **Sisters**, 20 miles east on US 20. (See appendixes 3 and 4 for more info.)

Camping

Good campsites with water are fairly common through much of the section, the majority being near lakes and perennial creeks. Not all of these campsites meet LNT requirements (100 feet from trail and/or water), so use your best judgment when selecting where to camp. Only one location—the camp area in Sunshine Meadow, in the Obsidian Limited Entry Area—requires an overnight permit. (See Passes and Permits in the introduction for more info.)

Water

Water is fairly plentiful and reliable through the majority of this section, with recommended camp areas beginning and ending at good sources, either in the form of lakes or perennial creeks. The exception to this comes at the end of the section where the PCT crosses the lava beds and burned forests of the Mount Washington Wilderness in a 16-mile dry stretch that can be quite brutal in summer for its heat and exposure.

1 WILLAMETTE PASS TO BOBBY LAKE

DISTANCE 9.5 miles

ELEVATION GAIN/LOSS
+1580 feet/–1240 feet

HIGH POINT 6360'

CONNECTING TRAILS AND ROADS
Willamette Highway (OR 58), Maiden Lake
Trail (#3841), Douglas Horse Pasture Trail
(#4382), Maiden Peak Trail (#3681), Bobby
Lake Trail (#3663, west), Bobby Lake Trail
(#40, east)

ON THE TRAIL

From Willamette Pass, the Pacific Crest Trail climbs easily to a cluster of pretty, forested lakes with ample camping opportunities. If you begin on a summer weekend, you will likely have lots of company for the first few miles. Past the lakes, the crowds will fade away as you journey deeper into the Willamette National Forest. This slightly shorter leg remains forested for much of the way, but a few viewpoints offer wider looks over the area you're crossing. Access to water is not so much an issue as it is in previous sections; however, it can present the problem of mosquitoes—*lots of them!*

The sparkling Rosary Lakes, a few miles from the Willamette Pass trailhead, are a worthy destination unto themselves.

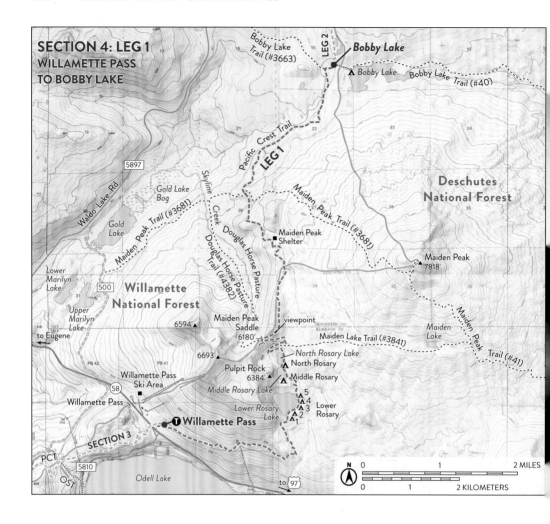

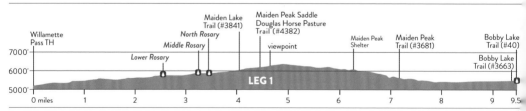

—if you journey into this area too early in the season (e.g., early July). The leg ends at a pretty lake just a short distance off the PCT, and sets you up for your entry into the Three Sisters Wilderness.

Before getting underway, be sure to fill out your wilderness permit. The Forest Service uses the information collected from these permits to identify how many people are hiking in the area and where they're coming from to do it. This in turn helps them secure funding for trail maintenance and upkeep—which you'll be thankful for when you don't have to bushwhack around blowdown

FOREST TRAIL MAINTENANCE

"Blowdown" and "deadfall" are terms commonly used to describe trees that have fallen across trails or on the forest floor. Burned sections of forest are usually littered with blowdown and deadfall as the fire weakens the soil securing the roots, making charred trees extremely susceptible to wind and gravity. Where a slice of a fallen tree has been cut away to allow hikers unimpeded passage is referred to as a "log-out." Depending on the area and the size of the tree, log-outs are done either by chain saw or crosscut saw. Trail maintenance crews carry this heavy equipment in by horse or by hand. If you happen across a trail crew while hiking, announce your presence so you don't sneak up on them—and be sure to thank them for the fine and challenging job they're doing to keep the trail clear of obstructions.

and deadfall. Once you're ready to go, take the trailhead spur 100 yards north to its junction with the PCT, set your GPS receiver odometer to 0, and plunge forward. Here, the rich forest of fir, pine, and hemlock welcomes you with a lush display of mosses, maidenhair fern, mountain strawberry, pearly everlasting, huckleberry, and lupine. The trail is soft and duffy, making the initial gentle ascent easy and enjoyable.

The trail climbs east, contouring upward on a south-facing slope. About a mile on, the forest becomes noticeably drier, with debris, deadfall, and log-outs littering the wooded floor. The trail then bends north, leveling to a pleasant walk in increasingly greener surroundings, mounts a small rise, and comes to the south shore of **Lower Rosary Lake (Camp)** ⦿ at 2.6 miles. The largest and prettiest of the Rosary Lakes, the lower lake is a vivid blue-green pool flanked on its west side by the steep slopes below 6384-foot **Pulpit Rock**. The PCT makes a sharp right (east) turn to circuit the east side of the

lake, passing several idyllic campsites with easy lake access over the next 0.5 mile. Camps contain fire rings, well-positioned logs for benches, and space for up to four tents in some of the larger sites.

The trail crosses the lake's rocky outlet channel (which usually diminishes later in the summer), passes one more good campsite, and begins ascending north on a moderately exposed slope. The trail levels at the forested shore of **Middle Rosary Lake (Camp)** ⦿ at 3.3 miles, where Pulpit Rock rises directly above; listen for pikas chirping in the talus below the peak. A bootpath breaks off to the left (west) to head around the middle lake's west shore to a secluded campsite; the PCT continues along the lake's east shore, the trail lined with huckleberry and heather. Approaching 3.4 miles, on a slight rise between Middle and **North Rosary Lake (Camp)** ⦿ is a large camp area with fire rings, log benches, and enough flat space to accommodate several tents. As opposed to the partial seclusion of the lower lake's individual campsites, this location is more of a community space with little privacy, but easy access to both the middle and upper lakes.

The PCT continues along the east side of the upper lake, then bends west to begin switchbacking up the increasingly more exposed, manzanita- and fireweed-draped northern slope above the lake. Halfway up the second switchback, at 4.1 miles, the **Maiden Lake Trail** (#3841) veers off to the right (southeast). At the top of the third switchback, at 4.5 miles, the PCT once again meets the Cascade Crest at a crossroads on 6180-foot **Maiden Peak Saddle**, marked by a large, weathered sign.

TRAIL TRIVIA

The **Rosary Lakes** were named for their resemblance to a string of beads. Curiously, the designator of these lakes did not think to keep the names of the lakes consistent with one another, otherwise they might be named Lower, Middle, and Upper Rosary, or South, Middle, and North Rosary.

A short walk east of the PCT, the Maiden Peak Shelter is a decent place to take a break.

Unfortunately, there's not much of a view from this high point. The **Douglas Horse Pasture Trail** (#4382) heads off to the west (see alternate route) while the PCT continues its switchbacking ascent. Nearing 4.7 miles, a faint bootpath right (south) leads a few paces to a rocky outcrop overlooking the Rosary Lakes below and Odell Lake in the distance. The PCT then reenters shady forest, contouring up around the east side of a nameless hill, and reaches the leg's high point at 4.9 miles as it returns to its northward heading. You'll get the sparest of glimpses of 7818-foot **Maiden Peak** through the trees.

ALTERNATE ROUTE: DOUGLAS HORSE PASTURE TRAIL

The Douglas Horse Pasture Trail (#4382), formerly a portion of the Oregon Skyline Trail, and the PCT prior to 1980, descends west from Maiden Peak Saddle into the valley below the northern slopes of the Willamette Pass Ski Area. There, it turns north to follow Skyline Creek down the valley until it meets the Maiden Peak Trail (#3681), 0.6 miles west of the PCT. Along the way, it crosses the creek twice and passes several good campsites.

As the trail begins its gentle descent, you may start to notice the blue diamond markers nailed high in the trees, indicating that this section of trail is used as a winter ski route. They remain fairly consistent for the next couple miles as the PCT continues north down the ridge, then meanders northwest into drier forest. At 6.3 miles, a side trail cuts off right (east) to the **Maiden Peak Shelter**, with a fire ring outside and a woodstove and chairs inside; unfortunately, there's no water nearby, and the adjacent terrain is not ideal for camping. Just 0.1 mile farther, another side trail—this one signed—leads to the same shelter. Continuing on, the PCT curves west through mostly healthy forest, with lupine lining the trailsides. Bearing north, the trail then traverses a west-facing slope high above the Gold Lake valley. At 7.2 miles, the PCT crosses the **Maiden Peak Trail** (#3681), which descends left (west) to the Douglas Horse Pasture Trail/OST and Gold Lake, and ascends right (east) to the summit of its namesake crest.

The PCT then tracks northwest in nicer forest carpeted with grouse whortleberry (smell blueberry muffins?), lupine, and mountain strawberry. Still on the west-facing slope, you'll get a partial view of the wide valley containing Gold Lake and Gold Lake Bog. The trail then levels in a more open, parklike section of forest, for a pleasant stroll all the way to the **Bobby Lake Trail** (#3663) junction at

MAIDEN PEAK

The highest point in Oregon's southern Central Cascades, between Diamond Peak to the south and Mount Bachelor to the north, Maiden Peak is an old shield volcano capped with a steep-sided cinder cone. From its junction with the PCT, the Maiden Peak Trail (#3681) climbs 3 miles and 2000 feet to a prime lookout point. The trail rises through fir and hemlock forest, then steepens as it climbs the lower flanks of the cindery summit cone, where it meets the other Maiden Peak Trail (#41) at a T-junction. Turn left (north) and continue 0.3 mile past gnarled whitebark pines and a small crater to the 7818-foot summit plateau that, until 1958, was the location of a Forest Service fire lookout. The expansive view from the top looks south over the glaciated basin containing Davis, Odell, and Crescent lakes, and beyond to Diamond Peak and Mount Thielsen; and north in a panorama that extends over Waldo Lake to the Three Sisters and Mount Jefferson. With the shorter mileage of this leg, and an early start, a detour to Maiden Peak's summit is very doable without needing to modify your itinerary.

9.4 miles. The first junction with the Bobby Lake Trail descends left (west) to the trailhead on Waldo Lake Road (FR 5897); the second junction, 0.1 mile farther, leads right (east) to the lakeshore and forested **Bobby Lake Camp ⬤**. (Note: Some maps may show the eastward Bobby Lake Trail as #40 in the Deschutes National Forest.) Now at the end of the leg, follow the lake trail 0.3 mile east, veering right at a fork, to the forested west shore of the lake. A few small, dispersed campsites can be found in the area, some with fire rings, some with logs for sitting; there's easy access to the lake for water or a refreshing dip. Mosquitoes can be a nuisance here in early summer, so be prepared. If there are clouds in the eastern sky, the view across the lake can be particularly colorful at sunrise and sunset.

CAMP-TO-CAMP MILEAGE

Willamette Pass to Lower Rosary Camp 2.6
Lower Rosary Camp to Middle Rosary Camp. . 0.7
Middle Rosary Camp to North Rosary Camp . . 0.1
North Rosary Camp to Bobby Lake junction . . 6.1
Bobby Lake junction to Bobby Lake Camp
   (off PCT) 0.3

2 BOBBY LAKE TO IRISH LAKE

DISTANCE 13 miles

ELEVATION GAIN/LOSS
+1870 feet/−1770 feet

HIGH POINT 6570'

CONNECTING TRAILS AND ROADS
The Twins Trail (#3595/#19), Charlton Lake Trail (#19), Charlton Lake Trail (#3593), FR 4290, Lily Lake Trail (#19.3), Harralson Trail (#4364), FR 600 (to Irish Lake Camp)

ON THE TRAIL

The next leg of the Pacific Crest Trail, from Bobby Lake to Irish Lake, is a pleasantly easy one, rolling gently (after an initial moderate ascent) on through the Willamette National Forest to the southern boundary of the **Three Sisters Wilderness**. Along the way, it skirts Charlton Lake (a popular recreation destination for weekenders), crosses several miles of the recovering Charlton Butte Fire area, then finally enters the southern Cascade Lakes region. Without crossing any major high points or ridges, views are limited to

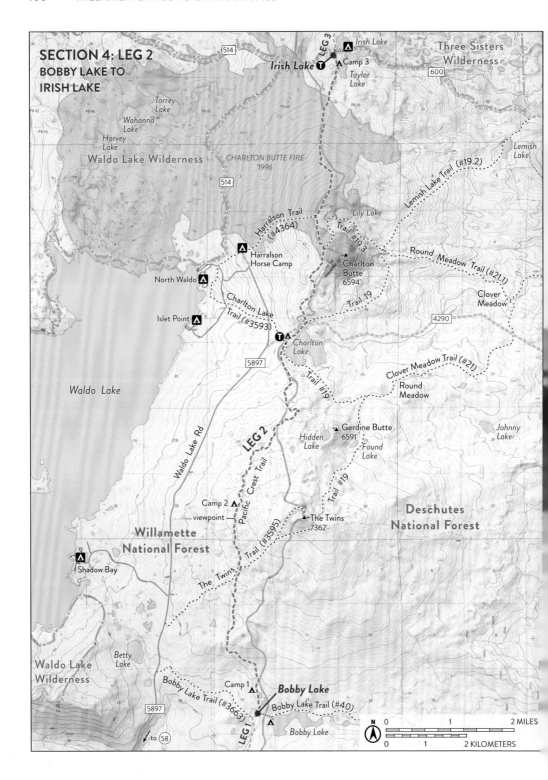

SECTION 4: LEG 2
BOBBY LAKE TO
IRISH LAKE

the surrounding mixed forest and the many lakes along the way—a significant and welcome change over the many miles of waterless trail in southern sections.

Returning to the PCT from Bobby Lake, the trail continues its northward march under cover of hemlock, pine, and fir forest. Shortly past 9.9 miles, the trail skirts a lakelet on the right (east), near which is a small campsite with a decent sitting log and space for a single tent (**Camp 1**) ⬛. Gradually, the trail begins curving northwest up around a forested butte, then turns north and begins a gradual ascent on the lower flank of **The Twins** (which remain largely unseen until you reach the shore of Charlton Lake). At 12.3 miles, the PCT crosses **The Twins Trail** (#3595), which climbs from **Waldo Lake Road** (FR 5897) to the left (west) and continues up right (east) toward The Twins' 7362-foot summit; just below the last stretch to this summit, the trail forks to meet other trails and destinations farther east.

THE TWINS

Named for the gap in the summit crater of this relatively young cinder cone, which has created dual peaks, The Twins rewards hikers with a sweeping panorama north to the Three Sisters, west over Waldo Lake, and south to Diamond Peak. The 3.4-mile roundtrip from the PCT climbs a little more than 1100 feet through mountain hemlock and whitebark pines to the summit viewpoint. Look for blooms of little pink elephant's head in the small meadow between the summit high points.

TRAIL TRIVIA

Named for Judge John B. Waldo, and surrounded on three sides by the Waldo Lake Wilderness, **Waldo Lake** is the second-largest natural mountain lake in Oregon. Filling an immense glacier-carved basin, the 10-square-mile lake and several smaller lakes were originally called the Virgin Lakes and, at one time, Pengra Lake. The PCT remains several miles east of both the lake and wilderness area.

The PCT continues, still ascending, through dry forest, where the slope gets increasingly rocky the higher you climb The Twins' western flank. Around 13.2 miles, look for a faint bootpath that breaks off to the left (west) to an exposed outcrop that offers the only look you'll get at **Waldo Lake** below (unless you opt for one of the summit side trips); less than 0.1 mile farther, the PCT reaches the leg's high point, rolling gently down from here on. As you start down, a small campsite can be found left (west) of the trail at 13.4 miles (**Camp 2**). There's no view or nearby water, but the space is big enough for a couple tents. Continuing on, the meandering trail passes two small, mucky ponds, then winds forward through forest dotted with jumbled volcanic rock mounds. Turning north, the trail reenters vibrant, mossy forest, granting quick peeks at **Charlton Lake** ahead.

In no time, the trail dips down to level ground and meets the **Charlton Lake Trail** (#3593/#19) at 17 miles. The left (#3593, north) branch leads 2 miles to the northeast shore of Waldo Lake; to the right (#19, south), the lake trail wraps around

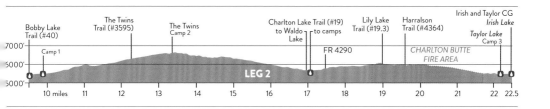

The ghosts of forest past stand as eerie sentinels over a young and thriving new forest in the Charlton Butte burn area.

the south side of Charlton Lake and continues on to Found Lake, Round Meadow, and other destinations east. Just 0.1 mile farther, the PCT crosses the Charlton Lake access trail (**Camp**) ⬤, with trailhead parking to the left (north) and lake access to the right (southeast). The short trail to the water's edge splits to circuit the west half of the lake in either direction. There are numerous campsites dispersed among the trees with fire rings and sitting logs. Too early in the day to call it quits, this spot makes a fine place to enjoy a snack or lunch and refill your water with a fine view across the large lake. The pointed mountain across the lake is 6591-foot **Gerdine Butte**, with the top of The Twins now visible to the south.

Continuing onward, the PCT climbs gently away from Charlton Lake amid dense and mossy old growth. At 17.5 miles it pops out of the forest to cross gravel road FR 4290, pass a junction with Trail #19 to Lemish Lake, then reenters forest. Meandering north, the trail crosses a small burned area with a view of a charred butte ahead, then it's back into the trees for a short stretch, coming at 18.7 miles to the southern edge of the area blackened by the 1996 **Charlton Butte Fire**; the scorched mound to the east is 6594-foot **Charlton Butte**. Far from a desolate, sullied wasteland, the area, after more than 20 years of recovery, is richly vegetated with small lodgepole pines taking hold among an abundance of fireweed, pearly everlasting, and other vibrant species that thrive following a forest wildfire. The trail forward through the burn area is clear and easy to follow. Obviously, much work went into logging out all the burned trees and deadfall to keep the trail open. At 19 miles, an unsigned fork splits the trail where the PCT continues left (west) and the **Lily Lake Trail** (#19.3) branches off to the right (north). When in doubt, look for the chiseled "i" blazes in trees marking the PCT's route.

There comes a short break in the blazed landscape when the trail passes through a small island of forest that survived the fire. Here, at 19.6 miles, the **Harralson Trail** (#4364) branches off to the left (west) to descend to a horse camp at the end of Waldo Lake Road. Then it's onward through the largest area of the burn, the ghosts of still-standing, but long-gone forest rising from a carpet of green, white, yellow, and pink. The scene is at once bleak, beautiful, and fascinating; the trail remains clear, gently winding and rolling along. Eventually, the edge of the burn area comes into view, and at 21.7 miles the PCT reenters mixed forest, descending northeast over an unnamed butte into lower lake country, leaving the crest proper to the west, where it rises north to the sharp ridge of 6893-foot **Irish Mountain**.

In no time, the trail reaches the southern branch of **Taylor Lake (Camp 3)** 🅾. The only access is via a small campsite right of the trail with

CHARLTON BUTTE FIRE

Set alight by a lightning storm in the summer of 1996, the high-intensity Charlton Butte Fire blackened more than 10,400 acres in the Willamette National Forest and Waldo Lake Wilderness, including burning across 3 miles of the Pacific Crest Trail. The area is being allowed to recover naturally, so reforestation is slow. Lodgepole pines, which rely on fire to release the seeds from their cones, adapt early following wildfire, but firs and hemlocks are slower-growing and rely on shade for their saplings to grow. On the exposed terrain around charred snags and remaining matchstick trees, the combination of rain and sun has allowed a variety of shrubs and wildflowers to thrive; at the peak of summer, the hillsides become a kaleidoscope of color.

room for a couple tents at 22.2 miles. Just beyond, at 22.5 miles, the trail crosses **FR 600** on the south side of **Irish Lake**. This fairly remote, modest-sized lake sees the occasional anglers and standup padddleboarders, but the forest road to get here is pretty rough, so it keeps the crowds at bay. Just northeast of the road crossing is a small trailhead parking area, and 0.3 mile east along the road is the small **Irish and Taylor Camp** 🅾, with six tent sites and a vault toilet. Depending on your energy level—and how much time you spent relaxing at Charlton Lake—this makes a good ending point for the day. But if you have a little gas left in the tank, it's worth proceeding on a few more miles into the next leg to a great camp at **Brahma Lake**.

CAMP-TO-CAMP MILEAGE

Bobby Lake junction to Camp 1. . . . . 0.4
Camp 1 to Camp 2. . . . . 3.5
Camp 2 to Charlton Lake Camp 3.7
Charlton Lake Camp to Camp 3 . . . . 5.1
Camp 3 to FR 600 . . . . 0.3
FR 600 to Irish and Taylor Camp (off PCT) . . 0.3

3 IRISH LAKE TO CLIFF LAKE

DISTANCE 13.6 miles

ELEVATION GAIN/LOSS
+1100 feet/–1530 feet

HIGH POINT 6070 feet

CONNECTING TRAILS
Elk Creek Trail (#3510), Winopee Lake
Trail (#16), Snowshoe Lakes Trail (#33),
Mink Lake Trail (#3526), Porky Lake Trail
(#4338), Cliff Lake spur trail

ON THE TRAIL

Lake lovers rejoice! Here is the section of trail
you've been waiting for. The stretch of Pacific
Crest Trail from Irish Lake to Cliff Lake is a comfort cruise through the central section of Oregon's
Cascade Lakes region of the **Three Sisters Wilderness**. Staying below and east of the crest proper
for several miles, this leg is decidedly lacking in
high points and big views. What you get instead
is a minimal ascent followed by mile after mile of
gently rolling downgrade through lush forest as
you pass one tranquil forested lake after another. If
you have additional time in your itinerary, you can
also explore the **Mink Lake Basin** on a network of
short, looping, and connecting side trails that take
in no less than ten additional idyllic azure pools—
many with secluded campsites. However, all this
water also means mosquitoes—*lots of them!*—in
early summer. Get out your bug net.

Beginning the leg at the Three Sisters Wilderness kiosk, on the southwest corner of Irish Lake,
just north of FR 600, fill out your self-register
permit and check the info board for any relevant
notices. The trail begins on level ground, with
glimpses of Irish Lake through the trees. Before you
know it, you're alongside **Riffle Lake (Camp 4)** ◐
at 23.3 miles. A short bootpath cuts right (east) to
a single campsite near the lakeshore. There is room
for a couple tents here, with a nice log for sitting
and enjoying the view; water access is fairly easy.
The trail continues north–northeast, an undulating stroll, reaching another small camp, this one
exposed and left (west) of the trail, at 23.7 miles
(**Camp 5**); here, you'll find space for a single tent.
The trail then veers northeast, passing a few small
ponds as it contours up around a forested ridge.

Just beyond this slight rise, the PCT skirts
the south shore of **Brahma Lake** at 25.2 miles. A
narrow, overgrown bootpath breaks off left (north)
to follow the shoreline to **Brahma Lake Camp** ◐,
but it's easier to continue on the PCT another 0.1
mile to a clear and obvious side trail that heads
left (west) just 60 yards to the camp area. The flat,
forested camp area is fairly large and spaced out, on
a small bluff above the lake. There's room for up
to six tents, with two fire rings and plenty of rocks
and logs for sitting; water access is easy for refilling
bottles or taking a refreshing dip. A narrow bootpath follows the lakeshore north from the main
camp area to a secluded single campsite with space
for one tent; the path continues to meet with the
PCT at the north end of the lake.

Following Brahma Lake, the PCT rises gently
northwest around the upper end of the lake and
over its trickling inlet stream. The sun-dappled

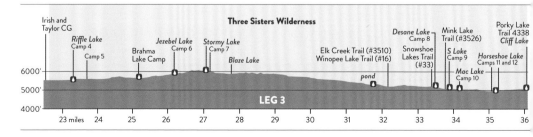

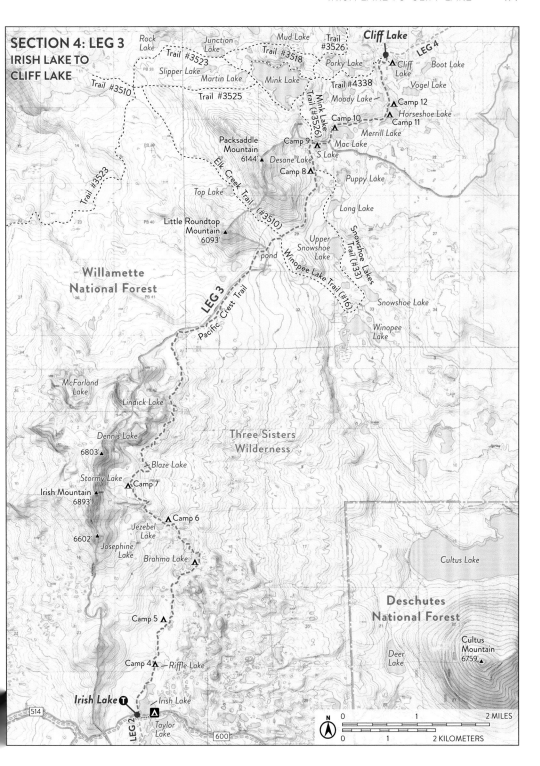

SECTION 4: LEG 3
IRISH LAKE TO
CLIFF LAKE

Rock Lake
Junction Lake
Mud Lake
Cliff Lake
Trail #3523
Slipper Lake
Trail #3518
Trail #3526
LEG 4
Martin Lake
Mink Lake
Porky Lake
Cliff Lake
Boot Lake
Trail #3510
Trail #3525
Trail #4338
Vogel Lake
Moody Lake
Camp 12
Mink Trail (#3526)
Camp 10
Horseshoe Lake
Camp 11
Merrill Lake
Packsaddle Mountain
6144'
Camp 9
Mac Lake
S Lake
Desane Lake
Camp 8
Puppy Lake
Trail #3523
Elk Creek Trail (#3510)
Top Lake
Long Lake
Willamette National Forest
Little Roundtop Mountain
6093'
pond
Upper Snowshoe Lake
Snowshoe Lakes Trail (#33)
Winopee Lake Trail (#6)
Snowshoe Lake
Winopee Lake
LEG 3
Pacific Crest Trail
McFarland Lake
Lindick Lake
Three Sisters Wilderness
Dennis Lake
6803'
Blaze Lake
Stormy Lake
Camp 7
Irish Mountain
6893'
Camp 6
Jezebel Lake
6602'
Brahma Lake
Josephine Lake
Deschutes National Forest
Cultus Lake
Camp 5
Deer Lake
Cultus Mountain
6759'
Camp 4
Riffle Lake
Irish Lake
Irish Lake
514
LEG 2
Taylor Lake
600

N
0   1   2 MILES
0   1   2 KILOMETERS

THREE SISTERS WILDERNESS

The second-largest wilderness area in Oregon, the Three Sisters Wilderness was established as part of the **1964 Wilderness Act.** The area currently encompasses more than 283,000 acres, straddling the Cascade Crest for nearly 30 miles at its widest (east–west), and extending along the range for more than 32 miles, from its boundaries with the Waldo Lake Wilderness to the south and the Mount Washington Wilderness to the north. The originally smaller area grew to its current size after the much-contested French Pete drainage was added in 1978, with a few additions made as part of the **1984 Oregon Wilderness Act.** The wilderness area is contained within the Willamette National Forest on the west side of the Crest, and the Deschutes National Forest on the east side.

Spanning so much area, the wilderness is comprised of highly diverse woodlands and ecosystems, ranging from low-elevation forests of Douglas-fir, Engelmann spruce, and western redcedar on the wetter west side of the mountains to ponderosa and lodgepole pines on the drier east side. The central higher elevations are home to mountain hemlock, subalpine fir, and whitebark pines. Intermingled among all this woodland are countless lakes, tarns, and ponds, and wildflower-filled alpine meadows. These contrast sharply to the barren, rugged lava flows and cinder cones that represent the area's relatively recent (geologically speaking) volcanic activity. The Three Sisters volcanoes form the centerpiece of the wilderness, along with several subordinate flanking volcanoes. Each measuring more than 10,000 feet in elevation and flanked by several active glaciers, the Three Sisters are a unique conglomerate of glaciated volcanic peaks, the like of which is unseen anywhere else in Oregon.

Several good highways border the wilderness, but the only access is via 260 miles of trails that crisscross the area, many leading to the picturesque lakes and meadows found on the flanks of the higher mountains. Of these, 53 miles of the Pacific Crest Trail navigate the entire length of the wilderness. Residing among the trees and meadows are creatures great and small. Black bears, black-tailed deer, and Roosevelt elk are the most common, though rarely seen. Seen even less are cougars, bobcats, coyotes, wolverines, and martens. Birds are plentiful, including woodpeckers, grouse, hummingbirds, owls, and bald eagles, and wildflowers are countless. All this draws a large number of hikers, backpackers, and campers to the area, and their impact is becoming apparent. The Forest Service is taking measures to mitigate some of this impact, but they ask that the public be good stewards of the land and follow Leave No Trace practices to help preserve the area's natural beauty.

forest abounds with lush flora: whortleberry, huckleberry, and strawberry. The trail winds forward, weaving around small and large ponds, then rises to **Jezebel Lake (Camp 6)** ⦿ at 26.2 miles; a small camp can be found amid the huckleberry and beargrass right of the trail. The trail continues its moderate ascent northwest up a drainage on good tread, making a short jog around a lateral ridge off Irish Mountain. The trail passes a murky pond to the right (east) and a grassy meadow to the left (west), then comes to a slight crest above the vivid blue-green **Stormy Lake** ⦿ at 27.1 miles; a side trail descends left (northwest) to the shoreline. The view across the lake is exceptional and the gentle slope above the water makes a fine place to break for a snack. Continuing around the lake, the trail crosses the lake's outlet, after which a bootpath breaks off left (west) to a

Morning mist hangs over Brahma Lake, where a large camp area invites PCT hikers to take a load off.

sheltered campsite above the northeast shore, with room for up to three tents (**Camp 7**). From this campsite, you have a view of rocky, 6893-foot **Irish Mountain** poking above the wooded canopy across the lake.

At this point you've reached the high point of the leg. The trail now curves east, descending the glaciated plateau holding Stormy Lake, then bends northwest to skirt **Blaze Lake** at 27.7 miles, then a smaller lake, and then an unappealing black pond. By now, huckleberries are everywhere. If you're passing through in season, you can enjoy a sweet and juicy snack. The PCT gradually descends, rolling gently northeast; upslope to the west, Dennis and Lindick lakes lay hidden in their shallow, crater-like basins.

SIDE TRIP: WINOPEE AND SNOWSHOE LAKES

Have the time and want to visit more lakes? Cut off the PCT onto the Winopee Lake Trail (#16) for a 4-mile side loop that meets back up with the PCT a mile ahead. The trail circuits a forested butte to large, marshy Winopee Lake. At a junction, veer left (north) on the Snowshoe Lakes Trail (#33) and stroll past Snowshoe, Upper Snowshoe, Long, and Puppy lakes, as well as along and over several creeks and drainages. The trail turns west past Puppy Lake to reconnect with the PCT at Desane Lake.

An old Pacific Crest Trail blaze marks the route through the Three Sisters Wilderness.

Following another quick ascent, the trail crests another lateral ridge, then plunges down into dense forest, becoming rough and rocky for a short stretch.

The trail levels onto a wide, once-glaciated plateau called **Cougar Flat** and passes a small, murky pond on the right (east), before bending east and passing a nicer lakelet in a shallow basin (no direct access). Returning northeast, the trail meets back up with the crest proper, walking the boundary between the Willamette (west) and Deschutes (east) national forests, and makes another descent amid viewless forest—but you're likely too busy looking down for berries, rather than up for views. At 31.8 miles, the trail pops out of the trees beside a large, clear, shallow pond ◐ resting in a wide, grassy meadow. (Some maps refer to this pond as Tadpole Lake.) There are no obvious campsites here, but a makeshift primitive site wouldn't be difficult to find on the flat ground nearby. The PCT then ducks back into the trees and makes a short,

gentle ascent to traverse the lower base of 6093-foot **Little Roundtop Mountain**, then descends to a four-way junction at 32.2 miles. Here, the **Elk Creek Trail** (#3510) heads off to the left (northwest) and the **Winopee Lake Trail** (#16) cuts off to the right (south).

Continuing on, the still closed-in and viewless forest becomes strikingly dry and barren, the shrubbery and berries now gone, replaced by debris and deadfall. It makes a short ascent to cross the lower slope of 6144-foot **Packsaddle Mountain** to the left (west, unseen), then descends, turning north, and reenters greener forest, the floor thick with huckleberry, bunchberry, and beargrass. Through the trees to the right you'll spy a small lakelet. Shortly past, at 33.4 miles, is the junction with the **Snowshoe Lakes Trail** (#33) which connects to the PCT from the right (east; see Snowshoe side trip). The trail then skirts the east side of **Desane Lake (Camp 8)** ◐, where a small, open camp can be found left (west) of the

174

rail at 33.5 miles. This site has nice sitting logs and can accommodate a couple tents; there's easy water access just below the camp, and the wooded lake is an agreeable sight. Past the lake and following a short descent, the PCT then meets the **Mink Lake Trail** (#3526).

Sticking with the PCT, the path ahead is equally crowded with idyllic forested lakes and good campsites for the next few miles. Turning east, the trail jogs west of the crest and immediately comes alongside **S Lake (Camp 9) ◐**; at 33.9 miles there is a good campsite right (south) of the trail near the lakeshore. The trail then curves north to **Mac Lake (Camp 10) ◐**, a large, pretty pool with a forested peninsula on its south side. The PCT remains high on the forested slope above this lake, but a side trail at 34.2 miles descends to the lakeshore and a large, open camp area with room for up to four tents. Passing Mac Lake, the trail continues, gradually descending and thick to the sides with berries and lupine, to round **Merrill Lake**. It then passes through a short section of drier forest with wide sky overhead, then reenters shady forest and comes to the west side of appropriately named **Horseshoe Lake (Camps 11 and 12) ◐**, backed on its east side by a steep, forested slope. At 35.1 miles, a side trail right (southeast) leads to a decent campsite with room for a few tents. An even nicer camp, with a great view across the lake, can be found by proceeding another 0.2 mile to the north side of the lake. This site has sitting logs and room for a couple tents; both sites have easy water access.

The PCT then bears northwest and passes **Moody Lake**, seen through the trees below to the left (west), then begins a gently ascending contour along a steep, west-facing slope, dense and overgrown with ferns and thimbleberry. The trail meets the top of the plateau and heads east to the base of a large, rocky jumble at 36.1 miles. Here, the PCT intersects the **Porky Lake Trail** (#4338), which descends to the left (west; see Mink Lake side trip). Just a few paces ahead, an unsigned trail breaks right (east) off the PCT—this is the trail to **Cliff Lake** and the end of the leg. Follow this spur 0.2 mile east along the lake's drainage, first beside the base of a rocky slope, then through dense forest

SIDE TRIP: MINK LAKE

Another worthwhile detour is the Mink Lake Trail, which leads less than a mile north to its namesake watery pool, the second-largest wilderness lake in Oregon and the headwaters of the South Fork McKenzie River; a shoreline trail circuits the entire lake with access to numerous well-used campsites. The lake loop also connects to no less than eight other trails and connectors for exploring several additional nearby lakes, including Martin, Slipper, Junction, Plumb, Mud, Porky, Goose, Corner, and Gnat lakes; dispersed campsites can be found at many of these. It's easy to customize an alternate route around a few or many of these lakes and meet back up with the PCT several miles ahead.

to **Cliff Lake Camp ◐**. Above the moderately accessible lakeshore is a wood-and-stone backcountry shelter near a wide camp area that can accommodate several tents. There's a large fire ring in the central area and a few logs for sitting. The view across the lake is a nice one, with rocky slopes intermingled with the forested shoreline. Listen for chirping pikas and yipping coyotes as you cook your dinner and watch the moon and stars fill the wide sky overhead.

CAMP-TO-CAMP MILEAGE

FR 600 to Camp 4 . . . . 0.8
Camp 4 to Camp 5 . . . . 0.4
Camp 5 to Brahma Lake Camp 1.5
Brahma Lake Camp to Camp 6 . . . . 1.0
Camp 6 to Camp 7 . . . . 1.0
Camp 7 to Camp 8 . . . . 6.3
Camp 8 to Camp 9 . . . . 0.4
Camp 9 to Camp 10 . . . . 0.3
Camp 10 to Camp 11 . . . . 0.9
Camp 11 to Camp 12 . . . . 0.2
Camp 12 to Cliff Lake junction 0.8
Cliff Lake junction to Cliff Lake Camp
(off PCT) 0.2

4 CLIFF LAKE TO ELK LAKE

DISTANCE 8.4 miles

ELEVATION GAIN/LOSS
+810 feet/−710 feet

HIGH POINT 5660 feet

CONNECTING TRAILS
Vera Lake Trail (#3526), Six Lakes Trail
(#14), Breezy Point Trail (#3517),
Red Hill Trail (#3515, OST), Sunset Lake
Trail (#3515.1), Island Meadow Trail (#3)

ON THE TRAIL

The final leg of the Pacific Crest Trail's passage
through the Cascade Lakes region continues to
roll through a forested landscape, passing more,
albeit smaller, lakes and ponds. Beginning with an

easy gradual ascent and finishing with a gradual
descent, it culminates with an inspiring mountain
view of what lies ahead. Throw in a few wide,
grassy meadows, even more berries, and a couple
pleasantly running streams, and it makes for an
enjoyable day. The leg finishes with a side trip to
Elk Lake Resort, a good rest and resupply location where you can camp, get a hot meal and cold
drink, and shower. You may even consider adding
in a "zero day" here to enjoy all the resort has to
offer on a charming lake with some incredible
mountain views.

Continuing on from the Cliff Lake junction,
the PCT crosses the lake's wide, rocky (likely dry)
outlet channel and moves northwest into dense
forest. As you find your pace, the trail veers east
to pass between a high, rocky slope to the right
(south) and a wide, grassy meadow with a large,

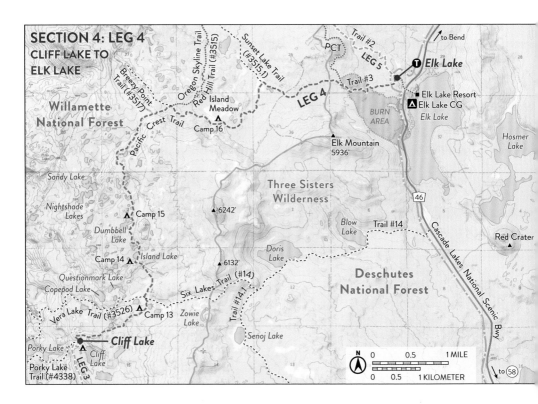

Dumbbell Lake is another of the delightful Cascade Lakes for taking a break, picking berries, and topping off water.

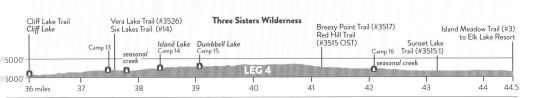

shallow pond to the left (north). The trail bends northeast on duffy tread under the trees, making a shallow ascent. At 37.5 miles, the trail passes a small, grassy pond on the right (east) with a tiny campsite nearby (**Camp 13**) ; there's room for one tent and a well-placed rock for sitting. Bending north, the PCT meets the **Vera Lake Trail** (#3526) and **Six Lakes Trail** (#14) at 37.6 miles. (Some newer maps might refer to the former as the Mink Lake Trail, and older maps refer to the latter as the Mink Lake Trail, #3526.1) The PCT then skirts the east side of **Reserve Meadow**, a grassy, slightly S-shaped depression that used to

hold a shallow lakelet. The trail meets the curving northern end of the meadow and crosses the grassy expanse where a small winding stream flows reliably into late summer.

Opposite the meadow crossing, the PCT bends northwest and begins climbing again, through a shallow saddle, to the edge of **Island Lake (Camp 14)** at 38.4 miles; a short bootpath leads left (northwest) to the lakeshore, continuing around to a couple of secluded campsites in the trees. The PCT winds along through the trees and past more ponds to an obvious side trail at 39.1 miles. This path cuts off left (west) to a large campsite beyond

A PCT hiker crosses a wide, grassy meadow just a few miles south of Elk Lake.

a narrow, rocky finger that juts out into **Dumbbell Lake (Camp 15)** ⓞ. The camp area can easily accommodate up to four tents, and has a fire ring and logs and rocks for sitting; access to the water is an easy scramble down the rocks to the lakeshore. The area is profuse with huckleberries. Several small ponds and lakelets follow in rapid succession as the trail gently undulates forward under shady, mossy forest.

The trail then bends east and descends to a fork in the road at 41.2 miles. Here, two trails branch off to the left. The **Breezy Point Trail** (#3517) heads 1.2 miles northwest to the **Fisher Lakes**, where it connects with the **McBee Trail** (#3523); the **Red Hill Trail** (#3515; part of the OST) heads northeast, then north for 1.7 miles to several trail junctions between Horse and Colt lakes. It then continues 4.2 miles past 6245-foot Red Hill and reconnects to the PCT at Sisters Mirror Lake.

WATER ALERT!

If you opt to forgo the resort on Elk Lake at the end of this leg, the next reliable water source after **Dumbbell Lake**, discounting the seasonal creek at mile 42.1, is a large pond at the PCT's junction with the Red Hill Trail (#3515) at mile 50.6, 11.5 miles ahead.

(Note: Some older maps refer to Trail #3515 as the Island Trail; see alternate route.) From this junction, the PCT continues right (east), snaking forward through more viewless forest, until it comes to the edge of **Island Meadow**, partially visible through the trees. From above, Island Meadow loosely resembles an eyeball, with the open, grassy meadow area the white part, the forested "island" in the middle the iris, and the hidden swampy

ALTERNATE ROUTE: OREGON SKYLINE TRAIL

This grassy pond at the junction of the PCT and OST offers one of your first peeks at South Sister.

If you don't plan on utilizing the Elk Lake Resort for rest and resupply, this 5.4-mile section of the **Oregon Skyline Trail** (Red Hill Trail #3515) is the better option for its access to water and decent campsites; there is little to be found of either along the mostly forested and viewless PCT between this junction and **Sisters Mirror Lake** (PCT mile 50.7). This alternate route shaves up to 4.1 miles off the section's mileage, and also gives the option of bypassing the hearty ascent and descent of Koosah Mountain.

From the junction at 41.2 miles, hop off the PCT and proceed northeast over rolling, forested terrain pocked with a few small ponds and lakelets. The first junction comes at approximately 1.5 miles, where the **Sunset Lake Trail** (#3515.1) joins from the right (east) and the **McBee Trail** (#3523) comes in from the right (west). Proceed another 0.2 mile to the next junction with the **Park Trail** (#3530), which breaks off to the left (west). This trail can be used to access the south and west sides of **Horse Lake** where dispersed campsites can be found near the lakeshore; camping is not permitted on the rocky peninsula. The route then crosses **Horse Creek 0** and splits again just 0.1 mile farther, with the **Horse Creek Trail** (#3514) veering off to the left (west). This trail can be used to access the north side of Horse Lake. Either side trail is a good option for water and camping to end your day, and there are some decent views of Mount Bachelor and Red Hill from the lakeshore.

To start the next leg and reconnect to the PCT, continue from the Horse Creek Trail junction on the **OST** (Red Hill Trail #3515) 0.2 mile east to another fork. Here, the **Horse Lake Trail** (#3516) continues east 1.5 miles to the PCT or 3 miles to **Elk Lake**. This is the quicker option to get back on the PCT. The alternative is to continue another 3.4 miles northeast on the OST, gaining gradual elevation through mostly pleasant forest. Midway through the stretch, about 2 miles from Horse Lake, the trail skirts the eastern flank of 6245-foot Red Hill, a large, tree-shrouded cinder cone. It then proceeds through an area festooned with numerous small lakes and ponds before reconnecting with the PCT at a well-signed junction near a pretty pond.

ELK LAKE RESORT

It's margarita time at Elk Lake Resort!

Conveniently located on the Cascade Lakes National Scenic Byway (OR 46), Elk Lake Resort is just a mile east of the PCT, and less than an hour's drive from Bend. Situated right in the middle of Section 4, it's the perfect place to take a break from the trail and kick back on a gorgeous lakeshore with spectacular mountain views while diving into a giant plate of nachos with a cold brew.

The resort features a small campground with 17 sites, three rustic camping cabins, and an assortment of small and large vintage cabins. Near the lakeshore, the resort restaurant serves up hearty breakfasts (try the huevos rancheros!) and tasty burgers and sandwiches. You can enjoy your food indoors, or out on their large deck. You can quench your thirst with a variety of sodas, beer, and cocktails; they also have ice cream and a coffee bar. The resort will accept and hold resupply packages, and offers bathrooms and showers for a small fee. Unfortunately, there are no laundry facilities, and the tiny store offers only a limited selection of snacks and drinks. On summer weekends, you'll be enjoying the lake and resort with lots of company, so try to plan your hiatus for mid-week when it's less crowded.

pond in the center the pupil. The trail circuits the southern side, staying in the trees, to a flowing creek **○** at 42.1 miles. The icy water is reliably refreshing, and it's a good place to top off your bottles before entering drier forest ahead. Near the creek, left (north) of the trail, is a small campsite with room for two tents (**Camp 16**).

Turning northeast from Camp 16, the PCT continues descending amid moderately pleasant forest. If hiking at the peak of summer, you'll be glad for the cool, shady conifers. At 43.1 miles, the trail suddenly pops out of the forest to cross another wide, grassy meadow—this one conspicuously drier

than the previous meadows. At the opposite end of the crossing, at 43.2 miles, the PCT comes to a junction with the **Sunset Lake Trail** (#3515.1), which veers off to the left (north) to nearby Sunset and Colt lakes, and just beyond, the trail to Horse Lake. Now the PCT turns east into drier forest, with much of the greener ground cover giving way to small patches of whortleberry amid mostly dry duff and debris. Here, on this wide and comfortable trail, you're likely to start encountering day hikers and equestrians venturing up from Elk Lake, your destination (not far now to that milkshake and fries!). At 44.5 miles the PCT pops out of the trees onto an open rise at the edge of a burn area. The wide panorama across the charred slope reveals **Mount Bachelor** to the east and peeks at **Broken Top** and **South Sister** to the north; **Elk Lake** fills the basin below.

Here amid the distracting vista, don't miss the junction with the **Island Meadow Trail** (#3), leading to Elk Lake and the end of this leg. This loose and sandy side trail heads down a moderately steep slope, with manzanita mixed amid charred deadfall and blackened tree ghosts. The descent eases about halfway down, leaving the burn area and entering dry, airy forest, where it exits the Three Sisters Wilderness, then finally turns north to bottom out at a junction with the **Horse Lake Trail** (#2), which you'll use to return to the PCT. Turn right (southeast) and head to the large trailhead parking area. To get to the resort, continue down the trailhead access road, cross the **Cascade Lakes National Scenic Byway** (OR 46) and enter **Elk Lake Resort**.

CAMP-TO-CAMP MILEAGE

Cliff Lake junction to Camp 13	1.4
Camp 13 to Camp 14	0.9
Camp 14 to Camp 15	0.7
Camp 15 to Camp 16	3.0
Camp 16 to Elk Lake junction	2.4
Elk Lake junction to Elk Lake Resort (off PCT)	1.3

5 ELK LAKE TO MESA MEADOW

DISTANCE 8.9 miles

ELEVATION GAIN/LOSS +1580 feet/–1160 feet

HIGH POINT 6450 feet

CONNECTING TRAILS
Horse Lake Trail (#2/#3516), Red Hill Trail (#3515), Nash Lake Trail (#3527), Mirror Lakes Trail (#20), Devils Lake Trail (#12.1), Le Conte Crater Trail (#12.3)

ON THE TRAIL

Moving into the second half of Section 4, the Pacific Crest Trail leaves behind the forested basins of the Cascade Lakes area and moves onto the high western flanks of the Three Sisters. Where significant views have been spare for many miles previous, they're now about to get big—*real big*—in what is arguably the most spectacular section of the PCT through Oregon. The leg begins with a moderate ascent over Koosah Mountain, is followed with a visit to a pleasant mid-elevation lake, and culminates with a traverse of the Wickiup Plain on the doorstep of Oregon's third-highest mountain: South Sister. The initial ascent is a healthy one, gaining nearly 1200 feet, but the terrain then eases to an effortless romp for the remainder of the leg. And with the relatively shorter mileage for the day, it allows you to spend extra time exploring along the way, or gives you an opportunity to get to camp early and kick back in an idyllic mountain meadow in the shadow of a 10,000-foot volcano.

Starting at the **Horse Lake Trailhead** on the west side of the Cascade Lakes National Scenic Byway, directly across from the Elk Lake Resort entrance, fill out your self-register wilderness permit at the kiosk and proceed to the trail fork just beyond. The trail to the left (south), the Island Meadow Trail (#3), proceeds steeply back up through the burn area you descended to get to Elk Lake; turn right (northwest) onto the **Horse Lake Trail** (#2), which climbs gradually under shady conifers to a junction with the PCT. After 1.2 viewless, but not unpleasant, miles, the trail crosses the PCT at a four-way junction. Straight ahead (west), the Horse Lake Trail continues on to its namesake lake (now as Trail #3516), with

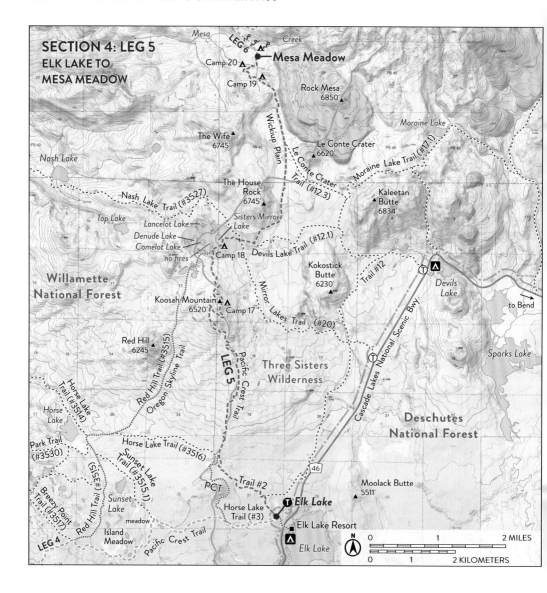

SECTION 4: LEG 5
ELK LAKE TO
MESA MEADOW

LEG 6

Mesa Creek

Camp 20

Mesa Meadow

Camp 19

Rock Mesa
6850'

The Wife
6745'

Le Conte Crater
6620'

Moraine Lake

Nash Lake

Le Conte Crater
Trail (#12.3)

Moraine Lake Trail (#17.1)

Wickiup Plain

The House
Rock
6745'

Kaleetan
Butte
6834'

Nash Lake Trail (#3527)

Top Lake

Sisters Mirror
Lake

Lancelot Lake

Denude Lake

Camelot Lake
no fires

Camp 18

Devils Lake Trail (#12.1)

Kokostick
Butte
6230'

Devils
Lake

Willamette
National Forest

Koosah Mountain
6520'

Camp 17

Mirror Lakes Trail (#20)

Trail #12

to Bend

Sparks Lake

Red Hill
6245'

LEG 5

Pacific Crest Trail

Three Sisters
Wilderness

Cascade Lakes National Scenic Bwy

Deschutes
National Forest

Horse Lake Trail (#3514)

Red Hill Trail (#3515)

Oregon Skyline Trail

Horse
Lake

Park Trail
(#3530)

Horse Lake Trail (#3516)

Sunset Lake
Trail (#3515.1)

Moolack Butte
5511'

Breezy Point Trail (#3517)

Red Hill Trail (#3515.1)

Sunset
Lake

PCT

Trail #2

46

Elk Lake

meadow

Horse Lake
Trail (#3)

Elk Lake Resort

LEG 4

Island
Meadow

Pacific Crest Trail

N

0   1   2 MILES

0   1   2 KILOMETERS

Elk Lake

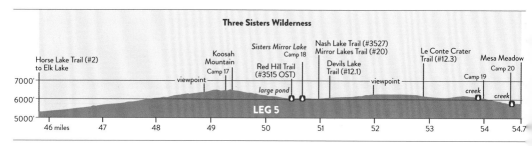

Three Sisters Wilderness

Horse Lake Trail (#2)
to Elk Lake

Koosah
Mountain
Camp 17

Sisters Mirror Lake
Camp 18

Nash Lake Trail (#3527)
Mirror Lakes Trail (#20)

Le Conte Crater
Trail (#12.3)

Mesa Meadow
Camp 20

viewpoint

Red Hill Trail
(#3515 OST)

Devils Lake
Trail (#12.1)

viewpoint

Camp 19

7000'

large pond

creek

creek

6000'

LEG 5

5000'

46 miles   47   48   49   50   51   52   53   54   54.7

KOOSAH MOUNTAIN

Koosah Mountain is the 16,524th-highest mountain in the United States, and the 381st-highest mountain in Oregon. This small shield volcano experienced significant glacial erosion during the ice ages, but the relatively intact condition of the summit scoria cone indicates that it may have had a final eruptive episode after the glaciers retreated.

connectors to Colt and Sunset lakes; left (south), the PCT wraps around an unnamed butte and continues into places already traveled. At this point, check and/or adjust your mileage (your odometer should read 45.8 miles), turn right (north), and press on.

The PCT continues along the crest on a nearly level track on comfortable tread, still under the cover of shady forest. The route meanders north between the Willamette National Forest (west) and the Deschutes National Forest (east). In the miles ahead, you will be able to tell which side trails are in which forests by their designator numbers: four digits in the Willamette and two digits (mostly) in the Deschutes. As the trail approaches the base of 6520-foot **Koosah Mountain**, it veers northwest to begin climbing a series of sweeping switchbacks. As the trail gains elevation, it alternates between open sections where manzanita adorns the slopes and shadier forested sections festooned with lupine, beargrass, and spiky, pink thistle; you may catch a peek south over forested ridges and valleys to Diamond Peak, now several days in your rear-view.

After the final rounding switchback, at 48.9 miles, the PCT curves around an open plateau of red cinders and small volcanic "lava bombs," just south of the summit proper. Here is your first "wow" view. **South Sister** and **Broken Top** form an impressive and imposing wall to the north, **Mount Bachelor** fills the scene to the east, and the view south extends over Elk and Lava lakes to **Diamond Peak**—and on clear days you may even spy the summit pinnacle of **Mount Thielsen**, some

60 miles distant. The trail then contours along the eastern slope, just below the summit. Trees once again block views, but at 49.3 miles look for a rocky outcrop to the right (east). Here, you'll find a small campsite with room for a couple tents and a killer view (**Camp 17**). While you still have many miles to go, this tempting spot is worth pausing for a few minutes—even long enough to chow down on an energy bar—just to absorb the immensity of the mountainous scene in front of you—and this is just a preview.

With your mountain appetite whetted for more, continue on. The PCT soon reaches its highest point on the mountain, still not touching the actual summit, then tips over to descend northwest on widening switchbacks into dense old-growth forest. As the trail levels through thinning forest, it crosses a pocket meadow brimming with lupine, heather, and huckleberry and bears north. At 50.4 miles, a tree-mounted sign indicates that you're entering the Sisters Mirror Lake no-campfire zone; 0.1 mile farther, the PCT arrives at a T-junction with the **Red Hill Trail** (#3515) near the shore of a large, pretty, clear pond ◐ surrounded by tall grass, with a peek of South Sister's upper slopes beyond 6745-foot **The House Rock**. *Ooohh*, it just keeps getting better.

Turning right (east) at the junction, the PCT rounds the pond on flat, open trail amid more heather and huckleberry with wide skies overhead. In no time, you're alongside **Sisters Mirror Lake**

TRAIL NOTE: CAMELOT LAKE

Some older guidebooks refer to this pond at Trail #3515's north junction as Camelot Lake; however, Camelot Lake is actually 0.2 mile northwest cross-country. However, there are several bootpaths that explore the many lakes in this area, including Camelot, Lancelot, Bounty, and Denude. If you choose to explore this area, be sure to use map and compass or GPS unit to track your location and find your way back to the PCT.

Take in a wide panorama of South Sister and Broken Top from the PCT's perch high atop Koosah Mountain.

(Camp 18) ⬤, at 50.7 miles. This large, shallow lake just begs to be visited—and a number of bootpaths make it that much easier to be lulled into a detour for a lunch stop or a quick dip. The lake doesn't actually mirror all Three Sisters, but South Sister can be seen over the forested ridge of The House Rock. Around the south and west shores, several campsites can be found among the trees and prolific huckleberry bushes—if you're passing through during berry season, you're in for a treat. Just be warned, in addition to the hordes of summer weekend campers out for a relatively easy getaway, Sisters Mirror Lake (as well as the other nearby lakes) is also popular with hordes of murderous mosquitoes. If you're passing through before August, come armored with long sleeves and pants, hat, head net, and plenty of repellent.

Once you manage to tear yourself away from the lake and continue on, the PCT proceeds along the forested eastern shore, gains a little elevation, then turns east into lodgepole pine forest on sandy tread. If you're on a longer trek and have hiked through the Crater Lake area (Section 2), you may have flashbacks of the Oregon Desert. At 50.9 miles, an unmarked trail veers west, leading to the north side of Sisters Mirror Lake and to some of the smaller lakes beyond. This is followed 0.1 mile later by a signed, yet somewhat confusing, four-way junction with the **Nash Lake Trail** (#3527) and **Mirror Lakes Trail** (#20). Straight ahead, the Mirror Lakes Trail descends southeast 3.4 miles to a trailhead on the Cascade Lakes National Scenic Byway; the nearer left, the Nash Lake Trail, proceeds 3.8 miles north to Nash Lake, and 3.1 miles farther to a junction with the Horse Creek Trail (#3514); the farther left, the PCT, turns east into greener forest. This point also marks the extent of the no-campfire zone. The final junction in this

SIDE TRIP: SOUTH SISTER

At 10,358 feet in elevation, **South Sister** is Oregon's third-highest peak, and is the highest non-technical peak accessible from the Pacific Crest Trail. A side trip to claim this high point requires at least one extra day, and while the climb doesn't demand specialized gear or experience, it may necessitate an ice axe and crampons earlier in the summer. The payoff at the top of this 4000-foot grind (from Moraine Lake) is an unparalleled—and unforgettable—view of Teardrop Pool, the highest lake in the state.

The best way to add this summit to your itinerary is to turn off the PCT onto the **Devils Lake Trail** (#12.1) for 1.7 miles, then turn onto the **Moraine Lake Trail** (#17.1) and climb 2.2 miles northeast to **Moraine Lake**. The route crosses the main climber's path and enters a picturesque, glacier-carved valley where the lake fills a sparsely vegetated basin. Set up camp at one of the few designated campsites and rest up for the next day's endeavor; campfires are not permitted here. Start early the next morning by returning to the climber's path using the trail on the south side of the lake, which climbs to a junction on the top of the ridge (moraine) above the lake. At this point, you have more than 3500 feet to ascend in 3.3 miles. Turn right (north) and get your climbing groove on.

The path climbs along the ridge to the head of Moraine Lake's valley, where a good viewpoint looks south over countless lakes and peaks below and off into the distance. Now the work really begins as the path steepens and becomes rougher, heading up a scree-covered slope to a sandy saddle, below which is a small cirque lake. The final stretch steepens even more and ascends the ridge between the **Lewis and Clark glaciers** to the rim of South Sister's summit crater. Continue around the rim counterclockwise to the summit proper, marked by a USGS benchmark. Peer down into the crater at icy blue **Teardrop Pool**, then take in the rest of the view, which spans almost the entire length of Oregon's Cascades. When you've soaked it all in, return to your camp by the same route, get a good night's rest, then return to the PCT the next morning and continue your journey.

Above Moraine Lake, there is no accessible water on the climb to South Sister's summit. Carry all you will need for the day, in addition to plenty of energy foods to keep you going up the steep climb. The path is fully exposed, and bright sunlight will be reflecting off of rocks and snow, so be sure to wear sunscreen. If the summit is in the clouds the morning of your climb, do not attempt. What looks like an innocent cloud may contain a snowstorm—and there aren't any views from inside a cloud, anyway.

---

cluster comes at 51.2 miles, where the **Devils Lake Trail** (#12.1) forks east while the PCT turns north. Want to bag Oregon's third-highest mountain? This is where you turn off for a side trip to South Sister (see sidebar).

Now east of the crest (momentarily), the PCT circuits the base of The House Rock, rising through a brief section of forest, then crosses a wide, grassy gully. The trail then gently contours to the top of a plateau and…*boom*! Here's your next "wow" moment—and this one's a doozy!

Now at 52 miles, in the big wide-open, the PCT enters the **Wickiup Plain**, an expansive "pumice meadow" blanketed with volcanic cinders and dotted with bunchgrass and small clumps of buckwheat and lupine, with only the occasional mountain hemlock or whitebark pine daring to take root. Taking center stage over the plain is

Big mountain views come into sharp focus where the PCT crosses the Wickiup Plain.

10,358-foot **South Sister,** capped with a very noticeable layer of red rock, under which are several immense glacial cirques; the large, southwest-facing snowfield is the Clark Glacier. In the distance, over its western flank, is pyramid-shaped **Middle Sister;** in the nearer distance is 6620-foot

> ### TRAIL TRIVIA
>
> **Teardrop Pool,** the icy blue melt pond in the summit crater of South Sister (and the highest lake in Oregon), was named in 1969 by the daughters of photographer David Falconer. Upon reaching the summit and spotting the pool, Patricia and Peggy asked what its name was. At the time, it had none. They chose the name "Teardrop Pool" and submitted the suggestion to the Oregon Geographic Names Board; it was then sent to and officially adopted by the United States Board on Geographic Names.

Le Conte Crater, and behind it the curiously sparkly **Rock Mesa.** If you suddenly have the urge to drop your pack at sit and marvel at this scene for a while, go for it. *This* is why you're hiking the PCT.

Proceed north across the plain, where the trail stretches out far in front of you. In early to midsummer, the plain will be a lovely shade of green with small, colorful blooms; by later summer and into the fall, it will be a rich golden red. Combined with the expansive mountain views, the crossing is simply joyful, and will doubtless be one of the most memorable parts of your journey. About midway across the plain, just northwest of Le Conte Crater, the PCT comes to an obvious junction marked by a large cairn and signpost. Here, the **Le Conte Crater Trail** (#12.3) splits off southeast for 3.6 miles to circuit 6800-foot **Kaleetan Butte** and end at the Devils Lake trailhead on the Cascade Lakes National Scenic Byway. Continuing through the plain, the PCT now comes alongside Rock Mesa, a rhyodacite dome formation that was extruded from a volcanic vent during an eruptive event around 2300 years ago. With a closer look, you can see that the sparkly effect is created by light reflecting off chunks of smooth, glassy obsidian mixed into the rocky matrix. Keep your eyes and ears perked for little pikas darting in and out of the rocks.

The PCT dips into a shallow gully, crosses it, then climbs gently out the other side to pass through a low, narrow saddle between Rock Mesa and a small rise—and right into a pleasant, grassy meadow filled with wildflowers and surrounded by green forest. The trail proceeds effortlessly northwest along the edge of the meadow and crosses a delightful little creek ⬤ on a small bridge at 53.9 miles; just beyond, a bootpath right (north) leads to a small campsite in the trees, with room for one tent (**Camp 19**). As the trail turns north, it starts a gentle switchbacking descent through a small stretch of burned forest to an easy rock-hop over a tributary of **Mesa Creek** ⬤ at 54.5 miles. Just across the creek, a bootpath veers left (north) to mount an ancient lava flow where two secluded campsites can be found in the trees (**Camp 20**); each site has room for one tent.

The end of the leg comes just 0.2 mile farther, at 54.7 miles, where the trail turns north again to skirt **Mesa Meadow (Camp)** in a glaciated basin. To the right (east), across the grassy clearing, South Sister rises above the forest, the massive cirque holding the remnants of Clark Glacier clearly visible. Left (west) of the trail, several dispersed campsites can be found in the trees at the edge of the meadow; water can be obtained on the north side of the meadow where **Mesa Creek** ⬤ meanders through. Drop your gear, set up camp, and watch for deer and marmots to venture into the meadow for their evening supper while the setting sun lights up South Sister in alpenglow glory.

CAMP-TO-CAMP MILEAGE

Horse Lake Trail junction to Camp 17 . . . . 3.5
Camp 17 to Camp 18 (Sisters Mirror Lake) . . . 1.4
Camp 18 to Camp 19 . . . . 3.3
Camp 19 to Camp 20 . . . . 0.5
Camp 20 to Mesa Meadow Camp 0.2

In summer months, the trail is lined with Indian paintbrush.

6 MESA MEADOW TO SUNSHINE MEADOW

DISTANCE 10.3 miles

ELEVATION GAIN/LOSS
+2010 feet/-1350 feet

HIGH POINT 6690 feet

CONNECTING TRAILS
James Creek Trail (#3546), Foley Ridge Trail (#3511), Linton Meadows Trail (#3547), Obsidian Trail (#3528), Glacier Way Trail (#4336)

ON THE TRAIL

If you're measuring your PCT journey in bang-for-buck, this next leg pays in spades. Now in the heart of the Three Sisters area, the route forward is a cornucopia of flower-filled meadows, rocky volcanic plateaus, and in-your-face mountain views. Elevation gain picks up a bit, as there are lateral ridges to mount, as well as age-old lava flows and glaciated basins to traverse. In this higher terrain, water becomes more scarce, especially later in the season when many of the smaller streams dry up—carry a little extra when leaving camp to stay hydrated in the widely exposed higher elevations, and don't forget to put your sunscreen on. The day promises scenery overload, but if you have the time to add a day to your itinerary, or stretch out a couple of others, the Linton Meadows side trip is highly recommended.

Before you can get to the good stuff, however, you have to contend with 2.3 miles of recently blackened forest. On the north side of the meadow, the PCT crosses Mesa Creek and its tributary at 54.8 miles, then plunges under cover of charred fir and hemlock. Burned in the summer of 2017, the forest turns dark and foreboding for the moderate northwest ascent onto the western flank of South Sister. At 55.3 miles, a small, seasonal creek **O** splashes across the trail. Just beyond, the trees part, momentarily granting a view west over 6455-foot **Sphinx Butte** and the massively glaciated Separation Creek valley. The trail then turns east and rises to meet the **James Creek Trail** (#3546), which branches off to the left (west) and proceeds to a five-way junction with several other trails. (Note: Some older maps indicate that this is Linton Meadow Trail #3547, which the PCT actually crosses much farther north.)

The PCT then crosses a small clearing, after which it makes a roundabout turn and comes to a minor crest at 55.9 miles, where a mucky pond fills a depression just below and right (west) of the trail. The trail crosses another clearing and rises northeast, meandering through bends and turns under cover of conifers, interrupted with occasional pocket meadows. Eventually, the trail levels out to track around the east side of an unnamed 6482-foot butte, dips through a slight

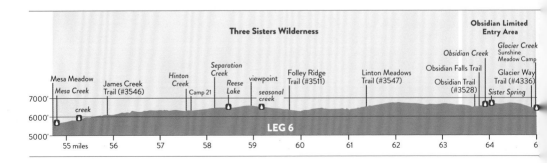

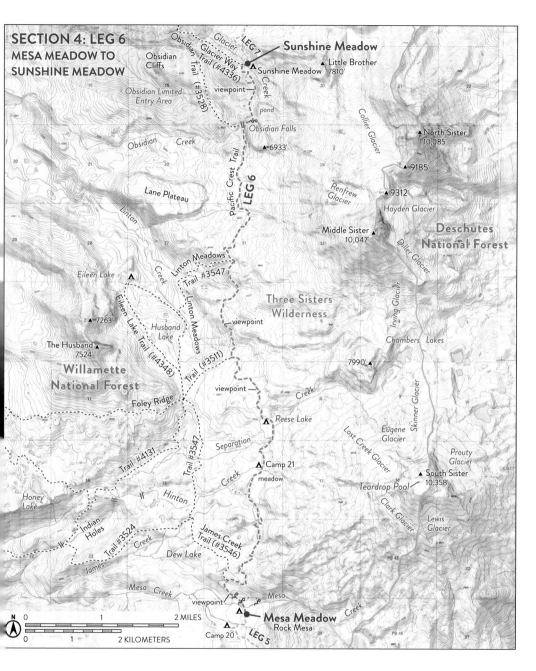

SECTION 4: LEG 6
MESA MEADOW TO
SUNSHINE MEADOW

drainage, then exits the burn area, and drops into an expansive high meadow. Here, you're presented with big views of both South and Middle Sister, the latter being your first full-profile view. Around this meadow, then through a grove of trees, head into the next meadow, this one opening up to the west for a look at jagged, 7524-foot **The Husband**. This becomes the norm for the next several miles of trail: forest, meadow, big view, forest, meadow, big view.

THE THREE SISTERS

Referred to as a "complex volcano," the Three Sisters are the 20-mile-long centerpiece of one of the highest concentrations of volcanic peaks and features in the state of Oregon, as well as the dominant feature of the Three Sisters Wilderness. Each peak measures more than 10,000 feet in elevation, with South Sister currently the tallest. The age range of the peaks varies substantially, indicating that this area has had a long and very active volcanic history. Despite their mid-state location at a fairly moderate latitude, the Sisters are home to fifteen of thirty-five named mountain glaciers, nearly half, the largest of which is the Collier Glacier, which continues to grind away at the north flank of Middle Sister and the south flank of North Sister. Not much is known about any Native American presence around the Three Sisters, or where the mountains' name even originated. Early settlers once called them Faith, Hope, and Charity, but those names did not stick, and now they're simply referred to as North, Middle, and South Sister.

The oldest of the complex, North Sister, at 10,085 feet and the fourth-highest peak in the state, is estimated to be more than 400,000 years old. As such, she is the most heavily eroded by the march of time and the glacial forces of numerous ice ages. In fact, it is estimated that North Sister may have stood more than 1000 feet taller than her current height, and that extensive glaciation ground off her top and revealed much of her inner structure, including volcanic dikes and sills. Built atop an even more ancient shield volcano, she is unique from her siblings in that her composition is basaltic andesite, rich in magnesium and iron, the source of her rosy hue. Atop it all, she is capped with a plug dome—now heavily eroded—which comprises her jagged double summits, Prouty Peak and South Horn. With North Sister's last known eruptive event having occurred approximately 55,000 years ago, she is considered an "extinct" volcano.

Just as North Sister's volcanic activity was winding down, the awkward Middle Sister started making her presence known around 100,000 years ago. Reaching 10,047 feet, Middle Sister is a composite volcano consisting mostly of andesite and dacite lavas, forming a nearly perfectly symmetrical cone—until glaciers started eating away at her, that is. While her western flank retains much of its original shape, the eastern flank has been deeply incised by the Hayden and Diller glaciers, along with smaller others, leaving behind deep cirques and sharp arêtes. Thick dacite lava flows on her south and north flanks give indication that her last eruption occurred approximately 14,000 years ago, and she's not expected to resume volcanic activity. From her general appearance and color, when not coated under a blanket of clean, white snow, she is often acerbically referred to as the "Gravel Pile."

The feisty South Sister's origin actually dates back more than 178,000 years, when an older shield volcano occupied the area. Then as recently as 30,000 years ago she started coming into her own with eruptions of rhyolite and dacite lavas, building her composite structure to 10,358 feet, well above her older sisters, and claiming the title of third-highest peak in Oregon. As the youngest, South Sister is not nearly as eroded as her siblings; however, she is draped with seven named glaciers, which are slowly but surely grinding away at her flanks. Still considered "active," South Sister last erupted a mere 2000 years ago, during which the Rock Mesa and Newberry Flow formations were extruded. Her unique summit crater, composed of reddish cinders, giving her the sobriquet "redhead" and adding to her feistiness, contains Oregon's highest lake, Tear-

Located right in the middle of Oregon, the Three Sisters are the centerpiece of a cluster of volcanic features that showcase nearly half a million years of volcanic activity.

drop Pool, at 10,218 feet. A steep, albeit nontechnical, path climbs from the Devils Lake trailhead on the Cascade Lakes National Scenic Byway to her lofty summit; this path can also be accessed from the PCT via the Devils Lake and Moraine Lake trails (see Leg 5).

The Three Sisters are one of the most attentively monitored volcanic centers in the Cascade Range. In 2000, satellite monitors detected volcanic swelling in the area just west of South Sister. A few years later, a swarm of small earthquakes occurred in the area, indicating movement of a magma body below, estimated at 4 miles below the surface. After reaching nearly a foot of uplift, activity slowed in 2007. The area continues to swell, but at a rate of less than 0.5 inch per year. The USGS has since installed GPS receivers and seismometers throughout the area to monitor the situation and, if necessary, issue potential eruption warnings. Welcome to the living Cascades.

At 57.6 miles, the trail crosses a shallow gully, which may or may not contain **Hinton Creek**, depending on the season and the previous winter's snowpack. Shortly past, at 57.7 miles in a grove of trees, a small campsite **(Camp 21)** can be found to the left (west); it has a couple nice rocks for sitting and room for two tents. Then it's back out in the open to cross the next meadow. The trail then veers northeast to ascend along the gully containing **Separation Creek**, which, like Hinton Creek, may or may not be running. After crossing the creek (or creekbed) at 58.2 miles, the trail flattens out and bends north into a shallow, wide-open basin where the scene is ridiculously spectacular with mountains, meadows, and flowers. The path parallels Separation Creek's channel for a ways, then bends away northwest. At this point, you may be thinking it can't get any better. At 58.5 miles it does, when the turquoise pool of **Reese Lake (Camp)** ⬤ comes into view, right (east) of the trail. A side trail cuts off to a slight bluff overlooking the lake where a large camp area begs to be used and enjoyed. The area has a good fire ring, room for up to four tents, and several rocks for sitting around

> ### TRAIL TRIVIA
>
> Not all place names in Oregon were designated hundreds of years ago. **Reese Lake** was only designated in 1987. It was named for Hamit Darwin Reese, a professor at Oregon State University and frequent Boy Scout trip leader. This small lake situated below South Sister was one of his favorite backcountry locations, so following his death, the Forest Service decided to honor the place with his name.

camp or overlooking the clear, blue-green lake backed by always-impressive South Sister.

Leaving the lake behind, the trail curves northwest on a gentle, 0.5-mile ascent to reach a 6530-foot crest with expansive views in almost every direction—Middle Sister to the northeast, The Husband to the northwest. Then it's an easy ramble down into, and across, a wide heather and huckleberry meadow, which transitions into a barren, rocky plain. On the north side of the

Little vegetation clings to the high, exposed flank of Middle Sister where the PCT crosses wide volcanic plains.

The idyllic Linton Meadows are worth a detour off the PCT—or even an extra day to explore.

SIDE TRIP: LINTON MEADOWS

The Three Sisters Wilderness boasts some of the most scenic and spectacular backcountry settings in all of Oregon, and the PCT doesn't come close to visiting even a fraction of them. For an experience more akin to the high country of the Sierra Nevada, take a stroll through the **Linton Meadows**. Turn off the PCT onto the **Foley Ridge Trail** (#3511) at 59.8 miles and descend 0.8 mile to a five-way junction in a glaciated notch. Turn right (north) on the **Linton Meadows Trail** (#3547) and climb easily 0.3 mile into the southern meadow area to a trail fork. Continue on the Linton Meadow Trail northward, with the edge of the forest to your left (west) and the glorious, wide-open meadows to your right (east). In midsummer, **Linton Creek** meanders musically through its channel surrounded by a carpet of brilliant green grasses and colorful wildflowers. There are numerous campsites to be found near the edge of the meadows and near the creek.

Where the trail forks again, with the **Eileen Lake Trail** (#4348), veer left (northwest) and descend to picture-perfect **Eileen Lake**, nestled right below the rocky spires of The Husband. Follow a footpath around the west side of the lake for stunning views of **Middle and South Sisters**, as well as more tempting campsites. In a setting like this, you may be inclined to call it a day right here and rejoin the PCT the next day. If so, reconnect to the PCT by returning to the previous junction, then turn left (north) and switchback steadily up 1.7 miles to rejoin the PCT at mile 61.4.

plain, at 59.2 miles, the trail crosses a seasonal creekbed in a green swath and turns sharply west, paralleling the creekbed through more heather and huckleberry.

At 59.8 miles the PCT intercepts the **Foley Ridge Trail** (#3511), a lateral route that descends 8 miles west to a trailhead on remote FR 2643, skirting The Husband, Substitute Point, and Proxy Point, with connections to Buck Meadows and Linton Meadows. You can't tell from this point how spectacularly inviting Linton Meadows is, but it makes a worthy side trip or alternate route that reconnects with the PCT less than 2 miles north.

Now the PCT turns north again, crosses a seasonal drainage in the next meadow, then hugs the hemlock-forested lower flank of Middle Sister on a gentle ascent. Around 60.4 miles, look for a faint bootpath breaking off the PCT that descends left (west) through the trees to a viewpoint overlooking Linton Meadows and The Husband rising high above—you just might consider heading back to that previous junction. The PCT continues forward, contouring the steep slope on loose, rocky tread, and becoming considerably narrower—though hardly treacherous—through short stretches. It then curves around the head of a glaciated drainage and ascends to meet the **Linton Meadows Trail** (#3547) at 61.4 miles. This trail switchbacks down and west into the drainage basin you just traversed, then crosses the central meadow area; it also connects to the Eileen Lake Trail (#4348).

The PCT keeps ascending gradually until it leaves tree cover behind and emerges onto a vast, rolling, rocky plain. Cinders and small lava bombs abound, and only small, hardy patches of heather, lupine, cinquefoil, and paintbrush hold on for dear life. The trail reaches its 6690-foot high point above this broad, volcanic expanse. The view is nearly endless in every direction; eastward, **Middle Sister** forms the entire scene. If you recall the views of her shape from points earlier, take note of how she has seemed to transform, no longer the symmetrical cinder pile, but now sculpted with obvious glaciated ridges and uneven slopes. In the opposite

direction, to the northwest, the flat expanse is 6552-foot **Lane Plateau**, a relatively young (geologically speaking) subglacial dacite extrusion.

The next mile is a fantastic traverse of volcanic alpine country, where the PCT crosses rocky plains and grassy meadows, interrupted only occasionally by small groves of stunted mountain hemlock and gnarled whitebark pine. In this wide-open environment on Middle Sister's high western flank, you definitely want to be well-protected from the sun, as it reflects off everything—especially if there's still lingering snow. Typically, despite its exposure, this area is one of the last portions of Oregon's PCT to melt out, so some routefinding may be necessary if crossing early in the season and the plain is still blanketed with cold white stuff. Look for cairns and post markers, and use your map and compass. Just before the trail reaches forest again, it crosses a wide cindery "meadow" speckled with

OBSIDIAN LIMITED ENTRY AREA

In order to minimize impact and preserve the natural features in this area, the Forest Service has implemented usage limits that require a special permit for both day hikers and overnight backpackers. PCT hikers are exempt from this permit requirement, but only as passers-through, and are required to stay within the "PCT Corridor," namely, within 300 feet of the trail. This inconveniently places the campsites near Obsidian and Glacier creeks off-limits to the typical PCT thru-hiker. However, conveniently—and highly recommended—for section hikers, you can reserve an Obsidian Limited Entry Area permit in advance of your trip. This will allow you legal access to camp in the Obsidian area and take advantage of good campsites near reliable water sources. (See Passes and Permits in the introduction for more info.)

Opposite: *Aptly named Obsidian Falls creates a fantastical scene as it cascades over c glassy, volcanic escarpment*

Just south of Sunshine Meadow, the PCT ambles alongside the melodic and refreshingly cool Obsidian Creek.

buckwheat and stonecrop, with another great view of Middle Sister. Take a good, long look, and notice the ragged peak just northeast: **North Sister**. That's what's coming next, but you have a few miles yet before you get there. At 63.4 miles, the PCT enters the **Obsidian Limited Entry Area**, marked by a large sign.

The PCT then makes a gentle descent into conifer forest adorned with pasqueflower along the west side of a 6933-foot knob to meet the **Obsidian Trail** (#3528) at 63.7 miles. Look down at the trail, and notice flecks of black, glassy rock in the trail tread—obsidian. Now the trail starts up again, climbing moderately northeast through a few switchbacks, where the sound of falling water becomes noticeable. Obstructed by the trees, **Obsidian Falls** doesn't come into view until you're almost upon it. At 63.8 miles, a side trail descends to the base of the 20-foot falls, a pretty curtain of water cascading down a mossy bluff. The PCT continues another 0.1 mile to the top of the

plateau above the falls where it crosses **Obsidian Creek ⬤**. If the seasonal creeks since Mesa Creek have all been dry, this icy cataract will be joyfully refreshing.

Now on level trail again, the PCT turns east alongside the creek toward a high lava escarpment, under which is a broad talus slope of shale-like rock. The trail then sweeps north along the base of the talus slope, where you'll find **Sister Spring ⬤** bubbling up right out of the rock. The tread then becomes noticeably rough and "crunchy" as the PCT parallels a low mound almost entirely composed of glassy black volcanic obsidian. The trail then drops slightly into a shallow basin holding a pretty pond ⬤ surrounded by grasses and heather, then ascends slightly to mount a low bluff at 64.4 miles. Here, you're presented with an impressive panorama over **Glacier Creek, Sunshine Meadow,** 7810-foot **Little Brother**, and the imposing, heavily glaciated western wall of 10,085-foot **North Sister**—plus, a preview northward of Mount

Washington, Three Fingered Jack, and Mount Jefferson.

The trail then makes a switchbacking descent into the forest on the north side of the bluff, passing the Prouty and Bronaugh memorial plaques, which are very easy to miss if you're not looking for them. At the bottom of the descent, the PCT meets the top of the **Glacier Way Trail** (#4336) at 64.9 miles. This steep side trail descends 0.5 mile northwest to connect with the **Obsidian Trail** (#3528), which, in turn, descends 3.2 miles through the Obsidian area to a trailhead on OR 242. Here, the PCT turns east and crosses **Glacier Creek (Camp)** ⬤ at 65 miles, amid the lower expanse of Sunshine Meadow.

This very popular backcountry destination—hence the limited entry regulation—has seen better days. Many of the campsites have been overused (and abused) and have been marked off by the Forest Service for rehabilitation. A few fair-game campsites are still accessible in order to take advantage of this pretty location and its good water source. If you have your overnight permit, look for an obvious side trail, just past the creek crossing, that heads right (west) up into the trees. Follow this path for 70 yards to a sheltered camp area with a large fire ring (though fires are prohibited), a few large logs for sitting, and room for three or four tents. Spend the evening creekside, enjoying the meadow and watching the sun fade off Little Brother. If you forgo the permit for the Obsidian LEA, take a break to top off your water at the creek and continue 1.8 miles to the next campsite at **Sawyer Bar**, free and clear of the limited entry area.

CAMP-TO-CAMP MILEAGE

Mesa Meadow Camp to Camp 21 . . . . 3.0
Camp 21 to Reese Lake Camp 0.8
Reese Lake Camp to Sunshine Meadow
    Camp (permit required) 6.5
Sunshine Meadow Camp to
    Sawyer Bar Camp (Leg 7) 1.8

7 SUNSHINE MEADOW TO MCKENZIE PASS

DISTANCE 9.5 miles

ELEVATION GAIN/LOSS
+1190 feet/−2260 feet

HIGH POINT 6900 feet

CONNECTING TRAILS
Scott Trail (#3531), Scott Pass Trail (#4068), Matthieu Lakes Trail (#4062), Lava Camp Lake spur trail

ON THE TRAIL

If you've ever wanted to reenact Sam and Frodo's journey through Mordor to Mount Doom, the next leg on the Pacific Crest Trail will help you fulfill your fantasy—or at least come pretty close to it. The way forward leaves the shelter of the forest to cross several rugged and geologically recent lava flows, originating from the cinder cones on the north flank of North Sister. The scene is both stark and fascinating, where jumbles of basaltic aa lava overlay entire swaths of the landscape for many miles, which is visible from several high viewpoints. But it isn't all bleak and barren. The last few miles reenter shady forest and skirt a pleasant lake—with the option to visit a second lake—before ending at a small campground just shy of McKenzie Pass. The trail forward is very exposed for many miles, and can get very warm in midsummer, so the usual sun protection is in order, as well as a good water supply.

Continuing northbound from **Glacier Creek**, the PCT proceeds back under the cover of forest and turns northwest to contour around the lateral ridge of **Little Brother**. This remnant of an

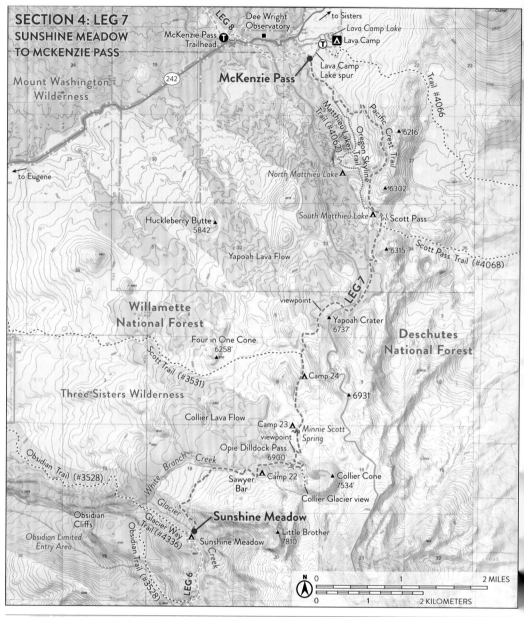

SECTION 4: LEG 7
SUNSHINE MEADOW
TO MCKENZIE PASS

LEG 8

Dee Wright
Observatory

to Sisters

Lava Camp Lake

McKenzie Pass
Trailhead

Lava Camp

McKenzie Pass

Lava Camp
Lake spur

Trail #4066

Mount Washington
Wilderness

242

▲6216'

Matthieu Lakes Trail (#4062)

Oregon Skyline Trail

Pacific Crest Trail

23

to Eugene

North Matthieu Lake ▲

▲6302'

Huckleberry Butte ▲
5842'

South Matthieu Lake ▲   ▲ Scott Pass

Yapoah Lava Flow

▲6315'   Scott Pass Trail (#4068)

**Willamette
National Forest**

viewpoint

LEG 7

Four in One Cone
6258'

▲ Yapoah Crater
6737

**Deschutes
National Forest**

Scott Trail (#3531)

Three Sisters Wilderness

▲ Camp 24

▲6931'

Collier Lava Flow

Camp 23 ▲   *Minnie Scott
Spring*

viewpoint

Opie Dilldock Pass
6900'

Obsidian Trail (#3528)

White Branch Creek

Camp 22

▲ Collier Cone
7534'

Sawyer
Bar

Collier Glacier view

Glacier

Obsidian
Cliffs

Glacier Way
Trail (#4336)

Sunshine Meadow

*Obsidian Limited
Entry Area*

Obsidian Trail
(#3528)

▲ Sunshine Meadow

▲ Little Brother
7810'

Creek

LEG 6

N   0   1   2 MILES

0   1   2 KILOMETERS

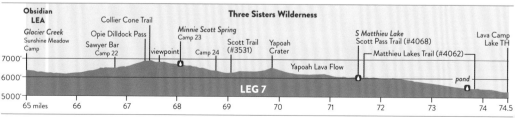

Obsidian
LEA

Three Sisters Wilderness

Glacier Creek
Sunshine Meadow
Camp

Collier Cone Trail

Opie Dilldock Pass

Sawyer Bar
Camp 22

Minnie Scott Spring
Camp 23

viewpoint

Camp 24

Scott Trail
(#3531)

Yapoah
Crater

S Matthieu Lake
Scott Pass Trail (#4068)

Lava Camp
Lake TH

Matthieu Lakes Trail (#4062)

Yapoah Lava Flow

pond

7000'

6000'

LEG 7

5000'

65 miles   66   67   68   69   70   71   72   73   74   74.5

From Opie Dilldock Pass, the PCT plunges into the wide, stark lava beds of Collier Cone and Yapoah Crater.

ancient volcano is actually the base upon which North Sister is built. Around the ridge, the trail bends northeast and begins a gentle ascent; the surrounding forest is lively and green, with plenty of bright yellow arnica decorating the shady slope. The trail then turns east at the edge of the gully containing seasonal **White Branch Creek**; across the gully, through the trees, you may notice a dark wall of lava rock. The PCT then exits the Obsidian Limited Entry Area at 65.4 miles and starts climbing earnestly alongside the gully until it exits the trees atop a bluff with a wide-open view of Little Brother and North Sister to the southeast and a vast and desolate ocean of craggy volcanic lava all ways north. In the distance, rising from the undulating sea of jagged black stone, **Mount Washington**, **Three Fingered Jack**, **Mount Jefferson**, and **Mount Hood** line up on the horizon.

The trail then descends to the rocky White Branch Creek gully and crosses to a little tree "island" called **Sawyer Bar (Camp 22)**, at 66.8 miles, where two small tent sites can be found tucked away in the trees. The location doesn't offer much else, and the White Branch Creek often runs dry by midsummer, but this makes a decent spot to make camp before entering the

COLLIER CONE

Collier Cone is a 1500-year-old cinder cone on the north flank of North Sister, whose western flank collapsed during a large lava outpouring. From the PCT, near mile 67.5, a loose, gravelly path climbs 0.5 mile and 700 steep feet to its 7534-foot rim summit. Views from the top include a stunning look at North Sister and the retreating Collier Glacier immediately south; the view north looks over more vast lava beds and takes in every high peak to Mount Hood.

barren wastes ahead if you don't have a permit to overnight in the Obsidian area at Glacier Creek. The trail then crosses a cindery flat and arrives at the gates of Mordor: a ragged, jumbly wall of reddish-black lava. The way forward, now a path of loose volcanic sand and cinders turns east and begins ascending the lowermost ridge extension of 7534-foot **Collier Cone**. The path then slides off the ridge and into a narrow gorge, continuing to ascend on tight switchbacks, surrounded by slopes of red cinders and jumbly black lava rock. Don't be surprised if you find yourself checking the shadows for lurking orcs. At the top of the gorge, at 67.4 miles, the PCT reaches 6900-foot **Opie Dilldock Pass**. Here, at the breach of Collier Cone, is an impressive view west over the vast lava field that this cinder cone spilled forth.

The PCT then proceeds into the interior of Collier Cone on a flat, rocky plain to an unsigned fork at 67.5 miles, marked by a large cairn. The fork right (south) climbs 0.4 mile to the top of Collier Cone's southern ridge for an incredible view over the Collier Glacier on North Sister's northwest flank, definitely worth a quick side trip. The fork left continues the PCT's journey north; where it turns northwest, a bootpath cuts off to steeply climb to Collier Cone's rim. The PCT then veers north out onto the spine of a narrow volcanic ridge. Just before the trail switchbacks down off the ridge onto the eastern slope, an incredible 360-degree panorama opens up over Oregon's entire Central Cascades region. This is quite possibly the biggest view in the entire state, another one of those humbling scenes where you suddenly realize how small you are in a very large environment.

Dropping down into the next basin, the trail continues north out of the moonscape and reenters

A southbound PCT hiker approaches Opie Dilldock Pass, leaving (from left to right) Mount Washington, Three Fingered Jack, Mount Jefferson, and Mount Hood behind him.

Yapoah Crater rises above cindery plains and lava flows, tempting PCT hikers to climb its slopes for big panoramic views.

(slightly) greener pastures, where **Minnie Scott Spring** ⬤ flows cheerfully across the trail at 68.1 miles. Left (northwest) of the creek crossing, a small campsite can be found at the edge of the trees (**Camp 23**). The trail then continues through a lightly forested saddle where blooms of magenta paintbrush bring splashes of vibrant color to the trailside. Then it's back out in the open to make a gentle, contouring descent across a steep slope of loose yellowish cinders before reentering sparse tree cover. At 68.8 miles, a short bootpath veers right (east) off the PCT to a nice, large campsite with room for a few tents (**Camp 24**) and a partial view over a wide, grassy meadow to the north.

Exiting tree cover once again, the PCT crosses a delightful meadow carpeted with lupine and aster, surrounded on all sides by colorful volcanic escarpments and cinder slopes. On the north side of the meadow, the PCT meets the **Scott Trail** (#3531) at 69.1 miles. This trail branches off westward for 5 miles to skirt Four in One Cone and parallel Frog Camp Creek to a trailhead on OR 242. Before ascending the next forested ridge, throw a look in your rearview for a peek at Collier Cone and North and Middle Sisters rising above the meadow that will

just make you want to smile. Then it's a quick up-and-over the ridge to the base of 6737-foot **Yapoah Crater** at 69.6 miles. The PCT makes a clockwise half-circuit around the black cinder cone, partway around crossing over the top of the lava flow that breached its lower flanks. From this high perch, the view north peers over Yapoah's

YAPOAH CRATER

Similar to Collier Cone, Yapoah Crater is a relatively young volcanic feature. It is the source of a massive lava flow more than a mile wide and nearly 8 miles long, estimated to have occurred around 2500 years ago. For a peek inside the cone's crater, as well as another high-point view over the surrounding area, a steep, crumbly path ascends to the rim. Look for the trail, which branches off the PCT at 69.6 miles and proceeds to contour the slope upward. The path enters a grove of trees on the northwest flank, then switchbacks up the cindery slope to the rim.

South Matthieu Lake makes a refreshing spot to pause for a water break after crossing the hot, dry moonscape below Yapoah Crater.

ALTERNATE ROUTE: MATTHIEU LAKES TRAIL (OST)

The 2.2-mile **Matthieu Lakes Trail** (#4062) parallels the PCT, but under cover of lively forest along the margin of the Yapoah lava flow. While the upper PCT route grants more views—albeit only for a short portion—the lower lake route, once a part of the Oregon Skyline Trail, offers more access to water—namely, a large lake with plenty of camping opportunities. To take this route, drop off the PCT at 71.7 miles and switchback 0.7 mile down into forest to the east shore of **North Matthieu Lake (Camp)** ⬤. There are seven designated campsites located around the lake—the first four sites are located right of the trail on the north and east sides; the remaining three sites on the west and south sides. As with the other lake, campfires are not permitted here. The trail continues past the lake and down a series of switchbacks into a lower basin where a small pond may be found right (east) of the trail. The trail levels out and skirts the edge of the lava flow to reconnect with the PCT at mile 73.7. This option adds only 0.2 mile to your day's total, and is an especially attractive—and refreshing—option in the middle of a warm summer day.

massive basalt flow that stretches all the way to McKenzie Pass; the now-familiar high peaks of Washington, Jack, Jefferson, and Hood can also be seen.

The trail then descends along Yapoah's northern slope and again turns to sandy cinders as it proceeds through the volcanic moonscape; sparse trees and tiny shrubs take root here and there among the jumble. If you ever wondered what it would look like to walk through a mountain of crumbled Oreo cookies (minus the cream filling), this is it. The PCT tracks north through the lava on sandy, level tread for a spell, then veers east to twist through a particularly jagged portion of spiky lava mixed with red volcanic rocks and cinders, finally dropping back down onto duffy forest floor under the shade of tall conifers. The shade doesn't last for long, however, as the trail emerges onto a moderate slope at the margin of the lava flow. The trail continues northward through an interesting corridor, contouring the slope on yellowish cindery tread among red cinders and lava rock, while paralleling the blocky black lava just to the left (west) and green forest just upslope to the right (east).

The PCT then pulls away from the lava and meets the **Scott Pass Trail** (#4068) junction at 71.6 miles, in a grove of shady trees. If the day has warmed considerably, you'll be thankful for every bit of shade you can find. Here, an information board welcomes you to the **Matthieu Lakes Area** and shows a map of the permissible campsites at the lakes ahead. The PCT continues left (northwest) while the Scott Pass Trail veers right (east) to numerous junctions and destinations. Just past the junction, the PCT skirts the north shore of **South Matthieu Lake (Camp)** ⬤, a glorious clear, blue pool in a shallow, tree-ringed basin. There are three designated campsites around the lake, one each on the north, west and south sides; campfires are not permitted here. After your sandy slog through the scorching lava, take a few moments to cool off lakeside, have a snack, and enjoy the setting—it's all going to change again very soon.

Pulling away from the lake, the PCT meets the southern junction with the **Matthieu Lakes Trail** (#4062) at 71.7 miles. Another portion of the old Oregon Skyline Trail, this alternate route drops down into a forested basin at the edge of the Yapoah lava flow (see alternate), while the PCT remains high on the ridge above. Sticking with the PCT, the trail makes a short, moderate ascent around an unnamed butte, gaining both elevation and exposure and granting ever-wider views over the surrounding landscape—brilliantly contrasted by green forest, black lava, and blue sky. Then the scene turns bleak again as the trail enters the 2017 **Milli Fire** area, where the once-vibrant forest has been reduced to a stand of blackened matchstick trees. The trail then winds down through a series of switchbacks, and passes a small basin, at 73.7 miles, which used to hold a nice pond. A short 0.1 mile farther, the PCT meets the northern junction with the Matthieu Lakes Trail.

The way forward once again parallels the Yapoah lava flow, winding north on a gradual descent through more burned woods over sooty, ashen terrain. The end of the leg comes along at 74.5 miles, where the **Lava Camp Lake (Camp)** ⬤ spur trail branches off 0.2 mile east to a large trailhead parking area. Across the parking area, a short bootpath leads through the trees to the camp area. Lava Camp Lake offers 12 fee-free campsites with picnic tables, fire pits, and tent spaces; there is a vault toilet, but water must be obtained by filtering from the lake. This is the last established campsite for nearly 10 miles, and the last reliable water source for nearly 16 miles. The final leg is a tough one, so take advantage of this location and get ready for the final stretch ahead.

CAMP-TO-CAMP MILEAGE

Sunshine Meadow Camp to Camp 22 (Sawyer Bar)	1.8
Camp 22 (Sawyer Bar) to Camp 23	1.3
Camp 23 to Camp 24	0.7
Camp 24 to South Matthieu Lake Camp	2.8
South Matthieu Lake Camp to North Matthieu Lake Camp (off PCT)	0.8
South Matthieu Lake Camp to Lava Camp Lake junction	2.9
Lava Camp Lake junction to Lava Camp Lake (off PCT)	0.2

8 MCKENZIE PASS TO SANTIAM PASS

DISTANCE 18.5 miles

ELEVATION GAIN/LOSS +2120 feet/ −2590 feet

HIGH POINT 6130 feet

CONNECTING TRAILS
OR 242, Little Belknap spur trail, Big Lake spur trail, Old Santiam Wagon Road, South Loop Trail (#3556), FR 860, Fireline Loop Trail (#3558), North Loop Trail (#3550), US 20/OR 126

ON THE TRAIL

Returning to the Pacific Crest Trail from Lava Camp Lake, the last leg of this section is one of the toughest—after three days of alpine bliss traversing the Three Sisters, it's time to pay the piper. Unlike the many miles to the south, shaped by water and ice, the miles ahead have been shaped much more recently by fire—exposed and waterless—making this passage challenging in the heat of midsummer. There are some redeeming elements to be enjoyed along the way, including big views of central Oregon's high peaks, a few slopeside meadows brimming with wildflowers, and a chance to look down the throat of a fairly recent volcanic event: **Little Belknap**. Due to the terrain, exposure, and lack of water, campsites are scarce. Your best bet is to start the leg early, push all the way through to your waiting ride at the Santiam Pass trailhead, congratulate yourself on a well-done hike, then drive to the town of Sisters to cool off with a refreshing drink.

Back at the **Lava Camp Spur** junction, hang a right (north) and ascend out of burned woods onto a wide lava flow, the same lava flow that you crossed 4 miles back that originated at Yapoah Crater. The trail meanders west across the lava on rough, cindery tread; vegetation is sparse, with just a few hardy grasses and other sprigs eking all they can out of the inhospitable terrain. Though the trail through the lava is well-developed, the surface can be quite dynamic, with loose ground ranging from the size of pebbles to small cobbles, many waiting to stub toes and turn ankles. If you're carrying trekking poles, they'll be put to good use here. Once you reach the plateau of the lava, the views open wide in all directions—a harsh and barren, yet surreal and intriguing landscape. To the south, North and Middle Sisters rise boldly above the aa; to the north, Belknap Crater and Little Belknap beckon while Mount Washington's pointed spire shoots skyward; farther north, glacier-capped Mount Jefferson climbs over the horizon.

At 75.7 miles, the PCT turns and comes to the **McKenzie Highway** (OR 242). The trail continues directly across, from a small turnout on the north side of the road. Depending on your itinerary, you may choose to walk the road 0.2 mile east to the **Dee Wright Observatory**; about halfway between the road crossing and the observatory is a well-maintained vault restroom. From the brink of the roadside, looking north, the scene

DEE WRIGHT OBSERVATORY

Completed in 1935 by the Civilian Conservation Corps, and named for the crew foreman who died the previous year, the Dee Wright Observatory sits atop the crest of 5325-foot McKenzie Pass. The squat, turret-shaped structure is built entirely of native lava rock. Windows within the shelter's walls are positioned precisely to frame views of the surrounding peaks. From the top of the observatory, unobstructed 360-degree panoramic views take in more than twenty mountains and high points, from Middle Sister to the south all the way to Mount Hood to the north. A paved, 0.5-mile interpretive trail loops through the nearby lava bed, highlighting some of the area's unique geology.

Notable for its vast, roiling lava beds originating from Belknap Crater and Little Belknap, Mount Washington Wilderness does not offer much shade.

is wide and bleak, a desert of black, jagged lava in all directions. Poking up out of the lava are two small, forested knobs, like tropical islands rising above a thrashing onyx sea. If you haven't already, now is the time to slather on a good helping of sunblock. For the next 3 miles, with the exception of the small, forested islands directly ahead, the only thing between you and the central Oregon sunshine is a lot of sky.

Winding west from the highway, the PCT begins crossing the main portion of the Belknap lava flow, generally paralleling the highway. The lava crossing ends soon enough and the trail drops onto the lower flank of the first forested "island," where it enters the **Mount Washington Wilderness** and quickly comes to a large trailhead parking area and permit kiosk at 76 miles. Here, fill out your free wilderness permit. The trail then continues northwest for a short spell on soft, near-flat, near-shady terrain. Under the shelter

of pine and fir forest, ferns, huckleberry, grouse whortleberry, and small purple penstemon thrive. The trail ascends slightly over the western flank of the hillock, then crosses the next petrified river of stone separating the two islands. Instead of crossing over the second forested hill, the trail circuits west around its base, in the margin between the shady forest and the jagged lava. Take a breather in the cool air under the trees—it will be the last shade you'll see for a while.

Leaving the forested island behind, the PCT begins ascending the southern slope of Little Belknap. The grade is shallow, which should be effortless, if it weren't for the loose and uneven lava trail surface. Take your time and watch your footing to avoid unwanted trips and turns. Despite its bleakness, the roiling, twisted terrain belies the youthful origins of Oregon's Cascades. As the trail climbs, the views become wider and better. The trail finally comes to a low crest at 78.2 miles.

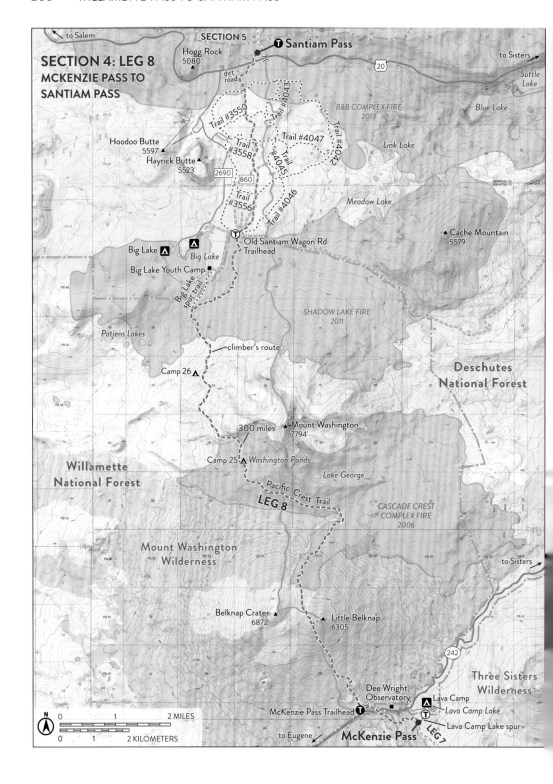

to Salem

SECTION 5

Santiam Pass

SECTION 4: LEG 8
MCKENZIE PASS TO
SANTIAM PASS

Hogg Rock
5080'

dirt
road

to Sisters

20

Suttle
Lake

Trail #4043

Trail #3550

Trail #4047

B&B COMPLEX FIRE
2013

Blue Lake

Hoodoo Butte
5597'

Trail
#3558

Trail
#4045

Trail #4042

Link Lake

Hayrick Butte
5523'

2690

860

Cache Mountain
5579'

Trail
#3556

Trail #4046

Meadow Lake

Big Lake
Big Lake

Old Santiam Wagon Rd
Trailhead

Big Lake Youth Camp

SHADOW LAKE FIRE
2011

Deschutes
National Forest

Big Lake
spur trail

Patjens Lakes

climber's route

Camp 26

300 miles

Mount Washington
7794'

Camp 25   Washington Ponds

Lake George

Willamette
National Forest

Pacific Crest Trail

LEG 8

CASCADE CREST
COMPLEX FIRE
2006

to Sisters

Mount Washington
Wilderness

Belknap Crater
6872'

Little Belknap
6305'

242

Three Sisters
Wilderness

Dee Wright
Observatory

Lava Camp
Lava Camp Lake

McKenzie Pass Trailhead

N
0   1   2 MILES
0   1   2 KILOMETERS

to Eugene

McKenzie Pass

LEG 7

Lava Camp Lake spur

The PCT winds over pressure ridges and crumbling lava tubes in the lava beds below (from left to right) Belknap Crater and Little Belknap.

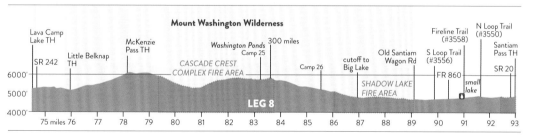

Here, a signed junction points the way to **Little Belknap**, a 0.2-mile side trail that ascends to the top of the volcano. This short detour is worth taking the time to explore a little.

The PCT then winds gently down across more lava, around more pressure ridges and past more collapsed lava tubes, and returns to normal ground at 78.5 miles. Here, the surface is a mix of dirt and cinders, where only sparse clumps of buckwheat withstand the arid conditions. Near here, a faint, unmarked bootpath breaks off the PCT westward to ascend Belknap Crater. Forest returns over the next 0.4 mile in the form of small, shady groves of lodgepole pines. There aren't any established campsites in the area, but the relatively flat surfaces in many places could easily accommodate

a tent for a primitive camping option in a pinch. Take comfort in a break from the sun here, as at 79.4 miles, the trail reenters a landscape twisted by fire—this time, wildfire.

Quickly the shade of green conifers gives way to a desolate dead forest of burned trunks, snags, and debris—the results of the **2006 Cascade Crest Complex Fire**. Trail conditions degrade significantly as the PCT continues its descent north; watch your footing over the rough, uneven path, dodging debris and skirting blowdowns. In some sections, the trail all but disappears, with no visible markers or blazes on the burned trees. Pay close attention and scan ahead for where the trail continues. The sparse shrubbery eventually gives way to barren lava where the topsoil has completely

LITTLE BELKNAP

Get an up-close view down the throat of a recent volcano at Little Belknap.

Geologically infantile, the Belknap lava flows are approximately only 3000 to 1500 years old, and cover more than 40 square miles. The majority of the dense, basaltic andesite lava originates from 6872-foot Belknap Crater, a shield volcano. This lava is intermingled with more lava originating from 6305-foot Little Belknap, a smaller shield volcano. The Pacific Crest Trail cuts its path directly between the two. The rugged terrain is marked by pressure ridges and collapsed lava tubes. From a slight ridge, a 0.2-mile side trail breaks off the PCT eastward for exploring Little Belknap. As you're heading up this side trail, take note of the difference in the lava's surface. The crumbly, blocky lava is aa; the smooth, ropy-looking lava is pahoehoe. Below the jagged summit, a portion of exposed lava tube makes a small cave—a nice shady spot for a snack or lunch break. The trail ends at a notch between a pinnacled mound and the summit proper.

From this notch, take the faint bootpath that wraps around the north side of the western mound to a cave with multiple lava arches overhead; this is the vent of Little Belknap. Use caution as you peer down the throat of this recently active volcano. To claim the summit for 360-degree views of central Oregon's Cascade peaks, scramble up the crumbly side of the eastern summit cone. There are no established trails to the summit, only a faint user trail that ascends the volcano's loose, cindery slopes.

eroded away. The going is rough until the trail bottoms out in a shallow gully near the edge of another lava flow. Here, the PCT turns east to skirt the extent of the jagged flow before turning back west to begin a wide circuit around Mount Washington.

As the PCT climbs west through salt-and-pepper burned forest, greenery returns to the floor, but there is no cover overhead. About halfway along the ascent, ferns become profuse on the exposed slope. The wide view to the south takes in Belknap

Crater and the inhospitable sea of lava surrounding it. Just past the 82-mile mark, the ascent reaches its high point and the trail levels out, undulating northwest. Among the standing ghosts of burned trees and deadfall, penstemon, lupine, beargrass, thistle, mariposa lily, and skyrocket decorate the open slope; the pointed peak of Mount Washington has long since disappeared behind the mountain's flank. Near the 83-mile mark, the peak comes back into view to the northeast, though mostly obstructed by standing burned forest. Better views are just ahead.

Now the PCT bears north as it continues to contour around the lower flanks of Mount Washington. At 83.2 miles you blissfully leave the burn area behind and reenter shady green forest on wide, comfortable trail—sometimes "green tunnel" is quite welcome. Just 0.1 mile into the sheltered forest, two small campsites can be found to the right (east) of the trail; spaces are large enough for a tent each (**Camp 25**). Just beyond the campsites, a large cairn marks an unsigned bootpath that breaks off to the east, leading to the **Washington Ponds**. In previous years, these two ponds were a reliable water source for passing hikers, but more recently have dwindled to nothing more than mucky puddles. Do not rely on finding good water here, but if you're looking to split this extra-long leg in half, do it here.

Following this short spell of delightfully shady forest, the trail once again departs the trees, but this time into a wide, grassy meadow with a good view of Mount Washington. Here, at 83.6 miles, you pass through the 300-mile point of the PCT's crossing of Oregon. If you're thru-hiking the whole state, you're two-thirds of the way done—congratulations! About halfway across the meadow, the trail crosses a long-dry stream gully. Beyond the meadow, the trail bends west, ducks briefly back under tree cover, then comes out in the open to traverse a wide south-facing slope, where manzanita adorns much of the surface. Once again, the view to the south takes in Belknap Crater's wide lava flows; to the west, the scene is a wide panorama of forested ridges and valleys.

Bending northwest again, the PCT returns to forest for the next couple of miles and begins what will be a long, gradual descent of Mount

TRAIL VISIBILITY

Some hikers, especially thru-hikers, choose to hike this stretch of the PCT between McKenzie and Santiam passes in the late hours of the evening or early hours of the morning to avoid the heat and exposure of summer days. In the low light and dark hours of the night, it can be extremely challenging to identify and stay on the trail across the lava fields and through the rugged burn areas. Attempting this stretch in the dark should only be done by those with night hiking experience and excellent navigation skills.

Washington's west and northwest slopes. Where the grade eases at 85.6 miles, a moderate campsite can be found left of the trail; nearer the trail is a small space for one tent, and beyond that a larger space can accommodate two tents (**Camp 26**). Here also, old maps indicate **Coldwater Spring**. This piped well can be found in a small clearing right of the trail, opposite the campsite, just through the trees; however, this seasonal water source has not been reliable in recent years. Continuing north, another unmarked side trail breaks off east at 86 miles. This is the climbers' path for Mount Washington. Gaining the summit requires technical expertise and climbing gear.

The PCT then enters a swath of forest scorched by the **2011 Shadow Lake Fire**, which intermittently charred the forest from medium rare to well done. Passage is quick, though largely exposed on relatively level tread. At 87 miles, a signed, 1.5-mile spur trail branches off to the left (north) to **Big Lake Youth Camp**. This lakeside resort offers some services, as well as resupply holds for PCT hikers (see appendix 4). Rising above Big Lake, the fire-ravaged slopes of **Hoodoo Ski Area** can be seen. The trail then traverses the blackened ridge on a wide circuit above Big Lake. The sounds of recreation civilization—e.g., motorboats—will rise to greet you as you proceed north to finally exit the Mount Washington Wilderness at 89 miles. Just beyond the wilderness boundary, the PCT comes

MOUNT WASHINGTON WILDERNESS

Located in the heart of central Oregon's Cascades, the Mount Washington Wilderness was established in 1964 and covers more than 54,000 acres. The area encompasses one of the largest and most recent lava flows in the United States. At its center, 7794-foot Mount Washington is the jagged core of a once-much-larger shield volcano. During the last ice age, immense glaciers eroded away much of the mountain, leaving behind a crumbling, andesitic plug. The summit can be attained by way of several technical climbing routes. Where hardened black aa and pahoehoe doesn't cover the ground, much of the wilderness is dominated by hemlock, fir, and lodgepole pine forest. Since 2003, several large wildfires have claimed large portions of forest throughout the wilderness, leaving it a patchwork of jagged lava, green forest, and scorched hillsides. There are several small lakes scattered around the wilderness; however, running water is scarce. The PCT is the primary trail that traverses the wilderness area from McKenzie Pass to Santiam Pass. A handful of shorter trails explore some of the area's geologic highlights.

to the **Old Santiam Wagon Road** and a large trailhead parking area.

The final 4 miles to Santiam Pass cross the **Ray Benson Sno-Park** and its spiderweb of trails, beginning with several old road crossings. The area is mostly dry, lodgepole pine forest interspersed with small, grassy meadows; the PCT is mostly flat with good, easy tread and decent shade from the sun. Between the Sno-Park trails are numerous old dirt roads, some still used, some decommissioned and covered with debris. The views here are limited to the immediate surroundings, so keep your eyes open for wildflowers, especially big white Washington lilies. At 89.9 miles, the PCT crosses the **South Loop Trail** (#3556); to either side, blue diamond blazes high on the trees mark the routes to the Sno-Park trailhead to the west and the Brandenburg Shelter to the east. Just 0.5 mile farther, the trail crosses **FR 860**, then at 90.9 miles, the PCT skirts the only reliable water source through the entire leg: a large pond ⬤ just west of the trail—a beautiful sight for overheated eyes. The water is shallow but clear near the grassy shoreline; across the lake is flat-topped, 5523-foot **Hayrick Butte**. If you need to filter water, be sure your sediment screen is working well, or strip off your boots and wade in a little deeper. This refreshing pool can be sweet relief on sweltering summer days.

The homestretch continues winding north, with huckleberry, grouse whortleberry, and pretty rosy spirea adorning the trailsides. The PCT then crosses the **Fireline Loop Trail** (#3558), then makes a short, gentle ascent and levels out again. At 91.6 miles, the PCT crosses the **North Loop Trail** (#3550), marked with a "You Are Here" signed trail map (posted high to be above winter snow). At 92.1 miles, the trail crosses the threshold into the southern extent of the **2003 B&B Complex Fire** burn area. (See more about the B&B Fire in Section 5.) The trail is once again fully exposed amid burned snags and debris. But the area is not fully desolate, blanketed with plenty of beargrass and pink thistle. In the near distance, flat-topped, 4872-foot **Hogg Rock** juts upward to the west; the jagged profile of Three Fingered Jack rises to the north.

WATER ALERT!

If you're thru-hiking the PCT into Section 5, you will want to top off all of your water sources at the pond at 90.9 miles. The next near-trail water is **Koko Lake**, 11.7 miles ahead, just south of Minto Pass, through more exposed, burned forest.

The pointed spire of Mount Washington rises above one of the few green meadows between barren lava beds and charred forest in its wilderness area.

The PCT crosses one final old, dirt road at 92.4 miles and bends northwest. The **North Santiam Highway** (US 20/OR 126) comes into view, and at 92.8 miles the PCT is unceremoniously spit out of the trees onto the shoulder of the highway. Use caution crossing the highway, as there is no obvious signage or roadside turnouts on either side alerting drivers that this is a major trail–road crossing. Across the highway, the PCT plunges back into more charred terrain, making a short, moderate ascent to the junction with the **Santiam Pass** trailhead spur at 93 miles. If this is the end of your journey, hang a left (west) and stroll down to the trailhead parking area and your waiting vehicle or ride.

Having just hiked nearly 100 miles through some of the most spectacular and varied wilderness in Oregon, give yourself a well-deserved congratulations—then hop in your car and drive 20 miles east to the town of Sisters and celebrate with frosty milkshakes!

CAMP-TO-CAMP MILEAGE

Lava Camp Lake junction to Camp 25 . . . . 8.8
Camp 25 to Camp 26 . . . . 2.3
Camp 26 to Big Lake Youth Camp junction . . 1.4
Big Lake Youth Camp junction to Big Lake
    Youth Camp (off PCT) 1.5
Big Lake Youth Camp junction to
    Santiam Pass 6.0

SANTIAM PASS TO TIMBERLINE LODGE

FROM HIGH RIDGES and forested valleys to the threshold of Oregon's tallest mountain, this stretch of the Pacific Crest Trail offers varied and fascinating scenery through this section of the Beaver State. Along the way you'll witness the effects of several devastating wildfires (and nature's efforts at recovery), ford rushing glacier-fed streams, and weave through parklike meadows beside glittering alpine lakes. There are plenty of ups and downs, but none too strenuous as the PCT continues north along the Crest between the Willamette (west) and Deschutes (east) national forests. From the north side of **Mount Jefferson**, the trail then tracks inside of the **Warm Springs Indian Reservation** for nearly 30 miles before finishing with a steady climb to an historic lodge in the **Mount Hood National Forest**.

The section begins at the Santiam Pass trailhead, an easy 20-mile drive west from the town of Sisters. The first 20-plus miles traverse the scarred hillsides and blackened forests resulting from the 2003 **B&B Complex Fire,** followed by several miles through the 2017 **Whitewater Fire** area. These stretches are arid and water is scarce, but unobstructed views showcase the ridges and basins of Oregon's eastern Cascades region with frequent looks at peaks near and far. From there, the scenery makes a welcome change to subalpine forest and parkland below the icy crown of Oregon's second-highest peak, Mount Jefferson, with a highlight being the stunningly scenic (and crowd favorite) **Jefferson Park**. Here, campsites dot the shorelines of numerous lakes, while copious huckleberries tempt the taste buds and oodles of wildflowers paint a tapestry of color over sprawling meadows. Then it's just a quick hop over Park Divide, through a region of forested lakes and ponds, to the vast Olallie Lake, where a small, lakeside resort offers cold drinks, salty snacks, cabins, and camping.

DISTANCE 96 miles

STATE DISTANCE 309.3–405.3

ELEVATION GAIN/LOSS
+16,350 feet/–15,360 feet

HIGH POINT 6890 feet

BEST TIME OF YEAR Aug–Sep

PCTA SECTION LETTERS F, G

LAND MANAGERS Willamette National Forest (Mount Jefferson Wilderness, west), Deschutes National Forest (Mount Jefferson Wilderness, east), Warm Springs Indian Reservation, Mount Hood National Forest

PASSES AND PERMITS NW Forest Pass required for parking at Santiam Pass, Frog Lake, Barlow Pass trailheads; limited-entry permit required to hike in Mount Jefferson Wilderness. For more information about PCT permit requirements, visit www.pctoregon.com/pct-info/permits.

MAPS AND APPS
- National Geographic PCT: Oregon North 1004, maps 4–11
- Halfmile PCT: Oregon F4–G1
- Guthook PCT: Oregon

Opposite: The PCT's passage around Mount Jefferson offers dramatic views of Oregon's second-tallest peak.

LEGS

1. Santiam Pass to Minto Pass
2. Minto Pass to Shale Lake
3. Shale Lake to Jefferson Park
4. Jefferson Park to Olallie Lake
5. Olallie Lake to Lemiti Creek
6. Lemiti Creek to Warm Springs
7. Warm Springs to Timothy Lake
8. Timothy Lake to Wapinitia Pass
9. Wapinitia Pass to Timberline Lodge

The second half of the section ventures onto the Warm Springs Indian Reservation. The mostly forested "green tunnel" may be short on views (you'll actually be thankful, as it traverses wide swaths of timber harvesting lands), but long on opportunities to become more acquainted with forest flora, including a variety of trees, shrubs, and flowers. After a few days in the woods, the trail comes to the doorstep of Oregon's tallest peak, **Mount Hood**, beginning with a leisurely romp around picturesque **Timothy Lake**, with its numerous camping options. The trail then crosses **Barlow Pass**, once known as part of the bygone Oregon Trail, before ascending the southern flank of Mount Hood, where wide panoramas explode into view as the PCT merges with the iconic **Timberline Trail** to circuit a portion of the mountain. The section ends at the historic **Timberline Lodge**, renowned for its rich Northwestern heritage. Here, you can toast a hike well done with cocktails in the spacious lounge, or in the dining room over one of their unique and mouthwatering meals. Of course, you'll probably want to wash off all the trail dust first, and one of their rustic yet elegant rooms will be just right for that—a royal treat at the end of a near-100-mile trek.

The challenges through this section are many—water, camping, exposure, mosquitoes—but none too difficult with proper planning. The terrain, much like the rest of the state, remains mostly gentle to moderate, with the largest ascent coming at the very end—all the more reason to take a well-earned break at the end of the section. In the middle of summer, be prepared for warm, dry days and, if you're hitting the popular camp areas, lots of weekend company. Unlike most of the rest of the PCT, where you can just load your pack and hit the trail, this section requires a little more advance preparation if you're going to take advantage of some of the better camp locations. This section definitely has some high highs, and low lows, but when you step above the treeline and stare face-to-face with Mount Hood, it will quickly erase the memory of the more lackluster trail miles behind and help you appreciate the effort that much more.

ACCESS
Santiam Pass
From Salem, take I-5 exit 253 for OR 22; turn and drive east for 80 miles. Continue east on US 20/OR 126 for another 5.4 miles to the signed PCT Trailhead; turn left onto the short spur to the parking roundabout. From Bend: Drive 19 miles north on US 20 to the town of Sisters; continue west on US 20/OR 126 for 20 miles to the trailhead.

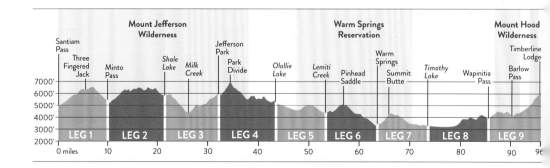

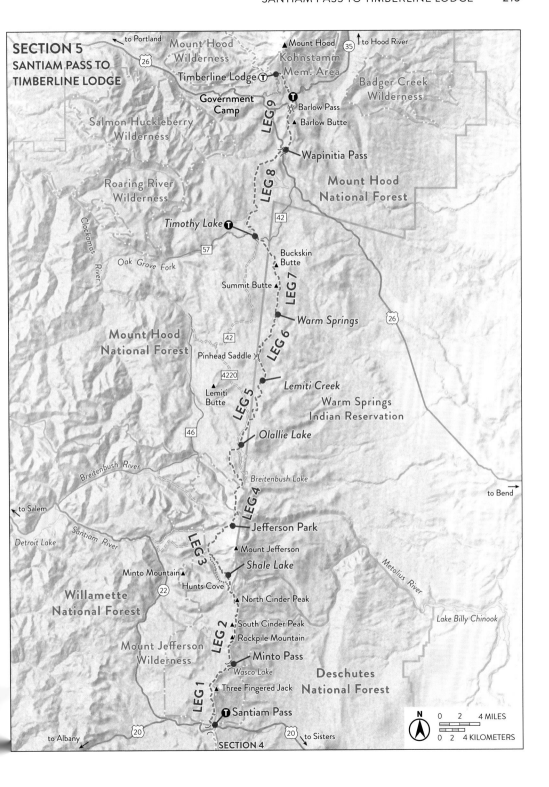

SECTION 5
SANTIAM PASS TO
TIMBERLINE LODGE

to Portland
Mount Hood
Wilderness
26
▲ Mount Hood   35   to Hood River
Kohnstamm
Mem. Area
Timberline Lodge   T
T
Barlow Pass
Government
Camp
Barlow Butte
Badger Creek
Wilderness

LEG 9

Salmon Huckleberry
Wilderness

Wapinitia Pass

LEG 8

Roaring River
Wilderness

Mount Hood
National Forest

42

Clackamas River

Timothy Lake   T

57

Oak Grove Fork

LEG 7

Buckskin
Butte ▲

Summit Butte ▲

Warm Springs

26

Mount Hood
National Forest

42

LEG 6

Pinhead Saddle

4220

Lemiti
Butte ▲

LEG 5

Lemiti Creek

Warm Springs
Indian Reservation

46

Olallie Lake

to Bend

Breitenbush River

Breitenbush Lake

LEG 4

to Salem

Santiam River

Detroit Lake

LEG 3

Jefferson Park

▲ Mount Jefferson

Shale Lake

Minto Mountain ▲

Hunts Cove

Metolius River

22

Willamette
National Forest

North Cinder Peak

LEG 2

South Cinder Peak
Rockpile Mountain

Lake Billy Chinook

Mount Jefferson
Wilderness

Minto Pass

Wasco Lake

Deschutes
National Forest

LEG 1

Three Fingered Jack

T   Santiam Pass

20

to Albany

20   to Sisters

SECTION 4

N

0   2   4 MILES

0   2   4 KILOMETERS

You may consider taking a "zero day" in Jefferson Park to enjoy its many lakes, meadows, and big mountain views.

Olallie Lake

This midsection access point requires a long drive to a remote location, but is worthwhile for breaking this extra-long section into two parts. From Government Camp (see next), take US 26 east/south for 11 miles. Turn onto Oregon Skyline Road (FR 42/4220) and continue 34 winding miles to the resort. The PCT crosses the road on the south side of Head Lake, just north of where the road forks.

Timberline Lodge

From Portland, drive east on US 26 for 52 miles to the town of Government Camp. Continue 1 mile east, then turn left on the Timberline Highway. Proceed 5.5 winding miles to the large parking area at Timberline Lodge.

From Bend, drive north on US 97 for 43 miles. Merge onto US 26 north and continue another 62 miles toward Government Camp. One mile before Government Camp, turn right onto the Timberline Highway and proceed up the mountain.

Hikers and backpackers should use the large, lower parking area, just southeast of the smaller main lodge parking area.

NOTES
Services

The southern trailhead at Santiam Pass is 20 miles west of the town of Sisters. There you'll find lodging, dining, groceries, and outdoor supplies. The northern trailhead, at Timberline Lodge, offers moderate and upscale dining and somewhat pricey lodge rooms. Government Camp, 6 miles down the mountain, has more moderately priced dining and lodging options, in addition to groceries and limited supplies. About midway through the section, Olallie Lake Resort offers rustic cabins, camping, and a decent store. (See appendixes 3 and 4 for more info.)

Camping

This section requires more planning than is usually needed along much of the PCT. The camping areas at Shale Lake (in addition to alternate camping at Hunts Cove and Pamelia Lake) and Jefferson Park all require overnight permits, which can be obtained in advance of your trip. Camping on the Warm Springs Indian Reservation is limited to just a few designated areas. (See Passes and Permits in the introduction for more info.)

Water
There are long stretches of exposed trail between water sources through several stretches of this section, especially in later summer when seasonal creeks and springs dry up. Plan to start with extra water, top off whenever possible, and stay hydrated. There are not usually any water caches to be found along this stretch of trail.

Hazards
There are two river fords on the west side of Mount Jefferson that can be treacherous during warm summer periods of high runoff or following summer thunderstorms: Milk Creek and Russell Creek. Try to ford these creeks in the morning, or wait until storms have passed. Always scout for the safest river crossing and exercise proper fording techniques. (See Planning and Preparation in the introduction for more info.)

SUGGESTED ITINERARIES

The following distances do not include off-PCT miles (up to 1 mile) to water sources, campsites, alternate routes, or resupply locations. For more information about trail distances, see How to Use This Guide.

9 DAYS

		Miles
Day 1	Santiam Pass to Minto Pass	10.1
Day 2	Minto Pass to Shale Lake	11.6
Day 3	Shale Lake to Jefferson Park	10.6
Day 4	Jefferson Park to Olallie Lake	12.4
Day 5	Olallie Lake to Lemiti Creek	8.9
Day 6	Lemiti Creek to Warm Springs	10.0
Day 7	Warm Springs to Timothy Lake (south)	10.2
Day 8	Timothy Lake (south) to Wapinitia Pass	11.8
Day 9	Wapinitia Pass to Timberline Lodge	10.4

7 DAYS

Day 1	Santiam Pass to Rockpile Lake	13.8
Day 2	Rockpile Lake to Whitewater Creek	18.1
Day 3	Whitewater Creek to Jude Lake	16.4
Day 4	Jude Lake to Warm Springs	15.3
Day 5	Warm Springs to Timothy Lake (north)	10.2
Day 6	Timothy Lake (north) to Wapinitia Pass	11.8
Day 7	Wapinitia Pass to Timberline Lodge	10.4

5 DAYS

Day 1	Santiam Pass to Shale Lake	21.7
Day 2	Shale Lake to Breitenbush Lake	16.7
Day 3	Breitenbush Lake to Lemiti Creek	15.2
Day 4	Lemiti Creek to Timothy Lake (north)	23.5
Day 5	Timothy Lake (north) to Timberline Lodge	18.9

1 SANTIAM PASS TO MINTO PASS

DISTANCE 10.1 miles

ELEVATION GAIN/LOSS
+1950 feet/–1650 feet

HIGH POINT 6510 feet

CONNECTING TRAILS
Old Summit Trail (#4014), Santiam Lake
Trail (#3491), Minto Pass Trail (#3437),
Minto Pass Tie Trail (#4015)

ON THE TRAIL

At the **Santiam Pass trailhead**, fill out your self-issue wilderness permit and prepare yourself to witness the effects—and recovery—of three devastating wildfires: the 2002 **Mount Marion Fire**, the 2003 **B&B Complex Fire**, and the 2006 **Puzzle Fire**. While much of the terrain is scorched and bleak, life is returning. Underneath the charred snags and matchstick trunks, small trees, shrubs, and an assortment of wildflowers have taken root. However, all this bleakness does little to detract from an eye-popping traverse below the jagged and imposing wall of **Three Fingered Jack**, where panoramic views overlook unburned mountain meadows and distant forested peaks. There are few reliable, easily accessible water sources until a few standing ponds and seasonal trickles near the end of the leg, so it's a good idea to carry as much water as needed to reach the camp at **Wasco Lake**, just below **Minto Pass**. Also, with much of this leg winding through exposed burn areas or on the rocky volcanic flanks of Three Fingered Jack (read: little shade), you will probably want to slather on sunscreen before heading out.

From the parking area, the PCT jogs northeast through open, burned forest, part of the massive B&B Complex burn area. Among the silvered remains of the once-verdant woodland, fern, huckleberry, and manzanita create a patchwork of vibrant undergrowth, while the seedlings of silver fir, mountain hemlock, and lodgepole pine have begun to establish the next forest to come; splashes of color come in the form of white pearly everlasting, yellow rabbitbrush, and pink fireweed. At 0.2 mile, the **Old Summit Trail** (#4014, signed for Square Lake) veers off to the right (east) for 1.8 miles to Square Lake, then 2 more miles to Booth Lake. This trail is popularly used to create an 18-mile loop around Three Fingered Jack. The PCT forks left (north) and enters the **Mount Jefferson Wilderness** just 0.1 mile farther. From here, the trail gradually climbs to wider panoramas showing the extent of the burn area—a vast wasteland of skeleton forest—as well as a peek at Mount Washington to the south.

Over the next couple miles, the scenery is fairly monotonous—broken only by a dirty standing pond at 1.1 miles—making it a good stretch to focus on the smaller details along the trail: birds, butterflies, and wildflowers. Take notice of the area's burned appearance. You will find that each section of charred forest bears remarkably

HUNTING SEASON

The wide and exposed burn areas north of Santiam Pass are popular buck hunting locations when the **High Cascade Hunt** happens in late summer. Deer frequent the area for the tender new growth of shrubs and grasses, while hunters favor the open hillsides and good visibility. Prepare for above-average company on the PCT as hunters toting scoped rifles pack in to the nearby lakes to basecamp. Don't let the presence of hunters frighten or discourage you from hiking during this season, just take the proper safety precautions. For more info about hiking during hunting season, see Planning and Preparation in the introduction.

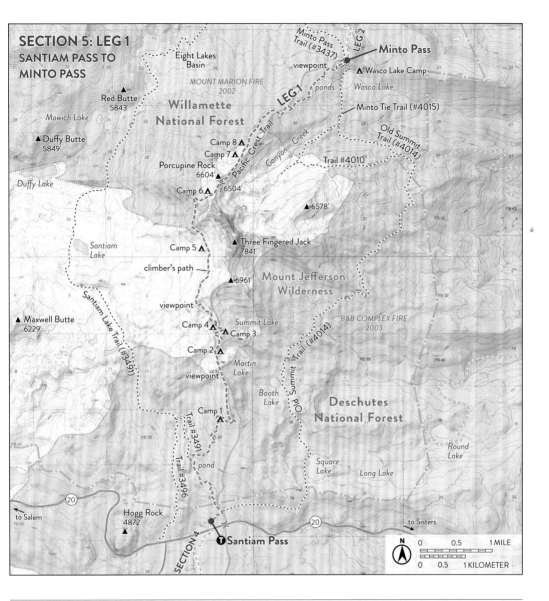

SECTION 5: LEG 1
SANTIAM PASS TO MINTO PASS

Minto Pass Trail (#3437)
LEG 2
Minto Pass
viewpoint
Wasco Lake Camp
Wasco Lake
Minto Tie Trail (#4015)
Eight Lakes Basin
MOUNT MARION FIRE 2002
ponds
LEG 1
Willamette National Forest
Red Butte 5843'
Mowich Lake
Pacific Crest Trail
Canyon Creek
Old Summit Trail (#4014)
Duffy Butte 5849'
Camp 8
Camp 7
Porcupine Rock 6604'
Camp 6
6504'
Trail #4010
Duffy Lake
6578'
Santiam Lake
Camp 5
Three Fingered Jack 7841'
climber's path
6961'
Mount Jefferson Wilderness
viewpoint
B&B COMPLEX FIRE 2003
Maxwell Butte 6229'
Santiam Lake Trail (#3491)
Camp 4
Camp 3
Summit Lake
Camp 2
Martin Lake
viewpoint
Old Summit Trail (#4014)
Booth Lake
Deschutes National Forest
Camp 1
Trail #3491
Round Lake
Trail #3496
pond
Square Lake
Long Lake
to Salem
20
Hogg Rock 4872'
SECTION 4
Santiam Pass
20
to Sisters

N
0   0.5   1 MILE
0   0.5   1 KILOMETER

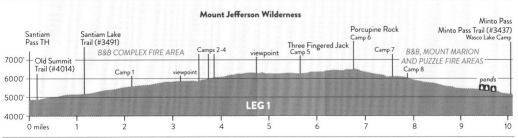

Mount Jefferson Wilderness

Santiam Pass TH
Old Summit Trail (#4014)
Santiam Lake Trail (#3491)
B&B COMPLEX FIRE AREA
Camp 1
Camps 2-4
viewpoint
viewpoint
Three Fingered Jack
Camp 5
Porcupine Rock
Camp 6
Camp 7
Minto Pass
Minto Pass Trail (#3437)
Wasco Lake Camp
B&B, MOUNT MARION AND PUZZLE FIRE AREAS
Camp 8
ponds

7000'
6000'
5000'
4000'

LEG 1

0 miles   1   2   3   4   5   6   7   8   9   10

High points en route to Three Fingered Jack offer long looks south at (from left to right): Broken Top, the Three Sisters, Mount Washington, and Hayrick Butte.

different characteristics, largely depending on how hot the wildfire burned. As you continue the moderate ascent, a jumble of rocky knobs creating an unnamed 5274-foot butte comes up on the west side of the trail. Just beyond, at 1.2 miles, the **Santiam Lake Trail** (#3491) breaks off northwest to descend to Santiam and Duffy lakes, and to connect to several trails that continue into the **Eight Lakes Basin**.

At 2.2 miles, a small campsite can be found right (east) of the trail (**Camp 1**). Just beyond, the PCT jogs east to begin a long, curving switchback before ascending Jack's southernmost extension. The trail returns north, continuing up the spine

CENTRAL OREGON'S BIG BURN

In summer of 2003, lightning ignited two separate wildfires on the east side of Oregon's Central Cascades. Burning individually at first, they were the Booth and Bear Butte fires. High winds, combined with warm temperatures and low humidity, fanned the flames into one raging conflagration that came to be called the **B&B Complex Fire**. The fire burned for nearly two months and consumed more than 90,000 acres of woodland. The largest portion of the burn occurred between Santiam Pass and Mount Jefferson, where it consumed huge swaths of Douglas-fir, western hemlock, and ponderosa, lodgepole, and jack pine forest, leaving a charred and barren landscape in its wake. The fire burned over nearly 20 miles of the Pacific Crest Trail, closing the area for much of the 2003 hiking season, and resulting in a massive cleanup to reopen the trail the following year.

THREE FINGERED JACK

Jack is a deeply glaciated shield volcano, consisting mostly of basaltic andesite lava, and is esti-mated to be around 150,000 years old. The more ragged upper reaches of unconsolidated tephra indicate a more explosive period of eruptions before going extinct. Close inspection of Jack's strata from the PCT reveals many of the multihued layers of volcanic deposition as the mountain was building itself. This is especially evident when viewing the peak from the northern flank. All this was laid bare after glaciers blanketed the Cascade Crest, as Jack has been worn away on every side, leaving a crumbling, finlike ridge towering above several deep cirques.

There are many stories as to how Three Fingered Jack came to be named. Tales include references to a local trapper named Jack who was missing two fingers, a pre-Vancouver explorer named Manuel Quimper who called the peak Tres Dedos ("three fingers"), and the Texas train robber Jack Dunlop, who was also missing a few digits. None of these accounts has been substantiated as official, so the true naming origin remains a mystery. However, it is known that prior to its current designation, the peak was known as Mount Marion. Regardless of who it was named after, some views of the peak leave one to wonder if the designator knew how to count, or had reached the bottom of his whiskey bottle, as there are certainly more than three distinct prominences along the summit spine.

Jack's summit—the smallest in Oregon, when measuring surface area—is a popular rock climb. It is most commonly approached using the southern route, which branches off of the PCT at 5.4 miles. The path ascends to the shoulder below the summit, from which technical rock climbing gear and experience are required to continue. Jack's northeastern face is considered one of the most treacherous rock climbs in Oregon, and is rarely attempted.

A PCT hiker traverses the wide talus slopes below Three Fingered Jack.

of the burned ridge. Just when the day starts to warm up and you start asking yourself why you've selected this burned-out eyesore of PCT to hike, you come to refreshing green forest. Stands of mature fir and hemlock provide a break from the sun while patches of beargrass add a splash of green to the trailside. At 3.6 miles, continuing the gentle ascent, a decent campsite can be found right (east) of the trail among the trees (**Camp 2**). Beyond that, an open section of thin vegetation and rocky soil presents a wide panorama eastward taking in 6436-foot **Black Butte**, a nearly symmetrical andesite cinder cone.

The trail then reenters open forest, passing another small campsite right (east) of the trail (**Camp 3**) before coming to a faint bootpath that breaks off to the right at 3.8 miles. This unmarked user path descends 0.25 mile to nearby **Summit Lake ◐**, a fairly reliable water source if your tanks run empty. The PCT then begins a series of long, lazy zigzags. At the corner of the first zig, at 3.9 miles, is a large open campsite in the trees left (west) of the trail (**Camp 4**), with space for a few tents. The trail continues through viewless, sun-dappled forest where, at 4.8 miles, a short bootpath jogs off to the left (west). At the end of this spur is a rocky outcrop—with a long, precipitous drop at the edge—that presents a panoramic view south and west. The scene takes in more of the vast B&B burn area and beyond to the open slopes of the Hoodoo Ski Area and farther to Mount Washington and the Three Sisters.

From here, the PCT meanders northwest through more open forest; windows through the trees offer occasional peeks westward of **Santiam Lake** and forested 6229-foot **Maxwell Butte**.

MOUNT JEFFERSON WILDERNESS

Designated in 1968 and located in the northern Central Cascades region, the Mount Jefferson Wilderness encompasses 104,000 acres of forested valleys, alpine meadows, and rocky volcanic features. The area fully envelops its second-highest peak, Three Fingered Jack, and surrounds its highest peak, Mount Jefferson, on three sides, sharing a border with the Warm Springs Indian Reservation on the east side. The higher elevations support mountain hemlock and fir forests, while several varieties of pine and cedar thrive in the lower elevations; typical ground cover is huckleberry, vine maple, and mountain rhododendron. There are more than 150 lakes in the area, and it is also home to a large number of animals, including black bears, cougars, deer, elk, and an abundance of birds. In addition to the PCT, more than 140 miles of hiking trails thread the area, most accessible by old forest roads. The most popular place to visit is Jefferson Park, on the mountain's northern flank, for its brilliant lakes and sprawling meadows.

In recent years, several wildfires have blackened large portions of the wilderness, the most damaging being the 2003 B&B Complex Fire, which charred more than 90,000 acres both within the wilderness and the surrounding forest lands, and burned across 20 miles of the PCT—nearly half of its total miles through the region. Several smaller fires, including two in 2014 and 2015, burned near the trail and blackened even more forest. Most of these originated with lightning strikes, which are common during summer thunderstorms. These fires have kept trail crews especially busy over recent seasons, as burned trees with weakened roots are extremely susceptible to wind and heavy snow and topple easily. Because it is a wilderness area, crews are limited to hand-powered tools—crosscut saws and axes; no chain saws—to clear snags and blowdown from the trail. The PCTA anticipates that this will be an ongoing challenge for the next several years as the area recovers.

If you're lucky, maybe you'll score this front-porch view of green meadows and far-below Santiam Lake from a campsite on the slopes of Three Fingered Jack.

Just when you're ready for a change of scenery, the PCT bends east for your first up-close view of **Three Fingered Jack**, showing how far—and how quickly—you've come from the trailhead. Now on fairly level tread, the PCT begins contouring Jack's southwest flank, through more forest to a cairn-marked junction at 5.4 miles. This marks the climber's southern route up Jack, veering off steeply to the right (east). After another 0.2 mile the scene opens up to the sheer, jagged slopes of 7841-foot Three Fingered Jack towering overhead, under which a wide talus slope of rocky debris extends west into the basin below.

Shortly after heading out into the open, at 5.7 miles, a bootpath descends left (west) to a small plateau and campsite (**Camp 5**). The expansive view from this site looks west over alpine meadows, forested lakes, Maxwell Butte, and 5849-foot **Duffy Butte**, making it a choice place to end the day if getting a late start. If hiking in early summer, you may get lucky and find running water nearby, streaming downslope from the snowpack above; later in the season, expect these streamlets to be completely dry. The PCT continues on a gentle ascent to the ridge extending from Jack's northern reaches. It passes through another small patch of green vegetation, then back into the next burn zone, this one rising up from the **Eight Lakes Basin** below to the northwest. At 6.5 miles, the trail crests the ridge and presents another wide panorama. To the west is a patchwork of forest and burn areas, to the east, Three Fingered Jack looms over your shoulder, and to the north Mount Jefferson beckons you forward.

The trail contours northeast, passing a small campsite at 6.8 miles, just left (north) of the trail (**Camp 6**), then crests the next ridge right beside 6604-foot **Porcupine Rock**. From this vantage point you can see the tilted, multicolored stratigraphy of Jack's volcanic anatomy. Look for mountain goats roaming on these high reaches. The PCT then dips east over the ridge and begins a steady switchbacking descent before heading northeast through a shallow saddle back to the west side of the ridge. Where the trail reenters another section of forest spared by the burn, a couple more small campsites can be found in the trees left (west) of the trail at 7.6 and 7.9 miles (**Camps 7 and 8**); each site has room for one tent. The trail continues to descend, passing a 6377-foot prominence, the final extension of Jack's northernmost ridge.

The last couple miles of the leg continue an easy descent through more burned forest. During early summer, beargrass stalks are topped with bulbs of tiny white flowers. Common throughout the western United States, beargrass leaves were often used by Native Americans for basket weaving. As the PCT approaches Minto Pass, it winds around Koko Lake and several small ponds ⬭. If hiking in the early summer, just after the snowmelt, the ponds will be cold and the water refreshing. Later in the season, they become tepid and murky. If your bottles are near empty and need a refill, first strain the water through a bandanna, then filter it.

At 9.9 miles, the trail reaches the edge of the bluff that overlooks **Wasco Lake**. The scene eastward is a stark one, with deep blue Wasco Lake contrasting sharply against the silvered matchstick forest. A few small patches of green dot the hillsides, as well as adorn the northern shore of the lake.

TRAIL TRIVIA

Minto Pass, as well as Minto Mountain and Minto Lake, were named for John Minto, a prominent transportation surveyor in the later 1800s. He was born in England in 1840, and migrated with his family to Oregon in 1844. He became an authority on Oregon's pioneer history and wrote for the *Oregon Historical Quarterly*.

The four-way junction at Minto Pass, at 10.1 miles, marks the end of the leg. Here, the **Minto Pass Trail** (#3437; signed for Marion Lake) breaks off to the left (northwest) where it descends 2.3 miles into the Eight Lakes Basin. To the right, the **Minto Pass Tie Trail** (#4015; signed for Wasco Lake) switchbacks steeply down 0.5 mile to the forested **Wasco Lake Camp** ⬭ on the unburned north shore of the lake. Proceed down to the lake where, near the bottom, the trail forks, with the **Old Summit Trail** (#4014) continuing right (west) to Wasco Lake. The Old Summit Trail used to continue north from this junction to small Minto Lake, but the trail has been abandoned and is no longer passable. Among the tall, shady conifers there are several large, designated campsites that can each accommodate a couple tents. Lake access is easy for refilling water bottles or taking a chilly dip in the clear blue water. Don't be surprised to be woken by the yip-yip-yipping of coyotes roaming the nearby hills in the wee hours of the night.

CAMP-TO-CAMP MILEAGE

Santiam Pass to Camp 1 . . . . 2.2
Camp 1 to Camp 2 . . . . 1.4
Camp 2 to Camp 3 . . . . 0.2
Camp 3 to Camp 4 . . . . 0.1
Camp 4 to Camp 5 . . . . 1.8
Camp 5 to Camp 6 . . . . 1.1
Camp 6 to Camp 7 . . . . 0.8
Camp 7 to Camp 8 . . . . 0.3
Camp 8 to Minto Pass/Wasco Lake junction . . 2.2
Minto Pass/Wasco Lake junction to
    Wasco Lake Camp (off PCT) 0.5

2   MINTO PASS TO SHALE LAKE

DISTANCE 11.6 miles

ELEVATION GAIN/LOSS
+2590 feet/–2050 feet

HIGH POINT 6460 feet

CONNECTING TRAILS
Old Summit Trail (#4014), Minto Pass Trail (#3437), Rockpile Lake Trail (#4005), Brush Creek Trail (#4004, unmaintained), Swallow Lake Trail (#3488), Shirley Lake Trail (#4003.1)

ALTERNATE TRAILS
Hunts Cove Trail (#3430), Hunts Creek Trail (#3440)

ON THE TRAIL

The first half of Leg 2 is much a repeat of Leg 1, with lots of burned forest standing over shoots of new growth. Conditions improve markedly along the way through stretches of healthy green forest and around some interesting volcanic features leading up to the front porch of Oregon's second-tallest peak, Mount Jefferson. The path forward is fairly effortless, starting with a short climb followed by undulating dips and rises to a junction where you can choose between two camping destinations to end the day. Adding to the enjoyment is the proliferation of trailside huckleberries for a refreshing, tasty snack as you ramble. There is still a shortage of accessible water through this stretch, along with lots of exposure, so be sure to top off your bottles and bladders and keep your sunscreen on.

From Wasco Lake, make your way back to the PCT junction at **Minto Pass**, hang a right (north), and head on. The trail contours around the unnamed 5674-foot butte that backs the west side of Minto Lake, a smaller lake 0.5 mile north of Wasco Lake. Since the 2003 B&B Complex Fire, the loop trail around this lake is no longer maintained and has altogether disappeared; around 10.7

miles, near the north end of the butte, you might spy the upper junction of the **Old Summit Trail** (#4014). Following this junction, the PCT begins a curving ascent to gain the ridgeline. As the route skirts the edge of another burn area, the result of the 2002 **Mount Marion Fire**, the trailsides and forest floor are littered with an abundance of blown-down and snags.

At 12.1 miles the trail skirts the edge of the ridge at the head of **Bear Valley** with a wide view east over another expanse of heavily burned woodland. The trail contours around the escarpment, rising to cross a narrow spur from another butte, then crosses a narrow saddle with 6559-foot **Rockpile Mountain** directly north. The trail then contours along the mountain's eastern slope where it strolls up to **Rockpile Lake (Camp 9)** ◐ at 13.8 miles. Near the southwest corner of the lake, the **Rockpile Lake Trail** (#4005) dips southeast into Bear Valley. A nice campsite can be found on the southeast side of the lake, and another good site on the north side; campfires are not permitted at this lake. A grassy bank on the south side of the lake makes a fine spot to drop your pack, filter some water, and have a snack while enjoying the view of the shallow lake reflecting the surrounding green trees—a little oasis to smile about amid the miles of burned devastation.

The PCT descends away from the lake gently north, and traverses another narrow ridge between opposing drainages. At 14.1 miles the PCT meets the upper junction of the **Brush Creek Trail** (#4004), which used to head east to connect with FR 900, but is no longer maintained since the fires. Just beyond, the PCT contours the west slope of a minor prominence, then makes a short ascent onto a wide-open plateau of reddish cinders, dotted with small patches of heather and dark lava rocks. At the south end of the plateau is a large cairn; to the west the rocky plain extends to a small rise punctuated with deep green forest, creating a vivid contrast on bluebird-sky days; the higher mount to the northwest, with green adorning its southern flank, is 6746-foot **South Cinder Peak**. In late summer,

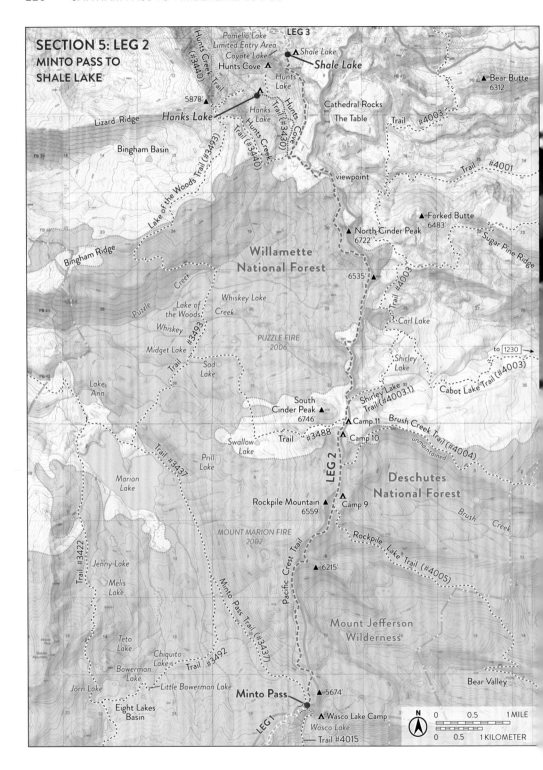

SECTION 5: LEG 2
MINTO PASS TO
SHALE LAKE

LEG 3

Pamelia Lake
Limited Entry Area
Coyote Lake
Hunts Cove
Shale Lake

Hunts Creek Trail (#3440)

Hunts Cove Trail (#3430)

Hunts Lake

Hanks Lake
5878'
Hanks Lake

Lizard Ridge

Bingham Basin

Lake of the Woods Trail (#3493)

Hunts Creek Trail (#3440)

Cathedral Rocks
The Table

Trail #4003

viewpoint

Bear Butte
6312'

Trail #4001

Forked Butte
6483'

North Cinder Peak
6722'

Sugar Pine Ridge

Willamette
National Forest

6535'

Trail #4003

Bingham Ridge

Creek

Puzzle

Whiskey Lake
Creek

Lake of
the Woods

Whiskey

Midget Lake

Trail #3493

Sad
Lake

PUZZLE FIRE
2006

Carl Lake

Shirley
Lake

to 1230 →

Cabot Lake Trail (#4003)

Lake
Ann

South
Cinder Peak
6746'

Shirley Lake
Trail (#4003.1)

Camp 11

Brush Creek Trail (#4004)

Trail #3437

Swallow
Lake

Prill
Lake

Trail #3488

Camp 10

unmaintained

Marion
Lake

Deschutes
National Forest

Brush

Creek

Rockpile Mountain
6559'

Camp 9

LEG 2

Trail #3422

Jenny Lake

Melis
Lake

MOUNT MARION FIRE
2002

Pacific Crest Trail

6215'

Rockpile Lake Trail (#4005)

Minto Pass Trail (#3437)

Mount Jefferson
Wilderness

Teto
Lake

Chiquito
Lake

Trail #3492

Jorn Lake

Little Bowerman Lake

Bowerman
Lake

Eight Lakes
Basin

Minto Pass

5674'

Bear Valley

Wasco Lake Camp
LEG 1

Wasco Lake

Trail #4015

N

0   0.5   1 MILE

0   0.5   1 KILOMETER

the path across the plateau is easy to follow. If early in the season and still covered with snow, just look for the matching cairn at the treeline to the north. There is a decent sheltered campsite in the trees just beyond the northern cairn, at 14.6 miles, just right (east) of the trail (**Camp 10**), with room for a couple tents.

The PCT continues under shady mature forest as it skirts the eastern flank of South Cinder Peak. Another small campsite, with room for one tent, can be found at 14.8 miles, right (east) of the trail (**Camp 11**). Around this point, you may notice a significant change in ground cover, with an abundance of vegetation. If hiking in late summer, you may also see a proliferation of strange and colorful fungi—puffballs, russulas, and artist's conks cling to decaying stumps or push their way up through rich, dark earth. Many of these are not edible, especially the extremely toxic fly and panther amanitas. Unless you can positively identify the species, it is best to leave fungi alone.

Around 14.9 miles, the PCT meets the **Swallow Lake Trail** (#3488) and at 15.1 miles the **Shirley Lake Trail** (#4003.1). The former descends left 3.3 miles west, wrapping around South Cinder Peak to Swallow, Sad, and Midget lakes, and points beyond; the latter descends right 1.2 miles north past small Shirley Lake to larger Carl Lake, where it forks into the Cabot Lake Trail (#4003). From Carl Lake the Cabot Lake Trail continues 4.1 miles north, paralleling the PCT to Table Lake on the eastern flank of Mount Jefferson, or east 4.1 miles past Cabot Lake and terminating at FR 1230. Proceeding north through these junctions, the PCT contours the forested western slope of the meandering crest. The trail is open, offering glimpses of red-hued South Cinder Peak as well as a couple of pocket lakes nestled in the basin below. At 16.1 miles, the PCT jogs west to round an unnamed point and crests a shallow saddle. Here you get your first peek at **Mount Jefferson** to the north.

Through the saddle, the PCT continues north, clinging to the western edge of the crest, on a fairly level grade. The way is open and pleasant, alternating between shade and sun, with peeks of Mount Jefferson urging you onward; huckleberry carpets the trailsides. The PCT then makes an abrupt turn east to contour across an open slope of rhyolite rockfall. Note the pinkish color of these exposed rocks and cinders belying the area's volcanic origins. At the margins of the slope, younger trees begin their encroachment. A low point along the crest offers a peek at Carl Lake, nearly 800 feet below. The path then proceeds through more burned and unburned forest, keeping to the western side of the ridge, with splashes of bright pink fireweed highlighting the trail in burned areas. Around 16.5 miles, the PCT emerges from forest again to another wide scene of fiery desolation.

Limp, silvered trees display where the 2006 **Puzzle Fire** hopped over the crest here, while a rocky knoll ahead displays colorful bands of volcanic cinders, strata alternating between reds and grays. If hiking on a warm summer day, you will likely reach this point about midday and may perceive a sudden rise in temperature. The PCT climbs across this knoll, rounding the exposed western slope to the crest of a bluff between the knoll and the southern ridge of 6722-foot **North Cinder Peak**. Here, at 17.5 miles, the scene opens up huge with some of the eye candy you've been waiting for.

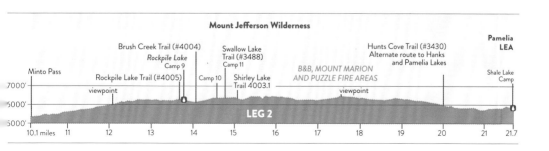

Grand views of Mount Jefferson greet you from the PCT near North Cinder Peak.

Directly north, 10,497-foot Mount Jefferson reaches for the sky. In early summer it will still be capped with a blanket of bright white snow; by season's end its slopes will be mostly bare and gray. Below the peak, the wide, flat plateau is **The Table**. Looking east you'll see two large, exposed basalt lava flows emanating from 6483-foot **Forked Butte**. The view west is blocked by the multihued cindery slopes and rocky outcroppings of North Cinder Peak's eastern escarpment. Just south of the trail, a nice flat spot in the trees could make a suitable campsite.

The PCT now jogs back and forth west and north, beginning its circuit around Mount Jefferson's western slopes. It dips below the crest for a meandering contour down around North Cinder Peak, losing much of the elevation recently gained. Where it reaches the peak's northwestern slope, it plunges back into mature, shady forest. Around 18.4 miles you'll find a large log resting alongside

CAMPING NOTE: PERMIT REQUIRED

Camping at **Shale Lake**, **Hunts Cove**, and **Pamelia Lake** requires a Limited Entry Area (LEA) permit, and, where posted, is allowed only at designated campsites. You can thank the people who have been carelessly trashing this location for the inconvenience. The alternative, if you can't secure a permit and want to have access to water, is to explore off trail east of Shale Lake for a suitable wilderness camp outside of the LEA boundary, approximately 0.2 mile east of the PCT. Be sure you're following LNT practices when choosing a campsite. (See Passes and Permits in the introduction for more info.)

the trail, just begging you to enjoy a sit. Why not? If your water bottles happen to be running low, there is a shallow pond **O** approximately 140 yards due east through the trees. The water will be fresher here in the early season, then questionable by late summer.

The trail reaches the edge of another escarpment, drawing ever closer to the ancient volcano. Below you, a glacial valley extends south from the foot of 7159-foot **Goat Peak** (see Leg 3). Lining the valley's west wall are the ragged **Cathedral Rocks**. The east wall is actually the western escarpment of The Table, its expansive meadow now visible, ringed by forest; directly south of The Table is a large unnamed cinder cone. From this point, the PCT leaves the crest and begins a westward, switchbacking descent to the head of a wide glaciated valley where, at 20 miles, it comes to a three-way junction.

Each of the trails forward was at one time part of the PCT. To the left, the **Hunts Creek Trail** (#3440; the "newer" Hunts Cove route) proceeds west around a knoll before contouring the valley's western slope, hopping over a ridge, then making a steep, switchbacking descent toward the valley floor and **Hanks Lake**. Straight ahead, the **Hunts Cove Trail** (#3430; the "old" route, originally part of the OST) descends directly into the forested valley, crosses a wide meadow, then descends again through forest to Hanks Lake. To the right, the PCT (the current "official" route) continues by turning north, traversing the valley's eastern wall below the colorful Cathedral Rocks, then ascending to the top of the ridge and proceeding

MOUNT JEFFERSON

The second-tallest volcanic peak in Oregon, Mount Jefferson was originally christened Mount Vancouver by English explorers. Its name was changed in 1806 by the Lewis and Clark Expedition in honor of then-president Thomas Jefferson. At one point, there was an attempt to rename all of Oregon's (and Washington's) peaks after American presidents, as well as name the Cascade Range the Presidential Range. The attempt was short-lived, and the only presidential names that remain are Mounts Jefferson and Washington in Oregon and Mount Adams in Washington. Before all the name-changing, its Native American designation was *Seekseekqua*.

Mount Jefferson resides in a deeply glaciated *graben* (a valley formed by the dropping of a block of land between parallel faults) in a remote section of Oregon's Cascades. The mountain has a long and violent volcanic history, dating back more than 1 million years. The main structure of the stratovolcano is composed of silica-rich andesite lava over a tephra cone core. Volcanic events continued building the mountain up to 35,000 years ago. Successive volcanic events occurred up to 6400 years ago, building many of the cinder cones on the north and south flanks, with the last eruption as recent as 950 A.D.

During the last ice age, glaciers covered the mountain and began their process of carving away the mountain's flanks. Estimated to have originally been over 12,000 feet, much of Mount Jefferson's western summit has been removed by glacial activity. The summit is actually a portion of the eastern slope. There are currently five active glaciers on Mount Jefferson's flanks: Waldo on the south; Russell and Jefferson Park on the northwest; little Milk Creek on the west; and Whitewater, covering much of the north and east. All of these glaciers are currently in retreat, and large moraines can be seen along their edges. There are several popular mountaineering routes that summit Mount Jefferson, but all require technical climbing experience.

ALTERNATE ROUTE: HANKS AND PAMELIA LAKES

The alternate route to Hunts Cove offers big mountain views, streaming springs, and pleasant campsites near picturesque lakes.

By the time you've made it to the PCT junction with the Hunts Cove trail alternates, you may be in the mood for a change of scenery. Take the **Hunts Cove Trail** (#3430) directly into the valley ahead. The trail is easy to follow as it makes a steady descent, first across open terrain before dipping under a shady conifer canopy. In season, huckleberries are everywhere. Go ahead—indulge in a snack or collect some for your breakfast the next morning. Approximately 0.7 mile from the junction, pass a wide, open meadow on the right side of the trail, with a grassy pond on the far end near the treeline. Just 0.1 mile farther, you are greeted by the joyous sound of running water—perhaps the first running water you may come across, depending on the time of year you're hiking. At the edge of another wide, grassy meadow, a deeply rutted stream 𝐎 cuts across the trail. This stream begins as a spring, high on the western flank of North Cinder Peak. Hop across and follow the tracked trail through the meadow to the opposite treeline.

The trail begins a steady curving descent into Hunts Cove, through dense, tangled forest. The faint sounds of the cascading creek will be over your left shoulder. Pay attention to the trail, which is easy to lose among the abundance of snags and blowdowns, as this section is not frequently maintained. Spying the lake through the trees, you'll come to another creek crossing 𝐎 and a single, secluded campsite. Keep heading down and west to arrive at a trail junction near the northwestern corner of **Hanks Lake**. This 0.4-mile spur trail heads north to secluded **Hunts Lake** with a handful of campsites; this could be an alternate camping destination if you're arriving at Hanks Lake on a crowded weekend. Otherwise, continue just a few hundred yards farther to **Hanks Lake Camp** with several campsites in a cluster above the grassy lakeshore, and one smaller secluded site in the trees opposite the trail. For fresh water, follow the trail around the camping area to the crossing of the lake's outlet 𝐎. All campsites on this route require a Limited Entry Area permit obtained in advance. (See Passes and Permits in the introduction for more info.)

If choosing this alternate route, see the directions for reconnecting to the PCT in the next leg.

on to **Shale Lake**. Now you get to choose where to end your day.

Proceeding on the official PCT route, the trail dives back under the cover of forest to make a descending contour along the valley's eastern wall. Where it crosses a couple open rock slopes, it offers a few views into the Hunts Cove lake basin and across the valley to the 5878-foot high point on **Lizard Ridge**. The trail then turns sharply east and pops up and over the edge of the valley to arrive at shallow **Shale Lake (Camp)** 🅾 at 21.7 miles. There are a few designated campsites (permit required; see camp note sidebar, p. 228) at Shale Lake, a delightful location in early summer to end your day, with Mount Jefferson reflected in

the still water. By the end of summer, however, there's not much left of Shale Lake, and the larger, forested lakes on one of the alternate routes may be more attractive.

CAMP-TO-CAMP MILEAGE
Minto Pass to Camp 9 (Rockpile Lake) 3.7
Camp 9 (Rockpile Lake) to Camp 10 . . . . 0.8
Camp 10 to Camp 11 . . . . 0.2
Camp 11 to Hunts Cove junction. 5.2
Hunts Cove junction to
   Shale Lake Camp 1.7
Alternate: Hunts Cove junction
   to Hanks Lake Camp (off PCT) 1.3

3 SHALE LAKE TO JEFFERSON PARK

DISTANCE 10.6 miles

ELEVATION GAIN/LOSS
+2680 feet/–2670 feet

HIGH POINT 5890'

**CONNECTING AND
ALTERNATE TRAILS**
Woodpecker Ridge Trail (#3442), White-water Trail (#3429) Pamelia Lake Trail (#3439), Hunts Creek Trail (#3440)

ON THE TRAIL
The next section of the Pacific Crest Trail, between Shale Lake and Jefferson Park, starts with a big descent, followed by an even bigger ascent. The nice thing is that both are fairly moderate, with a few switchbacks to ease the grade. (If you take the Hunts Cove alternate route, you will already have half of the descent behind you, with a nice level stroll along Pamelia Lake to give your legs a break before starting the climb back up.) But your attention will be on the ever-improving scenery through this next stretch, as you leave the wide burn areas behind. You'll traipse through

shady forest dense with undergrowth, cross streaming cataracts flowing from high glaciers, and finish the day by plopping yourself down lakeside in a subalpine paradise beneath Oregon's second-tallest volcanic peak.

From the plains around Shale Lake to the crossing at Milk Creek, the PCT loses nearly 1600 feet of elevation in a little less than 5 miles. Views are limited through this forested stretch as the trail descends the wall of a glaciated valley, transitioning from airy stands of silver fir and mountain hemlock into a denser canopy of Douglas-fir and western redcedar. Maidenhair fern, huckleberry (one of the best reasons for hiking in late summer!), and thimbleberry become predominant as ground cover, while mosses, lichens, and fungi decorate trees, rocks, and trailside. As you descend through sweeping switchbacks, breaks in the trees and exposed rock slopes offer a few views of the wide valley and Pamelia Lake below. The trail crosses a few springs 🅾 cascading down that will invite you to top off your bottles with cold, clear water.

Following this quick descent, the PCT meets the **Pamelia Lake Trail** (#3439) at 26.5 miles (the north end of the alternate route begun in

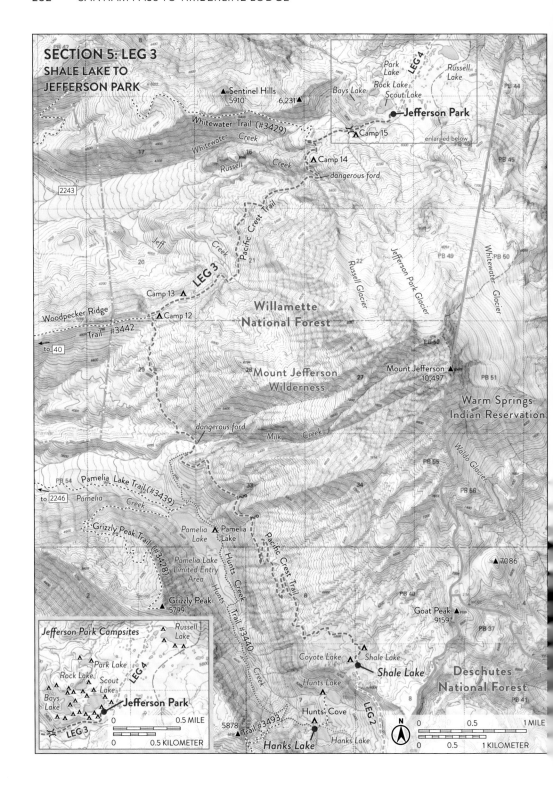

SECTION 5: LEG 3
SHALE LAKE TO
JEFFERSON PARK

LEG 4

Park
Lake
Russell
Lake

Bays Lake
Rock Lake
Scout Lake

Sentinel Hills
5910'   6,231'▲

Jefferson Park

enlarged below

PB 44

PB 45

Whitewater Trail (#3429)

Whitewater   Creek

Russell   Creek

▲ Camp 14

dangerous ford

☩ Camp 15

2243

Pacific Crest Trail

Russell   Creek

Jeff   Creek

17

16

21

22   PB 49

Jefferson Park Glacier

Russell Glacier

Whitewater Glacier

PB 50

20

Camp 13 ▲

Woodpecker Ridge

Trail #3442

to 40

LEG 3

29

28

Mount Jefferson
Wilderness

Willamette
National Forest

27

Mount Jefferson ▲
10,497'

PB 52

PB 51

Warm Springs
Indian Reservation

▲ Camp 12

dangerous ford

Milk   Creek

33

34

Wolda Glacier

PB 55

PB 56

PB 54

to 2246

Pamelia Lake Trail (#3439)

Pamelia   Creek

Grizzly Peak Trail (#3428)

Pamelia
Lake

▲ Pamelia
Lake

Pacific Crest Trail

▲ 7086'

Pamelia Lake
Limited Entry
Area

Hunts   Creek

Grizzly Peak ▲
5799'

Hunts Creek Trail #3410

PB 48

Goat Peak ▲
9159'

PB 37

Jefferson Park Campsites

Russell
Lake

Park Lake
Rock Lake
Scout
Lake

Bays
Lake

LEG 4

Jefferson Park

LEG 3

0   0.5 MILE

0   0.5 KILOMETER

Coyote Lake

Shale Lake

Shale Lake

Deschutes
National Forest

PB 41

Hunts Lake

Creek

LEG 2

5878 ▲

Trail #3493

Hunts Cove

Hunts Lake

8

Hanks Lake

Hanks Lake

N

0   0.5   1 MILE

0   0.5   1 KILOMETER

ALTERNATE ROUTE: HANKS AND PAMELIA LAKES
(CONTINUED FROM LEG 2)

If you opt for this alternate route, reconnecting to the PCT is a pleasant stroll with access to lots of water. From the **Hanks Lake** camp area, proceed west across the lake's outlet on the Hunts Cove Trail (#3430), which dives into lush forest, rich with fern, lichen, and fungi. The trail clings to the western wall of the valley, making a steady descent on a wide track. At the switchback junction with the Lake of the Woods Trail (#3493), veer right to continue down the valley on the **Hunts Creek Trail** (#3440). The steady, forested descent crosses several splashing springs to the bottom of the valley where it crosses **Hunts Creek ⬤** on a log bridge.

The trail continues northwest, crossing several bridges over more cascading tributaries, and arrives at the marshy head of **Pamelia Lake**. There are 14 designated campsites along the eastern shore of this wide, shallow lake. Some are in clusters, others are solitary sites; some have pleasant lake views, others are secluded in the trees. All require a Pamelia Lake LEA permit for camping. Across the lake is 5799-foot **Grizzly Peak**. The trail pulls away from near the lakeshore and begins a moderate, curving ascent to meet the **Pamelia Lake Trail** (#3439). Shortly past this junction this route reconnects with the PCT, just south of Milk Creek, at PCT mile 26.5.

the prior leg); this lateral heads west for 2.3 miles, crossing Pamelia Lake's outlet, to a trailhead at the end of FR 2246. At this junction the PCT veers east, bringing up a new view of Mount Jefferson. Below, you can begin to hear the gurgling of **Milk Creek** as the trail passes through head-tall stands of red-berried mountain ash leading to the rocky creek channel at 26.6 miles. This scene was dramatically different before November 2006, when a glacial outburst (flood), triggered by torrential rains, raced down this little canyon, scouring this deep, wide scar and wiping out the PCT crossing. The trail was never officially rebuilt here, but a makeshift bootpath descends to the creekbed for crossing and reconnects on the opposite bank. The water in Milk Creek is typically pale and ashy, hence its name, and not suitable for drinking.

At Milk Creek, the PCT has dipped to its low point in the leg. The next 6 miles are a sustained ascent (nearly 2200 feet) to reach Jefferson Park—beginning with a heart-thumping climb that gains nearly half of the elevation in less than 2 miles. The double-whammy comes in the fact that this stretch is also right through the 2017 **Whitewater Fire** area. The way forward is a gloomy trek through fire-mangled woods and ashen slopes, with little to inspire. You'll likely run into downed trees and snags along the way, so use caution, and make quick work of this stretch to get to greener pastures ahead.

The PCT now climbs east, away from the creek, on a narrow tread at the edge of a sheer, rocky escarpment and into burned woods before turning north again. The damage through this area was

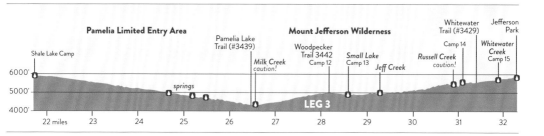

Milk Creek, the first of several stream crossings around Mount Jefferson, can be challenging during periods of high runoff or following sudden rainstorms.

extensive, so watch for trail markers and consult your map if you find yourself questioning the way forward. Also, watch your footing when detouring around fallen trees and snags. At 28.2 miles, the PCT meets the **Woodpecker Ridge Trail** (#3442) at a signed junction. This 1.8-mile lateral breaks west to a lesser-used trailhead at the end of FR 40. This point also marks the most westward extent of the PCT around Mount Jefferson. Fire laid waste to the campsite near here (**Camp 12**), so this location is no longer a suitable place to pitch your tent.

The PCT now begins heading northeast to get back on track with the crest, continuing its traverse around Mount Jefferson. Around 28.6 miles, following another moderate ascent, the PCT skirts a sooty pond **◑** at the base of a wide talus slope, with Mount Jefferson looming above. Listen for the telltale "eeep!" of pikas. The water here can be fresh in early summer, but by the end of the season starts getting murky. The two small campsites near here (**Camp 13**) were damaged badly in the fire, and so are no longer recommended. The trail

then traverses a wide talus slope under an exposed escarpment, and then turns southeast and comes to **Jeff Creek ◑** at 29.3 miles. This is a generally reliable source for cold running refreshment,

FORDING CREEKS

There are two unbridged creeks to cross as you contour around the western flank of Mount Jefferson: **Milk Creek** and **Russell Creek**. The flow of water down these narrow creek canyons can vary significantly depending on season, snowpack, temperature, and weather, making them easy rock-hops or treacherous fords. If possible, try timing your hike so that you're making these crossings early in the day, before it warms up and runoff from the snow and glaciers above increases. See more info about fording streams and rivers in Planning and Preparation in the introduction.

though it can be reduced to a mere trickle by the end of summer.

The PCT continues north, rising through gradually thinning forest, then veers northeast and begins a more strenuous climb, gaining several hundred feet of elevation over the next 0.75 mile. As it ascends, the route traverses a wide avalanche slope offering occasional peeks into the valley below, which reveals a wide path of tree-flattened destruction. Across the valley are the **Sentinel Hills**. The trail then reaches the crest of a low ridge, followed by a gentle descent to the rocky canyon of rushing **Russell Creek** ⬤ at 30.9 miles. There is no bridge over this creek, and it can be a challenging ford, even into late summer. During storms and high runoff periods it can be downright treacherous. If it is unsafe to cross right at the trail, search upstream for a place to cross. Downstream, the creek is funneled through a narrow slot, then plunges farther down into the canyon—*do not go that way to cross*. If you have to get into the water, practice proper fording techniques.

Once across, you're on the final stretch of this leg, and almost out of the burn area. The trail

TRAIL TRIVIA

Pamelia Creek was named in 1879 for Pamelia Ann Berry, a young lady who worked as a cook for the Marion County road surveyors. It was designated by John Minto, in recognition of her perpetual cheerfulness. Pamelia Lake, the source of Pamelia Creek, was later named by Judge John B. Waldo.

switchbacks up the opposite side, still climbing, but on a more moderate grade. As sullen as the scenery is, it does offer a glimpse of nature's regenerative power. In no time at all, green buds will begin poking through the soot-covered slopes. Fire-activated pine cones will begin to take root, ushering in the next forest that will grow and populate these slopes. With these good tidings in mind, cross a small creek at 31.1 miles. You might find an old campsite near here (**Camp 14**) badly burned, so keep pushing onward—you're so close to your day's destination. At 31.4 miles, the PCT

Crossing Hunts Creek on a fallen log

JEFFERSON PARK

Jefferson Park is one of the true gems in Oregon's Cascades wilderness. This subalpine paradise is renowned for its sparkling lakes and sprawling meadows bursting with summer berries and wildflowers, all at the foot of glacier-covered Mount Jefferson. If you're toting a camera, you'll delight in capturing the many moods and angles of the mountain, from across grassy fields or reflected in mirrorlike lakes and tarns. Sunsets often bathe the mountain in glorious alpenglow.

The downside to all this beauty is that the area has been heavily overused, with summer weekends often extremely crowded. To mitigate this overuse and repair some of the damage being done to this area, the Forest Service, in cooperation with the PCTA, has been rehabilitating the area, decommissioning many of the bootpaths and non-LNT campsites around the lakes. In order to help maintain this area's natural beauty and not exacerbate the overuse problem, hikers and campers should take extra measures to follow Leave No Trace practices in this area. Use only marked campsites and do not tromp through meadows.

If campsites around the lakes are filled, then you can also utilize primitive sites, so long as they are more than 250 feet from any water source and at least 100 feet from any trail. If you're doing this, then strict adherence to LNT practices is required to protect the area from further damage, namely: camp on durable surfaces (dirt, rock, snow); use preexisting spaces before making a new one; do not stomp through sensitive meadows or disturb fragile plants and flowers and dispose of waste properly; pack it in, pack it out. Campfires are not permitted anywhere within the Jefferson Park area.

Your best bet for an enjoyable visit would be to plan your stop in Jefferson Park during midweek, when crowds are fewer. With an overnight permit, you'll have access to numerous approved campsites around the shores of many of the park's lakes, the most popular being Scout Lake. Many of the sites on the north side of the lakes offer unparalleled views of Mount Jefferson. For more seclusion, try Bays or Rock lakes, or venture to the north end of the park area to Russell Lake.

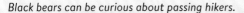

Black bears can be curious about passing hikers.

The massive Russell Glacier flows down the northwest face of Mount Jefferson.

exits the burn area and arrives at the junction with the **Whitewater Trail** (#3429). This trail breaks off west, over the Sentinel Hills, and connects to a trailhead on FR 2243 in 3.6 miles.

From here, the PCT turns east again and gently descends to a pleasingly bridged crossing of **Whitewater Creek** ⬤, where a couple campsites can be found near the creek, south of the trail (**Camp 15**). (If you don't have a permit to camp in the Jefferson Park area, this makes a suitable alternative.) The trail runs alongside a low ridge that separates the PCT from Bays and Scout lakes, with large rock outcrops protruding from the hillside. To the south, a wide, tree-ringed meadow opens up with a grand view of 10,497-foot Mount Jefferson. The large glacier covering the northwest flank of the mountain is the Russell Glacier. From this vantage point it's easy to see how glacial ice carved away the western summit and slopes of the mountain. Continuing east, a little stream trickles beside the trail until the path bends north, into the magnificent **Jefferson Park (Camp)** ⬤ at 32.3 miles. At a wide junction, side paths forks off to Scout, Rock, Park, and Bays lakes. Veer off the PCT and find your own idyllic campsite to drop your gear, take in the view, and call it a day well done.

CAMP-TO-CAMP MILEAGE

Shale Lake Camp to Camp 12 . . . . 6.5
Camp 12 to Camp 13 . . . . 0.4
Camp 13 to Camp 14 . . . . 2.5
Camp 14 to Camp 15 (Whitewater Creek) . . . 0.8
Camp 15 (Whitewater Creek) to Jefferson
     Park Camp 0.4

4 JEFFERSON PARK TO OLALLIE LAKE

DISTANCE 12.4 miles

ELEVATION GAIN/LOSS
+2100 feet/–3030 feet

HIGH POINT 6890 feet

CONNECTING TRAILS AND ROADS
South Breitenbush Trail (#3375),
Oregon Skyline Road (FR 4220),
Gibson Lake Trail (#708),
Horseshoe Lake Saddle Trail (#712), Ruddy
Hill Trail (#714), Red Lake Trail #719

ON THE TRAIL

When you're ready to move on from Jefferson Park, the next leg continues your journey north with a joyful stroll through mountain meadows, followed by a moderate climb to **Park Ridge**, the knife-edge arête that separates the Willamette and Mount Hood national forests. The PCT then meanders down through subalpine parklands into forested lake country. By getting an early start, you can knock out the 2-mile climb before the day warms up (the climb alone will warm you plenty), then descend to an optional camp location at a pleasant lake. Follow that with gently rolling terrain to finish at picture-perfect Olallie Lake. There will be plenty of water along the way, so no need to weigh yourself down with too much—plus, several of the small lakes make scenic rest stops.

From the south side of **Jefferson Park**, the PCT continues through the area on level ground carpeted with huckleberry and pink mountain heather; the meadows will likely be splotched with orange paintbrush, blue lupine, and purple aster (in season). You'll have a hard time facing forward with all the scenery around you—including majestic views of Mount Jefferson behind, tempting you to pause and pull out your camera for "just one more photo." Looking ahead, the exposed, rocky peak of 6851-foot **Park Butte** rises to the northwest. Less than a mile from your starting point, at 33 miles, the PCT crosses the **South Breitenbush Trail** (#3375). This lateral comes in 5.8 miles from the west, starting at a trailhead on FR 4685. It climbs nearly 3000 feet (passing the Bear Point Trail #3342, which switchbacks steeply to the summit of 6043-foot Bear Point) to connect with the PCT, making Leg 3's approach to Jefferson Park via the Whitewater Creek Trail (#3429) the shorter, easier option.

Just beyond the junction is the **South Fork Breitenbush River** 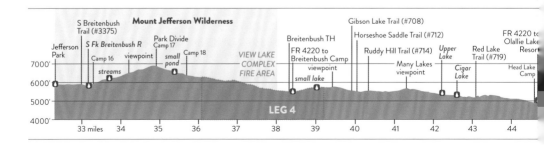, flowing out of nearby Russell Lake; a bootpath branches off east to the shallow lake and several designated campsites. The riverbed is wide and rocky with no bridge. Crossing in the early and peak season will likely get your boots wet, but later in the summer, it's an easy rock-hop. Once across, the trail proceeds fairly strenuously for a short distance north. Partway up the climb, at 33.3 miles, a fantastic campsite can be found in the trees just right (east) of the trail (**Camp 16**). As you're ascending, take a moment here and there to catch your breath and cast your gaze back over grassy slopes and through stands

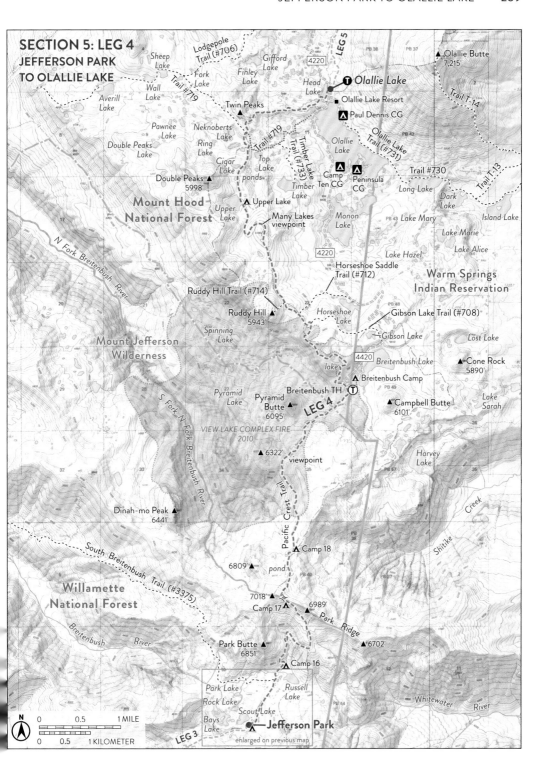

SECTION 5: LEG 4
JEFFERSON PARK
TO OLALLIE LAKE

LEG 5

Lodgepole Trail (#706)

Sheep Lake

Fork Lake

Finley Lake

Gifford Lake

4220

PB 38   PB 37

Olallie Butte 7,215'

Trail #719

Wall Lake

Averill Lake

Head Lake

T Olallie Lake

Trail T-14

Twin Peaks

Olallie Lake Resort

Paul Dennis CG

PB 42

Pawnee Lake

Neknoberts Lake

Ring Lake

Trail #719

Timber Lake Trail (#733)

Olallie Lake

Olallie Lake Trail (#731)

Double Peaks Lake

Cigar Lake

Top Lake

ponds

Camp Ten CG

Peninsula CG

Trail #730

Long Lake

Dark Lake

Trail T-13

Double Peaks 5998'

Upper Lake

Timber Lake

Island Lake

Mount Hood
National Forest

Upper Lake

Many Lakes viewpoint

Monon Lake

PB 43   Lake Mary

Lake Marie

Lake Alice

N Fork Breitenbush River

4220

Lake Hazel

Warm Springs
Indian Reservation

Horseshoe Saddle Trail (#712)

Ruddy Hill Trail (#714)

Ruddy Hill 5943'

Spinning Lake

Horseshoe Lake

PB 48

Gibson Lake Trail (#708)

Gibson Lake

Lost Lake

Mount Jefferson
Wilderness

lake

4420

Breitenbush Lake

PB 49

Cone Rock 5890'

Pyramid Lake

Pyramid Butte 6095'

Breitenbush Camp

Breitenbush TH T

LEG 4

Campbell Butte 6101'

Lake Sarah

S Fork N Fork Breitenbush River

VIEW LAKE COMPLEX FIRE 2010

6322'

viewpoint

Harvey Lake

PB 67

Dinah-mo Peak 6441'

PB 38

Creek

Shitike

South Breitenbush Trail (#3375)

Pacific Crest Trail

Camp 18

6809'

pond

PB 40

Willamette
National Forest

Breitenbush   River

7018'

Camp 17

6989'

Park Ridge

6702'

Park Butte 6851'

Camp 16

Park Lake

Rock Lake

Russell Lake

Whitewater   River

PB 44

Bays Lake

Scout Lake

Jefferson Park

LEG 3

enlarged on previous map

N

0   0.5   1 MILE

0   0.5   1 KILOMETER

From high atop Park Ridge, take in a wide panorama over Russell Lake and Jefferson Park, with Mount Jefferson rising majestically above all.

of conifers for dramatic views of the meadowy expanse of Jefferson Park with Russell Lake in the foreground, backed by Mount Jefferson.

At 33.6 miles, the grade eases as the trail descends slightly into a wide, meadow-filled cirque. Directly west is Park Butte's "summit," actually the high point of a north–south-trending arête that creates the western wall of the basin. Just ahead, a clear creek ⦶ cuts across the trail—an easy crossing—cascading down from a snowfield on the northeast side of the butte. Wildflowers are prolific through here. The PCT continues north to the back of the cirque, then turns sharply southeast and begins the second, less-strenuous part of its climb by contouring a forested escarpment, then turning northwest to climb across the back of the basin. At this corner, at 34.2 miles a small open patchwork meadow of rock and grass presents glorious views back at Mount Jefferson and east over central Oregon's high plains. A couple of small, exposed flat spots

could accommodate a tent or two for a primitive, albeit view-packed campsite.

The PCT continues its contouring ascent into the alpine zone, now bending northwest over open rocky trail. Stands of gnarled and stunted whitebark pines cling to the slopes, and trailside vegetation thins to patches of heather and tussock as the trail proceeds to a shallow saddle just below the ridge's high point at 34.9 miles. Just before reaching the crest, a small campsite can be found just off the trail (**Camp 17**). From atop the divide (another glacial arête), views are all-encompassing: to the south is a grand panorama over Jefferson Park and Mount Jefferson; to the north, an exposed moonscape of volcanic rock transitions to forested hills, with your next target, Mount Hood, glistening on the horizon. Take a break here to snack, get hydrated, and enjoy the views and the satisfaction of having completed most of your climbing for the day. Barring a few small rises ahead, the next 10 miles are a cruising descent.

PARK BUTTE

For an unforgettable view of Jefferson Park and Mount Jefferson, leave your pack and take the faint bootpath to the peak of 6851-foot Park Butte. The path climbs west from the Park Ridge saddle to the ridgetop, where it turns south and skirts along its rocky spine to its apex. Below, to the east (unseen from the PCT), a small lake fills a high cirque. The view from the summit will leave you breathless.

Continuing on, the PCT drops fairly steeply through rocky alpine terrain. Most years, lingering snow covers this exposed, north-facing slope late into summer. If the trail is buried, look for large cairns marking the route downward. After a short descent, the trail snakes around large jumbles of dark volcanic rock, and the grade eases near a small pond **0** at approximately 35.4 miles; by the end of summer, this pond may be nearly dry. Grasses begin to appear again trailside and the way opens up with a view over a patchwork of small meadows, rock gardens, and stands of hemlock. In the near distance, a burned ridge on the west side mars the continuity of the deep green forest ahead. The trail transitions from rock back to soft dirt and the way forward is blissful, descending through alpine parkland. In season, look for huckleberries to snack on. At 35.7 miles is another small, seasonal pond **0**, with a small campsite nearby (**Camp 18**).

The PCT contours the west side of a ridge and the forest begins closing in as the descent continues, offering sun-dappled shade. The wide glacial valley below to the west is the drainage for the **South Fork North Fork** (yes, both) **Breitenbush River**. The trail passes briefly through another burned area, and crests a low saddle between the ridge to the east and a butte to the west; it then bends northeast and enters another stretch of open forest. The trail eventually crosses a seasonal creek (by late summer this will be dry), then enters another swath of burned forest, this time the result of the 2010 **View Lake Complex Fire**, which burned across several sections of the PCT over the next 3.5 miles; to the northwest is 6095-foot fire-scarred **Pyramid Butte**. The trail then drops down into a dry gully ravaged by wildfire. Unlike the matchstick forests of burned trees seen earlier, this section looks as though it was bombed, with charred and twisted debris strewn all about. Prior to the fire here, the Pyramid Butte Trail, now abandoned, branched off to ascend the peak for some pretty nice views. Make quick work of this ugly section and take comfort in reentering green forest just beyond.

BREITENBUSH LAKE

If you get a late start out of Jefferson Park, or just decide to split this leg into two shorter sections, Breitenbush Lake makes a pleasant camping stop. There are 20 campsites near the west shore of the lake with picnic tables and fire pits. Vault toilets are available, and there is also a tapped spring for fresh, cold water. Unfortunately, there is no trash service here, so you'll need to continue to pack out all of your refuse. The campground is located on the **Warm Springs Indian Reservation**, so additional regulations are in effect as you are the guests of the reservation:

- Camp only in designated sites.
- Don't swim or bathe in the lake.
- Don't pick berries or other edibles.
- Don't cut or gather wood.
- Stay within the campground boundaries.
- Alcohol and firearms are prohibited.

To find the tapped spring, walk to the southeast corner of the campground loop and take the grassy path south, past the campsites. Cross a bridge over the outlet creek and proceed to a second bridge. A single pipe tapped into the side of a shallow gully delivers clean, cold water.

Take a load off at Olallie Lake where cold drinks and spectacular views await.

At 38 miles, the PCT tops a small rise to cross the boundary from the Willamette National Forest and Mount Jefferson Wilderness into the **Mount Hood National Forest** and **Olallie Lake Scenic Area**; this area also skirts the western edge of the **Warm Springs Indian Reservation**. As the trail descends, it traverses the base of an unusual volcanic rock projection, where a large shale-like mound of basalt culminates in an upturned wave-like formation—*cowabunga, dude!* It then levels and continues north through a low forest corridor to a trail kiosk and permit station. Here, hikers heading south to Jefferson Park and places beyond can self-register. The information board offers trail updates and park regulations; a short side trail right leads to a roundabout trailhead parking area. Continuing northwest, the PCT crosses the entry road and comes to Oregon Skyline Road (FR 4220) at 38.4 miles. Depending on the time of day, or what your itinerary allows, you can follow the

road to **Breitenbush Lake** for camping and water (**Breitenbush Camp**) ⭕, or keep pushing forward to Olallie Lake.

Directly across FR 4220, the PCT continues with a short, forested ascent to a bench above Breitenbush Lake. The trail then turns west, passes a small unnamed lake ⭕ at 39 miles, then passes through a gap between two minor buttes and comes to the western edge of the bench. The route then begins snaking around a larger butte, partially burned on the west side, then bears northwest over an exposed slope with a wide view of the valley below, and offers a glimpse ahead at rust-colored **Ruddy Hill**. A peek south reveals the pointed top of Pyramid Butte and Mount Jefferson rising above Park Ridge.

The PCT then passes through several trail junctions in quick succession: at 39.9 miles, the **Gibson Lake Trail** (#708) breaks off east to Gibson Lake; at 40 miles, the **Horseshoe Saddle Trail**

OLALLIE LAKE RESORT

Located on the shore of a sparkling mountain lake, and at the western base of 7215-foot Olallie Butte, the Olallie Lake Resort makes an ideal starting, ending, or layover destination for any trek along the PCT. Services here are limited, but they do offer just enough to help you relax your trail-weary legs. The small general store stocks a variety of snacks and camp foods, in addition to a small selection of hiking staples, first-aid supplies, and stove fuel.

The resort has ten cabin rentals, ranging from cozy units for couples, to larger units for groups up to six. Cabins have bedding, tables, and woodstoves. Running water is available via spigots outside, and vault toilets are nearby. There are no showers or laundry facilities, and the resort does not accept or hold resupply packages. For cheaper accommodations, the Paul Dennis Campground is just down the road past the resort. The campground offers 17 sites with tables, fire pits, and vault toilets. There is no running water at this site.

Camp Note
Many maps show the **Paul Dennis Campground** to be on Oregon Skyline Road between the Top Lake Trail and the resort. This is incorrect. The Paul Dennis Campground is actually on east side of the lake, just south of the Olallie Lake Resort.

For a change of pace from tent life, rent a rustic cabin at Olallie Lake Resort.

ALTERNATE ROUTE: TOP LAKE TRAIL

If you're planning a stay or layover at the Olallie Lake Resort, or one of the nearby campgrounds, you may want to take the Top Lake alternate route, the **Red Lake Trail** (#719). This 1.3-mile trail descends to the very pleasant Top Lake—complete with a little sandy beach for wading or sunning. Beyond the lake, the trail descends through forest, passing a few smaller lily ponds and pocket lakes, and the **Timber Lake Trail** (#733) to—you guessed it—Timber Lake, to end at **Oregon Skyline Road** (FR 4220) on the northwest shore of Olallie Lake. From this point, it's a pleasant 0.3-mile road walk around the lake to the resort.

(#712) descends northeast to Horseshoe Lake and a campground on FR 4220; and at 40.3 miles, the unsigned **Ruddy Hill Trail** (#714) breaks off west for a steep climb up and around its 5943-foot namesake. The PCT then continues northwest through a long stretch of cool, pleasant forest, where mature Douglas-fir, silver fir, and western hemlock filter the sun, which illuminates patches of trailside heather and huckleberry.

Quickly ascending an unnamed 5730-foot butte, the PCT works its way up the west slope, then curves around the east side. At the crest of the butte, at 41.3 miles, is the **Many Lakes viewpoint**. Here, a rocky outcrop invites you to drop your pack for a spell and enjoy a rest with a view east over the basin below, taking in **Olallie and Monon lakes** and several others nearby. Beyond the viewpoint, the PCT wraps around the butte to descend on the west side, making a U-turn at the edge of a wide, grassy meadow (likely a shallow lake basin at one time). Then, tracking north, the PCT skirts **Upper Lake (Camp)** ⬤ at 42.2 miles. A side trail right (east) leads to a couple of secluded campsites in the trees, while a side trail left (west) leads to an idyllic tent site between the trail and the lake. Another campsite can be found just a little farther north between the trail and the lake. The clear water will tempt you into taking a refreshing dip. If you're low on water, this would be the place to top off, as the water quality of the lakes ahead can be questionable depending on the season.

OLALLIE BUTTE

Olallie Butte is a Pleistocene-era shield volcano, and is the highest peak between Mount Jefferson to the south and Mount Hood to the north. Its sloping western flank is mostly forested while its eastern flank shows exposed rock in two glacier-carved cirques. The US Forest Service used to maintain a fire lookout atop the butte but abandoned it when the land was turned over to the Warm Springs Indian Reservation. Now the butte is largely on reservation land, with only the lower western flank on US Forest Service land. The name Olallie is derived from the Chinook word *klalelli*, which means "berries."

The southern flank of the butte is lined by a chain of lakes, the largest being **Olallie Lake**, followed eastward by Long, Dark, Island, and Trout lakes. To summit the butte, take the **Olallie Lake Trail** (#731) from the Paul Dennis Campground and proceed south along the western shore of the lake. Where the trail crosses onto reservation land, continue on **Trail #730** to **Long and Dark lakes**. Beyond Dark Lake, the route splits, with Trail #730 leading east to **Island Lake** and **Trout Lake** (location of a backcountry campground). Turn onto **Trail #T-13** and northeast to connect to the abandoned Trail #T-14, which climbs the southeast slope of the butte to the summit, where the vestiges of the old fire lookout remain.

Salmonberries have a very distinct flavor.

Continuing north, the trail meanders through a shallow basin of ponds and pocket lakes ◖, the largest being **Cigar Lake** at 42.6 miles. The water quality in these lakes varies, the larger staying fresh and clear into later summer, while the smaller get murky or dry up completely. Beyond the pocket lakes, the trail hugs the edge of a forested escarpment, below which is another lake basin, to arrive at the next trail junction, just south of the **Twin Peaks** at 43.1 miles. To the left, the **Red Lake Trail** (#719) veers left (northwest) toward Potato Butte and an assortment of lakes. Along its way, the Red Lake Trail connects with the Lodgepole Trail (#706), which proceeds northeast, paralleling the PCT for several miles, passing Middle and Lower lakes and the Cornpatch Meadows. To the right (southwest), it descends into a lower lake basin that includes pretty **Top Lake**. This is an alternate route to get to Olallie Lake.

The PCT continues north, before turning east to contour around the base of the Twin Peaks. It then meanders east, staying near the edge of the rocky escarpment above the lake basin below, before descending northeast, past a small pond, to circuit the southeast shore of **Head Lake** **(Camp)** ◖ at 44.6 miles, then once again meet Oregon Skyline Road (FR 4220). A few dispersed campsites can be found here, just west of the road crossing at 44.7 miles. The PCT continues on the other side of the road. Here, at the end of the leg, your options are to find a campsite near the lake, or proceed south 0.1 mile on FR 4220 to **Olallie Lake Resort (Camp)** ◖, where a small store greets hikers with cold drinks, snacks, campsite and cabin rentals, and a picture-perfect view across Olallie Lake of glacier-capped Mount Jefferson.

CAMP-TO-CAMP MILEAGE

Jefferson Park Camp to Camp 16 . . . . 1.0
Camp 16 to Camp 17 . . . . 1.5
Camp 17 to Camp 18 . . . . 0.9
Camp 18 to FR 4220/Breitenbush Lake
   junction 2.7
FR 4220 to Breitenbush Lake CG (off PCT) . . 0.3
FR 4220 to Upper Lake Camp 3.8
Upper Lake Camp to Head Lake Camp 2.4
Head Lake Camp to FR 4220/Olallie Lake
   junction 0.1
FR 4220 to Olallie Lake Resort (off PCT) 0.1

5 OLALLIE LAKE TO LEMITI CREEK

DISTANCE 8.9 miles

ELEVATION GAIN/LOSS
+660 feet/–1270 feet

HIGH POINT 5070 feet

CONNECTING TRAILS
Lodgepole Trail (#706), Olallie Meadow
Trail (#150), Russ Lake Trail (#716)

ON THE TRAIL

Beyond Olallie Lake, the scenery and terrain along the Pacific Crest Trail change dramatically—views are shrouded by alternating expanses of open and dense forest as the undulating trail winds its way northward. The trail leaves US Forest Service land and enters the **Warm Springs Indian Reservation**, with signs of logging activity and other indications of nearby civilization. There will be few water sources along the way, so you will be well served by topping off at Olallie Lake, and carrying a spare full bottle if you're hiking during a warm spell, or later in the summer. With this leg's mileage being low and fairly easy, you can enjoy a later start than what might be your norm—or you can get an early start and knock out this leg and the next to shorten your itinerary by a day.

Hopping back on the PCT, just across from Head Lake, the trail plunges back into brushy forest, lichen draping from the trees. For the first couple miles the trail contours down around the base of 7215-foot **Olallie Butte**, winding through an area of small lily ponds and pocket lakes. The most suitable pond ⚫ for obtaining water comes along at 45.4 miles; the rest are fairly murky and undesirable. You may occasionally hear the sound of a passing car or truck nearby, as the trail parallels the Oregon Skyline Road (FR 4220) not far off to the west. At 46.9 miles, the trail crosses a dirt service road where you'll start to notice a distinct buzzing sound. Here, a wide clear-cut swath in the forest serves as the conduit for a series of high-voltage powerlines. Make quick work of the exposed crossing and dive back into the quiet comfort of shady forest on the other side.

At 47.7 miles, the PCT meets the northern extent of the **Lodgepole Trail** (#706; signed for Triangle Lake), which breaks off west to cross Oregon Skyline Road to the Triangle Lake Horse Camp and Triangle Lake just beyond. This trail continues southwest, paralleling the road and the PCT, before veering off to Lower Lake and Potato

PCT blazes lead the way through a forested corridor on the Warm Springs Indian Reservation.

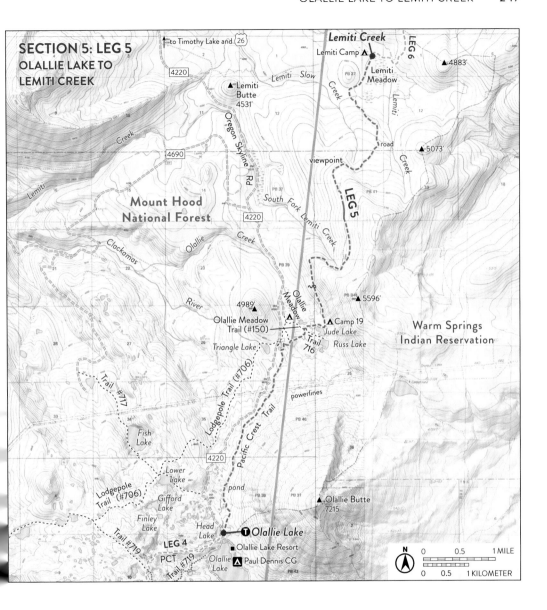

SECTION 5: LEG 5
OLALLIE LAKE TO LEMITI CREEK

to Timothy Lake and 26

Lemiti Creek

Lemiti Camp

Lemiti Meadow

▲4883'

4220

Lemiti Slow

Creek

▲Lemiti Butte 4531'

PB 37

LEG 6

Oregon Skyline Rd

4690

Creek

Lemiti

Creek

▲5073'

road

viewpoint

South Fork Lemiti Creek

PB 37

LEG 5

PB 41

Mount Hood National Forest

4220

Olallie

Creek

PB 39

Clackamas

Olallie

River

4989'

Olallie Meadow Trail (#150)

Olallie Meadow

▲5596'

PB 846

Camp 19

Jude Lake

Trail 716

Russ Lake

Warm Springs Indian Reservation

Triangle Lake

Trail #717

Lodgepole Trail (#706)

Pacific Crest Trail

powerlines

PB 46

Fish Lake

4220

Lower Lake

pond

PB 38

PB 37

▲Olallie Butte 7215'

Lodgepole Trail (#706)

Gifford Lake

Finley Lake

Head Lake

Trail #719

LEG 4

PCT

Trail #719

Olallie Lake

T *Olallie Lake*

■ Olallie Lake Resort

▲ Paul Dennis CG

PB 42

N 0 0.5 1 MILE
0 0.5 1 KILOMETER

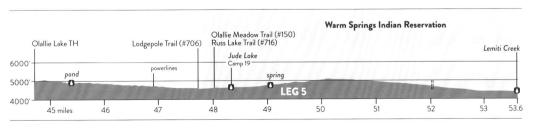

Warm Springs Indian Reservation

Olallie Lake TH

Lodgepole Trail (#706)

Olallie Meadow Trail (#150)
Russ Lake Trail (#716)

Jude Lake
Camp 19

spring

Lemiti Creek

6000'

5000'

4000'

pond

powerlines

LEG 5

45 miles   46   47   48   49   50   51   52   53   53.6

Watch out for gray jays—they'll happily share your trail mix!

Butte. Immediately following this junction, at 47.8 miles, the PCT bends northeast and crosses onto the Warm Springs Indian Reservation. The next junction comes up quickly where the **Russ Lake Trail** (#716) veers off to the right (southeast) for 0.3 mile to Russ Lake and a decent campsite. To the left (west) the **Olallie Meadow Trail** (#150) heads for the roadway and the **Olallie Meadow Campground**. Winding northeast, the PCT crosses a wooden bridge over the outlet of **Jude Lake ◐**. If you need to top off your water, draw it from the running water below the bridge instead of the silty water in the lake.

At this point the PCT has reached the bottom of its present descent. Proceeding around the north shore of Jude Lake, a nice campsite with room for a couple tents (**Camp 19**) can be found at 48.3 miles. The trail turns north and begins a gradual ascent of the forested lower flank of a winding ridge. Just under 49 miles, a freshwater spring ◐ crosses the trail, but by late summer it may be a mere trickle. The trail snakes around the ridge,

OLALLIE MEADOW CAMPGROUND

Trail #150 heads west 0.3 mile to the Olallie Meadow Campground. This small US Forest Service campground offers six small tent sites and makes a suitable alternate if you choose to bypass the busier Olallie Lake area as a camping destination. The campsites offer tent spaces, picnic tables, and grills, but there is no toilet, trash, or water available here.

crests a high point, then begins another steady descent. It then wraps around a northern extension of the ridge, at the edge of a clear-cut area, and offers a peek at Mount Hood in the distance—one of the few views to be had through this section.

The PCT then makes a wide curve westward. At the easternmost edge of the arc, the trail crosses a logging road at 52 miles, skirts the edge of a clear-cut area in recovery, then descends back into rich forest. Here the trees are tall and the trailside thick with vine maple, maidenhair fern, Pacific rhododendron, and Oregon grape. The path then curves northeast, passes a murky pond, and skirts around the base of a small rise. At this point the forest opens and becomes noticeably drier, as the trail continues to descend. Just as the forest starts to fill in again, **Lemiti Meadow** can be spied through the trees to the right (east), and the PCT arrives at **Lemiti Camp** at 53.6 miles. The campground is serviceable and offers three sectioned tent spaces under a tall forest canopy; water can be drawn from nearby **Lemiti Creek 🄾**. The area is fairly boggy, so if you're visiting or passing through early in the season, you'll want to make sure you have plenty of good mosquito repellent. Gray jays (camp robbers) are common here, so don't leave your snacks unattended.

CAMP-TO-CAMP MILEAGE

FR 4220 (Oregon Skyline Rd.) to Camp 19 .. 3.6
Camp 19 to Lemiti Camp 5.3

6 LEMITI CREEK TO WARM SPRINGS

DISTANCE 10 miles

ELEVATION GAIN/LOSS
+1110/−2120 feet

HIGH POINT 5100

CONNECTING TRAILS AND ROADS
Trooper Spring spur trail, Road 130 (abandoned), W-240 (unpaved)

ON THE TRAIL

As the next leg of the Pacific Crest Trail continues north from Lemiti Creek, you are still a guest of the Warm Springs Indian Reservation; permits are not required, but you should continue to observe their trail regulations. Much of the land you'll be passing through has been subject to timber harvesting and clear-cutting operations. Thankfully, the trail remains in a wooded corridor, befitting the Oregon PCT's "green tunnel" moniker, and these scars on the hillsides are only glimpsed through stands of mature and old-growth forest. The way forward begins with a moderate ascent, and a long, gradual descent brings you effortlessly to a camp area alongside the **Warm Springs River**. Access to water will be limited, so it is best to top off your bottles and bladders, and perhaps fill an extra bottle if hiking later in the summer.

Similar to the last leg, there are few views to be had along this stretch, but it does present an opportunity to observe an abundance of flora, and occasional fauna, to be seen through these lower Cascade mountains. If hiking in late summer or

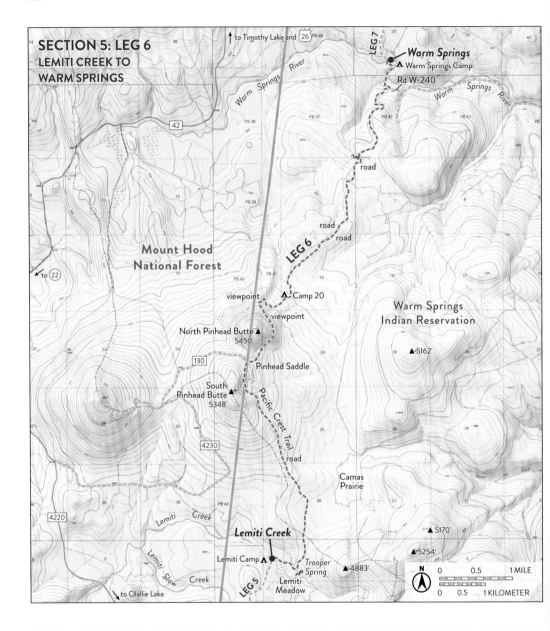

SECTION 5: LEG 6
LEMITI CREEK TO
WARM SPRINGS

to Timothy Lake and 26 PB 49

Warm Springs River

Warm Springs
△ Warm Springs Camp
Rd W-240

42

PB 38
PB 37
PB 42
PB 41

Warm Springs River

to 22

road

road

road
road

LEG 6

Mount Hood
National Forest

PB 42
PB 41

viewpoint
△ Camp 20

viewpoint

North Pinhead Butte ▲
5450'

Warm Springs
Indian Reservation

▲5162'

130

Pinhead Saddle

South
Pinhead Butte ▲
5348'

Pacific Crest Trail

4230

road

Camas
Prairie

4220

Lemiti Creek

PB 47

▲ 5170'

Lemiti Creek

▲5254'

Lemiti Camp △

Trooper
Spring

▲4883'

N
0   0.5   1 MILE
0   0.5   1 KILOMETER

LEG 5

Lemiti
Meadow

Lemiti Slow Creek

to Olallie Lake

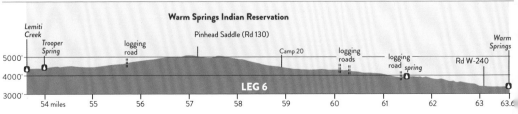

Warm Springs Indian Reservation

Lemiti
Creek

Trooper
Spring

logging
road

Pinhead Saddle (Rd 130)

Camp 20

logging
roads

logging
road   spring

Rd W-240

Warm
Springs

5000'

4000'

LEG 6

3000'

54 miles   55   56   57   58   59   60   61   62   63   63.6

TRAIL TRIVIA

Lemiti Meadow, as well as Lemiti Creek, were designated (supposedly) by Ephraim Henness, a Santiam River area pioneer and one of the first Cascade Range forest rangers, who may have been a little mixed up. The Chinook word *lemiti* actually translates to "mountain." He got closer when he (supposedly) named Lemiti Butte, which translates to "mountain butte." This is hardly the only incidence of a native word being misapplied to a geographic feature.

inviting rest stop bench for a drink and a snack. Just 0.2 mile beyond, the PCT crosses the first of several unmapped logging roads you'll encounter through this leg. From the road crossing, the trail climbs northwest, passing through a short stretch of forest charred by the **2014 Camas Prairie Fire**, then comes to a crest just below the peak of 5348-foot **South Pinhead Butte**. The path contours around the butte's forested eastern flank, reaching the leg's high point at 56.9 miles. Some maps indicate a spot called the **Chinquapin Viewpoint** near this location, but the views are nothing to write home about. From here, the trail drops into a saddle between the two buttes.

early autumn, many of the rich greens of mountain huckleberry, Oregon grape, and vine maple begin transforming into brilliant reds and yellows, creating a kaleidoscope of color, which can be just as captivating as any mountain view. You will likely also be accompanied by the calls and cries of a variety of birds making these lower hills their home. Take along a birding guide or app and see how many you can identify. Woodpeckers are common through this area.

Leaving Lemiti Creek, the PCT meanders east along the fringe of Lemiti Meadow; through the trees you can glimpse the marshy meadows and braided channels of Lemiti Creek. The trailside is thick with bunchberry and vanilla-leaf. Not long after getting under way, at 54 miles, a short side trail breaks off to **Trooper Spring ⬤**, a fairly reliable water source. Just beyond, the trail bends north and begins ascending the shallow southeast flank of **South Pinhead Butte**. The surroundings are pleasant, with tall conifers filtering the sunlight and beargrass and huckleberry lining the trail. You may be tempted to pick a handful of berries to snack on, but remember you're on reservation land and should respect their regulations and refrain here—there will be lots more berries in the miles ahead.

Around 55.5 miles, the route passes a noticeably huge lodgepole pine on the left side of the trail. This marks about the halfway point up the ascent. Just beyond this tree, a cut log makes an

When summer turns to fall, Oregon's Green Tunnel transforms into a Golden Tunnel.

Warm Springs River is one of the few places to refill water on the PCT's 30-mile passage through the Warm Springs Indian Reservation.

In the shallow gap between South and North buttes, at 57.2 miles, the overgrown remains of abandoned Road 130 descend west. This is no longer a reliable access way on or off the PCT. Here, a sign indicates that you are on Warm Springs Reservation land with mileage indicators for Warm Springs River to the north, and Lemiti Meadow to the south. Continuing on, the trail contours around 5450-foot **North Pinhead Butte**, briefly leaving the cover of forest to cross a wide, rocky slope. Here, the remnants of an andesite lava flow cover the hillside with a jumble of gray boulders. From the crevasses poke patches of hardy manzanita. Directly east of North Pinhead's peak, the trail reaches another minor crest. From this point, it's all downhill.

Rounding the northeast flank of the butte, the PCT begins a steady descent into the **Warm Springs Valley**. Along the way, you're offered a brief peek of what lies north. Only a few days' hike away, Oregon's tallest mountain, Mount Hood,

summons. A random trail post at 58.4 miles indicates "You Are Here." (*Thanks for the tip!*) Just beyond, the trees recede again as the PCT crosses another lava slope, switchbacking down through the rocks to the east. The open view over the forested valley below reveals several low peaks to the east, all scarred with a patchwork of timber harvesting. At the bottom of the switchback, the PCT turns northeast and slides back under the cover of forest. At 58.9 miles, a small campsite can be found left of the trail (**Camp 20**).

Descending a shallow ridge, the PCT crosses two more logging roads at 60.1 and 60.3 miles, then drops into the lower level of the river basin. After skirting the edge of a clear-cut area, the forest becomes richer and denser, the trees taller and fuller, reaching skyward. Shrubs of mountain rhododendron are thick along the trailside. The trail levels, turning north, and at 61.5 miles passes a seeping spring **O**, reached by a short spur trail to the left (west). By late summer, this spring won't have much to offer. The PCT then arcs east to cross one more logging road, W-240, at 63.1 miles, bears north, and in 0.5 mile arrives at the **Warm Springs Camp 0**.

Warm Springs Camp is considered the only "legal" PCT camping area between Lemiti Camp and the Forest Service campgrounds at Timothy Lake, 10 miles beyond. Of the six decent tent sites, half can be found on the south side of the river, the other half on the north side; the latter area is somewhat nicer (as primitive camp standards go)

with flat tent spaces, a community fire pit, and log benches. A log footbridge crosses the river between the two camp areas. Here, water can be easily obtained and you can cool your feet in the chilly stream. At the end of another short day, you can spend the afternoon kicking back and enjoying another evening of forested solitude.

CAMP-TO-CAMP MILEAGE

Lemiti Camp to Camp 20 . . . . 5.3
Camp 20 to Warm Springs Camp. 4.7

7 WARM SPRINGS TO TIMOTHY LAKE

DISTANCE 10.2 miles

ELEVATION GAIN/LOSS
+1110 feet/−1160 feet

HIGH POINT 4320 feet

CONNECTING TRAILS AND ROADS
Wilson Road (S-506D), Miller Trail (#534), Headwaters Trail (#522), Joe Graham Trail (#524), Oregon Skyline Road (FR 42), Timothy Lake Trail (#528), Southshore Trail (#529)

ON THE TRAIL
At this point, you're probably ready for a change of scenery. It's coming—just one more leg away. While this one takes you through more viewless forest, after an initial ascent the remainder is another gradually descending stroll. As soon as you leave the Warm Springs Indian Reservation and logging parcels behind and enter national forest again, the scenery markedly improves. And if you make quick time of this stretch, you can conclude your day lounging lakeside or enjoying a refreshing dip with a view of Oregon's tallest peak in the distance. There are no reliable water sources until nearly the end of the leg, so top off with whatever you need to get you through the day.

Heading north from the **Warm Springs Camp**, the Pacific Crest Trail wastes no time climbing up and away from the river valley as it contours around the eastern flank of 4970-foot **Summit Butte**. Shortly after getting underway, at 63.9 miles, a short side trail breaks off east to a trickling spring **0**—but you will likely have tanked up at Warm Springs. Although another day of viewless forest, this section is particularly pretty with the morning sun streaming in rays through the trees, illuminating mosses and lichens and setting the entire forest aglow. Watch the trailsides for a variety of wildflowers and fungi.

Approaching 65 miles, the PCT passes a particularly large Douglas-fir reaching for the heavens, and in 0.1 mile comes to an unmapped logging road. Take a short jog east to pick the trail back up again and resume your northward march through the "green tunnel." While the trees immediately surrounding the PCT are mature, the Oregon grape and maidenhair ferns are prolific, and the mountain rhododendrons are thick, it is easy to see the wide tracts of clear-cut and recovery areas just beyond. The trail bends northeast, reaching its apex on Summit Butte, amid a patchwork quilt of logging parcels. As the trail contours around the butte, bearing north, the descent toward Timothy Lake begins.

Another variety of PCT blaze indicates the route north to Mount Hood.

At 67.1 miles, just as you're starting down, you'll begin hearing the now-familiar buzz of high-voltage powerlines as the trail comes to another wide clearing. The route continues straight across, then bends northwest to jog around 4115-foot **Buckskin Butte**. Just south of the butte, at 68.4 miles, is an abandoned crossroads. Nearby, a large camp area can accommodate a few small tents (**Camp 21**). There is no water in the area, so you probably wouldn't want to stay here unless in a pinch. Continuing its contouring descent around the butte, the PCT crosses another unmapped logging road at 69.1 miles, and then **Wilson Road** (S-506D) at 69.7 miles.

Shortly after crossing the road, the PCT turns west and the forest begins filling in as you leave the logging areas behind, with clumps of beargrass lining the trail. Many maps indicate a seasonal

creek on this stretch, but don't count on fetching any water here. The PCT bends northwest, and at 70.8 miles leaves the Warm Springs Indian Reservation and reenters the **Mount Hood National Forest**. Now under the shade of tall conifers in a markedly pleasant and uncluttered stretch of forest adorned with ferns and mossy logs, the path proceeds forward, jogging north and west, with soft tread underfoot.

Entering the **Timothy Lake** recreation area, you'll likely begin seeing day hikers venturing onto the trail with you, connecting from a variety trail junctions ahead. At 71.6 miles, the PCT meets the **Miller Trail** (#534) and the **Headwaters Trail** (#522). The Miller Trail breaks off west for 0.25 mile to the **Clackamas Lake Campground** (Clackamas Lake is small and marshy and not really worth the side trip); the Headwaters Trail breaks

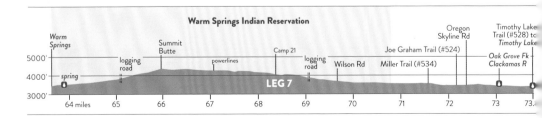

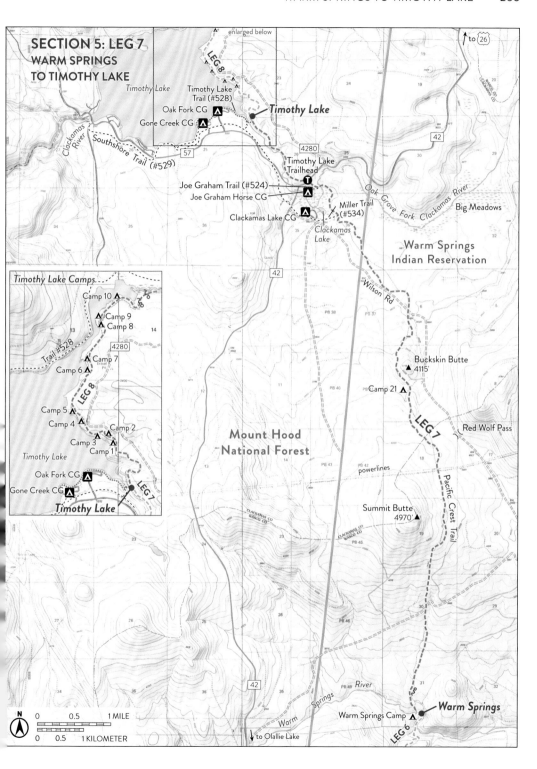

SECTION 5: LEG 7
WARM SPRINGS
TO TIMOTHY LAKE

to 26

enlarged below

LEG 8

Timothy Lake

Timothy Lake
Trail (#528)
Oak Fork CG
Gone Creek CG

Timothy Lake

Clackamas River

Southshore Trail (#529)

57

4280

42

Timothy Lake
Trailhead

Joe Graham Trail (#524)
Joe Graham Horse CG

Miller Trail
(#534)

Clackamas Lake CG

*Clackamas
Lake*

Oak Grove Fork Clackamas River

Big Meadows

**Warm Springs
Indian Reservation**

Wilson Rd

42

Timothy Lake Camps

Camp 10

Camp 9
Camp 8

Trail #528

4280

Camp 7
Camp 6

LEG 8

Camp 5
Camp 4

Camp 2
Camp 3
Camp 1

Timothy Lake

Oak Fork CG
Gone Creek CG

LEG 7

Timothy Lake

**Mount Hood
National Forest**

powerlines

Buckskin Butte
4115'

Camp 21

LEG 7

Red Wolf Pass

Pacific Crest Trail

Summit Butte
4970'

N

0   0.5   1 MILE

0   0.5   1 KILOMETER

42

Warm
Springs
River

to Olallie Lake

Warm Springs Camp

Warm Springs

LEG 6

South of Mount Hood, Timothy Lake is a popular, relaxing destination for hikers and campers.

off north toward the **Oak Grove Fork Clackamas River**, which the PCT will soon follow on its way to Timothy Lake (some maps may not show this trail). Bending north, the PCT skirts the forested edges of the wet meadows that indicate the extent of a once-larger Clackamas Lake, then crosses a meadow offering a clear glimpse into the area.

Turning west again, the PCT meets the **Joe Graham Trail** (#524) at 72.2 miles. This short spur branches off west to the **Joe Graham Horse Camp**. A quick 0.2 mile farther, the trail arrives at a large PCT trailhead and parking area on **Oregon Skyline Road** (FR 42). As you emerge from the trees, take note of the log archway with a hanging sign for the Pacific Crest National Scenic Trail. Whether you've hiked from far or near to get to this point, a photo under the signed arch makes a nice souvenir. At this point, you're also

OAK FORK AND GONE CREEK CAMPGROUNDS

These popular campgrounds can get quite full on summer weekends, so if your itinerary allows, try breaking here midweek. Or, if you're sticking to a set itinerary, make a campground reservation (recreation.gov) to ensure you can roll in hassle-free. Both of these campgrounds offer tent spaces, picnic tables, fire pits, drinking water, and vault toilets. It may be a bit of a culture shock coming into a bustling recreational camp area after days of quiet solitude on the PCT, but a few creature comforts like easily accessible drinking water, dinner at a table instead of a bumpy stump, and an opportunity to unload all of your trail trash can ease the adjustment. You just may be camping next to a party willing to share their juicy burgers and cold beer in exchange for tales from your journey.

TIMOTHY LAKE CAMPSITES

There are at least 10 established campsites along the forested eastern shore of Timothy Lake; Camp 6 is a particularly nice, secluded site at the edge of a halfmoon-shaped cove. All of these are accessible directly from the PCT, and range in size from small individual sites to large group sites that can accommodate several tents. Most have fire rings, logs for sitting, and easy access to the lakeshore for lounging, swimming, and filtering water. Following is a short description of the most notable campsites, from south to north, their size, and their PCT mileage. (See map for Leg 8 and inset shown of map for Leg 7 for exact locations.)

Camp locations from junction of PCT and Timothy Lake Trail:

Camp 1	Small site left	fire ring, logs	74.6 miles
Camp 2	Large site right, upslope	lake access on bootpath left	74.7 miles
Camp 3	Two large sites left	fire rings, lake access	74.8 miles
Camp 4	Large site left	fire ring, lake access	75.1 miles
Camp 5	Small site left	fire ring, lake access	75.2 miles
Camp 6	Medium site left	fire ring, logs, lake access at cove	75.8 miles
Camp 7	Several dispersed sites around cove	fire rings, logs, lake access	75.9 miles
Camp 8	Medium site left	fire ring, lake access	76.4 miles
Camp 9	Large site left	fire ring, rocks, lake access	76.5 miles
Camp 10	Medium site left	fire ring, logs, path to water	76.8 miles

on the final stretch of the leg. Crossing the road, it's just a short, shady ramble to the Oak Grove Fork Clackamas River **O** at 73.1 miles. The path proceeds alongside the river for a short spell, where you'll enjoy the sound of the babbling creek. The final stretch climbs away from the water to meet the **Timothy Lake Trail** (#528) at 73.8 miles. From a small clearing just off the trail, you have a picturesque view over wide, blue Timothy Lake.

At this point, you have the option of ending the leg at an established campground, complete with picnic tables, restrooms, and piped water, or proceeding on a little farther to one of many primitive campsites along the eastern lakeshore, which stretch into the next leg. To take advantage of the **Oak Fork or Gone Creek campgrounds** (with 47 and 50 sites, respectively), on the southeast shore of pretty Timothy Lake, veer off the PCT onto the Timothy Lake Trail, cross the high bridge over the Oak Grove Fork, then immediately turn onto the **Southshore Trail** (#529) for 0.5 mile to Oak Fork,

or 1 mile to Gone Creek. If you'd prefer a little more solitude and more of a wilderness experience, you'll find the first of the east shore campsites in just under 1 mile farther on the PCT. (See the campsites marked on the map and the beginning of the next leg for more info.) Either way, once you've selected a campsite, spend the rest of your day kicking back lakeside.

CAMP-TO-CAMP MILEAGE

Warm Springs Camp to Camp 21 . . . . 4.8

Camp 21 to Miller Trail/Clackamas Lake
   CG junction. 3.2

Miller Trail to Clackamas Lake CG
   (off PCT). 0.5

Miller Trail to Timothy Lake Trail junction 2.2

Timothy Lake Trail junction to Oak Fork CG
   (off PCT) 0.5

Timothy Lake Trail junction to Gone Creek CG
   (off PCT) 1.0

Timothy Lake Trail junction to Timothy Lake
   Camps (see sidebar) . . . . 0.8+

8 TIMOTHY LAKE TO WAPINITIA PASS

DISTANCE 11.8 miles

ELEVATION GAIN/LOSS
+1400 feet/–790 feet

HIGH POINT 4200 feet

CONNECTING TRAILS AND ROADS
Old 1916 Trail (#537), Timothy Lake Trail
(#528), Little Crater Lake Trail (#500),
FR 5890 (unpaved), Jackpot Meadow
Trail (#492), FR 58, FR 240 (unpaved),
Blue Box Trail (#483), Warm Springs
Highway (US 26), Frog Lake trailhead spur

ON THE TRAIL

As in the last few legs, most of this next one stays
under cover of forest—although some nice views
do come into play in the latter half. The first 5
miles are an easy, pleasant romp along and above
the watery basin of Timothy Lake, with numerous
camping options (in case you choose to forgo the
larger, busier campgrounds on the southern shore).
Once the lake is in your rear-view, you might opt
for a short side trip to a spectacular little scenic
gem—Little Crater Lake—before the trail starts
ascending to Wapinitia Pass. While some stretches
of forest to the south have been a mixed bag, the
way forward is within lush and lively forest for mile
after mile. Mountain rhododendron, vine maple,
and Oregon grape abound; huckleberry, salmonberry, and lady fern become dense in places. And
wildflowers become more prolific; among the many
varieties, look for pretty pink rose spirea, hedge
nettle, and purple shrubby penstemon.

From the Pacific Crest Trail's junction with
the **Timothy Lake Trail** (#528), 0.5 mile east of
the Oak Fork Campground and 1.4 miles north of
FR 42 (this is PCT mile 73.8), the PCT continues
north, meandering across a shallow drainage. By
midseason, there's likely nothing flowing through
here. Passing through 74.5 miles, the trail comes
alongside the lakeshore with partial views through
the trees, passing the first of the **Timothy Lake
Camps** at 74.6 miles (see Leg 7). From here,
the trail curves gently up and down along the
lakeshore, where campsites and lake access are
plentiful.

The PCT completes its lakeside stroll around
77 miles alongside a wide, grassy delta at the head
of the lake where several small springs flow into
Timothy Lake's upper arm. Along the treeline,
you may notice a string of small birdhouses (or, are
they bathouses?) mounted on short posts. The trail
then dips south and crosses a small, cold spring 0.1

TRAIL TRIVIA

Prior to 1967, **Timothy Lake** was Timothy
Meadows. Then the Portland General Elec-
tric (PGE) utility company dammed the Oak
Grove Fork Clackamas River and flooded
the basin, which was a popular sheep grazing area. The name derives from the timothy grass (also known as cat's tails) that was
planted around the basin. The Timothy Lake
recreation area is still administered by PGE.

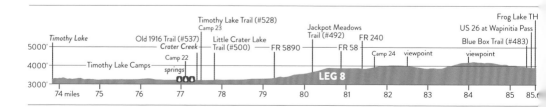

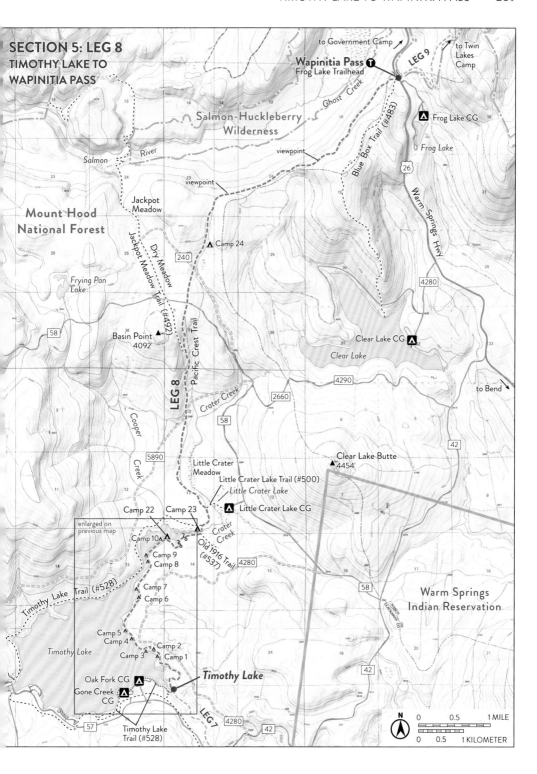

SECTION 5: LEG 8
TIMOTHY LAKE TO
WAPINITIA PASS

to Government Camp

LEG 9

to Twin
Lakes
Camp

Wapinitia Pass
Frog Lake Trailhead

Frog Lake CG

Ghost Creek

Salmon-Huckleberry
Wilderness

Blue Box Trail (#483)

Frog Lake

viewpoint

Salmon River

26

viewpoint

Warm Springs Hwy

Jackpot
Meadow

Mount Hood
National Forest

Dry Meadow

240

Camp 24

4280

Jackpot Meadow Trail (#492)

Frying Pan
Lake

Clear Lake CG

58

Basin Point
4092'

Clear Lake

Pacific Crest Trail

LEG 8

4290

Crater Creek

to Bend

2660

Cooper Creek

58

42

5890

Little Crater
Meadow

Clear Lake Butte
4454'

Little Crater Lake Trail (#500)

Little Crater Lake

Camp 22   Camp 23

Little Crater Lake CG

enlarged on
previous map

Camp 10

Crater Creek

Old 1916 Trail (#537)

Camp 9
Camp 8

4280

Warm Springs
Indian Reservation

Timothy Lake Trail (#528)

Camp 7
Camp 6

58

Camp 5
Camp 4

Camp 2
Camp 1

Timothy Lake

Camp 3

42

Oak Fork CG

Gone Creek
CG

Timothy Lake

LEG 7

57

Timothy Lake
Trail (#528)

4280

42

N

0   0.5   1 MILE

0   0.5   1 KILOMETER

Big views of Mount Hood over Ghost Creek and the Salmon River meadows highlight the traverse to Wapinitia Pass.

mile farther. Where it swings back north, the trail hooks up and over another small spring , then returns to its previous course. (The campsite once near here, Camp 22 on the map, was decommissioned by the Forest Service in 2017.)

The way forward then takes several waypoints in quick succession: First, the trail passes a small running spring  at 77.2 miles, which flows right out from the rocks beside the trail. Just beyond, the trail skirts a swampy area filled with dark, mucky water; if it's mosquito season, you'll want to be well protected through here. The PCT then meets the **Old 1916 Trail** (#537) at 77.4 miles. This mountain-biking trail branches off right (south) for 4.2 miles, connecting to several other side trails to end at the Oregon Skyline Road (FR 42). This is the route used by mountain bikers to complete a loop around Timothy Lake, since bikes aren't permitted on the PCT—though don't be surprised if you catch a few on the PCT regardless. Just beyond this junction, over a pair of puncheons (boardwalks), the trail crosses

well-flowing **Crater Creek**  on a sturdy wooden bridge. In season, splashes of bright yellow monkeyflower adorn the creeksides. This will be the last access to running water until Frog Lake at the end of the leg. A good water access point can be found just left (west) of the trail, on the north side of the bridge. A handful of paces beyond the bridge, just before another section of puncheon, a bootpath breaks off left (west) to a small, secluded campsite in the trees (**Camp 23**). Finally, the PCT meets the wide, northern junction of the **Timothy Lake Trail** (#528) at 77.5 miles. This trail proceeds 7.4 miles around the western side of the lake and reconnects to the PCT at the start of this leg. (This loop makes a pleasant weekend outing for a quick trail fix.) A posted sign here gives information on area permit and camping requirements.

Still on fairly level ground, with tall conifer above, bunchberry and mountain strawberry below, the PCT resumes its lazy northward heading, and soon meets the multisigned junction with the **Little Crater Lake Trail** (#500) at 77.8 miles. If you have the time, it's worth the 0.2-mile (one way) side trip to check out this incredibly deep, cold blue pool. A short 0.2 mile beyond is the **Little Crater Lake CG**. This drive-in campground has 16 tent sites with picnic tables and fire pits; there is also piped water and vault toilets. The route then heads northwest, then north through pleasantly forested terrain, meeting and crossing gravel FR 5890 at 79.3 miles.

From this point, the PCT gets down to its business for the day, beginning a steady ascent north to a fork at 80.2 miles. Here, the PCT continues right (north), while the **Jackpot Meadow Trail** (#492) branches off to the left (northwest). The trail continues climbing in earnest, now in more open, airy forest, reaching a viewless high point on the eastern flank of 4092-foot **Basin Point**. It then levels off in denser forest, the trailsides lined with beargrass, huckleberry, and rhododendron, before meeting paved FR 58 at 80.9 miles.

LITTLE CRATER LAKE

Not so much a "lake" as it is a deep, spring-fed pool, Little Crater Lake is so pure that its deep azure color almost rivals that of its big brother in the southern part of the state. Unlike other bodies of water in Oregon's volcanic Cascades that fill basins and glacial depressions with rain and snowmelt, this pool formed when underground springs forced their way to the surface along a fault line. As the water continued to jet its way upward, it began to dissolve away the surrounding siltstone, enlarging its opening on the surface until it eventually formed a 100-foot-wide pool. Because the lake is still fed from underground springs, it maintains its clarity and a constant 34 degrees year-round. The lake is mostly surrounded by dense shrubbery, but a small viewing platform at the edge lets you peer down into its 45-foot depths.

A sturdy bridge crosses Crater Creek, a good place to top off water bottles, with a good campsite nearby.

Now bearing northeast, the PCT continues rising through drier, open forest with an abundance of beargrass. During this plant's blooming season (every other year) hundreds of tall flower stalks make a spectacular sight. The trail dips to cross gravel FR 240 at 81.4 miles, with a very old trail sign indicating Highway 26 is 4 miles ahead. After another short, easy stretch, the trail passes **Camp 24** at 81.7 miles. This large camp, just right (east) of the trail, can accommodate up to five tents, and has fire rings and logs for sitting; the better tent sites are farthest from the trail. The PCT then jogs between two low hills before turning northeast at the edge of a wide, deep, forested valley. An open viewpoint at 82.5 miles presents an unobstructed panorama, taking in the **Salmon River** and meadows below, and glacier-draped Mount Hood rising above.

For the next 1.5 miles, as the PCT makes a gradual contouring ascent to Wapinitia Pass, you'll be treated to more occasional views of the big scene to the north. In actuality, these open "viewpoints" are the edges of clear-cut patches on the forested slope below. In the days ahead, when you're ascending Mount Hood, looking south, these patches will help you identify where you contoured this ridge above the valley. The PCT comes to a crest at 84.1 miles, well below

Look for a variety of woodland wildflowers near streams and lakesides, including bog gentian.

FROG LAKE CAMPGROUND

Frog Lake is a popular summer destination for car campers, anglers, kayakers, and standup paddleboarders. The 33-site campground accepts reservations (recreation.gov) and is often filled on summer weekends; on weekdays visitation is slim, so it's much easier to drop in on the fly—and have a little more peace with fewer crowds. Each site has a picnic table, fire pit, and tent space, and the campground has vault toilets and potable well water. There is also a day-use space (no camping) on the southwest side of the lake, as well as a few primitive campsites dispersed around the perimeter of the campground and lake that can be used without a nightly campground fee. A short trail at the south end of the camp loop leads through a lakeside meadow profuse with blue gentian to the shallow, tree-ringed lake for relaxing or taking a cool summer dip.

a 4600-foot peak to the southeast, then offers a last look at the sprawling Salmon River meadows below with Mount Hood opening up above. The next time you see Mount Hood, you'll be standing high upon it.

From this point, the trail begins a steady, contouring descent under cover of dense forest. You'll probably make quick work of this stretch, arriving at the junction with the **Blue Box Trail** (#483) at 85.4 miles. This 3.7-mile trail heads southwest, paralleling the PCT on higher ground—actually reaching the 4600-foot peak the PCT traversed under a short ways back—before descending south to Clear Lake. Just beyond this junction, the PCT spills out of the forest onto the shoulder of the **Warm Springs Highway** (US 26), at **Wapinitia Pass**, at 85.5 miles. Cars and trucks race over this pass, paying little attention to hikers, so proceed across with caution. On the opposite side of the highway, the trail dives back under the cover of forest, and less than 0.1 mile farther arrives at the cutoff junction to the **Frog Lake Trailhead and**

CAMP NOTE: TWIN LAKES CAMP

If you choose to forgo the frontcountry campground at Frog Lake, the nearest alternative is the camp area at Lower Twin Lake. This will add 2 more miles to the end of Leg 8, making for a 13.8-mile day, but the tradeoff is fewer crowds (though this lake's relative proximity to the trailhead still makes it fairly popular on weekends) on a nicer lake, in a pleasant wilderness setting. Numerous campsites can be found at the end of the short spur trail that descends to the northern edge of the lake. A 0.9-mile trail circuits the entire lake, with the Frog Buttes Trail (#530) branching off to the south. (See map in Leg 9.)

Campground (Camp) ⬤. There's a conveniently placed picnic table and trashcan at this junction.

Having reached the end of the leg, turn right (south) off the PCT to the wide trailhead and Sno-Park parking area. Here you'll find a vault toilet and another trash receptacle. On the other side of the paved parking area you'll find the signed campground road, which winds 0.5 mile south to the drive-in campground. The alternative to this established campground (especially on weekends) is to continue another 1.3 miles along the PCT, then detour onto the **Twin Lakes Trail** (#495) for 0.7 mile to the Lower Twin Lake camp area (see Camp Note). At either location, find a spot, drop your gear, and get a good night's rest for the last leg of the section, which culminates in a big climb to even bigger views—a just reward for your long-distance efforts.

CAMP-TO-CAMP MILEAGE
Timothy Lake Trail junction to
    Timothy Lake Camps (see Leg 7) 0.8
Timothy Lake Camps to Camp 22. . . . . 2.5
Camp 22 to Camp 23 . . . . 0.4
Camp 23 to Little Crater CG junction 0.3
Little Crater Lake CG junction to
    Little Crater Lake CG (off PCT) 0.4
Little Crater Lake CG junction to
    Camp 24 . . . . 3.9
Camp 24 to Frog Lake Trailhead
    junction 3.9
Frog Lake Trailhead junction to
    Frog Lake CG (off PCT) 0.5

Little Crater Lake is a short side trip off the PCT.

9 WAPINITIA PASS TO TIMBERLINE LODGE

DISTANCE 10.4 miles

ELEVATION GAIN/LOSS
+2750 feet/–620 feet

HIGH POINT 6050 feet

CONNECTING TRAILS AND ROADS
Twin Lakes Trail (#495), Palmateer Trail
(#482), Barlow Butte Trail (#670), Barlow
Pass Road, Mount Hood Highway (OR 35),
Timberline Trail #600

ON THE TRAIL

The final leg of Section 5 culminates with one of
the longest sustained climbs of the Pacific Crest
Trail's journey through Oregon, gaining nearly
3000 feet over the next 10 miles. The grade stays
fairly moderate through the course of the leg,
with few downright steep sections, allowing you
to maintain a reasonable pace for most of the
day. The only descent comes midway through the
leg, making you wonder why you're going *down*
when you still have so much *up* to do. The payoff
comes near the end of the leg when you burst
out of the forest onto the doorstep of Oregon's
highest volcano, **Mount Hood**. The views are
at once immense and impressive, as unlike the
PCT's respectable passage around Oregon's other
iconic mountains, you now find yourself high on
the mountain, nearly toe-to-toe with a massive
glacier-covered peak.

As for scenery, the trail stays mostly in the
trees until the very end—but oh, how lovely it is.
At the peak of summer, this stretch of lush and
lively forest is positively bursting with berries and
wildflowers. Look for an abundance of mountain
rhododendron, lady fern, beargrass, and huckleberry lining the trails underneath a canopy of
mostly mountain hemlock forest. Sprinkled here
and there are splashes of color in the form of purple
penstemon and lupine, orange Indian paintbrush,
and pink bleeding heart, to name a few. Higher
elevations showcase whitebark pines surrounded
by purple aster, bright yellow goldenrod, and pink
mountain heather.

From the Frog Lake junction, the PCT sets forth
on comfortable, level tread, making a wide curve
from northeast to southeast in the first 0.5 mile. Just

TRAIL TRIVIA

Bird Butte, just north of the Twin Lakes,
was named for George Bird, a local forest
ranger who bled to death near this location from an unspecified accident. This is
one of the more grisly designations among
Oregon's geographic place names.

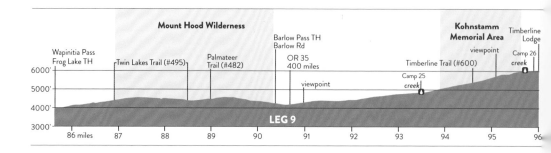

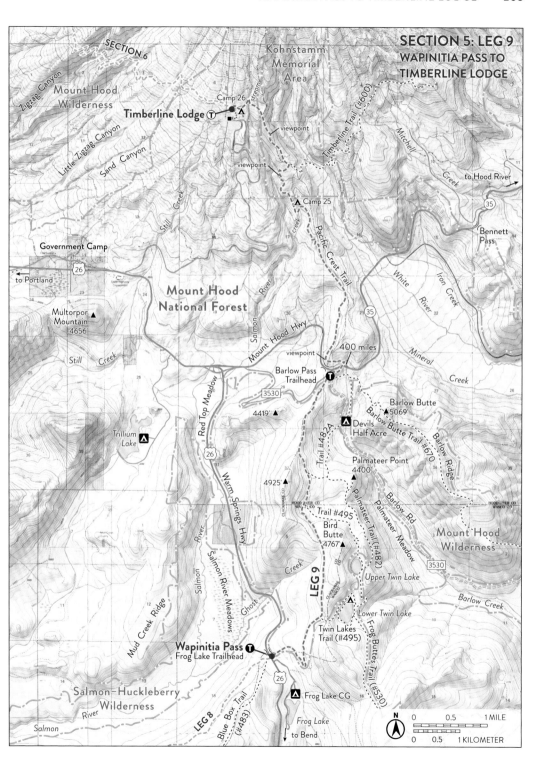

ALTERNATE ROUTE: TWIN LAKES TRAIL

For adding some scenery to your PCT journey through this section, you may consider one of the alternate routes on the **Twin Lakes Trail** (#495). Branching off the PCT at the southern junction (PCT mile 86.9), the forested Twin Lakes Trail crosses a saddle between two hills, then descends into the lower lake basin, where a short spur trail leads to the lake and camp area. The trail then proceeds through several switchbacks to gain some elevation and turn north, where it meets the southern shore of **Upper Twin Lake**—with a peek at Mount Hood's snowy cap—on the southeast flank of Bird Butte. Just beyond, the **Palmateer Trail** (#482) forks right (north) to a prime clifftop view over the wide, glacial **Barlow Creek Valley**; the **Palmateer Meadows** are far below, with Barlow Ridge creating the eastern horizon.

At this fork on the east side of Upper Twin Lake, you have the option of returning to the PCT by reconnecting with the **Twin Lakes Trail** and proceeding west to the northern junction of the side loop, or continuing north on the Palmateer Trail to ascend 4400-foot **Palmateer Point**. From this high perch, take in panoramic views of Barlow Creek valley, Palmateer Meadows, Barlow Peak, and Mount Hood. This route also skirts a few wide meadows bursting with summer wildflowers. Reconnect to the PCT by continuing on the Palmateer Trail (passing Trail #482A) to the PCT junction. The Twin Lakes side loop is 2.9 miles, and cuts out 1.4 miles of mostly viewless PCT; the Twin Lakes and Palmateer side loop—including the jaunt to Palmateer Point—is 4.2 miles, and cuts out 2.1 miles of forested PCT.

as the incline starts becoming noticeable, the trail switchbacks to make an even wider curve northeast and quickly gain some elevation, contouring up to a saddle between two low hills. Here, at 86.9 miles, the **Twin Lakes Trail** (#495) breaks off to the east (right). This well-signed junction presents the option for a couple of side loops to the pretty, forested Twin Lakes—including the large **Lower Twin Lake Camp**—as well as a couple notable viewpoints (see Alternate Route). Just beyond the junction, a large posted sign indicates entry into the **Mount Hood Wilderness**. There are no permit requirements here, but the sign does indicate wilderness regulations (Leave No Trace) and recent area notices.

Heading north, the PCT continues gaining elevation as it contours along the western slope of 4767-foot **Bird Butte**. You won't see any trace of the butte's upper reaches, as the forest, transitioning to more fir and pine, restricts any views upward. But if you look down, you might catch a glimpse of little Douglas squirrels darting here and there gathering nuts and seeds. As the trail curves

northwest between Bird Butte and a butte to the west, the sounds of the nearby highway finally fade away and the PCT meets the northern junction of the Twin Lakes Trail at 88.5 miles; just 0.5 mile farther, it meets the **Palmateer Trail** (#482).

BARLOW BUTTE

It's unlikely, with the leg's already considerable elevation gain, that you're going to want to add a side trip of 4 miles and 1100 more feet of gain to your day's total. But for you fervent peak-baggers, Barlow Butte offers some pretty spectacular views south and east. The overgrown summit, once the site of a Forest Service lookout, showcases bird's-eye views over the Barlow Creek valley, Barlow Ridge, and Bonney Ridge, as well as a distant look at Mount Jefferson. There are views of Mount Hood, but they are partially obstructed by trees.

As the PCT approaches Barlow Pass on Mount Hood, it crosses the historic Barlow Road.

Following a short ascent around another unnamed butte, the PCT bears northeast to begin the only moderate descent of this leg, down a north-trending ridge. At first, the slopes to both sides fall away steeply, but as the grade eases, the path meanders to the edge of the Mount Hood Wilderness, arriving at the **Barlow Pass Trailhead** at 90.4 miles. At this wide trail junction, a tall, weathered sign displays a portion of the Twin Lakes area; the wide trail that breaks off to the east is the **Barlow Butte Trail** (#670), which climbs 1.4 steep miles to 5069-foot **Barlow Butte**, before descending 3.7 steep miles to a trailhead at Barlow Road (FR 3530). This junction offers a decent picnic table, a place to relieve yourself of your load for a few minutes and fuel up for the big climb ahead.

When you're recharged and ready to move on, pick up the PCT on the north side of the Barlow Pass junction. The trail dives back under forest

for just a few paces before crossing the historic **Barlow Pass Road**, where a large sign offers some historical facts about the old Oregon Trail wagon road. Back under the trees, the path curves east, paralleling the trailhead access road before coming out onto an old, overgrown side road. Veer right (northeast) and proceed to the shoulder of the **Mount Hood Highway** (OR 35) at 90.7 miles. This location marks the PCT's 400-mile point from the California–Oregon border. As with the previous highway crossing, this one also sees a lot of speeding car and truck traffic, but it's at a bend with limited visibility, so proceed to the other side with extreme caution. The trail picks back up again near the end of the guardrail on the highway's north shoulder.

Now it's time to put your climbing face on. The PCT immediately ascends the slope on a moderate incline, surrounded by dense vine maple. It makes

267

SANTIAM PASS TO TIMBERLINE LODGE

a sharp switchback to keep gaining elevation, turns west, then breaks out into the open, now high above the highway; the view looks southwest over forested **Buzzard Point** and **Mud Creek Ridge**. Turning north, the trail contours up across an increasingly steep conifer-covered slope to where it becomes a narrow catwalk between an exposed rock escarpment and a precipitous drop into the head of a densely forested drainage. Following another short, moderate ascent, the grade eases, the forest flattens out, and the trail becomes surrounded by thick huckleberry and beargrass under a canopy of mountain hemlock draped with Methuselah's beard.

Climbing northwest, the trail zigs and zags up the next ridge, staying within sun-dappled forest. Here more trailside wildflowers begin to present themselves: lupine, bunchberry, mountain strawberry, and daisy-like aster. If there were a window through the trees to the east, you would see that the trail is climbing parallel to the wide White River canyon. Passing through 4800 feet, the PCT curves west around the head of another drainage. Here, you may begin to hear the sweet sound of running water. The trail crosses a dry creek culvert, bends a little more, then comes to a nice campsite just upslope of the trail at 93.5 miles (**Camp 25**); the space is big enough to accommodate a couple tents, and has a few logs for sitting. Just beyond the campsite, where the trail bends again, a good creek **◊** flows down the mountainside.

Pulling away from the camp and creek, the PCT starts climbing steadily again, first southwest, then turning sharply northwest to gain the next ridge. At 93.9 miles, the PCT enters the **Richard L. Kohnstamm Memorial Area**, marked by a couple of large, tree-mounted signs. As you continue onward and upward, small peeks through the trees indicate a deep, wide valley to the west. At 94.3

The PCT merges with Mount Hood's Timberline Trail high on its volcanic slopes, then proceeds through alpine meadows boasting huge panoramic views.

TIMBERLINE LODGE

Opened to the public in 1938, Timberline Lodge was constructed as a Depression-era Works Progress Administration project, built from local timber and stone. It was dedicated shortly before opening by President Franklin D. Roosevelt, who declared, "Those who will follow us to Timberline Lodge on their holidays and vacations will represent the enjoyment of new opportunities for play in every season of the year."

The lodge saw a period of recreation through the 1940s, but began to fall into disrepute and disrepair by the early 1950s. In 1955 it was closed by the US Forest Service, who revoked its operating permit. The closure didn't last long, as Richard L. Kohnstamm applied for a new operating permit, began renovating the establishment, and reopened it to the public. After extensive renovation and additions, Timberline Lodge was designated a National Historic Landmark in 1977. It has since become one of the Northwest's most popular year-round vacation destinations, most notably for its Magic Mile chairlift, which whisks skiers and snowboarders high onto Mount Hood for epic winter—and summer!—snowplay.

The interior of Timberline Lodge is adorned with hand-carved ornamentation, mosaic artwork, and stone arches. Its lower level houses a small museum displaying photos and relics from the lodge's early years. For guests, the lodge offers charming, well-appointed rooms, a heated swimming pool, a hot tub, and a selection of dining options. The **Cascade Dining Room** is the main, upscale restaurant offering a fine choice of Northwest-inspired cuisine. Of most interest to PCT hikers is the moderately priced, not-to-be-missed breakfast buffet. The **Ram's Head Bar** on the top floor offers a variety of craft beers, cocktails, and coffee drinks, as well as a selection of appetizers, sandwiches, and entrées. And hidden in the basement is the **Blue Ox Bar**, perfect for grabbing a slice of pizza and local microbrew. Unfortunately, the more hiker-friendly (and affordable) Black Iron Grill and Market Café, both in the adjacent Wy'East Day Lodge, are only open during the winter ski season.

For PCT hikers, Timberline Lodge offers a limited number of services. They will accept and hold resupply packages at the Wy'East store for a small fee. Camping is not permitted on lodge grounds, or in the parking areas; however, there is a small camping area on the PCT above the lodge (Camp 26), just east of the paved ski area service road. Hikers are welcome to visit any of the dining establishments and the small gift shop, but showers and laundry services are restricted to lodge guests only. If you're in the mood to splurge, reserving a room at the lodge for the end of your hike is a luxurious and well-deserved reward. (See appendix 4 for more info.)

miles, the **Salmon River Canyon** comes into full view, its steep lower slopes rocky and exposed, barren of any vegetation. Across the chasm, you'll spy **Timberline Lodge** on the ridge above. From here, the trail turns again, winding northeast on a gentler grade. The tree cover starts noticeably thinning, and small pocket meadows begin to appear, choked with pretty violet aster and clumps of northern goldenrod. Just a little farther, at 94.5 miles, 11,240-foot **Mount Hood** bursts into full and spectacular view.

Now above treeline in the wide open subalpine, the PCT meets the **Timberline Trail** (#600) at 94.6 miles. The scene is all-encompassing. Taking center stage is the vast, stark head of the White River canyon. Above the canyon, the **White**

Don't stand too close to the edge where the PCT skirts a high ridge above the White River canyon.

River Glacier spills down the mountainside. Streaming from the glacier, a large cascade tumbles down the wide, rocky basin to begin forming the White River. To the west, the groomed **Palmer**

RICHARD L. KOHNSTAMM MEMORIAL AREA

The Richard L. Kohnstamm Memorial Area was established as part of the 2009 Mount Hood Wilderness Act. The expansion designated this 126-acre ribbon of mountainside in honor of Kohnstamm, who, in 1955, began renovation of the then-derelict Timberline Lodge. With the assistance of the US Forest Service, he expanded the lodge building in 1975, and shortly thereafter, with the aid of Friends of Timberline, began restoration of the lodge's original art and furnishings. In 1977, Timberline Lodge was designated a National Historic Landmark. The wilderness area in his name was created to memorialize "the man who saved Timberline Lodge."

Glacier blankets the visible slope; to the east, year-round snowfields drape ridges and fill valley depressions. At this junction, the PCT and Timberline Trail become one to proceed clockwise around the mountain. Above the treeline, the trail surface becomes soft and sandy. Goldenrod and aster carpet the ridgetop, along with lupine, penstemon, paintbrush, and buckwheat, intermingled with gnarled whitebark pines.

Proceeding northwest, the trail ascends the spine of the ridge separating the White River canyon from the Salmon River canyon, eventually becoming narrow enough that the slopes fall away sharply to both sides. You may find your progress slowed by the deep, soft volcanic sand, even becoming a bit of a slog up some of the steeper sections. But you'll be busy taking in the immense views that will seem to improve with every foot of elevation you gain—Mount Hood right in your face to the north; Mount Jefferson, beyond countless forested ridges, on the southern horizon. Here's the place to look back and spy those clearcut patches that afforded your few ridgetop views in the previous leg. At 95.1 miles, the PCT brushes

a precipitous clifftop high above the White River canyon for more "wow" views—don't stand too close to the loose, sandy edge, though.

The path continues up along a shallow drainage, as the ridgetop blends into the slope above, and begins turning west. Crossing near the head of the (likely) dry drainage, the PCT/Timberline Trail exits the Kohnstamm Area at 95.6 miles. The trail crosses another drainage gully, this one likely running, streaming from the Palmer Glacier ❶; the crossing is usually an easy rock-hop. Climbing, the trail curves again to the west and the Timberline Lodge comes into clear view. At 95.8 miles, the trail forks, with the PCT/Timberline proceeding to the right (west), and an access trail to the parking area veering off to the left (south). Just 0.1 mile beyond, in a grove of trees, a decent camp area can be found just south (left) of the trail (**Camp 26**). A minimalist site, it has room for a few tents, but not much more; this location is well-suited for camping near the lodge to take advantage of its services. The trail then crosses one more small, seasonal stream and comes to a paved service road at 96 miles.

Here, at the end of the leg, head down the road to **Timberline Lodge** where a cold, refreshing drink awaits in the **Ram's Head Bar**. If your PCT journey ends here, there's probably no better place. Take some time to explore the historic lodge, its artwork, carvings, and historical relics. Kick back in one of the big, cozy lounges in front of huge picture windows looking up at Mount Hood. Congratulate yourself on a hike well done. If your journey is just pausing here, before finishing the state with Section 6, you should still do all that. Then you'll be refreshed and ready for the roller-coaster ride that awaits between Mount Hood and the Columbia Gorge.

CAMP-TO-CAMP MILEAGE

Frog Lake Trailhead junction to Twin Lakes Trail junction	1.3
Twin Lakes Trail junction to Lower Twin Lake Camp (off PCT)	0.7
Twin Lakes Trail junction to Camp 25	6.6
Camp 25 to Camp 26	2.4
Camp 26 to Timberline Lodge junction	0.1
Timberline Lodge junction to Timberline Lodge (off PCT)	0.2

TIMBERLINE LODGE TO CASCADE LOCKS

THE FINAL SECTION of the Pacific Crest Trail through Oregon, from Mount Hood to the Columbia River Gorge, winds northwest through a roller-coaster of mountain ridges and deep river canyons. The route remains largely in forest, most of it exceptionally lively and verdant. Trailsides are dense with seasonal shrubs, berries, and wildflowers, while canopies of moss- and lichen-draped evergreens filter summer sunlight, keeping trail passage cool and comfortable. Where the trail does emerge from forest cover, the scenes are wide and impressive, showcasing several faces of the iconic Mount Hood, replete with glistening glaciers and rugged volcanic features.

From the historic **Timberline Lodge** high on the flanks of Mount Hood, the PCT wends its way through the Timberline Ski Area before entering the **Mount Hood Wilderness** on its clockwise semi-circuit of the big volcano's southwestern flanks. The fun really begins with the big descent into Zigzag Canyon, where the untamed Zigzag River pours from the Zigzag Glacier, high on the mountainside. Through this dynamic landscape, you'll witness the effects of the mountain coming down upon itself as you cross debris flows and skirt precipitous cliffsides above deeply scoured canyons where the anatomy of the mountain is exposed for all to see—layer upon layer of pyroclastic and debris flows. The mountain traverse offers two scenic alternate routes, both highly recommended: one to a sprawling subalpine wildflower meadow, the other to a beautiful cascading waterfall in a lush grotto.

At **Lolo Pass** the PCT leaves the wilderness area behind and enters the **Bull Run Watershed** protected area. Views become limited as the trail undulates though conifer forests, traversing high slopes and skirting narrow ridges, most lined with

DISTANCE 49.8 miles

STATE DISTANCE 405.3–455.2 miles

ELEVATION GAIN/LOSS
+9290 feet/–15,130 feet

HIGH POINT 6090 feet

BEST TIME OF YEAR Aug–Sep

PCTA SECTION LETTERS F, G

LAND MANAGERS Mount Hood National Forest (Mount Hood Wilderness, Bull Run Forest Reserve, Mark O. Hatfield Wilderness), US Forest Service (Columbia River Gorge National Scenic Area)

PASSES AND PERMITS NW Forest Pass required for parking at Bridge of the Gods and Eagle Creek trailheads; also required at most connecting trailheads; self-issue wilderness permits for Mount Hood and Mark O. Hatfield wilderness areas.

MAPS AND APPS
- National Geographic PCT: Oregon North 1004, maps 1–3
- Halfmile PCT: Oregon G1–G8
- Guthook PCT: Oregon

LEGS
1. Timberline Lodge to Muddy Fork River
2. Muddy Fork River to Salvation Spring
3. Salvation Spring to Wahtum Lake
4. Wahtum Lake to Cascade Locks
3/4A. Indian Springs to Cascade Locks (via Eagle Creek Trail)

Opposite: *Tucked away in a lush grotto that is a short side trip from the PCT, Ramona Falls is like a scene out of a fairy tale.*

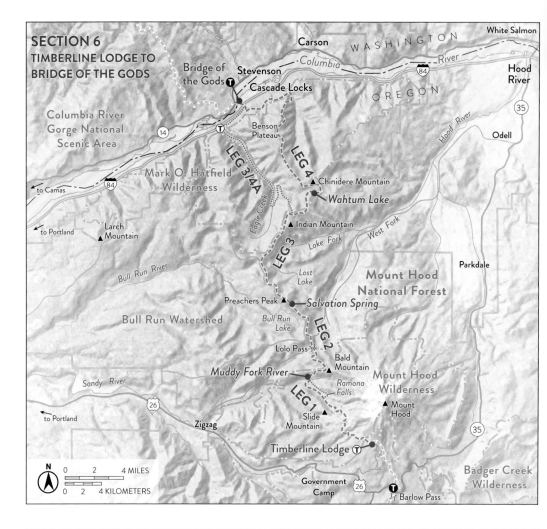

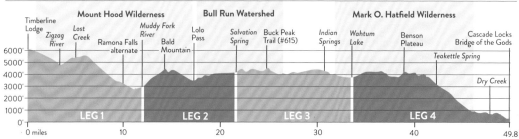

berries and an assortment of wildflowers. Reaching the rock garden flanks of Indian Mountain, you'll have panoramic views over the **Eagle Creek Canyon**. You'll then have the choice of continuing on the official PCT route over the **Benson Plateau**, or detouring onto the outrageously scenic **Eagle Creek Trail** and descending along a rushing creek and past a series of remarkable waterfalls. Similar to the option presented at Crater Lake National Park, the majority of PCT hikers at this point opt for the more scenic route. If you don't mind some trail company, you should too. If quiet solitude is more your gravy, take the official route, which offers a few impressive views, followed by a climactic descent that rivals some of the highest passes in California and Washington to drop you at the finish line just above sea level at the **Columbia River**.

The PCT's final miles in Oregon are among its most challenging. The ascents are long and steep, and the descents are longer and steeper, all on trail tread that varies between soft forest duff and rough, rocky scree. Plus, the crossing—or fording—of three rushing, possibly swollen, cataracts will add to the thrill. Water and campsites are fairly common through the first half of the section, but fewer and farther between through the second half. Also, weather around Mount Hood and into the Columbia River Gorge can be extremely fickle, where rain, and even snow, are possible at any time during the summer.

Because of Mount Hood's proximity to the Portland–Vancouver metro areas and their outdoor-loving populations (in addition to the section's starting point being a popular year-round vacation and recreation destination), you are likely to see more trail traffic though some legs, mostly in the Mount Hood and Eagle Creek areas. This can potentially mean crowded campsites, so be prepared to share known camp areas. For solitude, you can always venture off trail (where permitted) and find some of the hidden-gem campsites in the Paradise Park and Benson Plateau areas. The less-welcome company comes in the small, buzzing variety. Early summer finds these lush forested areas populated by gazillions of bloodthirsty mosquitoes. By August, you should have more comfortable passage.

Following all the ups, downs, heat, cold, and two-, four- (watch for marmots, deer, and black bears!), and six-legged trail companions, you'll have reason to celebrate upon reaching the trailhead at the **Bridge of the Gods** and shrugging off your pack and kicking off your boots. Regardless of whether you're doing just this section, continuing from several sections prior, or thru-hiking from California or into Washington, you'll have plenty of bragging rights to share about your epic adventure on Oregon's Pacific Crest Trail.

ACCESS
Timberline Lodge
From Portland, drive east on US 26 for 52 miles to the town of Government Camp. Continue 1 mile east, then turn left on the Timberline Road. Proceed 5.5 winding miles to the large parking area at Timberline Lodge.

From Bend, drive north on US 97 for 43 miles. Merge onto US 26 north and continue another 62 miles toward Government Camp. One mile before Government Camp, turn right onto the Timberline Road and proceed up the mountain. Hikers and backpackers should use the large, lower parking area, just southeast of the smaller main lodge parking area.

Bridge of the Gods
From Portland, drive east on I-84 for 42 miles to exit 44. Stay right to turn onto the Bridge of the Gods ramp to Stevenson, Washington. Partway up the ramp, turn right into the trailhead parking area. The PCT spills out of the trees and across the road on the south side of the trailhead area; it proceeds north directly across the bridge.

NOTES
Services
The Timberline Lodge, at the southern trailhead, caters mostly to guests with accommodations and dining options, with only limited services to hikers, mostly by way of accepting and holding resupply packages. The towns of Sandy, Welches, and Government Camp, on the way up Mount Hood, offer a variety of lodging, dining, and grocery services; there is an outdoor supply store in Welches and a post office in Government Camp. The town of Cascade Locks, at the northern trailhead, has a few lodging, dining, and grocery services. (See appendixes 3 and 4 for more info.)

Camping
There are several established camp areas and primitive campsites through both this section of the PCT and the adjoining alternate routes. Some of the closer-in locations—Lolo Pass, Wahtum Lake, and Eagle Creek—usually see crowding on weekends, so plan accordingly. Camping restrictions are

imposed within the Bull Run Watershed (end of Leg 2), and along the Eagle Creek alternate route.

Water

Water is fairly regular through the first half, thanks to snowmelt and glacial runoff streaming down Mount Hood and numerous perennial springs. Water gets scarcer in the second half, with most reliable sources at or near popular camp locations. There is a 12.6-mile (potentially) dry stretch near the end (Leg 4), so plan accordingly.

Hazards

There are three significant river crossings around Mount Hood that are not serviced by bridges. Two require fords, while the other requires a precarious log crossing. Both the Zigzag and Sandy rivers are often at flood stage in the spring and early summer.

Scout for the safest crossing, exercise proper fording techniques, and use extreme caution. The current Muddy Fork River crossing is via two parallel downed trees. The Forest Service does not plan to install new bridges. (See Planning and Preparation in the introduction for more info.)

Wildfire Damage

In the summer of 2017, the massive Eagle Creek Fire burned several miles of the PCT between Wahtum Lake and Cascade Locks, as well as most of Eagle Creek Canyon, causing extensive damage to these trails and throughout the Columbia River Gorge. Expect extended closures or detours. The Eagle Creek alternate route may remain closed through 2018. Contact the Columbia River Gorge National Scenic Area office for the latest on trail accessibility.

SUGGESTED ITINERARIES

These distances do not include off-PCT miles (up to 1 mile) to water sources, campsites, alternate routes, or resupply locations. For more about trail distances, see How to Use This Guide.

4 DAYS (VIA PCT)

		Miles
Day 1	Timberline Lodge to Muddy Fork River	11.9
Day 2	Muddy Fork River to Salvation Spring	9.7
Day 3	Salvation Spring to Wahtum Lake	11.7
Day 4	Wahtum Lake to Cascade Locks	16.5

4 DAYS (VIA EAGLE CREEK TRAIL)

Day 1	Timberline Lodge to Muddy Fork River	11.9
Day 2	Muddy Fork River to Salvation Spring	9.7
Day 3	Salvation Spring to 7.5-Mile Camp	14.2
Day 4	7.5-Mile Camp to Cascade Locks	10.5

3 DAYS (VIA PCT)

Day 1	Timberline Lodge to Lolo Pass	17.2
Day 2	Lolo Pass to Wahtum Lake	16.1
Day 3	Wahtum Lake to Cascade Locks via PCT	16.5

3 DAYS (VIA EAGLE CREEK TRAIL)

Day 1	Timberline Lodge to Lolo Pass	17.2
Day 2	Lolo Pass to 7.5-Mile Camp	18.6
Day 3	7.5-Mile Camp to Cascade Locks	10.5

Opposite: *The west side of Mount Hood features several deeply scoured river canyons where cataracts from the Reid and Zigzag glaciers spill down the mountainside.*

1 TIMBERLINE LODGE TO MUDDY FORK RIVER

DISTANCE 11.9 miles

ELEVATION GAIN/LOSS
+1400 feet/–4650 feet

HIGH POINT 6090 feet

CONNECTING TRAILS
Mountaineer Trail (#798), Hidden Lake
Trail (#779), Paradise Park Loop (#757),
Paradise Park Trail (#778), Timberline Trail
(#600), Sandy River Trail (#770),
Ramona Falls Trail (#797)

ON THE TRAIL

The first stage of the PCT around Mount Hood starts high and ends low—with a few good dips and rises in between that can really get the heart pumping. Namely, the trail crosses all the major drainages flowing from the glaciers on the southwest side of the mountain. What this means is lots of big views, big water, and big forest. Traversing the largest portion of the **Mount Hood Wilderness**, this leg offers two popular alternate loops: the side loop up through **Paradise Park**, and the parallel loop to **Ramona Falls**. Both are definitely worth hopping off the PCT to add some dramatic scenery to your day with minimal additional mileage.

From **Timberline Lodge**, proceed up the ski lift service road on the east side of the building.

About 0.2 mile up, the PCT crosses the road. Look for the large sign indicating Canada 550 miles to the left and Mexico 2108 miles to the right. The largely barren alpine environment is a mixture of volcanic sand, gravel, and rock, supporting patches of grasses, hardy small shrubs and wildflowers, and windblown whitebark pines. Turn (left) west and put boots to trail.

Heading away from the lodge, the PCT traverses the **Timberline Ski Area**, rolling over open ski slopes—Gordo's Mile, Blossom, Norm's, and Kruser—and passing under a couple of chairlifts. Where the trail crosses these exposed slopes are views aplenty—upslope, Mount Hood's ragged summit rises toward the clouds; downslope, wide panoramas showcase the **Salmon River Meadows** (if you hike Section 5, you get a close-up look at these from the ridge above) and **Trillium Lake**. On clear days, **Mount Jefferson** may be spied on the southern horizon; and on really clear days, you may be able to pick out the **Three Sisters** even farther south. Just west of the ski area, the trail enters open, sunny forest, replete with small flower-filled pocket meadows dotted with volcanic boulders and colored with purple aster and blue lupine.

The first of the leg's many trail junctions comes in an exposed area where the **Mountaineer Trail** (#798) crosses the PCT at 0.6 mile. This narrow, 2.7-mile loop trail climbs steeply (almost 1000

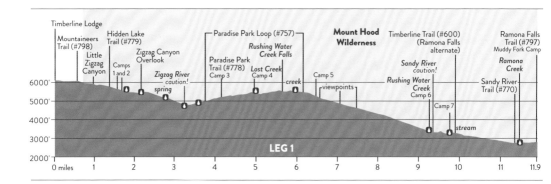

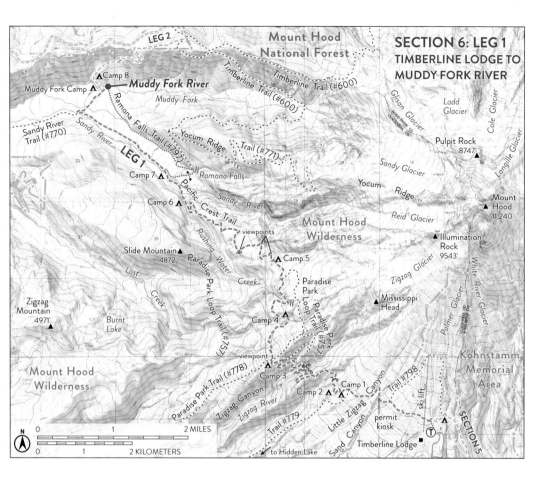

SECTION 6: LEG 1
TIMBERLINE LODGE TO MUDDY FORK RIVER

feet in less than 1 mile) to the **Silcox Hut**, near the base of the Palmer Glacier. A quick 0.1 mile farther, the PCT enters the largest portion of the **Mount Hood Wilderness**, where a trailside kiosk asks all hikers to complete a self-register wilderness permit. The Forest Service uses this information to determine how many people are hiking in the area, which helps to secure funding for trail maintenance and upkeep projects—like (hopefully) replacing washed-out bridges.

The PCT ambles westward, crossing a couple small drainage gullies, usually dry by midsummer. The next drainage, **Little Zigzag Canyon**, at 1 mile, is considerably larger and often has water in it. This water is often cloudy with volcanic silt, so not suitable for filtering or drinking.

WATER ALERT!

The larger streams and rivers around Mount Hood are glacial runoff and snowmelt, flowing down the mountain in canyons and channels of volcanic sediment. Many of these cataracts pick up the loose, fine particles of this sediment, making the water silty and cloudy. Because volcanic ash and sediment contains high concentrations of silica (i.e. glass), this water is not ideal for drinking, even when filtered. Most of the smaller streams and springs run clear and cold and are the best options for refilling as needed.

MOUNT HOOD

Known to the Multnomah tribe as *Wy'east*, 11,240-foot Mount Hood dominates the horizon in northwestern Oregon. In addition to being the most prominent mountain peak in Oregon—and fourth-highest among the entire Cascade Range (following Mounts Rainier, Shasta, and Adams), Mount Hood also has the distinction of being the most recently volcanically active—behind Mount St. Helens, of course. Mount Hood is also unique in that its history as a volcanic epicenter dates back more than 1 million years—much older than many of the other Cascade peaks. The composite structure of Mount Hood is primarily from the eruption of recurring andesite and dacite lava domes and flows, accompanied by the deposition of pyroclastic flows and tephra fallout. The most recent mountain-building event occurred as little as 235 years ago, the results witnessed shortly thereafter by the Lewis and Clark Expedition. Presently considered "dormant," Mount Hood is still geologically active. Fumaroles on the mountain's upper slopes continue to emit sulfurous gases from deep within the earth, indicating that Mount Hood is still very much alive.

What intermittent eruptions continue to build on Mount Hood, ice and water work to tear down. Blanketing Mount Hood's flanks are 11 named glaciers and snowfields, with numerous additional perennial snow features. Over the course of several ice ages, Mount Hood's glaciers once radiated up to 9 miles from the mountain's crown, carving and gouging the major drainages known today. Presently, the largest glaciers on the mountain are the Coe and Eliot glaciers on the north and northeast flanks, respectively. An estimated 3 million cubic meters of ice and snow combined remains on the mountain—and that translates into a lot of meltwater streaming down its mountainsides. Adding to the deterioration of Mount Hood's flanks, massive lahars (debris flows), the result of the geologically recent Crater Rock eruption events, scoured the southern and western drainages—White River, Zigzag River, Rushing Water Creek, and Sandy River—ever deeper, stripping away all forms of vegetation. The Sandy River lahar was so massive that it reached the Columbia River. As you stand over, and hike through, these canyons, you can examine the denuded walls and make out the varying layers of Mount Hood's anatomy laid bare.

The actual elevation of Mount Hood has been a point of contention among the scientific and exploratory fields. According to the USGS, the present elevation of the mountain, based on a 1993 expedition in which they hauled 16 pounds of measuring equipment to the summit, is 11,240 feet. This height varies by up to 10 feet, based on previous and other measurement calculations that place the mountain's elevation at either 11,239 feet or 11,249 feet. Prior to modern-day measuring equipment, early explorers greatly overestimated the mountain's height, with the most lofty approximation being 19,400 feet and designating Mount Hood as the highest mountain in North America. For the purpose of this guidebook, we are using the USGS designation of 11,240 feet. However, if you look up the elevation in other books, online resources, and topographic maps, you are likely to find a variety of "official" heights.

In addition to its geologic history, Mount Hood also possesses a colorful and romantic local history. According to the ancient Multnomah peoples, Wy'east is a monument created by the Great Spirit

Sahale. Legend says that Sahale's two sons, Wy'east and Klickitat, fought for the love of a beautiful maiden, Loowit. The battle resulted in great destruction to forests and villages. This enraged Sahale, inciting him to smite all three. In his grief, he erected three mountains as monuments to the fallen lovers: Loowit (Mount St. Helens), Klickitat (Mount Adams), and Wy'east (Mount Hood). More recent history states that Mount Hood was "discovered" by Lieutenant William Broughton, a member of Captain George Vancouver's Discovery Expedition of the 1790s. Broughton christened the "high, snowy mountain" after Lord Samuel Hood, an admiral in the British navy. A few years later, the mountain was sighted by the Lewis and Clark Expedition, who, at the time, dubbed the peak Timm Mountain, translated "Falls Mountain" according to the local natives, for its proximity to Celilo Falls on the Columbia River. Shortly after, they realized this was the previously named Mount Hood, to which they deferred, and which continues to carry that name.

Presently, Mount Hood is a beacon for outdoor recreation in the Northwest, most notably for its ski resorts and hiking trails, in addition to being one of the most-climbed mountains in the United States. Among six different ski resorts, Mount Hood offers more than 4600 acres of skiable terrain—and the country's only year-round ski slope on Palmer Glacier. More than 10,000 climbers attempt Mount Hood's summit every climbing season, typically April through June. The most popular and "easiest" southern Hogsback route can be completed in a single day, using semi-technical equipment. In recent years, with changing weather and snow patterns, that route seems to be migrating, making the final ascent more challenging. The mountain's signature hiking trail, the Timberline Trail, built in the 1930s by the CCC, circumnavigates the mountain on a 41-mile loop, of which the PCT utilizes 11 miles. Unfortunately (as of 2016), the Timberline continues to be in a sad state of disrepair, most notably for the washout below the Eliot Glacier—which occurred in 2006!—and the significant, and hazardous, erosion of the trail above the Muddy Fork River. Otherwise, there are hundreds of miles of trails on and around Mount Hood, with some of the most popular hiking destinations being Ramona Falls, Paradise Park, Elk Meadows, McNeil Point, Mirror Lake, Zigzag Mountain, Lookout Mountain, and Badger Creek.

The centerpiece of this mountain wonderland is the historic Timberline Lodge. Built in the 1930s, and with a storied and colorful history (see Section 5 for more info), the Timberline Lodge is nestled high on the volcano's southern slopes between the Richard L. Kohnstamm Memorial Area to the east and the Mount Hood Wilderness to the west. The larger area is home to three designated wilderness areas—Mount Hood (which includes the Kohnstamm area), Salmon–Huckleberry, and Badger Creek—in ten different land tracts, totaling nearly 160,000 acres of preserved ridges, valleys, lakes, rivers, and alpine environments. The first area to be established was the Mount Hood Wilderness in 1964, with the Salmon–Huckleberry and Badger Creek wilderness areas following in 1984; in 2009, the Mount Hood area was expanded, and the Kohnstamm area was designated by renaming a portion of the Mount Hood Wilderness. On its journey around Mount Hood, the PCT passes through approximately 22 miles of the Mount Hood and Kohnstamm wilderness areas.

Fuzzy mariposa lilies are among the variety of wildflowers that pop up on the slopes around Mount Hood in summer.

Following a moderate descent into the canyon, the crossing is usually easy, with just a couple of quick boulder-hops. Then the trail proceeds up and out along the opposite canyon wall, ducks back into denser hemlock, pine, and fir forest, and resumes its previous course. The next junction comes along at 1.4 miles, where the **Hidden Lake Trail** (#779) descends 4.2 miles to a trailhead on FR 2639 (just off US 26, a few miles west of Government Camp). Halfway down this ridgeline route, it passes tiny, forested **Hidden Lake**.

The route twists and turns downward, passing a couple decent campsites (**Camps 1 and 2**). The first small site, at 1.6 miles, is just left (south) of the trail above a lush draw; there's room for a couple tents, but not much more. The second site, at the bottom of a looping bend at 1.7 miles, is tucked away in a grove of trees. Look for an obvious bootpath breaking left (south) off the PCT to this nice, secluded camp with room for a couple tents. Just 0.1 mile farther up the trail, through a stretch of thick huckleberry, there's a fairly reliable water source from a clean spring **O**.

After circuiting another sizeable drainage, the trail makes a contouring ascent above the treeline to the narrow ridge overlooking the mighty **Zigzag Canyon**. Here, at 2.2 miles, the view is wide and impressive. This is usually the point where most visiting day hikers, casually exploring from Timberline Lodge, get intimidated and decide to turn back. To the northeast, the canyon rises to its origin below **Mississippi Head**, noted by its sheer, vertical wall of columnar lava rock. Above the head, the **Zigzag Glacier** leads your view past **Illumination Rock** to Mount Hood's summit. Looking across the canyon, you can spy a portion of the wide, green meadows in **Paradise Park**. And downward—700 feet downward—the frothing **Zigzag River** tumbles and cascades down its rocky, denuded channel. Yes, you have to get across this—but it's easier than it looks.

Proceeding on, the PCT dips below the rim, reducing your view to the immediate surrounding forest, then casually slides over the ridgetop and descends into the canyon under a dense evergreen canopy on long, sweeping switchbacks. The effortless descent, while viewless, is adorned with trailside vegetation thanks to numerous seeps dribbling out of the slope: spiky orange Indian paintbrush, pretty pink and yellow monkeyflower, and trumpet-like purple penstemon, in addition to a variety of ferns, salmonberry, and other moisture-loving mountain shrubs. At 2.8 miles, the trail crosses a spring **O** flowing down the hillside in a narrow, rocky, mossy chute. The trail crosses this spring two more times on the successive switchbacks, then levels before exiting the forest through thick brush and comes to the rocky channel of the **Zigzag River O** at 3.3 miles.

TRAIL TRIVIA

It is believed that the **Zigzag Canyon** received its name from a journal entry belonging to Joel Palmer, a pioneer who crossed the river canyon in the fall of 1845. He describes his descent as "turn directly to the right, go zigzag . . . then turn short around, and go zigzag . . . until you come under the place where you started from . . . and so on . . . ."

In late summer, and during low runoff years, the river crossing is usually inconsequential, just a simple rock-hop across the braided channel. At these times, the water is usually clear, refreshingly cold, and safe for filtering and drinking. In early summer, and during high runoff years, it may be trickier and

Watch for fairyslippers (calypso orchids) along the trail near Mount Hood.

Paradise Park is a wonderland of flower-filled meadows and gurgling streams on the high slopes of Mount Hood.

require a ford. Then too, it is usually cloudy with silt and not a desirable water source. If this is the case, and you're in need of a refill, backtrack to the spring and tank up there. The trail picks up again on the other side of the river and begins making a steep westward ascent. In some places, the trail is exceptionally narrow, clinging to the steep slope above increasingly precipitous drops on loose, sandy tread. Partway up the climb, a trickling spring dribbles across the trail at 3.6 miles ⬥.

Switchbacking upward to regain elevation, you may notice a dramatic change in the trail-side vegetation. On this drier, south-facing side of the canyon, the shrubbery is largely beargrass, huckleberry, and mountain strawberry. Midway through the third switchback, the PCT meets the southern junction of the **Paradise Park Loop Trail** (#757) at 3.8 miles, which climbs away northeastward. This highly recommended alternate route climbs above the treeline to traverse spectacular wildflower meadows with in-your-face views of Mount Hood. Near this junction, a small trailside sign indicates that you have just entered

a no-campfire zone. Proceeding away from the junction, the PCT continues gaining elevation through a few more forested switchbacks. Near the top, an opening in the forest presents a wide view south to Mount Jefferson. The trail then curves at 4.2 miles, at the edge of a steep, barren slope, and presents a panoramic view west over 4971-foot **Zigzag Mountain** and the canyons holding **Lady Creek** and **Lost Creek**. A few paces beyond this viewpoint, the trail seems to fork at an unsigned junction. The path left (west) proceeds through thick huckleberry to a small, unassuming campsite near the edge of a high cliff (**Camp 3**); the path right continues north on the PCT.

Back on gentle, forested, near-level trail, the PCT crosses the **Paradise Park Trail** (#778) at 4.3 miles. To the left (west), this trail descends steadily on a forested ridge to a trailhead at the bottom of Zigzag Canyon on FR 2639-021; to the right (east), it climbs 0.5 mile to meet the Paradise Park Loop, then another 0.5 mile to a high viewpoint over the meadows. If you were undecided and skipped the previous opportunity to take the Paradise Park alternate, here's your second chance. The PCT meanders north under shady forest on soft, comfortable tread for a spell, then bends east, gently ascending to cross **Lost Creek** ⬤ at 5 miles. The crossing is just above where the creek converges with a smaller tributary—giving you two opportunities to refill your tanks with cold, refreshing mountain water, or dunk your hat or bandanna and cool your sweaty brow. Just beyond the creeks a good, small campsite can be found in the trees to the right (east) of the trail (**Camp 4**).

The next 0.5 mile curves up around the next ridge, shady forest intermingled with small, open pocket meadows, until it comes to the exposed edge of **Rushing Water Canyon**. This wide drainage is barren of vegetation on much of its upper, angled slopes leading up to the canyon's head where a narrow waterfall spills over a high promontory. Rising above the open, meadowy slopes above the canyon's head, Mount Hood's upper, glacier-clad flanks and summit are clearly visible. The PCT circuits this drainage, contouring into the basin on loose, narrow tread, and crosses just below the falls at 5.7 miles. Similar to many of the water sources on Mount Hood, the flow in Rushing Water Creek is highly dependent on the snowpack and time of summer. During heavy runoff, you may have to splash or rock-hop across; during low runoff, it may be barely a trickle, or nothing at all. After crossing, the trail

ALTERNATE ROUTE: PARADISE PARK

This scenic route parallels the PCT above the treeline between the Zigzag and Sandy river canyons to wander among sprawling alpine meadows enhanced by huge panoramic views. Even nicer, this option only adds a moderate amount of elevation gain, and no extra mileage. Be aware, however, that this is one of the most popular day hikes on Mount Hood, especially at the peak of wildflower season—so you're likely to have lots of company on this short stretch. If you're just passing through for the views, it shouldn't impact your itinerary too much; if you're modifying your itinerary to spend more time exploring and plan to camp in the park area, finding a campsite on a weekend may be challenging. Backpackers and thru-hikers who plan to camp in the park area are encouraged to use established sites to minimize impact on the fragile meadows.

The detour begins at 3.8 miles, at the southern junction with the **Paradise Park Loop** (#757), where it turns sharply off the PCT. The trail ascends a drainage canyon that feeds the **Zigzag River** before topping out in open, green meadows—the same meadows you observe from across the Zigzag, before beginning the big descent. The route meanders north across flowery slopes where, in early summer, the mountainside is carpeted with white avalanche lily; by midsummer, the meadows turn into a fireworks display of blue lupine, orange paintbrush, and purple aster. The trail crosses the upper branches of **Lost Creek** in verdant gullies, often overflowing with pink and yellow monkeyflower. Around this area, numerous campsites—in addition to the remains of the Paradise Park Shelter—can be found near the trail and at the end of short bootpaths.

The views get better as the trail contours north through ever-wider meadows offering unobstructed and in-your-face views of Mount Hood's western features: **Mississippi Head**, **Illumination Rock**, and **Zigzag Glacier**. While the big mountain will likely be drawing most of your attention, don't forget to cast a glance to the south and west. The panorama extends across the forested ridges and valleys surrounding the triple peaks of **Zigzag Mountain**, and farther out across the **Salmon–Huckleberry Wilderness**. The trail eventually descends back into the trees to reconnect with the PCT at 6.2 miles.

climbs steeply out of the canyon and returns to its meandering, northward track.

Passing briefly through open woods thick with paintbrush, aster, buttercup, and pearly everlasting, the forest closes in again and the trail starts descending. At 6 miles, it crosses a small, seasonal stream **O**, then at 6.2 miles meets the north end of the Paradise Park Loop Trail (#757). From here, the PCT descends in earnest, switchbacking northwest. Around the 6.5-mile mark, a sandy bootpath leads off the trail right (east) to a small, open campsite with a fire ring (**Camp 5**). Following, it bursts out in the open to cross a wide slope thick with mountain ash. Where the trail curves west at 6.2 miles, a bootpath leads right (north) to a viewpoint at the top of a high cliff. Here, you get a vertigo-inducing look at a wide, flood-scoured canyon, where a frothing river tumbles and falls down a rocky chasm, eventually feeding into the Sandy River. Similar to the previous river canyons, this one is also the result of water gouging its way down through layers of pyroclastic deposits. High above the snowfields feeding this cataract, the **Reid Glacier** fills the basin between Illumination Rock to the south and **Yocum Ridge** to the north.

The next jaw-dropping view comes at 7.1 miles, following a few more forested switchbacks downward. This one is at the precipitous brink of the same canyon, a little farther down, above what appears to be a bottomless abyss. The wide scene illustrates the immense power of earth, and its ability to build mountains, as well as water, and its ability to carve mountains and tear them down. Eastward, up the mountain,

TRAIL TRIVIA

Yocum Ridge, one of the prominent ridges on the west slope of Mount Hood, was named for Oliver C. Yocum, who immigrated to Oregon in 1847. With a great fondness for Mount Hood, he opened the Government Camp Hotel in 1900, where he lived and guided visitors to Mount Hood's summit.

the deeply incised canyon looks even bigger, the barren walls even higher; the immense rock escarpment across the gorge reveals the andesite and dacite building blocks of Mount Hood's upper flanks. Northward, down-canyon, reveals the even deeper Sandy River Canyon, and its multiple layers of lava and pyroclastic deposits—as if Mount Hood were a layer cake with a big slice cut away, revealing alternating layers of cake, frosting, and fruit filling. (Mmm . . . cake.) The scene is at once awe-inspiring and intimidating, placing you as a very small person at the edge of a vast and dynamic landscape.

At the end of the next switchback, at 7.5 miles, you are presented with another wide view, this time north and west, peering across the deep incision created by Rushing Water Creek. Across the canyon, the stripped-away slopes of 4872-foot **Slide Mountain** dominate the horizon. The trail then peels away from the edges of the ridge and plunges down under the cover of cool, increasingly dense forest; the ridgetop is carpeted with rhododendron and huckleberry, and lichen hangs from the trees, filtering the sunlight and casting an enchanting glow through the trees. Try not to speed down this ridge too fast, as this is one of the most pleasant stretches of forest, and you might find yourself imagining all manner of mystical forest denizens curiously watching your passage, from just out of sight.

Nearing the bottom of the descent, after the forest loses a bit of its charm and becomes thick with debris—and right about when your knees are ready for a break—the grade eases, and the trail switchbacks south into the shallow bottom of the Rushing Water Creek drainage. The sound of water will perk up your ears, and you'll notice a sudden profusion of trailside shrubbery—ferns, strawberry, vanilla-leaf, and more—and soon enough, the stream comes into view, paralleling the trail just below. At 9.3 miles, a short, steep path descends left (west) to the stream **O**; across the stream, a large camp area has several logs for sitting and room for a few tents (**Camp 6**). The PCT continues downstream, contouring the slope, the sound of the gurgling and splashing water like sweet music. Just 0.1 mile farther, the trail bursts

The Sandy River on Mount Hood is one of the more challenging water crossings in Oregon.

out of the forest onto the wide, rocky floodplain of the **Sandy River**.

The view up the floodplain shows the wide canyon of the Sandy River, with Mount Hood and its western slope peaks and glaciers clearly visible. The route across is marked by rock cairns. A large cairn directly across the floodplain, near the treeline, indicates where the trail continues. Now you just have to find a safe place to cross. In early summer, or during high runoff, the Sandy is potentially hazardous and uncrossable; later in the season, crossing may require you to scout up- and downstream for a safe ford. The alternative, since you are likely to get to this point of the leg later in the day, is to backtrack to the camp area beside Rushing Water Creek and attempt a crossing the next morning when the river flow is likely lower. If the river looks just too dangerous, don't risk it—turn around and head back. If the river is safe enough to ford, cross carefully, then look for the cairns on the opposite side. You're on the right track if your heading is slightly northwest into the trees. The trail comes to the base of an exposed, southwest-facing slope, becomes more obvious, then veers northwest along the base of the slope.

SANDY RIVER

The Sandy River Canyon was initially carved by ice age glaciers, then scoured deeper by massive, volcanic lahars (debris flows). The relatively flat canyon floor is actually a stack of debris flows that buried the forest and settled in the river basin. High above the canyon is the Reid Glacier—source of the Sandy River—nestled between Illumination Rock and Yocum Ridge. From its origin, the Sandy flows 56 miles west and north to drain into the Columbia River. Its name is derived from the large quantities of pyroclastic sand deposits washed downstream to its outlet at the Columbia, where William Clark (of Lewis and Clark fame) proclaimed the river crossing "a quick sand, and impassable."

The PCT then reenters forest and begins climbing out of the river basin. At 9.8 miles, it comes alongside a small, trickling stream of cold, clear water ⬤. Just beyond, where the trail bends, are

ALTERNATE ROUTE: RAMONA FALLS

The gorgeous cascades of Ramona Falls

Hidden away in a lush grotto, Ramona Falls is arguably one of the prettiest waterfalls in the North-west. It cascades 120 feet down a wall of columnar basalt, creating a multitiered veil of lacy water. To get an up-close look at this watery spectacle, it's just a short detour off the PCT. From the junction with the **Timberline Trail** (#600) at 9.9 miles, veer right (southeast) onto the Timberline and climb easily through dry lodgepole pine forest for 0.5 mile. The trail passes through an equestrian control gate, then drops down into Ramona Falls' shady hollow. Camping is not permitted near the falls, but a wide viewing area has plenty of logs and rocks for sitting and admiring the scene. A sturdy log bridge crosses the wide creek at the base of the falls and offers a fantastic view up the streaming cascade.

To return to the PCT, proceed across the bridge and veer left (east) on the **Ramona Falls Trail** (#797) to follow **Ramona Creek** downstream through delightful green forest. Ignore the Timberline Trail that forks steeply uphill to the right (northeast; see Trail Note). The creek pulls away from the trail after about a mile. If you need to top off your water for camp and the next morning, it's best to do it here. The final stretch of the detour crosses another section of dry forest before reentering healthier woodland, passes through another equestrian control gate, and reconnects with the PCT at mile 11.9, just north of **Muddy Fork Camp.**

two large camp areas (**Camp 7**). To the left (west) of the PCT, a large space offers a couple sitting logs and room for a couple tents. A few paces farther around the bend, an even larger area to the right (east) offers a few dispersed sites with fire rings and space for a few tents in each. The nicest site is farthest from the trail. Just 0.1 mile farther, at 9.9 miles, the PCT reaches a T-junction. This is where the PCT and **Timberline Trail** (#600) part ways; the PCT continues left (northwest) while the Timberline breaks away right (southeast). At this junction, you have the option of detouring to **Ramona Falls** on an alternate route that parallels the PCT and rejoins it just south of the **Muddy Fork River**. This side trip to one of Oregon's prettiest waterfalls is definitely worth taking, and adds only 0.3 mile to your day. Between the falls and the stroll along enchanting **Ramona Creek**, it's surprising this more appealing route is not an official part of the PCT.

Continuing away from the Timberline Trail (#600) junction, the PCT proceeds northwest, slightly above the Sandy River basin. Views are spare and the forest is dry and uninspiring, due in large part to a debris flow that spilled over the banks of the Sandy and inundated the surrounding forest. The gentle downgrade makes it easy to speed along until the trail splits again at 11.4 miles. Here, the PCT turns sharply northeast, as the path continuing west becomes the **Sandy River Trail** (#770), leading 1.9 miles to the large Ramona Falls trailhead on FR 1825-380.

Just 0.1 mile along, the PCT crosses **Ramona Creek** ◯ on a sturdy wooden bridge before it dives back under healthier, shadier forest, once again thick with rhododendron and huckleberry. The walk is easy and pleasant all the way to the junction with the **Ramona Falls Trail** (#797) at 11.9 miles, where the Ramona Falls alternate route rejoins the PCT. Just beyond the junction is **Muddy Fork Camp**. This decent, large camp area has space for several tents, a few fire rings, and lots of logs for sitting. The nearest water is across the **Muddy Fork River** at a small spring that trickles across the trail (the Muddy Fork, akin to its name, is usually brown and silty, so not suitable for drinking or filtering). At this point, your knees are probably ready for a break. Drop your gear and call it a day.

CAMP-TO-CAMP MILEAGE

Timberline Lodge to Camp 1	1.6
Camp 1 to Camp 2	0.1
Camp 2 to Camp 3	2.5
Camp 3 to Camp 4	0.8
Camp 4 to Camp 5	1.5
Camp 5 to Camp 6	2.8
Camp 6 to Camp 7	0.5
Camp 7 to Muddy Fork Camp	2.1

TRAIL NOTE: TIMBERLINE TRAIL (OLD PCT)

Many older topo maps show the PCT (still as part of the Timberline Trail) as climbing northeast from Ramona Falls to circuit Yocum Ridge, cross several branches of the Muddy Fork, and make a gradual contouring ascent to Bald Mountain. The PCT was changed to its present course (bypassing Ramona Falls to the east) in the early 2000s to make the trail more accessible to stock users (one of the mandates of the PCT). Many hikers continue to take this older route—part of the Timberline Trail—for bigger views from Yocum Ridge, and an easier ascent of Bald Mountain. This section of the Timberline, however, is in extremely poor condition. Many sections have washed or eroded off the steep slopes, making for a treacherous passage; other sections are heavily overgrown and require nothing short of bushwhacking your way through. In addition, the upper crossing of three branches of the Muddy Fork can be extremely confusing across the rocky, unmarked floodplain—not to mention dangerous during periods of high runoff. Until improvements and repairs are made to this stretch of trail, it is recommended that you avoid this route.

2 MUDDY FORK RIVER TO SALVATION SPRING

DISTANCE 9.7 miles

ELEVATION GAIN/LOSS
+3120 feet/–1800 feet

HIGH POINT 4410 feet

CONNECTING TRAILS AND ROADS
Timberline Trail (#600), Top Spur Trail
(#785), Lolo Pass Road (FR 18), Huckleberry Mountain Trail (#617)

ON THE TRAIL

The next leg, from the Muddy Fork to a nice camp area at Salvation Spring, continues the Pacific Crest Trail's up-and-down course around Mount Hood—beginning with a huge grind up Bald Mountain. From that point, the PCT veers away from the mountain to traverse the Bull Run Watershed in Mount Hood National Forest. The day affords a few big views of volcanic peaks in both Oregon and Washington, as well as more interesting geology, but otherwise remains in the trees for much of the way. The forest itself is pleasantly full of berries, wildflowers, and curtains of lichen draping from aged conifers. Water is sporadic through this stretch, so start with a good supply.

If you spent a little time exploring the **Muddy Fork Camp** area the previous day, you likely got a look at the river crossing—it's not as bad as it seems. Carefully make your way across the log bridge (current as of 2016) and hang a left to thrash through a section of dense, overgrown thimbleberry. The trail crosses a small spring ⬭, then comes to a small camp area at 12.1 miles (**Camp 8**). This serviceable site has a few well-placed logs, and room for two tents on gently sloping ground—a good alternative if the larger camp area on the south side of the Muddy Fork is crowded.

Just beyond the camp area, the trail turns sharply northwest and gets down to business, starting a steep, contouring ascent to the crest of **Bald Mountain**. The first stretch of densely forested south slope is littered with deadfall and debris, but as the trail gains elevation, the vegetation increases substantially—lots of sword fern, rhododendron, and huckleberry. The heart-pounding grade eases slightly, giving you a short respite to cross a rocky avalanche chute, followed by a tiny sign posted on a tree that reads, "Please do not cut switchbacks." Yep, they're coming. After this, the trail crosses a pretty, cascading stream ⬭ at 13.1 miles. This water source, in a verdant, narrow crevice choked with thimbleberry, vanilla-leaf, fern, and strawberry, is a good place to top off your containers (if you haven't already) to get you through the remainder of the climb; the next reliable source is another 4.5 miles ahead.

The trail resumes its upward trajectory, now through a series of switchbacks. The grade varies from one switchback to the next, some steep and demanding, others more moderate and easygoing. The consolation for all this climbing is that the trail tread is smooth and easy on the feet. The surrounding high conifers keep the trail shady, but as you get higher on the slope, you may notice that the sky through the trees seems to be getting lower and lower, indicating you are nearing the top. Just when your quads start screaming for a break, the trail makes a sudden turn east at the top of the final switchback, leveling out among a thick patch of rhododendron at 13.6 miles. A large, logged-out tree rests beside the trail and invites you to take your load off for a few minutes.

Now atop the western ridge of Bald Mountain, the PCT continues east, ascending the northwest slope on a shallow grade. The trailside vegetation becomes lively again, with lots of rhododendron, beargrass, and bunchberry (all spectacular when blooming)—but still no views. At this point you may begin to see increased trail traffic, with day hikers venturing onto the PCT and Timberline Trail from the nearby Top Spur and Lolo Pass trailheads. The trail tops out at a wide junction at 14.4 miles, a few hundred feet below **Bald Mountain**'s 4591-foot peak. A large map and

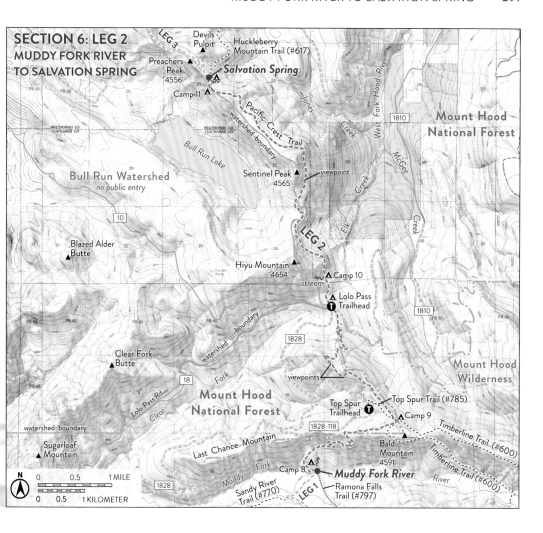

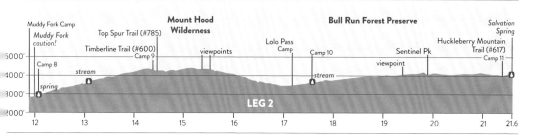

info sign are located here, as well as a self-register wilderness permit kiosk. On the right (east) side of the junction, the **Timberline Trail** (#600) makes a tight U-turn around the info board; the southeast branch contours the south slope of Bald Mountain, through rock gardens with spectacular views, to an upper crossing of the Muddy Fork, then circuits Yocum Ridge to Ramona Falls (the latter half of this stretch is in serious disrepair; see Trail Note in Leg 1); the northeast branch contours the north slope of Bald Mountain, and continues the Timberline's circuit of Mount Hood to McNeil Point, Cairn Basin, and places beyond. If you're not pressed for time, it's worth taking the southeast branch for 0.5 mile to a stellar viewpoint overlooking the Muddy Fork canyon, a huge waterfall streaming from the Sandy Glacier, and an in-your-face look at Mount Hood. The PCT continues left (northwest), with a modest campsite just right (north) of the trail (**Camp 9**).

Now on a gentle downslope, the PCT passes the **Top Spur Trail** (#785) at 14.5 miles, which descends 0.5 mile to a trailhead on FR 1828-118. The PCT's descent is short-lived, however, as the trail rises up the spine of the ridge. The tree cover remains fairly closed-in, enticing you with potential grand views just beyond; salmonberry and cow parsnip become dense and overgrown, encroaching on the trail in places. Finally, at 15.4 miles, the trees part and give you a first-class view of Mount Hood over the wide Muddy Fork canyon. From

TRAIL TRIVIA

The name **Illumination Rock** commemorates an Independence Day celebration in 1887, when a group of climbers hauled 100 pounds of red fire (strontium salt, which burns bright red) to light up the mountain. The burning light was seen from Portland and everywhere that had a view of the mountain.

this vantage, it's easy to pick out the **Sandy Glacier** and 9543-foot **Illumination Rock** (see Leg 1).

The PCT then quickly circuits an unnamed 4534-foot point, slides to the north side of the ridge, and begins gently descending. Before diving back under forest cover, a window in the trees presents a wide view northward. The impressive scene of **Mount Adams** in the distance is juxtaposed with a patchwork of timber harvest tracts

Put your balance beam skills to work on the log crossing over the Muddy Fork River.

Mount Hood stands sentinel above forested slopes.

splayed across the valley and ridges below. Then it's down—down, down, down 1000 feet, through pleasant forest as the trail sweeps down the wide at first, then increasingly tightening switchbacks. The trail tread, however, becomes rough, rocky, and rooty—not the soft, pleasant cruise of coming up the other side. The trail finally bottoms out, exits the Mount Hood Wilderness, and bursts into the sunlight amid a brushy area thick with rhododendron and fireweed. It then briefly ducks back under tree cover to arrive at **Lolo Pass** at 17.2 miles, a popular trailhead on **Lolo Pass Road** (FR 18). Opposite the information board, on the right (east) side of the trail, a large campsite (**Lolo Pass Camp**) can be found in the trees. This space has a picnic table, a couple fire rings, space for several tents, and usually lots of abandoned trash. It makes a good enough lunch stop, but the disappointing accommodations will likely prompt you to keep your visit short.

Moving north, the PCT crosses Lolo Pass Road and enters the **Bull Run Watershed**, where a signboard gives information and regulations about the area ahead. The trail then pops out into the big wide-open again to cross a brushy swath where a series of powerlines pass overhead. Despite the eyesore, there are plenty of sun-loving wildflowers to be seen, including daisies, fireweed, and Oregon

BULL RUN FOREST RESERVE

For 11.4 miles, north from Lolo Pass Road, the PCT traverses the 102-square-mile Bull Run Watershed Management Unit, the source of Portland's drinking water. The majority of the land is federally owned, and unauthorized entry is prohibited. The PCT proceeds through a narrow corridor just opposite the north ridge above Bull Run Lake, one of the main reservoirs. Warning signs are posted at regular intervals reminding hikers to stay on the trail and not do any off trail wandering.

The rocky path around Hiyu Mountain grants a few big views of Mounts Hood and Adams.

goldenrod. The trail then makes a lazy bend northeast, starts gaining elevation again, and ducks under tall conifers. This is the start of the next ascent—much milder than earlier—continuing through the rest of the leg. At 17.6 miles, where the trail makes a sharp right (north) turn, a small creek **O** splashes down a rocky chute and across the trail. This is a good spot to top off your bottles with cold, clear water and wipe the dust and sweat from your face. Just beyond the stream, a small campsite can be found below the trail in the trees to the right (east), with some good logs for sitting and room for one tent (**Camp 10**).

The PCT then contours across a steep slope on the eastern flank of 4654-foot **Hiyu Mountain**, where the trail turns to a narrow ledge and passes underneath a high rock escarpment. Here, you're treated to some good views of Mount Hood and Mount Adams. Then it's back into the trees, winding north, the trail periodically flirting with the edge of the ridge. The forest remains pleasant, full of the same lively and colorful varieties as seen in miles past—the abundance of huckleberries is especially nice in late summer. You're offered one more fleeting view of Mount Hood at 19.4 miles, as the trail passes under 4565-foot **Sentinel Peak**. Near 19.9 miles, shortly after the trail makes a decisive turn west, the trail crests the north side of the peak, then descends northwest just below the spine of the ridge. At 21.4 miles, the PCT meets the **Huckleberry Mountain Trail** (#617), which descends to the right (northeast). This trail drops more than 800 feet in 2.1 miles to **Lost Lake** in the valley below (see Leg 3). There is also a mediocre campsite near the junction large enough for two tents (**Camp 11**).

Continue another 0.2 mile north on the PCT to an obvious side trail that descends to the right (northeast) at 21.6 miles. Look for a small hand-lettered sign indicating **Salvation Spring Camp** on a tree opposite the side trail. The trail descends 100 feet through overgrown berry bushes to a wide forest clearing. Small Salvation Spring **O**, reliably runs—albeit lightly—through summer. Across the spring, a large camp area offers several tent sites, a fire ring, and good logs for sitting. There aren't any panoramic views from this camp location, but it does offer an open sky for stargazing. Plus, depending on your pace in making this leg's big ups and downs, it might be nice to quit early for the day, set up camp, and enjoy hanging out in a nice, forested glen.

CAMP-TO-CAMP MILEAGE

Muddy Fork Camp to Camp 8	0.2
Camp 8 to Camp 9	2.3
Camp 9 to Lolo Pass Camp	2.8
Lolo Pass Camp to Camp 10	0.4
Camp 10 to Camp 11	3.8
Camp 11 to Salvation Spring Camp	0.2

3 SALVATION SPRING TO WAHTUM LAKE

DISTANCE 11.7 miles

ELEVATION GAIN/LOSS
+2030 feet/–2410 feet

HIGH POINT 4510 feet

CONNECTING TRAILS
Buck Peak Trail (#615), Indian Mountain Trail (#416), Indian Springs Trail (#435), Eagle Creek Trail (#440)

ON THE TRAIL

Now on the second-to-last leg of the Pacific Crest Trail through Oregon, you'll finish traversing the Bull Run Watershed and enter the Mark O. Hatfield Wilderness. Most of the day's mileage continues to trace near the spine of a forested ridge, skirting several high points, but with sparing peeks at the wider world. The big payoff comes in the second half of the leg when the trail contours along the rock garden slopes of **Waucoma Ridge**, which offers huge panoramic views over **Eagle Creek Canyon**. Then it's decision time. Where the trail meets the abandoned, yet still service-able, **Indian Springs Camp**, you have the option of continuing on the official PCT to **Wahtum Lake**, or veering onto the ridiculously scenic **Eagle Creek** alternate route. Most of the leg is devoid of reliable water sources, so tank up before departing Salvation Spring. The consolation is that the day's terrain is generally mild and shaded, allowing you to cruise along at a casual pace.

Pulling away from Salvation Spring Camp, the PCT dives back into hemlock-and-fir forest on a moderate, switchbacking ascent up the flank of 4556-foot **Preachers Peak**, reaching its high point in less than a mile in a shaded saddle, with 4462-foot **Devils Pulpit** to the east. The story behind the naming of these neighboring peaks is that if the preacher is present, the devil is likely nearby. If you find yourself feeling weary, anxious, or frustrated at this point of your PCT journey, you can utter a little prayer, or lob a few curses—nobody's judging.

Making a wide, northwest circuit around a deep, forested basin, the trail quickly becomes overgrown with berry shrubs and clings to a narrow ledge above a harrowing drop. Far below, well out of sight, **Inlet Creek** flows into Lost Lake. The ridge traverse continues to a point where an opening in the trees offers a brief look down on Lost Lake before the trail makes an abrupt westward turn. This is followed by more viewless traverse to another saddle at 24.3 miles. In inclement weather, you may find the wind racing through this low point between two unnamed peaks. On the right (north) side of the saddle, a medium-sized campsite has room for a couple tents, with a decent log for sitting nearby (**Camp 12**).

Shortly past the camp, the trail slides below the ridgeline, bending north and contouring under another unnamed high point. A window in the trees looks northeast over the **Lake Branch Valley**, 4066-foot **Raker Point**, and 4162-foot **Sawtooth Mountain**. Just a little farther, the route comes to an unsigned fork at 24.8 miles. Veering up to the right (northeast), the **Buck Peak Trail** (#615) climbs to its namesake crown. The PCT continues left (north), contouring the western flank of the peak (note a PCT marker on a tree several yards beyond the fork), high above little **Blue Lake**, of which you might be able to steal a

TRAIL TRIVIA

Waucoma Ridge is the natural divide between the Eagle Creek and Benson Creek drainages. Its name is derived from a local native word translated as "cotton-wood tree." It is uncertain how this ridge, bereft of any cottonwood trees, came to be named as such. It may be another example of white settlers choosing a name whose meaning they didn't truly understand.

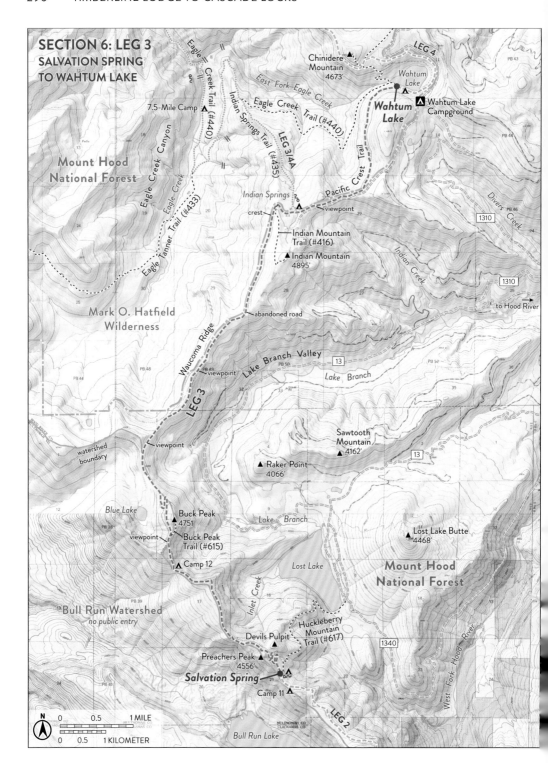

SECTION 6: LEG 3
SALVATION SPRING
TO WAHTUM LAKE

What strange things lurk in the foggy forest between Preachers Peak and Devils Pulpit?

peek. The trail then switchbacks down over rough, rocky tread, returning northwest. Where the trail begins a sweeping turn northeast, it exits the Bull Run Watershed at 26.4 miles and ascends gradually onto the forested spine of **Waucoma Ridge**. Now back on smooth, duffy tread, the trail skirts the border of the Mark O. Hatfield Wilderness.

The next few miles of trail undulate along the ridgetop, alternating between the east and west sides. Occasional pockets in the trees open up views of the valleys on either side. Where there aren't wider views, the trailside fern, huckleberry, vanilla-leaf, columbine, and devil's club offer plenty to admire. At 27.6 miles, the trail reaches a viewless crest, slides to the west side of the ridge with another brief view, then crosses to the east side and begins descending; at 28.8 miles, the trail comes alongside an overgrown, abandoned road, just below the trail on the left (west) side of the ridge. The trail crosses the old road, dipping lower on the forested ridge. About now, you're probably ready for a change of scenery, and here it comes.

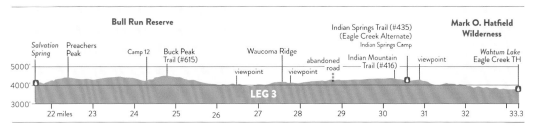

Summer brings purple hedge nettle to moist lakesides.

BUCK PEAK

This little-used and lesser-known side trail off the PCT climbs 0.5 mile to the summit of 4751-foot Buck Peak, once the site of a Forest Service fire lookout, and named for the large buck spied on its summit in summer of 1906. The lookout is long gone, but the expansive views from this highest point in Oregon's Clackamas County remain. On clear days, you can take in a stellar view of five Cascades peaks: Mounts Hood and Jefferson in Oregon, and Mounts Adams, Rainier, and St. Helens in Washington. You can also peer far below to sparkling Lost Lake. Because this detour off the PCT sees little traffic (and even less maintenance), it is often brushy and overgrown.

The trail momentarily pops out of the forest at 29.3 miles to cross a wide rock slope. Here, amid pockets of vine maple, thimbleberry, and penstemon, you're presented with a big view over the upper **Eagle Creek Canyon**. On the far side of the valley, 4500-foot, pyramid-shaped **Tanner Butte** rises high above the valley floor. These open rock slopes are the preferred habitat of cute little pikas, usually extremely skittish—but watch carefully and listen for their "eeeeep!" and you may see them. After crossing a couple more rock slopes, rich with gardens of paintbrush, fireweed, and penstemon, the trail breaks out into the open on the western flank of **Indian Mountain**, where the view becomes all-encompassing. The wide valley below contains the upper reaches of Eagle Creek, as well as the countless small tributaries that feed into it. The scene extends to the north where you can easily identify the **Columbia River Gorge**, and beyond, **Table Mountain** and the **Red Bluffs**.

INDIAN MOUNTAIN

Another lesser-traveled trail in the Mount Hood National Forest between Mount Hood and the Columbia River Gorge, Indian Mountain is the site of another bygone fire lookout. The 1-mile summit trail veers off the PCT at its well-marked junction at mile 30.3. The path begins as a faint bootpath, gently ascending open slopes adorned with wildflowers—look for clusters of avalanche lily and mountain pennycress, as well as the usual open-slope varieties. The view north becomes more expansive as the trail gains elevation. The path then begins following an old service road into the forest, where the views fall back until it turns to the east and climbs the final stretch to the 4895-foot summit. From the open, rocky top, you're offered a 360-degree panorama of every peak in northern Oregon and southern Washington.

The PCT then sweeps around the northern slope of Indian Mountain where it meets the **Indian Mountain Trail** (#416) at 30.3 miles, marked by a signpost in a large rock cairn.

From the junction, the PCT continues its circuit around Indian Mountain, descending an open slope a short distance south before turning east and reentering forest, momentarily dominated by beargrass and green alder. At 30.6 miles, a side trail veers left (north) to the **Indian Springs Camp** ⬤. This long-abandoned camp area is hardly a first-class accommodation, but is serviceable for tired hikers. A picnic table offers a place to drop your load and have a sit in what used to be the camp and trailhead parking area. A handful of dispersed, secluded campsites can be found below the parking area, tucked away in shady pockets of trees among a network of bootpaths. On the north side of the camp, the **Indian Springs Trail** (#435) crosses the trickling spring (can be very light in later summer) and begins its steep descent to Eagle Creek.

At this point, you have to choose how you want your PCT adventure to come to its conclusion.

The path across the open, rock garden slopes of Indian Mountain offer long views over the upper Eagle Creek Canyon and beyond.

MARK O. HATFIELD WILDERNESS

Originally designated as the Columbia Wilderness in 1984, the Mark O. Hatfield Wilderness (renamed in 1996) occupies nearly 66,000 acres in the Mount Hood National Forest, at the edge of the Columbia River Gorge National Scenic Area. The area's geologic history—which includes massive lava flows, volcanic mountain building, glacial scouring, and the great Missoula Floods (which carved the Columbia River Gorge)—created a striking area punctuated by deep river canyons, volcanic plateaus, and a north-facing escarpment of basalt cliffs laced with streaming waterfalls. With an annual average rainfall of 150 inches in the high country and 75 inches in the lower elevations, the mostly wooded

wilderness is a rich rainforest of old-growth western hemlock and Douglas fir over carpets of fern, salal, rhododendron, and huckleberry. In addition to its abundant common flora, the area is also home to a dozen endemic plant species, including Columbia kittentails and Barrett's penstemon. The wildlife population is almost as diverse, ranging from pikas and pine martens, to black-tailed deer and black bears, to bald eagles and water ouzels.

Interestingly—or ironically—the area's name change from Columbia to Mark O. Hatfield was quite a point of contention. Hatfield, a multiterm Oregon senator, was a strident proponent of commercial timber harvesting, and had a history of opposing any wilderness bill that involved the preservation of big trees. Through political maneuvering, he managed to obtain huge subsidies for the timber industry, and only supported wilderness efforts if it took attention away from the areas he was apt to turn over for logging interests. In the book *Oregon's Wilderness Areas*, author George Wuerthner remarks, "A more appropriate legacy for the former senator would be a sign on the largest clear-cuts . . . commemorating his efforts to erase Oregon's natural heritage." Was the name changed out of spite, or as a means of redemption? Regardless, the Columbia (Hatfield) Wilderness has become a mecca for tree-loving recreationists in the Northwest.

Presently, more than 200 miles of hiking trails weave through the ancient trees in this wilderness area, including 14 miles of the Pacific Crest Trail. Many of these trails vault from the near-sea-level elevation of the Columbia River to over 4000 feet on Larch Mountain and the Benson Plateau, and nearly 5000 feet on Mount Defiance. Located only 45 driving minutes from the Portland metro area, this translates into lots of hikers, backpackers, trail runners, photographers, campers, and anglers heading for the Gorge's gorgeous hills—most significantly concentrated on the historic waterfall highway (from Crown Point to Ainsworth State Park; this includes Latourell, Bridal Veil, Wahkeena, Multnomah, and Ponytail falls) and the extraordinary Eagle Creek (a much-preferred PCT alternate route; see Leg 3/4A).

Essentially, what kind of dessert do you want? Are you satisfied with a scoop of no-frills vanilla ice cream? Then you should continue on the official PCT to **Wahtum Lake** and complete the trail via the **Benson Plateau**. Or do you prefer a big brownie sundae, complete with hot fudge, whipped cream, sprinkles, and a juicy red cherry on top? In that case—wanting gobs of eye-chewing scenery—you should take the alternate route down **Eagle Creek**. The following description will continue to detail the PCT's official route forward, which, in itself, offers a few perks, namely a few big views you won't get on the alternate Eagle Creek route (see Leg 3/4A).

Continuing from the spring on the PCT's official route, the trail briefly parallels the camp area's rough access road, crosses into the forest, then traverses an exposed, south-facing slope above the Indian Creek basin and below an unnamed forested pyramid. Here, among patches of manzanita and tracing alongside FR 660, you're offered another fleeting view of Mount Hood. Following an easy rise, the trail resumes its gentle descent, slipping below the level of the road, and traversing a saddle between two deep basins, where it finally enters the **Mark O. Hatfield Wilderness** at 31.6 miles. The PCT then curves north onto the forested flank of a 4615-foot butte where the slopes are pleasantly adorned with fern, vine maple, vanilla-leaf, false lily of the valley, and Oregon grape. You may also begin to notice the presence of mossy rocks pocking the hillsides, belying the area's volcanic origins. Continuing to gently lose elevation, a few breaks in the trees offer peeks of 4673-foot **Chinidere Mountain** to the north, across the East Fork valley.

TRAIL TRIVIA

Wahtum Lake is another chuckle-worthy geographic place name, designated in 1901 by H.G. Langille, on a survey party for the USGS. He was obviously unaware that *wahtum* is the Sahaptin word for "lake." Enjoy your stay at Lake Lake.

WAHTUM LAKE CAMPGROUND

At the junction of FR 660 and FR 1310, the Wahtum Lake Campground is a small, primitive campground offering five tent sites and a vault toilet; there is no water or trash service here, but a nightly fee is required. It can be accessed by a 0.3-mile, switchbacking spur that veers off the PCT at an unsigned fork (33.6 miles) and climbs to the Wahtum Lake trailhead. This is a popular campground and trailhead (despite the rough road to get here) for weekenders and day-trippers, so not an ideal destination for thru-hikers—but may be serviceable in a pinch. (See Leg 4 for more info.)

As the PCT bends east approaching **Wahtum Lake**, the sound of running water—**East Fork Eagle Creek**—rises to meet your ears from the valley below. As the trail enters the wide, forested amphitheater containing the lake, a marker indicating a designated campsite can be found at 33.2 miles. The path leads left (north) to a large space with good log benches and several dispersed tent sites; there is no direct access to the lake for water from this site, but you can see it through the trees. This is the first of many sites at **Wahtum Lake Camp** ⬤. Shortly ahead, at 33.3 miles, the PCT meets the **Eagle Creek Trail** (#440); this is another option for connecting to the alternate Eagle Creek route (see Leg 3/4A). Near this junction, a few more campsites can be found near the trail and in the trees. Some have fire rings, logs for sitting, and access to the lake for water and swimming. Unfortunately, many of these camps will likely also have plenty of discarded trash left by careless campers.

For the next 0.25 mile along the south shore, there are several campsites of varying sizes. Some have recently (as of 2016) been marked with "No Camping" signs in order to rehabilitate overused sites. Having reached the end of the leg, choose a site that serves you well. If the site doesn't have direct water access, there is access from a few points along the trail. The lake is cool and clear and perfect for a refreshing dip after a sweaty day on trail—just be careful not to step on the little crayfish skittering around the rocks near shore. With only one more leg to go, enjoy a good night's rest on your (perhaps) last night on Oregon's PCT.

CAMP-TO-CAMP MILEAGE
Salvation Spring Camp to Camp 12 . . . . 2.7
Camp 12 to Indian Springs Camp 6.3
Indian Springs Camp to Wahtum Lake Camp. . 2.7

4 WAHTUM LAKE TO CASCADE LOCKS

DISTANCE 16.5 miles

ELEVATION GAIN/LOSS
+2260 feet/–5780 feet

HIGH POINT 4300 feet

CONNECTING TRAILS AND ROADS
Eagle Creek Trail (#440), Herman
Creek Trail (#406), Chinidere Cutoff
Trail (#406M), Chinidere Mountain Trail
(#445), Eagle Benson Trail (#434), Benson
Way Trail (#405B), Ruckel Creek Trail
(#405), Benson Ruckel Trail (#405A),
Herman Bridge Trail (#406E), Dry Falls
Trail, Gorge Trail (#400), Harvey Road,
Interstate 84

ON THE TRAIL
Just like any roller-coaster—or mountain climb, for that matter—what goes up, must come down. And in the case of the Pacific Crest Trail, on its final leg to **Cascade Locks** in the **Columbia River Gorge**, it comes *way* down. As the trail rises and falls through the forest, the route between big views (mainly in the second half) is far from boring, with plenty of smaller trail features to pique your interest, including berries, wildflowers, a (suspected) haunted forest, and a handful of geologic curiosities. As you lose elevation in the latter portion of the leg, the day will warm up considerably, so carry plenty of water and stay hydrated.

Beginning at the junction with the **Eagle Creek Trail** (#440), the PCT continues along the forested and shrubby southern shoreline of **Wahtum Lake ◑**. If you wind up having to scout for a campsite the day before, you may already be ahead of this junction. At 33.6 miles, the trail comes to an unsigned fork. The PCT proceeds left (east), while the side trail right (southeast) climbs to the **Wahtum Lake Campground** on FR 660. Past the fork, the PCT begins pulling away from the lakeside, gently gaining elevation in hemlock forest on a wide, contouring circuit around the lake basin. At the back of the basin, on the lake's east side, the trail crosses several seeps and becomes heavily overgrown with berry shrubs, columbine, bleeding heart, and hedge nettle. Lake views are reduced to just a few flashes of watery blue through the trees. On the north side, the trail starts ascending more earnestly. At 35.3 miles, the first of several rapid-fire trail junctions appears, beginning

WATER ALERT!
Water can be exceptionally limited on this leg, with the first seasonal source (Teakettle Spring) 8.7 miles ahead, and the first usually reliable source (a small stream across the trail) 12.6 miles ahead. Otherwise, it's 14.5 miles to **Dry Creek**, just a few miles from the end of the section. In short: tank up at Wahtum Lake.

High atop the Benson Plateau, take in long views over the Herman Creek valley to distant Mount Adams.

with the **Herman Creek Trail** (#406), branching right (northeast).

This 10.5-mile trail parallels the PCT northward in the valley to the east and reconnects with the PCT (via the Herman Bridge Trail spur) near the end of the leg. Just 0.1 mile farther, the **Chinidere Cutoff Trail** (#406M) drops sharply to the left (south). This steep, 0.7-mile shortcut descends to the valley bottom, just west of Wahtum Lake, to cross East Fork Eagle Creek and connect to the Eagle Creek Trail (#440). At the final junction (for now), just around the bend from the cutoff trail, the **Chinidere Mountain Trail** (#445) forks off to the right (north) and climbs heartily to a grand viewpoint.

Still gently ascending, the trail wraps clockwise around the flank of Chinidere Mountain, along a narrow, burned ridgeline. At 36.5 miles, just below the crest of a low rise, the PCT reaches its highest point in the leg—but it's not all downhill yet. Continuing on its northwest course, the trail descends gently along the ridge, weaving through a few shallow notches. At 36.9 miles, a faint bootpath veers off 30 yards to the right (east) to an open viewpoint atop a high cliff. The expansive view looks east over the **Herman Creek**

CHINIDERE MOUNTAIN

The fairly steep side trail up 4673-foot Chinidere Mountain—named for the last chief of the Wasco Indians—climbs 400 feet in 0.3 mile through several forested switchbacks to reach its open, rocky summit plateau. Views from the top take in Mounts Hood, Jefferson, Adams, Rainier, and St. Helens, as well as Eagle Creek Canyon, Benson Plateau, and the Columbia River Gorge. If you forgo the summit points in the previous leg (Buck Peak and Indian Mountain), this one is worth claiming for a knock-your-Smartwools-off panorama.

Canyon to 4555-foot **Tomlike Mountain**, from which **Wooley Horn Ridge** extends to the north. Looking north, the flat expanse of the **Benson Plateau** is clearly seen, beyond which Mount Rainier's and Mount Adam's glacier-capped peaks sparkle on the horizon. The trail dips through a few short switchbacks to the west side of the ridge,

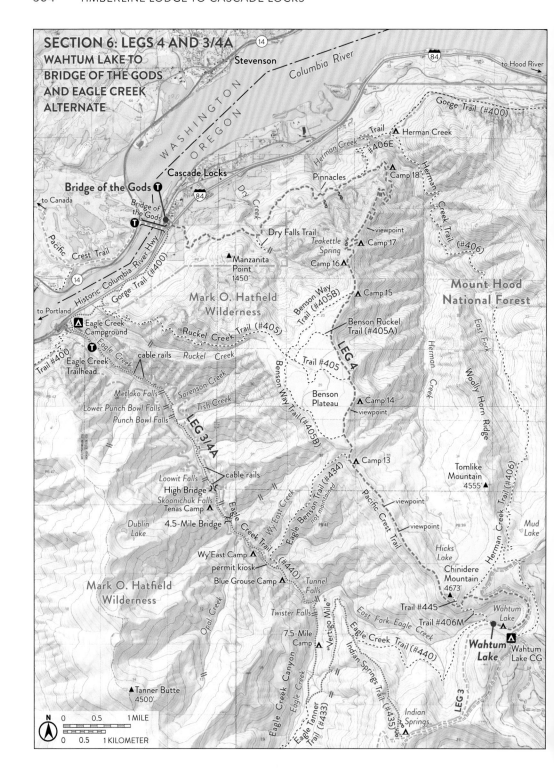

SECTION 6: LEGS 4 AND 3/4A
WAHTUM LAKE TO
BRIDGE OF THE GODS
AND EAGLE CREEK
ALTERNATE

14

Stevenson

Columbia River

to Hood River

84

WASHINGTON

OREGON

Gorge Trail (#400)

Herman Creek Trail

Herman Creek

#406E

Cascade Locks

Pinnacles

Camp 18

Bridge of the Gods

84

Bridge of the Gods

to Canada

Pacific

Crest Trail

Dry Creek

Dry Falls Trail

viewpoint

Herman Creek Trail (#406)

Teakettle Spring

Camp 17

Camp 16

Mount Hood
National Forest

14

Historic Columbia River Hwy

Gorge Trail (#400)

Manzanita
Point
1450'

Benson Way Trail (#405B)

Camp 15

Benson Ruckel
Trail (#405A)

to Portland

Mark O. Hatfield
Wilderness

Eagle Creek
Campground

Ruckel Creek Trail (#405)

LEG 4

East Fork

Trail #405

Eagle Creek
Trailhead

Trail #400

cable rails

Ruckel   Creek

Benson Way Trail (#405B)

Benson
Plateau

Herman Creek

Woolly Horn Ridge

Metlako Falls

Sorenson Creek

Camp 14
viewpoint

Lower Punch Bowl Falls

Tish Creek

Punch Bowl Falls

LEG 3/4A

Camp 13

Tomlike
Mountain
4555'

Mud
Lake

Loowit Falls

cable rails

High Bridge

Eagle Benson Trail (#434)
not maintained

viewpoint

Skoonichuk Falls

Tenas Camp

4.5-Mile Bridge

Eagle Creek Trail

Wy'East Creek

Pacific Crest Trail

viewpoint

Hicks
Lake

Dublin
Lake

Wy'East Camp

Chinidere
Mountain
4673'

permit kiosk

(#440)

Tunnel
Falls

Blue Grouse Camp

Mark O. Hatfield
Wilderness

Opal Creek

Twister Falls

Trail #445

Trail #406M

Wahtum
Lake

7.5-Mile
Camp

"Vertigo Mile"

East Fork Eagle Creek

Eagle Creek Trail (#440)

Wahtum
Lake

Wahtum
Lake CG

LEG 3

Tanner Butte
4500'

Eagle Creek Canyon

Eagle Creek

Eagle Tanner
Trail (#433)

Indian Springs Trail (#435)

Indian
Springs

N

0   0.5   1 MILE

0   0.5   1 KILOMETER

then passes through a brushy notch to the east side of the ridge where it traverses an open, rocky slope under a castle-like crag (with another good view to the north and east); it then undulates down to a ridgetop saddle at 38.3 miles. Here, a moderate trailside campsite has room for several tents and a few logs for sitting (**Camp 13**). Opposite the campsite, the **Eagle Benson Trail** (#434) descends 2.7 steep miles west atop a forested ridge to connect to the Eagle Creek Trail. (Visit www.pctoregon.com for the latest information regarding trail and camping restrictions related to the 2017 Eagle Creek Fire.)

Hiking away from the campsite, the trail contours up a steady grade to reach the top of the **Benson Plateau** at 38.8 miles. This geologic oddity—a nearly flat, forested tableland—is a remnant of the area's original lava depositions, unaffected by glaciation or river erosion. Look for pretty little pale bellflowers along the trail. At the southern edge, where the PCT mounts the plateau, is the little-used and easy-to-miss **Benson Way Trail** (#405B), which veers off to the left (west). Now on easy, level ground, the PCT meanders north along the plateau's eastern edge into what can only be described as a haunted forest. The spindly, gnarled trees close in around the trail, keeping little sunlight from reaching the beargrass- and debris-littered forest floor. You may almost sense creatures lurking in the shadows. The nightmare forest doesn't last for long, and you're soon back in verdant, green surroundings where the good faeries keep the wicked spirits at bay.

TRAIL NOTE: EAGLE BENSON TRAIL

Due to its steep grade and the general lack of maintenance that occurs on the Eagle Benson Trail (#434), this is not a recommended connector for reaching the Eagle Creek Trail from the PCT. Trail conditions are often poor and heavily overgrown.

Around 39.2 miles, look for a bootpath that veers right (east). This short path leads to the verge of the plateau and a tiny, open viewpoint that offers a grand view over Herman Creek Canyon, as well as your final peek of Mount Hood far to the south, rising over Waucoma Ridge. Just 0.1 mile farther north, a decent campsite can be found to the right (east) of the trail (**Camp 14**); this forested site can accommodate a couple tents.

Continuing its easy path north under a canopy of lichen-draped forest with thick beargrass carpeting, the PCT meets the **Ruckel Creek Trail** (#405) at 39.6 miles. Another of the many trails that explore the Benson Plateau, this one branches off left (west) to the central area of the plateau, the headwaters of **Ruckel Creek**, and the **Benson Campsite**. Beyond this, it connects to several other trails, many of which loop back to connect to the PCT both north and south. After another casual jog along the plateau's edge, at the brink of a deep basin, the PCT intersects the **Benson Ruckel Trail** (#405A) at 40.4 miles. This overgrown spur

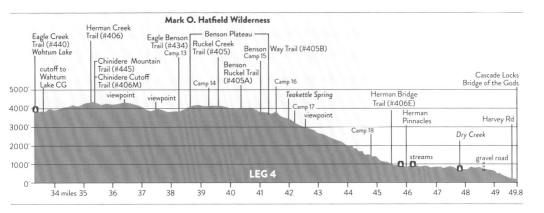

The Columbia River comes into view as the PCT descends to Cascade Locks.

branches off left (southwest) to Ruckel Creek and **Hunters Campsite** at its junction with Ruckel Creek Trail. From this junction, the PCT heads for the northeastern rim of the plateau, coming to its tipping point at 40.9 miles. Here, beside a tree bearing a diamond-shaped PCT marker, the trail begins its long dive to the Columbia River—a plunge equal to descending from the rim of the Grand Canyon to the Colorado River.

It begins with a steep, rapid decline to a narrow ridgetop where, at 41.1 miles, the PCT meets the north end of the **Benson Way Trail** (#405B). This is the last of the plateau trails, leading southwest to the same destinations as the previous Benson Ruckel Trail. Just beyond the junction is a nice

TRAIL TRIVIA

Ruckel Creek was originally named Deadman Creek. It was later changed to less-macabre Ruckel Creek to honor J. S. Ruckel, the man who incorporated the Oregon Steam Navigation Company, and built a tramway along the Columbia River.

trailside camp area with a couple fire rings and room for up to three tents (**Camp 15**). The trail then rolls north along the ridgetop, through a notch, to the verge of the ridge beside a small point at 41.6 miles. Here, a decent campsite can be found left (west) of the trail (**Camp 16**); this space is large enough to accommodate a few tents. Following this campsite, the business ahead is down, down, *down*. Over the next 4 miles, the PCT drops nearly 3000 feet on a steady grade, turning and switchbacking down a fire-scorched ridge.

Shortly after the big descent begins, roundabout through the second switchback, a large sign indicates **Teakettle Spring** ◖, just below the trail to the left (north), at 42 miles. This may be your first access to fresh water since leaving Wahtum Lake—depending on the season. This small spring may dwindle to nearly nothing later in the season or in drier years. At the end of this same switchback, at 42.2 miles, a small campsite can be found below the trail to the right (east); this site has room for one tent and a pretty nice view over Herman Creek Canyon (**Camp 17**). At this point you may become aware of your proximity to civilization once again, with the sound of train traffic rising from the gorge below. A few more knee-grinding switchbacks continue down the ridge, where the trailside shrubbery—fern, bunchberry, thimbleberry, Oregon grape, vanilla-leaf, and more—returns robustly, until the trail bursts out of the forest onto an open point at 42.6 miles. Here, you're presented with a huge panoramic view north, taking in Mounts St. Helens, Rainier, and Adams, and east, over the Herman Creek Canyon.

Following this visual treat, the trail dips over the ridge for another series of winding switchbacks. Under shady conifers and tall vine maple (which you'll be very happy for if the day is warming up), unless you are tracking your direction by compass, you may wind up not knowing which direction you're facing by the time you reach the bottom. As long as you're going down, you're going the right way. Near the end of the descent, the PCT exits the Mark O. Hatfield Wilderness and enters the **Columbia River Gorge National Scenic Area** at 44.3 miles. Finally, at the second-to-last switchback, a small trailside campsite can be found at 44.8 miles (**Camp 18**). You may be able to hear Herman Creek gurgling in the valley below.

At 45 miles, your knees will sigh in relief as the trail eases to a gentler grade. There's still more descending ahead, but on much easier terrain. Here the PCT turns southwest and begins contouring the base of the high ridge just descended. Where it crosses an open rock slope below a high, narrow slot, you're offered a view of the Columbia River and the town of Cascade Locks, still far below. Your destination is a mere 4.5 miles away—and those remaining miles are exceptionally enjoyable.

At 45.5 miles the PCT meets the **Herman Bridge Trail** (#406E), a 1.2-mile spur to the lower reaches of the Herman Creek Trail (#406), which leads 0.6 mile to the Herman Creek trailhead at the **Herman Creek Campground**. As the PCT continues its parallel course along the base of the ridge and high above the Columbia River, it dips into a verdant notch at 45.9 miles, which can only indicate one thing—water **◐**! Here, a lively stream cascades down a rocky, mossy cleft and splashes across the trail. The trickling sound is like sweet music, and the cold, clear water is like fine mountain wine. Drink your fill (filtering first), top

off a bottle, and march on, refreshed and newly invigorated.

The trail then dips along the contour and you may notice a proliferation of mossy, volcanic boulders dotting the forest floor. This indicates that you are near the **Herman Creek Pinnacles**. Heading west, you won't see them directly from the PCT, but look for an obvious side trail that branches off right (north) at 46 miles. Two 50-foot-tall basalt spires—the remnants of volcanic vents—rise out of their bases of loose talus. A fairly easy path through the talus circumnavigates the western pinnacle for an up-close view. The PCT then crosses another, smaller, dribbling stream **◐** at 46.2 miles, before making a winding, rising, dipping traverse around an extension of the ridge's lower base.

This continues until the trail bends south and the sound of big running water fills your ears—**Dry Creek ◐** at 47.8 miles. Quite opposite its name, Dry Creek runs plentifully year-round, streaming from springs on the northern slopes of the Benson Plateau. A sturdy wooden bridge crosses the creek, immediately after which the **Dry Falls Trail** (actually an old roadbed) crosses the PCT. If you're in

The end of the line at Cascade Locks

the mood for a scenic detour, turn left (north) and hike 0.3 mile up the trail/old road to **Dry Falls**, where a 74-foot horsetail waterfall plunges out of a narrow gorge of mossy columnar basalt. This falls is actually the last of a series of five cascades that tumble more than 230 feet down this rocky slot. If the day is warm, you can rock-hop right up to the base of the falls and enjoy a shower of cool mist—*aaaaahhh!*

From this point, you're on the homestretch. The PCT continues west under the cover of pleasant, fern-choked forest, then rises to traverse the base of 1450-foot **Manzanita Point**, where the previously smooth, duffy tread degrades to a rough, rocky surface—watch out for ankle-rollers. At 48.6 miles, the trail doglegs right (northwest) across a gravel service road under buzzing powerlines, then dives back under the trees to make a gently descending circuit around 895-foot **Cascade Point**. The rough tread eventually returns to smoother hard pack and the route turns and meanders idly north, then west, down through fern, devil's club, and columbine until it meets paved **Harvey Road** at 49.6 miles. Here, the PCT continues north on the road; across the road, the **Gorge Trail** (#400) reaches its eastern extremity, also spilling onto the road. (If you opt for the Eagle Creek alternate route, this is where it reconnects with the PCT.) Proceed the final 0.2 mile along the road under the Highway 84 overpass, where the PCT veers off the road to the left (west). The trail then cruises through the trees alongside the highway until spilling out onto the shoulder of the road at the **Bridge of the Gods**.

CAMP-TO-CAMP MILEAGE

Wahtum Lake Camp to Camp 13 . . . . 5.1
Camp 13 to Camp 14 . . . . 1.0
Camp 14 to Camp 15 . . . . 2.0
Camp 15 to Camp 16. . . . . 0.3
Camp 16 to Camp 17. . . . . 0.6
Camp 17 to Camp 18. . . . . 2.6

3/4A   ALTERNATE

INDIAN SPRINGS TO CASCADE LOCKS
(VIA EAGLE CREEK TRAIL)

DISTANCE 15.7 miles

ELEVATION GAIN/LOSS
+1830/–5860 feet

HIGH POINT 4220 feet

CONNECTING TRAILS AND ROADS
Eagle Creek Trail (#440), Eagle Tanner Trail (#433), Eagle Benson Trail (#434), Eagle Creek Loop road, Columbia Gorge Trail (#400), Harvey Road, Pacific Crest Trail, Interstate 84

Note: See map on p. 304.

ON THE TRAIL

To add some spectacular scenic flavor to the end of your PCT journey, veer off the PCT at **Indian Springs Camp** and finish your route via the popular **Eagle Creek Trail** (#440). Instead of following the PCT's high ridgelines and traversing the geologic anomaly that is the Benson Plateau, this alternate course plunges into a deep, lush canyon and follows Eagle Creek downstream past several spectacular waterfalls—including the extraordinary **Tunnel Falls**—and a selection of nice (albeit heavily used) backcountry camps. The final few miles of this route tracks the **Gorge Trail** (#400) east to reconnect to the PCT within 0.2 mile of its northern Oregon terminus at the **Bridge of the**

ALTERNATE START: EAGLE CREEK TRAIL FROM WAHTUM LAKE

Another way to finish via the Eagle Creek Trail is to take it downward from its upper terminus at Wahtum Lake. This is the more advisable alternate route if there has been recent rainfall, as the Indian Springs Trail can be treacherously slippery when wet and muddy. While less strenuous than the Indian Springs route, you would need to finish Leg 3 at Wahtum Lake and then take the Eagle Creek Trail west, contouring several wide drainages high above East Fork Eagle Creek. This route does not offer any exceptional views, and would add nearly 9 miles and perhaps another day to your itinerary.

Gods. Because of its remarkable scenery, most PCT section and thru-hikers opt for this route instead of the official Benson Plateau course. The trade-off is sacrificing several bird's-eye views of wide valleys and Cascade peaks for a glorious riverside walk in what is arguably the Columbia River Gorge's most scenic canyon. Just be prepared to have company on this trail—and if on a weekend, make that *lots* of company.

This alternate route begins at **Indian Springs Camp**, at 30.6 miles, where the steep and brushy **Indian Springs Trail** (#435) descends into the trees from the north end of the parking area. The trail immediately crosses **Indian Springs ⬦**, which may be but a faint trickle in low runoff years or late in the season. If you have enough water to carry you for a few miles, you needn't worry about refilling here. There will be plenty of water in the miles ahead—actually, more than on any other stretch of the PCT through Oregon.

The initial descent is narrow, steep, and often overgrown, with the trail losing nearly 2000 feet in just 2 miles—a real knee-grinder. Take it slow, and take care to save your legs and remain on the trail. The trail drops north following the drainage channel of the spring and remains largely closed-in by dense forest, with lots of familiar shrubbery lining and encroaching on the path. After 0.2 mile, the trail contours down along an east-facing ridge where it comes out into the big wide-open and traverses a wide rock slope. The view from this point, under a 4075-foot lower extension of the Indian Mountain ridge, is northeast over the East Fork canyon and across to 4673-foot

Chinidere Mountain. The trail wraps around the northern tip of the peak to the top of the ridge and continues descending earnestly northwest. At 32.5 miles, the Indian Springs Trail comes to an end at a T-junction with the **Eagle Creek Trail**

The "Vertigo Mile" of the Eagle Creek Trail was carved right out of the canyon walls.

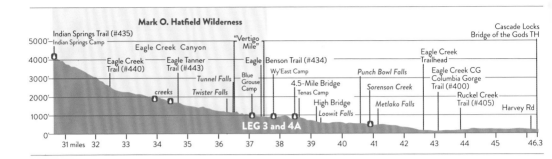

(#440). To continue down into the canyon, fork left (west); the right (east) fork proceeds 6 miles to Wahtum Lake.

Continuing down on the Eagle Creek Trail, the route heads north and slips below the ridgetop to the east side. Around the 33-mile mark, it hangs a U-turn over the ridge and continues descending, now on the west side, heading south. At the crux of this turn, listen for water flowing below in the narrow canyon directly north—this is the upper portion of the **East Fork Eagle Creek** that, just shortly below, will be plummeting over a high, rocky escarpment as Tunnel Falls. The grade eases as the trail contours along the west side of the wooded ridge. At 34 and 34.5 miles, the trail veers into a couple of lush drainages and crosses a couple of healthy tributaries **O** cascading down to add their volume to the main Eagle Creek. Just 0.2 mile farther, the trail reaches the canyon bottom, meeting the **Eagle Tanner Trail** (#443), which continues south up Eagle Creek before crossing and looping high around **Tanner Butte**. This is a popular, albeit challenging, loop route for weekenders that combines the beauty of Eagle Creek with the eye-popping views from a 4500-foot perch. At this junction, hang another U-turn to remain on the Eagle Creek Trail, now following the river north.

Back on a comfortable grade, trace Eagle Creek downstream. Around 35.3 miles, the trail re-crosses the two streams **O** from higher up, now closer together as they nearly converge before spilling into Eagle Creek. With the campsite at the end of the leg just ahead, this is the ideal location to refill your water containers, as the camp area

does not have direct or easy access to water. You won't need to overfill to carry you through much of the next day, as water will continue to be plentiful along the way. Beyond the streams, the trail descends gently, coming closer to Eagle Creek, and arrives at **7.5-Mile Camp** at 35.8 miles. Camping along Eagle Creek is only permitted in designated campsites, this being the farthest location from the trailhead. Its moderate distance beyond Tunnel Falls (southward)—the common turnaround point for day hikers and weekenders—makes this the most ideal campsite for PCT hikers. The camp area offers six decent sites near the trail and above the creek. This is the only camp area along Eagle Creek that permits campfires; but having a campfire is generally discouraged.

After choosing a site and dropping your gear, shake the jelly out of your legs and settle in for the evening. If you have any energy left, you may want to wander a little farther down the trail—sans backpack—for your first peeks of **Twister Falls** and **Tunnel Falls**, 0.5 and 0.7 mile downstream, respectively. And this is just the tipping point for your next day full of gushing-water eye candy.

On continuing the next day, the trail proceeds downstream past no fewer than six spectacular named waterfalls, and numerous more unnamed falls, cascades, and slides. The trail, mostly a steady, gradual descent, alternates between wide, comfortable tread alongside the river, and narrow, cliff-hugging ledges blasted out of sheer rock walls, precipitously high above. The sheer amount of water and its magnificent falling displays will surely make you giddy. Prepare to be wowed—*seriously*.

The Eagle Creek Trail passes through a tunnel blasted right out of the rock behind Tunnel Falls.

Pulling away from **7.5-Mile Camp**, the trail traces north alongside Eagle Creek. A short 0.5 mile from the camp, the trail skirts the vertigo-inducing upper brink of **Twister Falls**, aptly (and unofficially) named for the way the river splits through a narrow, twisting slot before plunging nearly 100 feet into a mossy amphitheater of high columnar basalt walls. *Don't even think about getting into the tempting pool above the falls!* There will be opportunities for chilly dips later on. Viewing these falls is challenging due to the location of the trail and the way the river zigzags through the multiple tiers of the falls. The upper tiers are visible from the trailside above the main falls, while the misty main plunge is visible from the trail alongside the basin. Use extreme caution near these falls.

The trail then contours around the basin on a high, narrow ledge, beginning what is chillingly referred to as the "Vertigo Mile." Blasted out of the sheer basalt walls, the trail edges precariously onward, more than 200 feet above the river.

Several lengths of steel cable handrail have been bolted into the wall to assist in traversing the rocky cliff, often slippery from the spray coming off the falls. The trail, still high above the river, then turns into a narrow hanging valley of more sheer columnar basalt where you're presented with a picture-perfect view of **Tunnel Falls** at 36.5 miles. This is where the East Fork Eagle Creek finishes its journey from Wahtum Lake with a 165-foot plunge into a large pool before flowing into the main Eagle Creek. While the falls are glorious, the main attraction is the tunnel carved out of the solid rock behind the falls so the trail could circuit the basin. Now a mere 60 feet above the rushing outlet below—but no less harrowing—the narrow trail continues to cling to the walls on a slippery rock ledge (with more cable rails for assistance) to pass through the dripping tunnel and circuit the opposite wall. Depending on the amount of runoff coming out of Wahtum Lake and the higher feeder streams, Tunnel Falls can be a light curtain of water spilling down the rocks, or a gushing monster filling the entire basin with spray.

The trail then turns out of Tunnel Falls' side canyon—where a large, unnamed block waterfall pours over a step in the creek's channel, just below the convergence of the East Fork with Eagle Creek—and proceeds northwest, dropping down to near-riverside, where it follows the creek downstream to **Blue Grouse Camp O** at 37.1 miles. This camp area offers four sites between the trail and the river; the large, open space is partitioned by downed logs, so there's not much seclusion to be had here. A short side trail from the northernmost campsite descends steeply to a small beach area with water access. A short 0.2 mile beyond the camp area, the overgrown **Eagle Benson Trail** (#434) veers off northward. This 2.7-mile connector climbs steeply on unmaintained tread to a junction with the PCT in a saddle just north of the Benson Plateau (not recommended). Continuing along the river, just under 37.6 miles, the trail crosses a sturdy bridge over a cascading stream and comes to the boundary of the **Mark O. Hatfield Wilderness**. Here, a signed kiosk asks hikers heading south (into the wilderness) to complete a self-register permit. The trail now proceeds within

a narrow channel of the **Columbia River Gorge National Scenic Area**.

The next camp area, **Wy'East Camp O**, comes along at 37.8 miles. This is the largest (and most popular) camp area along Eagle Creek, with eight individual campsites, some large, some small, some open and near the trail, some secluded and tucked away in the trees. Despite the presence of fire rings, campfires are prohibited at this camp. Water access is easy, but the wide, rocky creek at this location doesn't offer any swimming holes. Just past the camp, **Wy'East Creek O** tumbles down the eastern wall and streams under a good wooden bridge; a short way upstream, wispy **Wy'East Falls** spills over a lip of volcanic rock. Continuing along the musical waterway, don't forget to keep your eyes peeled for moisture-loving wildflowers that line the trail- and creeksides, such as larkspur, monkey-flower, bleeding heart, sea blush, columbine, and coast manroot. Around 38.3 miles, look for **Opal Creek** to come pouring into Eagle Creek from the opposite side of the canyon; just beyond, an unnamed tributary gushes into the creek in two side-by-side falls.

At 38.5 miles, the trail crosses Eagle Creek on **4.5-Mile Bridge O**, a sturdy wood-and-metal trestle spanning the creek about 20 feet above the water, and then continues along the creek on the western side. At 38.8 miles, **Tenas Camp** offers four tent sites in a forested pocket; fires are not permitted, and there is no water access. From this point north, camping is not permitted along Eagle Creek, so if you're thinking of extending your trek for additional exploring, this is your last chance at a campsite. Just beyond the camp area is the broad, two-tiered **Skoonichuk Falls**. For the best view of this falls, look for a short side trail right (east) to an overlook.

The trail stays on the west side of the creek for less than a mile, then crosses to the east side at 39.2 miles, on the **High Bridge**. True to its name, this sturdy double-rail bridge spans a 120-foot-deep slot where Eagle Creek rapidly funnels through far below. Opposite the bridge, the trail turns downstream and follows a narrow, very exposed ledge, still high above the river. This section of trail has had safety cables bolted into

Just off the Eagle Creek Trail, Punchbowl Falls is one of the most photographed waterfalls in Oregon.

the rock wall for aid. Along this high, exposed stretch is a view of **Loowit Falls** at 39.3 miles, where, on the opposite canyon wall, this lacy cascade streams 100 feet from its tipping point down to Eagle Creek. The tightrope walk along the cliffside continues for a spell, with more cable rails for a little added security, then the trail dips into a side gully and crosses a steadily running stream ⓞ on a wooden bridge.

Just 1.2 miles farther, the trail crosses **Tish Creek** ⓞ in another side gully, on another small bridge, then meets the side path to the **Punch Bowl Falls** overlook at 40.6 miles. The viewpoint is just a few paces off the main trail at the top of a bench over the river. Below, the exceptionally photogenic Punch Bowl Falls pours out of a rocky slot and into a deep, wide bowl—hence its name.

At just 36 feet, it's hardly the tallest falls in the gorge, but it is one of the most photographed for its idyllic setting—matched in its beauty by its danger. Every year (even since becoming illegal in 2011) people are injured jumping into the pool below the falls—despite posted warning signs. If you're looking for that perfect swimming hole, you only have to proceed another 0.2 mile down the trail and find the spur to **Lower Punch Bowl Falls**. This short side trail descends a fairly steep 0.2 mile to the riverside, where Eagle Creek spills over a terrace of volcanic rock into another large pool. If the water is at a moderate flow—not during high spring runoff—adventurous explorers can walk a short distance up the creek above the lower falls for another view of Punch Bowl Falls. On weekends, expect to find lots of people here.

Continuing downstream, the trail crosses **Sorenson Creek** ⬤ at 40.9 miles, then reaches the final major falls on Eagle Creek, **Metlako Falls**, at 41.2 miles. Similar to Punch Bowl Falls, Metlako Falls plunges 82 feet into a pool within a lush grotto, and is perhaps the most fantastical-looking waterfall in the gorge—something not too far removed from what you might expect to find in Middle Earth. Unfortunately, the viewpoint for a peek at Metlako Falls collapsed in the winter of 2016, and the falls is inaccessible.

The final 1.5 miles of the Eagle Creek Trail continue down the gorge. From the falls, another narrow cliff catwalk traverses the high cliffside, but as the trail descends the valley widens. The last stretch is across a wooden boardwalk just above river level; if you're in need of water, the creek is easily accessed here. The trailhead, complete with restroom, comes along at 42.7 miles. At this point, there's still about 3.5 miles to the Bridge of the Gods, so if you don't break before reaching this point, several spots along the creekside make fine lunch stops.

The route from this point follows the Eagle Creek Loop road down toward the fish hatchery and **Eagle Creek Campground**. Around 43.1 miles, look for the **Gorge Trail** (#400) to break off the road westward (left); just beyond, a side road to the campground curves off east (right). Walk this road about 0.1 mile and veer east onto the Gorge Trail, passing between the campground and the fish hatchery. The trail then turns northeast to meander through a forested corridor, alternating between easy stretches of duff-covered trail and paved sections of the **Historic Columbia River Highway**. At 43.9 miles, the **Ruckel Creek Trail** (#405) veers off to the right (southeast) to climb along the creek to the Benson Plateau. The next 2 miles parallel Interstate 84, where you're lulled along by the sound of speeding cars and trucks until you finally reach the end of the line at gravel **Harvey Road** in Cascade Locks at 46.1 miles. Just across the road you'll see where the PCT spills out of the brush.

Now back on the official PCT, turn left (north) and hike the final 0.2 mile along the road and under the highway overpass. Before emerging on the other side, the PCT veers off to the left (west), then cruises through the trees alongside the highway until spilling out onto the shoulder of the road at the **Bridge of the Gods**.

CAMP-TO-CAMP MILEAGE

Indian Springs Camp to 7.5-Mile Camp 5.2
7.5-Mile Camp to Blue Grouse Camp 1.3
Blue Grouse Camp to Wy'East Camp 0.7
Wy'East Camp to Tenas Camp 1.0

CONGRATULATIONS!

You have just reached the end of the Pacific Crest Trail's passage through Oregon. If you want to touch the official Oregon–Washington border to call your journey complete, walk halfway across the bridge (being mindful of traffic!) and take in the view from high above the Columbia River. Below the road, a large trailhead parking area has a sheltered picnic patio, a water fountain, and a restroom. If a burger and icy soda are calling your name, proceed down the bridge road to Wanapa Street, where a small selection of diners and drive-ins offer hot, cold, and tasty refreshments.

And while you're gorging on salty fries and frosty milkshakes, take a few moments to consider your achievement, no matter whether you started 50 miles, 150 miles, or 450 miles south of this point. Your journey on Oregon's PCT has taken you around glacier-capped peaks, over icy rivers, around gemlike lakes, and through some of the most spectacular wilderness forest to be found in the western United States. With lush and lively woodlands sprawling across dynamic glacial and volcanic landscapes; Oregon's PCT presents its own unique peace, magic, and inspiration. It's a place that can't be fully experienced in just one passage, in just one year, as its appearance and attitude change with the seasons, and from one year to the next. You never know what you may discover on your next hike on Oregon's PCT.

RESOURCES FOR OREGON'S PCT

GENERAL

Pacific Crest Trail Association
www.pcta.org

Pacific Crest Trail: Oregon
www.pctoregon.com

MAPS

US Forest Service PCT maps
www.fs.usda.gov/main/pct/maps-publications

US Forest Service Oregon National Forests maps
www.nationalforestmapstore.com/category-s
   /1848.htm

National Geographic Trails Illustrated: Oregon
www.natgeomaps.com/trail-maps/trails
   -illustrated-maps/oregon

Green Trails maps
https://greentrailsmaps.com/maps/map/OR

Halfmile PCT maps and apps
www.pctmap.net

FOREST REGULATIONS

US Forest Service
www.fs.fed.us/visit/know-before-you-go/hiking

Oregon Department of Fish and Wildlife
www.dfw.state.or.us

Crater Lake National Park
www.nps.gov/crla/planyourvisit

Warm Springs Indian Reservation
www.warmsprings.nsn.gov

PERMITS

National Forests
A Northwest Forest Pass is required for parking at maintained National Forest trailheads throughout Oregon; available at ranger stations, REI, and select outdoor retailers.

Crater Lake National Park
Required for backcountry camping within national park boundaries (Section 2); obtain in person at the Steel Visitor Center or Rim Village visitor center.

Obsidian Limited Entry Area
Required for camping within the Obsidian area in the Three Sisters Wilderness (Section 4); obtain permits at www.recreation.gov.

Pamelia Lake Limited Entry Area
Required for camping in the Pamelia Lake, Hunts Cove, and Shale Lake areas in the Mount Jefferson Wilderness (Section 5); obtain permits at www.recreation.gov.

Sunlight illuminates an understory of vine maple under tall Oregon conifers.

SUGGESTED READING

Asars, Tami, *Hiking the Pacific Crest Trail: Washington*, Seattle: Mountaineers Books, 2016.

Curtis, Rick, *The Backpacker's Field Manual*, New York: Three Rivers Press, 2005.

Hughes, Rees, and Corey Lewis, eds., *Pacific Crest Trailside Reader: Oregon & Washington*, Seattle: Mountaineers Books, 2011.

Kramer, Philip, *Hiking the Pacific Crest Trail: Northern California*, Seattle: Mountaineers Books, 2018.

McArthur, Lewis L., *Oregon Geographic Names*, Portland: Oregon Historical Society Press, 2003.

Orr, Elizabeth L., and William N. Orr, *Oregon Geology*, Corvallis: Oregon State University Press, 2012.

Salabert, Shawnté, *Hiking the Pacific Crest Trail: Southern California*, Seattle: Mountaineers Books, 2017.

Sullivan, William L., *Atlas of Oregon Wilderness*, Navillus Press, 2009.

Turner, Mark, and Phyllis Gustafson, *Wildflowers of the Pacific Northwest*, Portland: Timber Press, 2006.

Turner, Mark, and Ellen Kuhlmann, *Trees and Shrubs of the Pacific Northwest*, Portland: Timber Press, 2014.

Zangle, Libby, *Rabid: The Pacific Crest Trail.* Amazon Digital Services, 2014.

APPENDIX 2

OREGON PCT LAND
MANAGERS (SOUTH TO NORTH)

ROGUE RIVER–SISKIYOU NATIONAL FOREST
Sky Lakes Wilderness, west
www.fs.usda.gov/main/rogue-siskiyou

Siskiyou Mountains Ranger District
6941 Upper Applegate Road
Jacksonville, OR 97530
541-899-3800

High Cascade Ranger District
47201 Highway 62
Prospect, OR 97536
541-560-3400

CASCADE-SISKIYOU NATIONAL MONUMENT
Soda Mountain Wilderness
www.blm.gov/or/index.php

Medford District BLM
3040 Biddle Road
Medford, OR 97504
541-618-2200

FREMONT-WINEMA NATIONAL FOREST
Sky Lakes Wilderness, east
www.fs.usda.gov/main/fremont-winema

Klamath Ranger District
2819 Dahlia Street, Suite A
Klamath Falls, OR 97601
541-883-6714

Chemult Ranger District
110500 Highway 97 N.
Chemult, OR 97731
541-365-7001

CRATER LAKE NATIONAL PARK
www.nps.gov/crla
Steel Visitor Center
Munson Valley Road
Crater Lake, OR 97604
541-594-3000

UMPQUA NATIONAL FOREST
Oregon Cascades Recreation Area, west
www.fs.usda.gov/contactus/umpqua

Diamond Lake Ranger District
2020 Toketee Ranger Station Road
Idleyld Park, OR 97447
541-498-2531

DESCHUTES NATIONAL FOREST
Oregon Cascades Recreation Area, east
Diamond Peak Wilderness, east
Three Sisters Wilderness, east
Mount Washington Wilderness, east
Mount Jefferson Wilderness, east
www.fs.usda.gov/detail/deschutes

Crescent Ranger District
136471 Highway 97 N.
PO Box 208
Crescent, OR 97733
541-433-3200

Sisters Ranger District
Pine Street and Highway 20
PO Box 249
Sisters, OR 97759
541-549-7700

WILLAMETTE NATIONAL FOREST

Diamond Peak Wilderness, west
Waldo Lake Wilderness
Three Sisters Wilderness, west
Mount Washington Wilderness, west
Mount Jefferson Wilderness, west
www.fs.usda.gov/detail/willamette

Middle Fork Ranger District
46375 Highway 58
Westfir, OR 97492
541-782-2283

McKenzie River Ranger District
57600 McKenzie Highway
McKenzie Bridge, OR 97413
541-822-3381

Detroit Ranger District
44125 N. Santiam Highway SE
Detroit, OR 97342
503-854-3366

MOUNT HOOD NATIONAL FOREST

Mount Hood Wilderness,
Kohnstamm Memorial Area
Bull Run Forest Reserve
Mark O. Hatfield Wilderness
www.fs.usda.gov/detail/mthood

Clackamas River Ranger District
595 NW Industrial Way
Estacada, OR 97023
503-630-6861

Zigzag Ranger District
70220 E. Highway 26
Zigzag, OR 97049
503-622-3191

Hood River Ranger District
6780 Highway 35
Parkdale, OR 97041
541-352-6002

COLUMBIA RIVER GORGE NATIONAL SCENIC AREA
www.fs.usda.gov/crgnsa

Multnomah Falls Visitor Center
53000 Historic Columbia River Highway
Corbett, OR 97019
503-695-2372

Headquarters
902 Wasco Street, Suite 200
Hood River, OR 97031
541-308-1700

SERVICES NEAR TRAILHEADS
(SOUTH TO NORTH)

The following references cover the cities and services nearest the trailheads, listing those most convenient and accessible for PCT hikers. Large towns are best for stocking and gearing up prior to your PCT hike. Resorts and small towns near trailheads offer limited services and supplies. Establishments indicated with (*) are popular resupply locations, with more information in appendix 4. National Forest campgrounds can be reserved at www.recreation.gov.

SECTION 1:
NEAR DONOMORE PASS

The largest city nearest where the PCT crosses from California into Oregon is **Medford**, located on I-5, 30 miles north of the California border, and 275 miles south of Portland. Medford has all the amenities of a big city—groceries, lodging, restaurants, outdoor gear shops (including an REI), gas, and a post office. On the way to the trailhead, 5 miles west of Medford, **Jacksonville** is a smaller town with a few lodging options, grocery store, and gas. **Ashland**, a popular resupply town for thru-hikers (12 miles from the PCT), is located on OR 99, 13 miles south of Medford. Ashland has groceries, lodging, restaurants, outdoor gear, gas, and a post office. If bypassing the first 26 remote miles of the PCT in Oregon and starting where the trail crosses I-5, **Callahan's Mountain Lodge*** has several hiker-friendly services.

Lodging and Camping

Callahan's Mountain Lodge* has 19 comfortable lodge rooms with hot tubs, and a restaurant with live music and a full bar. This very hiker-friendly establishment offers a variety of services, including camping, showers, laundry service, and their famous bottomless spaghetti dinner! Learn more: www.callahanslodge.com.

Jackson Campground is located on Upper Applegate Road, 23 miles southwest of Medford and just past the turnoff for FR 20. This small, year-round campground has 12 first-come, first-served sites with water, restrooms, and garbage service. Learn more: www.fs.usda.gov/activity /rogue-siskiyou/recreation/camping-cabins.

Mount Ashland Campground, on FR 20, 11 miles from I-5 (exit 6), is a summer-only campground with nine sites and a vault restroom; water and trash are not available here. This campground is 0.5 mile off the PCT, 18 miles from the border crossing and 8 miles from the I-5 crossing. Learn more: www.fs.usda .gov/activity/klamath/recreation/camping-cabins.

Ranger Station

The **Star Ranger Station** for the Rogue River–Siskiyou National Forest is located on Upper Applegate Road, 14 miles south of Jacksonville and 8 miles north of FR 20 (see appendix 2). The **Medford BLM Office** for the Cascade-Siskiyou National Monument is located in Medford, on Biddle Road near I-5.

SECTION 2:
NEAR FISH LAKE (OR 140)

The PCT crosses the Lake of the Woods Highway (OR 140) near the Cascade Crest trailhead, just south of Mount McLoughlin, and 2 miles east of **Fish Lake Resort**.* This busy summer resort is a popular rest and resupply location for thru-hikers. The trail crossing is 41 miles east of **Medford** and 39 miles northwest of **Klamath Falls**. Both cities offer all the services you might need prior to embarking on your PCT adventure, including groceries, lodging, restaurants, gear shops, gas, and post offices. These are your best bets for stocking and gearing up before getting underway.

Trail sign at the southern border of Crater Lake National Park

Lodging and Camping

Fish Lake Resort* has 11 cabins, in addition to tent and RV campsites. The **Tadpole Café** has a shaded deck overlooking the lake and serves hearty meals, plus ice cream and milkshakes. In addition to their well-stocked store, they also offer showers and a laundry room; there is no phone or Wi-Fi service available here. Learn more: www.fishlakeresort.net.

    Fish Lake and Doe Point campgrounds, just west of Fish Lake Resort, are open May through October with 20 and 30 campsites, respectively, some of which can be reserved in advance. Campgrounds have drinking water, restrooms, and trash service. **North Fork Campground**, on the west side of Fish Lake, has nine first-come, first-served campsites. This campground has drinking water and vault toilets. Learn more: www.fs.usda.gov/activity/rogue-siskiyou/recreation/camping-cabins.

    Lake of the Woods Resort, 7 miles east of the PCT, has 32 nicely appointed cabins, in addition to a small store that carries a selection of groceries, beverages, and camping supplies. The **Lake House Restaurant** offers a sizeable menu of breakfasts, lunches, and dinners; in summers they host a Saturday night BBQ buffet with live music. Learn more: http://lakeofthewoodsresort.com.

    Aspen Point and Sunset campgrounds, on the west side of Lake of the Woods, offer 60 and 64 campsites, respectively. Each campground has drinking water, restrooms, and trash service, as well as day-use areas, boat ramps, and RV dump stations. Campgrounds are typically open May through October, and some sites can be reserved in advance. Learn more: www.fs.usda.gov/activity/fremont-winema/recreation/camping-cabins.

Ranger Stations

The **Prospect Ranger Station** for the Rogue River–Siskiyou National Forest is located in the town of Prospect; this office is not near the PCT. Within **Crater Lake National Park** the **Steel Visitor Center** is located on Munson Valley Road, between Rim Village and Mazama Village (see appendix 2).

SECTION 3:
NEAR CASCADE CREST (OR 138)

The nearest services to this trailhead north of Crater Lake National Park are found at **Diamond Lake Resort.*** This popular fishing and watersport destination has lodging, camping, and three restaurants. The small town of **Chemult** on US 97, 24 miles northeast of the trailhead (10 miles north of Diamond Lake Junction), has a few hotels, restaurants, gas, and a small grocery. **Bend**, another 65 miles north, has all the services of a large city, including an REI. The nearest city to the west is **Roseburg**, 80 miles distant at the junction with I-5. Another option is to enter Crater Lake National Park (fee required) and proceed 30 miles south to **Mazama Village,*** which has camping, lodging, a small grocery store, and gas.

Lodging and Camping

Diamond Lake Resort* on OR 138, 10 miles northwest of the Cascade Crest trailhead, offers a 38-room motel, 42 cabins, and 10 small studio units. They also have three restaurants: **Diamond Lake Café**, **Mt. Bailey Grill & Sports Lounge**, and **South Shore Pizza**, in addition to a small store and watersport rentals, www.diamondlake.net.

    Diamond Lake, Thielsen View, and Broken Arrow campgrounds are three Forest Service campgrounds at Diamond Lake that offer more than 450 campsites. All locations have drinking water, toilets, and garbage service; Diamond Lake and Broken Arrow also have showers, boat ramps, and RV dump stations. Campgrounds are open for the summer season, usually beginning on Memorial Day. A limited number of reservations can be made in advance. Learn more: www.fs.usda.gov/activity /umpqua/recreation/camping-cabins.

Mazama Village,* in Crater Lake National Park, has 40 cabins and a 214-site campground with drinking water, restrooms, garbage service, and an RV dump station; reservations are recommended. A grocery store, gas, showers, laundry, and the Annie Creek Restaurant can be found nearby; Wi-Fi service is available for a small fee. Upscale lodging and dining can also be found in the Rim Village at the Crater Lake Lodge; reservations are required well in advance. Mazama Village services are typically open from mid-June to mid-October; Rim Village services are open in the summer, weather permitting. Learn more: www .craterlakelodges.com.

Ranger Stations
The Chemult Ranger Station for the Fremont-Winema National Forest is 24 miles northeast of the Cascade Crest trailhead in the town of Chemult on US 97. The Toketee Ranger Station for Umpqua National Forest is 27 miles northwest of the trailhead, located on Toketee–Rigdon Road, just off OR 138. Crater Lake National Park has a small visitor center/ranger station in Rim Village. The Steel Visitor Center is located on Munson Valley Road, between Rim Village and Mazama Village (see appendix 2).

SECTION 4:
NEAR WILLAMETTE PASS (OR 58)
There are two resorts on Odell Lake near the PCT's crossing on OR 58: Shelter Cove Resort* and Odell Lake Lodge & Resort. Both are popular summer fishing destinations, the former also a good PCT hiker resupply location. There are also several Forest Service campgrounds in the area at Odell Lake and nearby Waldo Lake. To the east, the largest town is La Pine, 42 miles northeast on US 97. Here you'll find lodging, restaurants, groceries, and gas. Bend, with its outdoor gear shops, is another 30 miles north. To the west, your best bets for trip preparation are in the large metro areas of Eugene and Springfield, 70 miles distant near the junction with Interstate 5, where you will find ample services and supplies.

Lodging and Camping
Shelter Cove Resort,* 2 miles southeast of the trail and 2.3 miles south of the trailhead, is largely an RV campground, but they do have eight rustic cabins, a large four-unit lodge, showers, and a laundry room. Their moderate store carries a decent selection of groceries and fishing supplies; however, they do not have an on-site restaurant. Learn more: www.sheltercoveresort.com.

Odell Lake Lodge & Resort, 6 miles east of the PCT trailhead at Willamette Pass, has 13 rustic cabins, seven lodge rooms, and a 30-site tent and RV campground. The campground has drinking water and restrooms, and all facilities have easy access to the lakeshore and restaurant; the small store only sells snacks and souvenirs. Learn more: http://odelllakeresort.com.

Trapper Creek Campground is a Forest Service campground on the west end of Odell Lake, 2 miles from the trailhead, on FR 5810. This 29-site campground has drinking water, vault toilets, and trash service, and is a short walk from the store and other amenities at Shelter Cove Resort. Learn more: www.fs.usda.gov/recarea/deschutes/recreation /camping-cabins.

North Waldo, Islet, and Shadow Bay campgrounds are popular Forest Service sites located on the east side of Waldo Lake, off FR 5897, up to 17 miles from the Willamette Pass trailhead. There are more than 200 campsites available between the three locations, each with drinking water, vault toilets, and trash service; North Waldo and Islet campgrounds are 2 miles west of the PCT at Charlton Lake, and are usually open July through September; Shadow Bay usually opens in mid-June. Reservations can be made for North Waldo in advance, but most sites at Islet and Shadow Bay are first-come, first-serve. Learn more: www.fs.usda.gov/recarea/willamette/recreation /camping-cabins.

Ranger Stations

The **Middle Fork Ranger District Station** for the Willamette National Forest is located on the Willamette Highway (OR 58), 33 miles west of the Willamette Pass trailhead. The **Crescent Ranger District Station** for the Deschutes National Forest is located at the junction of FR 61 and US 97, 23 miles east of the trailhead (see appendix 2).

SECTION 4:
NEAR ELK LAKE (MIDPOINT)

Midway through Section 4 is a good starting/stopping point if you want to cut this larger section in half. It's also a good opportunity to relax and resupply on a longer trek. The **Elk Lake Resort*** on the Cascade Lakes National Scenic Byway is just a short jaunt off the PCT, and there are a couple National Forest campgrounds nearby as well. The city of **Bend** is approximately 33 miles east of this point, and has all the services you would need for stocking and gearing up for the trail.

Elk Lake Resort,* 1.3 miles east of the PCT, has a small, 18-site campground, three rustic camping cabins, and seven vintage log cabins. The campground can accommodate tents and RVs, and has drinking water and restrooms. The lakefront restaurant serves plenty of comfort foods and has a full bar. You can also rent kayaks and standup paddleboards and take a day off the trail and spend it on the water—the views are fantastic! Learn more: www.elklakereservations.net.

Elk Lake and Point campgrounds are 0.1 and 1 mile south, respectively, of Elk Lake Resort. Elk Lake has 22 campsites and Point has nine; both are first-come, first-served. Both campgrounds have vault toilets, but only Elk Lake has drinking water and trash service. Both can also accommodate small RVs, but there are no hookups or dump stations. These campgrounds are typically open May through late September. Learn more: www.fs.usda.gov /activity/deschutes/recreation/camping-cabins.

SECTION 5:
NEAR SANTIAM PASS (US 20/OR 126)

The nearest services to the trailhead at Santiam Pass can be found in the town of **Sisters**, 20 miles east. There you will find a couple lodging options, restaurants, groceries, gas, and limited camping supplies; they also have a post office. Between the trailhead and Sisters is **Black Butte Ranch**, with upscale lodging and dining, and **Camp Sherman**, with family-friendly accommodations and outdoor recreation. The **Big Lake Youth Camp*** on Big Lake is not open to the general public, but there are numerous National Forest campgrounds in the area. From the west side of the Cascades, the cities of **Salem**, **Albany**, and **Eugene** are all approximately 110 miles distant. There are several small towns and establishments with limited services on these western approaches. **Bend** is 22 miles southeast on US 20.

Black Butte Ranch, 13 miles east of the trailhead on US 20/OR 126, is a large golf and spa vacation destination. They have a variety of overnight accommodations, from lodge rooms to vacation homes. On the grounds are numerous restaurants, including **Robert's Pub, Aspen Lounge**, and the **Lakeside Bistro**. Recreation opportunities include golf, tennis, horseback riding, mountain biking, and a variety of watersports. Reservations are recommended. Learn more: www .blackbutteranch.com.

Camp Sherman, on the Metolius River and 11 miles east of the trailhead on SW Suttle-Sherman Road, has 20 comfortable, fully equipped cabins. Meals and entertainment can be found at the **Lake Creek Lodge**, and they have a small store that stocks groceries and fishing supplies. On-site recreation includes a variety of sports courts, walking trails, and swimming. Nearby, the Forest Service operates the **Camp Sherman Campground** with 15 campsites, with drinking water, vault toilets, and trash service; this campground is open year-round. Learn more: www.lakecreeklodge.com, www.fs.usda.gov/activity/deschutes/recreation /camping-cabins.

Big Lake Youth Camp,* a few miles southwest of the trailhead, is a good resupply point for thru-hikers, but that's about it. The camp does offer limited meals, showers, and laundry facilities to hikers passing through. Donations for each are suggested, usually $5. Learn more: http://biglake.org.

Big Lake, Big Lake West, and Link Creek campgrounds are the nearest camping facilities to the Santiam Pass trailhead, up to 5 miles south and east, respectively. Together, they offer a total of 90 campsites; Link Creek (at Suttle Lake) also has three yurts. All campgrounds have drinking water, restrooms, and trash service. Limited reservations can be made in advance for Big Lake and Link Creek; Big Lake West, the smallest facility with 11 tent-only sites, is first-come, first-served. Big Lake campgrounds are usually open mid-May through summer; Link Creek is open mid-April through November. Learn more: www.fs.usda.gov/activity/deschutes /recreation/camping-cabins.

Lost Lake, Scout Lake, Indian Ford, and Riverside campgrounds, as well as several more sites along the Metolius River north of Camp Sherman, can be found in the wider area around Santiam Pass. **Cold Springs Campground** can be found 4 miles west of Sisters on the McKenzie Highway (OR 242); this route leads to Lava Camp Lake, near the end of Section 4. Open times for these campgrounds vary; check website for latest information. Learn more: www.fs.usda.gov/activity/deschutes /recreation/camping-cabins.

Ranger Stations
The **Sisters Ranger District Station** for the Deschutes National Forest is located in the town of Sisters, on US 20, 21 miles east of the Santiam Pass trailhead. The **Detroit Ranger District Station** for the Willamette National Forest is located on the North Santiam Highway (OR 22), 40 miles northwest of the trailhead (see appendix 2).

SECTION 5:
NEAR OLALLIE LAKE (MIDPOINT)
Halfway through Section 5, Olallie Lake makes a good, albeit remote, location for splitting the section in half and/or enjoying a little downtime from the trail. The tiny **Olallie Lake Resort*** is just a short walk from the trail, and there are several Forest Service campgrounds located around the lake. As inviting as it looks, swimming is not permitted in Olallie Lake, but you can take a refreshing dip in nearby Head Lake. There are no other towns or

Go for some tasty grub at one of the resorts near the PCT.

services nearby, so come prepared with everything you need—including water.

Olallie Lake Resort* is just 0.1 mile from the PCT on FR 4220. This small summer resort offers 10 rustic cabins and two yurts at very modest prices. They also host the nearby **Paul Dennis Campground** with 17 sites near the lakeshore. The moderate store here stocks a decent selection of groceries, camp supplies, and stove fuel. Learn more: www.olallielakeresort.com.

Camp Ten and Peninsula campgrounds are located near the south end of Olallie Lake, 1.2 and 1.7 miles, respectively, from the PCT. Camp Ten has 10 campsites and Peninsula has 35. Both locations have vault toilets, but no water or trash service; sites are first-come, first-served. These facilities are typically open June through September. Learn more: www.fs.usda.gov/activity/mthood/recreation /camping-cabins.

SECTION 6:
NEAR TIMBERLINE LODGE (US 26)
Just steps away from the PCT Trailhead, the historic **Timberline Lodge*** offers the nearest lodging and dining accommodations on Mount Hood—but be prepared to pay for the indulgence. The small town of **Government Camp**, 6 miles from the trailhead, has more moderately priced lodging

and restaurant options, as well as a small grocery store and gas. On the way up the mountain (from Portland), the town of **Welches**, 13 miles west of Government Camp, has a grocery store, gas, and an outdoor gear shop. There are post offices in both Welches and Government Camp. **Portland** is approximately 60 miles west of the PCT, and has all the services of a big city, including an REI. To the southeast, the nearest city is **Madras**, located at the junction of US 26 and US 97; **Bend** is 40 miles farther south. There are also numerous Forest Service campgrounds on Mount Hood.

Timberline Lodge* offers luxury accommodations in a rustic and relaxed style. There are three restaurants in the lodge that serve moderate and upscale dining selections—the breakfast buffet in the **Cascade Dining Room** is a PCT hikers' favorite. This year-round destination offers summertime skiing and snowboarding on the Palmer Glacier—a unique novelty worth trying before, after, or on a break from the trail. Learn more: www.timberlinelodge.com.

Still Creek and Trillium Lake campgrounds are the nearest camping facilities to the PCT Trailhead. Still Creek, 2 miles east of Government Camp along US 26 (8 miles from the PCT), is a small location with 27 sites; Trillium Lake, 10 miles south of the PCT on Trillium Lake Road, is a popular lakeside campground with 52 tent and RV sites. Both have drinking water, vault toilets, and trash service, and are open during the summer season; advance reservations are available. Learn more: www.fs.usda.gov/activity/mthood/recreation/camping-cabins)

Camp Creek and Frog Lake campgrounds are located on US 26 7 miles west and 8 miles southeast, respectively, from Government Camp. Camp Creek has 25 sites with drinking water and vault toilets; this location is not suitable for large RVs. Frog Lake has 33 sites near the lake, with drinking water, restrooms, and trash service. This campground is just 0.5 mile from the PCT at Wapinitia Pass; both accept reservations. Learn more: www.fs.usda.gov/activity/mthood/recreation/camping-cabins.

Ranger Stations

The **Zigzag Ranger District Station** for the Mount Hood National Forest is located on US 26 in the town of Zigzag, 11 miles west of Government Camp, and 17 miles from the PCT Trailhead at Timberline Lodge (see appendix 2).

SECTION 6:
NEAR CASCADE LOCKS (I-84)

The small town of **Cascade Locks** is just a short walk from the PCT Trailhead at the Bridge of the Gods. There a few lodging options here, as well as restaurants, a couple small grocery stores, gas, and a post office. Oregon's biggest city, **Portland**, is 45 miles west on I-84, where you will find countless services to help you prepare for your trek. Approaching from the east, you will pass through the towns of **Hood River** and **The Dalles**, 20 miles and 45 miles east, respectively, both of which have a good selection of general services. Farther east, it's slim pickings.

Cascade Locks Marine Park and KOA campgrounds offer camping locations within the town of Cascade Locks. The Marine Park has 14 sites and is 0.7 mile from the PCT Trailhead, off SW Portage Road. The KOA has 90 tent and RV sites, in addition to camping cabins, and is 2 miles from the trailhead, on Forest Lane. Both locations have drinking water, restrooms, showers, Wi-Fi service, and will accept reservations. Learn more: http://portofcascadelocks.org, http://koa.com/campgrounds/cascade-locks/.

Ranger Stations

The **Multnomah Falls Visitor Center** for the Columbia River Gorge National Scenic Area is located on I-84 at the **Multnomah Falls Lodge** and scenic area, 13 miles west of the Bridge of the Gods trailhead at Cascade Locks (see appendix 2).

APPENDIX 4
RESUPPLY SERVICES
(SOUTH TO NORTH)

The following locations offer resupply services and other amenities for PCT hikers. They can be easily accessed from the PCT, typically no more than 2 miles from the trail. All of these establishments will accept and hold mailed packages (see requirements) for free or a small fee. When labeling your package, in addition to the location's address, write your name and expected pickup date on all sides of your package so it can be easily organized and located by staff.

In addition, most of these locations have stores and/or restaurants that can help you improvise a resupply plan if you're interested in a little "slackpacking," hiking more than one section, or thru-hiking the whole state—or more. Fresh food can be a nice addition to your menu, and may even allow you to skip cooking for a night or two. If you plan to purchase as you go, pack along extra plastic bags to store your food. (TIP: When ordering food to go, ask for condiments and spreads on the side so your food won't get soggy while you hike.) If you plan to purchase stove fuel along the way, call ahead to inquire about what fuels they keep in supply.

SECTION 1:
DONOMORE PASS TO FISH LAKE

Callahan's Lodge is located 0.8 mile off the PCT (section mile 26) at Siskiyou Pass on I-5. The lodge's tiny gift shop stocks just a small selection of candy bars and beverages. For resupply, Callahan's restaurant serves sandwiches and wraps to go. They will hold resupply packages **mailed via USPS or UPS** for a small fee. The lodge's reception desk is usually open for package pickup from 7 a.m. to 10 p.m.; the restaurant is open from 8 a.m. to 9 p.m. (541-482-1299, www.callahanslodge.com)

Send resupply packages to:
Your Name Here
PCT Hiker, ETA: mm/dd/yy
c/o Callahan's Lodge
7100 Old Highway 99 S.
Ashland, OR 97520

Green Springs Inn is a small resort on OR 66, 1.8 miles east of the PCT's highway crossing at Siskiyou Summit (section mile 43.7). They have a tiny store that stocks a selection of beverages and sundries. The restaurant at Green Springs Inn serves a variety of meat and veggie sandwiches, ideal for purchasing a few to wrap up and take with you. They will hold resupply packages **mailed via USPS or UPS** for free. Summer hours for package pickup and the restaurant are typically 9 a.m.–9 p.m. (541-890-6435, www.greenspringsinn.com)

Send resupply packages to:
Your Name Here
PCT Hiker, ETA: mm/dd/yy
c/o Green Springs Inn
11470 Highway 66
Ashland, OR 97520

Camper's Cove at Hyatt Lake is a small resort on Hyatt Prairie Road, 1.4 miles northwest of the PCT (section mile 51). The resort's claim to fame is having "the smallest store on the PCT"—and that's no joke. You'll find a few snacks, candy bars, and beverages, but don't expect to purchase a worthwhile resupply here. If you time your visit right, you can hit the small café and purchase a sandwich or two, or pizza, to pack along. They will hold resupply packages **mailed via UPS** for free. Store and office hours for package pickup are 8 a.m.–5 p.m.; check website for café hours. (541-482-3331, www.hyattlake.com)

Send resupply pages to:
Your Name Here
PCT Hiker, ETA: mm/dd/yy
c/o Hyatt Lake Resort
7900 Hyatt Prairie Road
Ashland, OR 97520

Fish Lake Resort on Lake of the Woods Highway (OR 140) is 2 miles west of the PCT (section mile 81.5). This is one of the better locations for dining and resupplying. They have a large store that carries a variety of camp and trail foods, snacks, candy, beverages, sundries, and stove fuel. The **Tadpole Café** offers some suitable sandwiches and other items to pack up and take with you. They will hold resupply packages **mailed via UPS** for a small fee. Summer office, store, and restaurant hours are 9 a.m.–7 p.m., with slightly longer hours on weekends. (541-949-8500, www.fishlakeresort.net)

Send resupply packages to:
Your Name Here
PCT Hiker, ETA: mm/dd/yy
c/o Fish Lake Resort
State Highway 140, Mile Marker 30
Medford, OR 97503

SECTION 2:
FISH LAKE TO CASCADE CREST

Mazama Village in Crater Lake National Park is 1 mile from the PCT (section mile 47.1), and located at the junction of OR 62 and Munson Valley Road. The large store stocks a variety of camping and hiking foods, snacks, treats, beverages, and sundries, so purchasing a few days' resupply here is just as easy as mailing one. They also sell guidebooks, maps, some hiking supplies, and stove fuel. **Annie Creek Restaurant** serves a few good wraps and sandwiches that could be purchased to go, and if cold pizza is your thing, they offer several good pies at reasonable prices. You may also find a hiker donation box outside of the village store. The store will hold resupply packages **mailed via UPS** for a small fee. Summer hours for the store and restaurant are 7 a.m.–9 p.m. (888-774-2728, www.craterlakelodges.com)

Send resupply packages to:
Your Name Here
PCT Hiker, ETA: mm/dd/yy
c/o Mazama Village Store
700 Mazama Village Drive
Crater Lake, OR 97604

Rim Village in Crater Lake National Park is 0.2 mile from the Dutton Creek trailhead on Rim Drive (section mile 51.1 on recommended rim route). The **Rim Village Café**, attached to the gift shop, offers a limited selection of premade sandwiches, drinks, and candies; the tiny visitor center (where you pick up wilderness camping permits) sells guidebooks and maps. The dining room at the historic **Crater Lake Lodge**, at the far end of the village, offers a selection of upscale sandwiches at fairly moderate prices that could be taken on the trail. Summer café hours are 9 a.m.–8 p.m. Lodge dining room lunch hours are 11:30 a.m.–2:30 p.m. There is nowhere to send resupply packages to Rim Village. (888-774-2728, www.craterlakelodges.com)

Diamond Lake Resort, north of Crater Lake National Park is 10 miles from the PCT (section mile 69.5), just off of OR 138. They also have three restaurants that offer a large selection of easily-packable sandwiches and pizzas that would make great additions to your trail menu. Their small store stocks a selection of camping foods, snacks, treats, beverages, and some supplies. The resort post office will hold resupply packages **mailed via USPS** for free. Post office hours for package pickup are 8 a.m.–4:30 p.m. (closed noon–1 p.m.) Monday through Friday, and 8 a.m.–12:30 p.m. on Saturday; store and restaurant hours vary. (541-793-3333, www.diamondlake.net)

Send resupply packages to:
(Your Name Here)
PCT Hiker; ETA: mm/dd/yy
c/o Diamond Lake Resort
350 Resort Drive
Diamond Lake, OR 97731

SECTION 3:
CASCADE CREST TO
WILLAMETTE PASS

Shelter Cove on Odell Lake is 1.8 miles from the PCT (section mile 58.2) on FR 5810, 2 miles south of OR 58. This hiker-friendly resort is home of **The General Store**, one of the best resupply outlets along the PCT in Oregon. It carries a good selection of camp and hiking foods, snacks, candy, and beverages. There are no dining options here, but they do offer hot dogs and microwave pizzas. A hiker donation box can usually be found on the deck outside the store. The store will hold resupply packages **mailed via UPS or FedEx** for free. Summer store hours, and for package pickup, are typically 7 a.m.–6 p.m. (541-433-2548, www .highwaywestvacations.com)

> Send resupply packages to:
> Your Name Here
> PCT Hiker, ETA: mm/dd/yy
> c/o Shelter Cove Resort
> W. Odell Lake Road, Highway 58
> Crescent, OR 97733

SECTION 4:
WILLAMETTE PASS TO
SANTIAM PASS

Elk Lake Resort, on the Cascade Lakes Scenic Byway, is 1.3 miles from the PCT (section mile 44.5), and at about the halfway point through Section 4, making this a good resupply stop. The resort doesn't have a substantial store, only selling a few snacks, candy, and beverages. The restaurant—a PCT hikers' favorite—offers a decent selection of meat and veggie sandwiches that can be ordered to go. The resort will hold resupply packages **mailed via UPS** for a small fee. Summer office and restaurant hours vary by day, but they are usually open 11 a.m.–7 p.m., with longer hours on weekends. (541-480-7378, www.elklakeresort.net)

> Send resupply packages to:
> Your Name Here
> PCT Hiker, ETA: mm/dd/yy
> c/o Elk Lake Resort
> 60000 Century Drive
> Bend, OR 97701

Big Lake Youth Camp, a few miles south of US 20/OR 126 at Santiam Pass, is 0.8 mile from the PCT (section mile 87). The camp store only stocks a small selection of snacks and beverages, so this location is primarily beneficial for multi-section and thru-hikers to send packages to resupply for the next stretch of trail. The camp will hold packages **mailed via USPS or UPS** for free. Packages can be retrieved from the Headquarters building near the camp entrance, which is usually open 8 a.m.–7 p.m. (503-850-3583, biglake.org /pct-hikers)

> Send resupply packages to:
> (Your Name Here)
> PCT Hiker; ETA: mm/dd/yy
> c/o Big Lake Youth Camp
> 13100 Highway 20
> Sisters, OR 97759

SECTION 5:
SANTIAM PASS TO
TIMBERLINE LODGE

Olallie Lake Resort, midway through Section 5, is just 0.1 mile from the PCT (section mile 44.7) on FR 4220. The resort has a small store that stocks a decent selection of camping foods, snacks, candy, beverages—enough to put together a few days' menu if needed. They also carry a small supply of sundries, trail supplies, and stove fuel. Due to its remote location, this resort does not accept or hold resupply packages. (503-853-3481, www .olallielakeresort.com)

Timberline Lodge on Mount Hood is just 0.2 mile from the PCT (section mile 96). The small store only sells gifts and souvenirs, so plan on mailing everything you might need. The **Ram's Head Bar** offers a few upscale sandwiches that could be taken on the trail, or grab a pizza to-go from the **Blue Ox Bar**. Bacon lovers can order the breakfast bacon sampler plate (so good!) and a few orders of toast, and chow down on sandwiches for a few days. The **Wy'East Store**, across the parking area from the lodge, will hold resupply packages **mailed via USPS** for a small fee. Summer store hours for package pickup are 8:30 a.m.–4 p.m. (503-272-3311, www.timberlinelodge.com)

Send resupply packages to:
Your Name Here
PCT Hiker, ETA: mm/dd/yy
Wy'East Store
c/o Timberline Lodge
27500 E. Timberline Road
Government Camp, OR 97028

SECTION 6:
TIMBERLINE LODGE TO
CASCADE LOCKS

Cascade Locks, the small town on the Columbia River where the PCT leaves Oregon, is 0.1 mile from the trailhead at the Bridge of the Gods. This is a major resupply location for thru-hikers proceeding north into Washington. There are a handful of grocery and restaurant options for purchasing a resupply here. Your best bets are **Columbia Market** and **A&J Select Market**. The **Bridgeside Inn**, at the bottom of the bridge ramp below the trailhead (and with great views of the river and bridge), offers a selection of deli sandwiches that can be ordered to go. The Cascade Locks post office, 0.3 mile north of the trailhead on Wanapa Street, will hold resupply packages **mailed via USPS** for free. Post office hours are 8:30 a.m.–5 p.m., Mon.–Fri. (541-374-5026, www.usps.com)

Send resupply packages to:
Your Name Here
PCT Hiker, ETA: mm/dd/yy
c/o General Delivery
461 NW Wanapa Street
Cascade Locks, OR 97014

INDEX

ABOUT THE AUTHOR

ELI BOSCHETTO grew up in sunny Southern California, where he developed his hiking legs in the southern Sierra Nevada, tromping trails and climbing mountains along the Kern River and in Yosemite and Sequoia–Kings Canyon national parks. In 2005, he relocated to Portland, Oregon, where he and his wife Mitzi continued exploring the great outdoors, and racking up the trail miles. All the while, Eli's pack grew heavier with all the camera gear and recording equipment that began to accompany him on his adventures.

In 2008, after working for more than a decade in commercial publishing and marketing, Eli shifted his attention and professional experience to full-time trail writing and photography. He quickly became a regular contributor to *Backpacker*, *Sierra*, and numerous Northwest travel publications. He also served as the editor and art director of *Washington Trails* from 2011 to 2016. This experience then led to writing full trail guidebooks. To date, Eli has three Oregon hiking guides under his boots: *Hiking the Pacific Crest Trail: Oregon*, *Urban Trails: Portland*, and *Day Hiking: Mount Hood*.

After completing his PCT guide, Eli founded PCT: Oregon, an online resource for Oregon's PCT hikers, and supplement to this guidebook. In addition to trail news and gear reviews, he posts regular updates by rehiking sections of Oregon's PCT every year. Eli was also a member of the 2018 Granite Gear Grounds Keepers, serves as a National Geographic maps ambassador, and is on the advisory board for the Oregon Trails Coalition. When he's not on the PCT, Eli's favorite places to hike are Oregon's Eagle Cap Wilderness, California's Ansel Adams Wilderness, and Scotland's Isle of Skye. You can connect with Eli at www.pctoregon.com.

ABOUT THE SERIES

The Pacific Crest National Scenic Trail meanders north from California's border with Mexico to the entrance of Manning Provincial Park in British Columbia, on the Washington State–Canada border. This rigorous trail has evolved since its earliest envisioning in 1926 to encompass approximately 2650 miles, traveling through some of the West Coast's most stunning country. Now with the new series **Hiking the Pacific Crest Trail** hikers and other adventurers can enjoy beautiful, full-color guides to section hiking the entire trail.

- All new guides, focused on section hiking the PCT
- Each volume researched and created by an experienced hiker and backpacker
- Inspirational full-color guides with more than 150 photographs
- Section-by-section routes for day hikers, backpackers, and thru-hikers
- Four volumes in series: Washington, Oregon, Northern California, and Southern California

MOUNTAINEERS BOOKS is a leading publisher of mountaineering literature and guides—including our flagship title, *Mountaineering: The Freedom of the Hills*—as well as adventure narratives, natural history, and general outdoor recreation. Through our two imprints, Skipstone and Braided River, we also publish titles on sustainability and conservation. We are committed to supporting the environmental and educational goals of our organization by providing expert information on human-powered adventure, sustainable practices at home and on the trail, and preservation of wilderness.

The Mountaineers, founded in 1906, is a 501(c)(3) nonprofit outdoor recreation and conservation organization whose mission is to enrich lives and communities by helping people "explore, conserve, learn about, and enjoy the lands and waters of the Pacific Northwest and beyond." One of the largest such organizations in the United States, it sponsors classes and year-round outdoor activities throughout the Pacific Northwest, including climbing, hiking, backcountry skiing, snowshoeing, camping, kayaking, sailing, and more. The Mountaineers also supports its mission through its publishing division, Mountaineers Books, and promotes environmental education and citizen engagement. For more information, visit The Mountaineers Program Center, 7700 Sand Point Way NE, Seattle, WA 98115-3996; phone 206-521-6001; www.mountaineers.org; or email info@mountaineers.org.

Our publications are made possible through the generosity of donors and through sales of more than 800 titles on outdoor recreation, sustainable lifestyle, and conservation. To donate, purchase books, or learn more, visit us online.

OTHER TITLES AVAILABLE FROM MOUNTAINEERS BOOKS

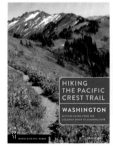    

Mountaineers Books is proud to be a corporate sponsor of the Leave No Trace Center for Outdoor Ethics, whose mission is to promote and inspire responsible outdoor recreation through education, research, and partnerships. • The Leave No Trace program is focused specifically on human-powered (nonmotorized) recreation. • Leave No Trace strives to educate visitors about the nature of their recreational impacts and offers techniques to prevent and minimize such impacts. • Leave No Trace is best understood as an educational and ethical program, not as a set of rules and regulations. • For more information, visit www.lnt.org or call 800-332-4100.

$24.9

A LIFETIME OF OREGON WILDERNESS ADVENTURES!

THE PACIFIC CREST NATIONAL SCENIC TRAIL stretches roughly 2650 miles from Mexico to Canada, passing through the rich and varied terrain of California, Oregon, and Washington. While each year many hikers attempt to cover that distance in a single, months-long epic journey, most of us are lucky to have even a week to devote to hiking. So how can we get out on the most famous trail in the West?

With boots-on-the-ground trail beta from one of Oregon's most experienced hikers, *Hiking the Pacific Crest Trail: Oregon* breaks down the state's more than 450 miles of the PCT into manageable sections—stunning routes that can be easily knocked off in three days, a week, or more. Author Eli Boschetto details everything a section hiker needs to know, including access points, camp-to-camp mileages, and best places to stake a tent, from the rolling grasslands of the Soda Mountain Wilderness to the barren volcanic plains of the Central Cascades to the doorstep of Oregon's tallest peak, Mount Hood.

Whether you plan to tackle the PCT section by section, use the companion guides to Washington and California (see inside) to plan a full PCT thru-hike, or explore the route within Oregon at your leisure—this unparalleled guide will help you find your way.

Former editor of *Washington Trails* magazine and Northwest trail correspondent for *Backpacker* magazine, **ELI BOSCHETTO** lives in Portland. Visit Eli at www.pctoregon.com.

FEATURES INCLUDE:

- 6 trail sections broken down into 3- to 8-night trips
- 41 trail legs—many are great weekend outing
- Easy-to-understand maps and elevation prof
- Engaging route descriptions, including sites, history, flora, and fauna
- Camp-to-camp mileages
- Details about campsites and water sources
- Alternate routes, desirable detours, and connecting trails
- Permits, hazards, and restrictions
- Clear references to PCTA section letters
- Suggested itineraries
- More than 150 full-color photos

978-1-59485-876-5

MOUNTAINEERS BOOKS

Outdoor books by the ex